GREEN BUILDING MATERIALS

A GUIDE
TO PRODUCT
SELECTION
AND
SPECIFICATION

Second Edition

ROSS SPIEGEL • DRU MEADOWS

WILEY

JOHN WILEY & SONS, INC.

The numbers and titles referenced in this product are from *MasterFormat*™ 1995 Edition and *MasterFormat*™ 2004 Edition and are published by the Construction Specifications Institute (CSI) and Construction Specifications Canada (CSC), and used with permission from CSI, 2005. For those interested in a more in-depth explanation of *MasterFormat*™ and its use in the construction industry contact:

The Construction Specifications Institute (CSI)
99 Canal Center Plaza
Alexandria, VA 22314
(800) 689-2900; (703) 684-0300
CSINet URL: http://www.csinet.org

The authors advocate the use of environmentally friendly (green) building products, systems and materials; and believe that green products and innovative technology can enhance the outdoor and indoor environment, improve the quality of life of the user, and in general, perform as well and even outperform their baseline competition. This book is intended to be a guide for researching environmental issues relative to building products. No warranty is made as to completeness or accuracy of information contained herein. References to manufacturers do not represent a guaranty, warranty, or endorsement thereof.

50% Recycled content. Elemental chorine free.

This book is printed on acid-free paper. ♾

For general information on our other products and services or for technical support, please contact our Customer Care Department within the United States at (800) 762-2974, outside the United States at (317) 572-3993 or fax (317) 572-4002.

Wiley also publishes its books in a variety of electronic formats. Some content that appears in print may not be available in electronic books.

Library of Congress Cataloging-in-Publication Data:

Spiegel, Ross, 1947–
    Green building materials : A guide to product selection and specification /
  Ross Spiegel and Dru Meadows.—2nd ed.
    p.   cm.
    Includes index.
    ISBN-13: 978-0471-70089-0 (cloth)
    ISBN-10: 0-471-70089-4 (cloth)
    1. Building materials—United States—Catalogs. 2. Green products—United States—
  Catalogs. I. Meadows, Dru. II. Title.
  TH455.S65   2006
  691—dc22
                                                        2005020000
Printed in the United States of America.

10 9 8 7 6 5 4 3 2 1

CONTENTS

PREFACE TO THE SECOND EDITION

When we set out over seven years ago to write "a guide to product selection and specification" for green building materials, the extent of design and construction professionals' knowledge of green or environmentally friendly buildings was fairly limited. The variety of green building materials was similarly limited. In these few short years, the industry has expanded exponentially. Today, there are hundreds (if not thousands) of green building products. There are green journals, green conferences, and green committees in nearly all building trade and professional organizations. There are numerous green building rating programs, not least of which is the U.S. Green Building Council's LEED® (Leadership in Energy and Environmental Design). There are now well over 100 ASTM standards related to sustainability in buildings. Spurred by the mounting public interest in green buildings, municipalities, states, and national governmental agencies are implementing green initiatives and adopting one rating system or another with increasing rapidity.

The years between the publication of the original edition and the second edition have seen an explosion in the knowledge base supporting green buildings, green building materials, and sustainability. The science informing environmental decision-making continues to grow. Manufacturers are researching and developing new green product lines as well as improvements to existing products. With the increasing number of completed green, sustainable or high-performance buildings, real-life statistics about cost and energy usage are becoming available. Not only is it possible to find a definition of "sustainability" in your dictionary today, but also it is difficult to pick up a newspaper or magazine or read an electronic newsletter that does not mention "sustainability."

In light of the progress at all levels in the green building industry, it became clear to us that an updated edition was overdue. We are grateful that our editor at John Wiley & Sons agreed. We hope that readers will find this second edition even more helpful than the first edition and will continue to use it as a "toolkit" in their daily practice and learning.

Ross Spiegel
Shelton, Connecticut

Dru Meadows
Tulsa, Oklahoma

ACKNOWLEDGMENTS
TO THE SECOND EDITION

The latest edition of *Green Building Materials*, which you are now holding in your hands, is the result of much hard work and the product of encouragement and input from many people. Although limited space does not permit me to thank them individually I would like to recognize the following groups: my "green" friends and fellow members in The Construction Specifications Institute; my friends in the U.S. Green Building Council; and the special people who believed in this project from the start . . . to the finish: my co-author Dru Meadows, my wife and daughters, Dorine Shirinian Spiegel and Erica Shirin Spiegel; thank you all.

In the end, my passion about green buildings and sustainable design remains undiminished. When you finish reading this edition, sit back and remember that "a greener future is in your hands." Make good use of the time you have.

Ross Spiegel
Shelton, Connecticut
September 2005

* * * * *

For my colleagues, clients, family, and friends—all of whom have inspired me to find more sustainable solutions. And especially for the readers who care enough to act on their convictions. Thank you.

Dru Meadows
Tulsa, Oklahoma
September 2005

PREFACE TO THE FIRST EDITION

Much has been written in the last 25 years about the philosophical and moral impetus to design and construct green or environmentally friendly buildings. Although more and more building owners are demanding that their design professionals take environmental concerns into account for new buildings, knowledge about the process of selecting and specifying green building materials has remained sketchy.

In this book, the reader will find not only a discussion of why one should use green building materials and what green building materials are but a guide to their selection and specification as well. The reader will also find information about the construction process and how to guard against the substitution of non-green building materials. The information contained in the appendices and glossary serve to round out the package, providing the reader with valuable reference material, sample specifications, and a kit of tools to use on green building projects.

This book was a labor of love for the authors, and its creation and birth were made possible by the encouragement and understanding of their families, friends, professional colleagues, and members of the green building movement. Our thanks also go out to the editors and staff at John Wiley & Sons, who made the birthing process as painless as possible.

Ross Spiegel
Fort Lauderdale, Florida

Dru Meadows
Tulsa, Oklahoma

CHAPTER 1

Introduction

No man is an Island, entire of it self; every man is a piece of the Continent,
a part of the Main; if a clod be washed away by the sea, Europe is the less,
as well as if a promontory were, as well as if a manor of thy friends or of thine
own were; any man's death diminishes me, because I am involved in Mankind;
And therefore never send to know for whom the bell tolls; It tolls for thee.

—*Devotions upon Emergent Occasions, Meditation 17*
John Donne

In *Devotions upon Emergent Occasions,* the seventeenth-century English metaphysical poet John Donne wrote, "No man is an Island, entire of it self." Through this statement, Donne asserted that we all share a common humanity. In today's increasingly complex and interrelated world, not only is no man an island but, similarly, no building stands alone. Every building exists within an environmental context upon which it not only acts but which also has an impact upon the building. Due to today's increased complexity and interrelatedness, no building can be constructed as a microcosm. The people in charge of every building project must consider the impact it will have on the environment into which it will be placed, locally and globally.

Donne's assertion that no man is an island is also an affirmation of sustainability. *Sustainability* is commonly interpreted to mean living in such a way as to meet the needs of the present without compromising the ability of future generations to meet the needs of the future.[1] It is frequently compared to the Native American concept of consultation with the as yet unborn future generations for their input on significant decisions—decisions that might affect them. Sustainability is a social concept in that it considers the needs of the unborn. It is an environmental concept in that it addresses the effect of pollution and resource management (or lack thereof) on Earth's ecological systems. Further, it is an economic concept in that it seeks to quantify the tolerable limits for consumption such that we can live on Earth's interest instead of depleting the principal. It is a perspective that focuses on systems and relationships instead of objects.

The term *sustainability,* once rare to find in a dictionary, has in the last few years begun to appear with more regularity. While the spell check on your personal computer may stumble over the word, many online dictionaries such as yourdictionary.com and OneLook.com now include the term. *Sustainability* can also now be found in online encyclopedias such as Wikipedia. Use of the term has quickly become widespread. Another term that has come into common usage is *high-performance building*. A high-performance building is one whose energy, economic, and environmental performance is substantially better than one designed by standard practice. It is a building that is healthy to live and work in and that has a relatively low impact on the environment.[2] The term *green* has also become part of our working vocabulary. It is now used not only as a name for a particular color but as an adjective meaning "environmentally friendly." It refers to the color of lush, healthy, unpolluted vegetation. Some local and regional programs use *blue* in a similar manner to indicate the idea of cool, clean, unpolluted water or air. *Brown* is indicative of dirty, barren, polluted areas, and has entered the industry vocabulary as a term referring to contaminated sites, *brownfields*. Like the terms *sustainability, green,* and *high-performance building, integrated design* is now in common usage. Integrated design describes a process used to design and construct a building in such a manner so as to promote sustainability. The integrated design process encourages all members of the building team to work together from the earliest stages of project development to achieve high performance and sustainability in the design. *Green,* like the other terms, has entered the vernacular. Thus, *a green building* is not, the shade of paint, but on the impact the building has on the environment. Simply stated, a green building is one that is located and constructed in a sustainable manner and that is designed to allow its occupants to live, work, and play in a sustainable manner.

The growth of interest in green buildings has led to the development of rating systems such as the U.S. Green Building Council's Leadership in Energy and Environmental Design (LEED®) Green Building Rating System and in green building material rating systems such as the National Institute of Standards and Technology's (NIST) BEES (Building for Environmental and Economic Sustainability) program.

Over the last decade, interest in green issues among those in both the building industry and the general public has grown considerably. Today, the proliferation of green articles, conferences, publications, websites, electronic newsletters, and projects attest to an increasing consciousness. We have been made aware, in no uncertain terms, that we are a dirty and wasteful species. Each of us has had to accept responsibility for our part.

The United States generates more waste than any other nation. Each day, we produce enough garbage to fill 63,000 garbage trucks, which "lined up . . . would stretch from San Francisco to Los Angeles (about 400 miles)."[3] For many American schools, the amount of money spent on trash disposal is at least equal to that spent on textbooks.[4] The building industry alone accounts for approximately 20 percent of the waste stream.[5] "The U.S. Environmental Protection Agency (EPA) estimates that approximately 136 million tons of building-related [Construction & Demolition (C&D)] debris were generated in 1996—the majority from demolition (48 percent) and renovation (44 percent). New construction generated only 8 percent of building-related C&D debris."[6] "The United States Geological Survey has estimated that construction accounts for 60 percent of all materials used in the United States for purposes other than food and fuel."[7]

We waste energy. The U.S. Department of Energy has estimated that improvements in the energy efficiency of buildings, utilizing existing and readily available technologies, could save $20 billion annually in the United States and create 100,000 new jobs.[8] A significant percentage—40 percent—of the world's energy usage is dedicated to the construction and operation of buildings.[9] Even more is indirectly mandated by the thoughtless siting of buildings relative to each other. Urban sprawl has been denigrated for its negative impact on quality of life. People regularly complain about the time devoted to traveling across town or the unfortunate aesthetics of their surroundings. However, as environmentalists will quickly tell you, urban sprawl is guilty of damaging the environment both directly and indirectly. It directly damages the environment as inexpensive fringe property is hastily and wastefully paved over, and indirectly as the hundreds of thousands of energy-burning vehicles drive past to conquer the next bit of fringe real estate.

We also waste our natural resources. Over 50 percent of the wetlands of the contiguous United States have been destroyed—filled, contaminated, or otherwise "reclaimed."[10] The destruction of wetlands and other natural resources has become much more efficient with technological advances. In recent decades, " . . . the average annual rate of deforestation worldwide was approximately equivalent to an area the size of the state of Georgia."[11] James Lovelock, creator of the GAIA theory[12], has predicted that, at current rates of deforestation, we will have lost 65 percent of all the forest of the tropics by the end of this century. This is a critical threshold. "When more than 70 percent of an ecosystem is lost, the remainder may be unable to sustain the environment needed for its own survival."[13] The building industry commandeers 3 billion tons of raw materials annually—40 percent of total global use.[14] It uses almost half of all the mined, harvested, and dredged raw materials each year! It also diverts 16 percent of global fresh water annually.[15] Most of the earth's water is located in our oceans and is too salty for residential, commercial, or industrial use. Only 3 percent of the water on the planet is fresh, and most of that is located in polar ice. Of all the water on the planet, only about 0.003 percent is readily available as fresh water for human use.[16] The 16 percent annual usage estimate accounts for the quantity of water required to manufacture building materials and to construct and operate buildings. It does not reflect the impact of the building industry on the quality of water. It is entirely possible that future estimates of the percentage of available fresh water will decrease as we continue to contaminate our limited supply.

At some point, with continued unlimited growth, demand will exceed our resources. But at what point? There is a great deal of debate over the exact numbers. How much fossil fuel do we have left? Enough for 10 years? 100 years? Determining the exact limit causes genuine concern because we want to know how much we can use—and, of course, how much is it going to cost.

According to the United Nations Population Fund reports, from the beginning of time until 1950, the world population grew to almost 2.5 billion people; from 1950 to 1990, that population doubled; and by 2050, the world will add almost 2.5 billion people, an amount equal to the world's total population in 1950.[17] The same resources we are now using will have to support nearly 9 billion people. Each additional person requires food, clothing, shelter, and assorted amenities. Most of this growth is anticipated in Asia and in developing countries. Currently, these areas do not have the same standard of living that developed nations do, but they are actively attempting to acquire it. Also, these areas produce the majority of the raw materials, the renewable and nonrenewable resources that developed nations use to achieve their higher standard of living. As available resources per capita decrease, the costs will increase; there is even a question as to whether or not the developing nations, as they industrialize and acquire not only the need for but also the capacity to process their raw materials, will continue to supply raw materials to the previously developed nations.

A simple objective comparison of available resources to increasing human demands indicates that the system, as currently functioning, cannot continue indefinitely. Use of nonrenewable resources must stop, either voluntarily or involuntarily. Proponents of sustainability opt for the voluntary method.

Sustainable approaches focus on two questions:

1. What are we using?
2. How well are we using it?

What we are using may be perpetual resources, resources that are "virtually inexhaustible on a human time scale,"[18] such as solar, wind, or tidal energy; renewable resources, resources that can be replenished through natural processes in a relatively short time, such as trees and water; or nonrenewable resources, resources that require millions or billions of years to be replenished through geological, physical, and chemical processes, such as aluminum, coal, and oil.

The law of conservation of matter states that matter can be neither created nor destroyed. What we have inherited—perpetual (exclusive of the solar input), renewable, or nonrenewable—is, ultimately, all we've got. We can take some from here and move it there, reshape it, burn it, bury it—but it's all we are going to get. What existed at the beginning of time is what we have now.

A significant ecological aspect of the law of conservation of matter is that matter goes through cyclical transformations. Matter cycles from physical reservoirs into biological reservoirs and back again. Water, for example, regularly travels through rivers, lakes, oceans, and the atmosphere, making detours through plants and animals (e.g., humans). Through transpiration, plants transfer water from the soil to vapor in the air. The rising vapor condenses to form clouds; rain falls, trees grow. Water vapor also condenses over the ocean. Algae in seawater produce dimethyl sulfide, which provides cloud-condensing nuclei, the particles that water condenses around to form clouds. The cloud cover lowers the temperature, causing differentials in temperature and air movement. The cloud collides with a land mass—rain.

There are some interesting environmental corollaries to the law of conservation of matter. If matter cannot be created, we never really get anything new, and we never really throw anything away. We just move it around and combine it with different materials. Therefore, we are drinking the same water that has traveled through the cycle over and over and over since day one. And, if we deposit chemicals into a stream, they are likely to travel with the water to the next location in the cycle, and the next. Ultimately, everything is in your own backyard. The time a water molecule stays at any one point in the cycle is as follows:[19]

Location	Residence Time
Atmosphere	9 days
Rivers	2 weeks
Soil moisture	2 weeks to 1 year
Large lakes	10 years
Underground water at slight depth	10s to 100s of years
Ocean mixed layer to a depth of 55 yards	120 years
Seas and oceans	3,000 years
Underground water at depth	up to 10,000 years
Antarctic ice cap	10,000 years

The question of how well we use our perpetual, renewable, and nonrenewable resources must be answered in terms of our effect on the quality of the resource and our impact on the cycle of the resource (rate of flow, diversion, etc). According to the EPA, "In 2000, states, tribes, territories, and interstate commissions report that about 40% of streams, 45% of lakes, and 50% of estuaries that were assessed were not clean enough to support uses such as fishing and swimming."[20] That survey included only 19 percent of the nation's 3.7 million miles of rivers and streams, and only 43 percent of the nation's 40.6 million acres of lakes, reservoirs, and ponds. According to the Index of Watershed Indicators for 2002, only 15 percent of the nation's watersheds had relatively good water quality.[21] Hose down your driveway and you have diverted a portion of the daily one-third of flowing water in the country and added to it an assortment of petroleum products, pesticides, herbicides, and debris that will flow down the street into the stormwater system. Thermoelectric power generation is responsible for nearly half of the annual water withdrawals in the United States, amounting to approximately 195 billion gallons per day in 1990.[22] A significant pollutant that power plants add to the water is waste heat.

The options for greener use of a resource are often complicated by political and economic factors. Water quite visibly travels across borders and is subjected to a variety of social, economic, and political values along the way. Of the 200 largest river systems in the world, 120 flow through two or more countries. Access to shared resources has triggered numerous conflicts over the centuries. Witness the tension in the Middle East. The 1967 Arab-Israeli war was fought, in part, over water rights to the Jordan River. The conflicting demands of agricultural, industrial, and urban uses are felt not only between countries but also between and within states. The Los Angeles aqueduct project infuriates Northern California. The mighty Colorado River has so many users that it is virtually dry at its end.

While sustainable approaches could benefit from political advances and new technologies, many simple and innovative options are currently available. Many not only improve the manner in which we use our resources but also have financial benefits. For example, a water recirculation system reduced the amount of water the Gillette Company used to make razor blades from 730 million gallons to *156 gallons* per year. Companywide, Gillette now saves approximately $1.5 million a year in water and sewage bills.[23]

Harrah's Hotel and Casino in Las Vegas asked its customers whether they wanted their sheets changed every day. Most said no. Harrah's reduced "its energy and water costs for cleaning sheets by $70,000 per year."[24] By utilizing a landscaping technique called *xeriscaping*, which relies on native plants instead of water-intensive imported plants, Valley Bank in Tucson, Arizona, realized a $20,000 per year savings.[25]

The Earth has evolved thousands of intricate, delicately balanced cycles, each of which is woven into increasingly more complex systems to create the overall single system that is our world. The prospect of living sustainably in the midst of such complexity can be overwhelming. Some respond with a deus ex machina confidence that technology will "solve" the problems, whatever they are, or that nature will adjust as necessary. Others, overwhelmed by the enormity of the challenge, reassure themselves by asserting that the impact one individual can make is negligible. Technology may solve *some* problems, but only if we focus our attention on those problems and seriously endeavor to understand them. Nature *will* undoubtedly adjust; the question is whether or not that adjustment will involve the eradication of our species. And individual impact *does* add up, regardless of whether or not you choose to see the aggregate. Furthermore, history books are full of individuals who had tremendous cultural, economic, political, and environmental impact. As the anthropologist Margaret Mead pointed out, "Never doubt that a small group of thoughtful, committed citizens can change the world. Indeed, it is the only thing that ever has." Solving all the problems simultaneously is as unrealistic as avoiding them. A more constructive approach is to do what you can and continue improving. Maintain the deep dark green goal, but don't let the fact that you are a few shades lighter stop you from achieving even that much.

Can you, as a designer or building owner, envision a building that neither imports nor exports material or energy during construction? during operation? If not, can you envision a trade for the imported or exported material that will balance in a larger picture? To determine how closely you come to this goal, ask these questions: What am I using? How well am I using it?

With a basic appreciation of the law of conservation of matter, the answer to the first question will have implications for the impact of your choice on our natural resources and on the relative healthfulness of our environment. These two topics—resource management and toxicity—are valuable tools for evaluating materials. The answer to the second question will have implications for the performance of the material. Performance issues include durability, energy efficiency, amount of waste generated, and potential for reuse or recycling. Performance is also a valuable tool for evaluating the greenness of a material.

Life Cycle Assessment (LCA) is the formal methodology for answering these questions. LCA is a process that investigates the impact of a product at every stage in its life, from preliminary development through obsolescence. At each stage, you look at the materials and energy consumed and the pollution and waste produced. Life stages include extraction of raw materials, processing and fabrication, transportation, installation, use and maintenance, and reuse/recycling/disposal. To date, there is no single accepted LCA methodology. Experts are still trying to define precisely what is meant by *life cycle assessment*. Groups as diverse as the EPA, ASTM International, the Society of Environmental Toxicology and Chemistry (SETAC), the National Institute of Standards and Technology (NIST), and the International Organization of Standardization (ISO) each have worked on creating an outline of the process. Nevertheless, there is general consensus regarding the concept of LCA and its usefulness in quantifying sustainability.

Selection of materials is only one part (albeit an important one) of making a green building. The LCA methodology helps us visualize the link between the big picture and the details while bringing us that much closer to the goal of living sustainably. This point is emphasized by inclusion of the LCA approach specified in ISO 14000 standards in the BEES software. A future version of the LEED Green Building Rating System is scheduled to include LCA methodology as well.

Every human endeavor has as its basis a condition or state of being we wish to attain. Call it an ideal of perfection for which we strive. In order to make our struggle more manageable, we break our efforts into smaller pieces called *goals*. Goals are the steps we can take on the path toward our ideal. Within the context of the subject of this book, our ideal can be described as a world of buildings that are located, constructed, and designed in a sustainable manner and that allow their occupants to live, work, and play in a sustainable manner.

An inherent quality of an ideal, of perfection, is that it is unattainable. This should not discourage us from making changes in the status quo. With a limited investment of time, money, and research, it is relatively easy to make measurable improvements. That is the crucial point: If you shift your paradigm from simple black-and-white answers to shades of gray (or should we say green), then the possibilities for environmental successes are unlimited.

The subject of green buildings has been widely discussed and often written about. This book does not attempt to be an exhaustive text on the pros and cons of going green. It also does not try to engage in a detailed discussion of green buildings. Many fine books are available on both subjects.

The goal of this book is to help designers and other members of the building construction team better understand the green building material selection and specifying process. By attaining this goal, we hope to take one more step toward reaching our ideal.

Notes

1. In the words of the landmark World Commission on Environment and Development (the Brundtland Commission), we should "meet the needs of the present without compromising the ability of future generations to meet their own needs." Cited in Joel Darmstadter, *Global Development and the Environment: Perspectives on Sustainability,* Resources for the Future, Washington, D.C., 1992.

2. U.S. Department of Energy, Office of Energy Efficiency and Renewable Energy High Performance Buildings, http://www.eere.energy.gov/buildings/highperformance.

3. Valerie Harms. *The National Audubon Society Almanac of the Environment: The Ecology of Everyday Life* (New York: G.P. Putnam's Sons, 1994), 93.

4. *The Denver Post 1991 Colorado Recycling Guide.*

5. EPA Municipal Solid Waste Programs Division.

6. EPA Document EPA530-N-02-003, "WasteWise Update: Building for the Future," 2002, http://www.epa.gov/wastewise/pubs/wwupda16.pdf.

7. USGS Fact Sheet FS-068-98, "Materials Flow and Sustainability," 1998, http://pubs.usgs.gov/fs/fs-0068-98/fs-0068-98.pdf.

8. Department of Energy, "North American Energy Measurement and Verification Protocol," March 1996, DOE / EE-0081, p. 1.

9. David Malin Roodman and Nicholas Lenssen, Worldwatch Paper 124, "A Building Revolution: How Ecology and Health Concerns Are Transforming Construction" (Washington, D.C.: Worldwatch Institute, March 1995), 23.

10. National Science and Technology Council, *Technology for a Sustainable Future: A Framework for Action* (Washington, D.C.: Government Printing Office, 1994), 32.

11. Ibid.

12. James Lovelock first put forth the Gaia Hypothesis in 1969, and published the theory in his book *Gaia: A New Look at Life on Earth* in 1979. With the Gaia Hypothesis, Lovelock proposed that our planet is not just a space occupied by a variety of living things, but is a collection of living things that act together as a single living organism.

13. James Lovelock, *Healing Gaia: Practical Medicine for the Planet* (New York: Harmony, 1991), 157.

14. Roodman and Lenssen, "A Building Revolution," 22.

15. Ibid.

16. G. Tyler Miller, *Living in the Environment: An Introduction to Environmental Sciences*, 7th ed. (Belmont, Calif.: Wadsworth, 1992), 334.

17. United Nations Population Fund, "State of World Population," 2004.

18. Miller, *Living in the Environment*, 10.

19. World Resources Institute, *1994 Information Please Environmental Almanac* (New York: Houghton Mifflin, 1994).

20. EPA Document EPA-841-R-02-001, National Water Quality Inventory, 2000 Report, www.epa.gov/305b.

21. EPA Office of Wetlands, Oceans, and Watersheds, "Index of Watershed Indicators: An Overview," 2002, www.epa.gov/iwi/.

22. Stephen A. Thompson, *Water Use, Management, and Planning in the United States* San Diego, Calif.: Academic Press, 1999), 125, 127.

23. Joel Makower. *the e factor: the bottom-line approach to environmentally responsible business*, (New York: Tilden Press, 1993), 217.

24. Joseph J. Romm, *Lean and Clean Management: How to Boost Profits and Productivity by Reducing Pollution* (New York: Kodansha, 1994), 4.

25. Makower, *the e factor*: the bottom-line approach to environmentally responsible business, New York, NY; The Tilden Press, 1993, p. 217.

CHAPTER 2

Why Use Green Building Materials?

An ounce of prevention is worth a pound of cure.

—Anonymous

Using green building materials can help divert indoor air quality (IAQ) liability claims, respond to consumer demand, and provide for compliance with certain regulatory requirements. And, oh yes, it's the right thing to do.

Liability concerns regarding healthy buildings and healthy sites are rising in proportion to our growing understanding of the potential hazards associated with certain materials. Asbestos and lead are classic examples. Green building products, especially those fabricated from nontoxic, natural, and organic materials, can reduce IAQ contaminants and the accompanying complaints and claims.

Consumer demand for healthy buildings and for energy-efficient structures also drives manufacturers and designers to explore options for green products. Meeting consumer demand is good business. Failure to meet consumer expectations is likely to remind you about the liability concerns.

As more and more green buildings are completed and begin to welcome both occupants and visitors, they are demonstrating why using green building materials pays benefits beyond avoiding liability claims. These buildings can result from a desire to be altruistic or to obtain a financial return on investment. Examples of buildings that exhibit "the right thing to do" are:

The Chesapeake Bay Foundation's Philip Merrill Environmental Center[1] in Annapolis, Maryland. The building incorporates an external shading system made from salvaged wood from old pickle barrels that helps the building control the sun for natural heating and lighting; structural insulated panels as an alternative to conventional framing; cork flooring and wall panels from cork oak trees, wood that is Forest Stewardship Council (FSC) certified or obtained from sustainably managed forests; and metal siding and roofing panels made locally from recycled steel. In these ways the building leads the way in conserving raw materials as well as energy and water. Located on the Chesapeake Bay, the building physically demonstrates the Foundation's efforts to restore the natural habitat of the bay, reduce pollution, and replenish fish stocks. By locating the building on the site of a former beach club, previously undisturbed portions of the site were left untouched and the building's impact on the bay minimized. The building also minimized the use of raw materials by simply using less. This was achieved by exposing much of the structure to view with a design calling for a minimal amount of interior walls. The building also avoids the use of finishes wherever possible. The resulting built environment is a healthy and energy-efficient one that offers occupants natural ventilation and light and views of the bay. Upon completion, the building received the U.S. Green Building Council's LEED® Green Building Rating System's platinum rating, its highest.

The Solaire, a 27-story, 293-unit residential building located in Battery Park City in New York, was built on landfill on the west side of the City's financial district. The building includes a green roof, materials containing recycled content, and materials that are healthy for the occupants. All of the materials incorporated into the building are free of formaldehyde and contain low or no Volatile Organic Compounds (VOCs). A prospectus for the building touts its green features by prominently featuring the words *natural materials* and *live naturally*. The building was so successful in attracting occupants that a second building with the same features is planned nearby.

Four Times Square, located in midtown Manhattan, is a 48-story, 1.6-million-square-foot office building that demonstrates energy efficiency, excellent indoor air quality, and the use of green building materials. The developer of the building, the Durst Organization, knew from the start that the building would be ecologically responsible. They used the building's environmental features as a marketing device while conserving resources and making a healthy place to work. Technologies installed in the building include fuel cells, CFC- and HCFC-free HVAC systems, and photovoltaic panels integral with the curtain wall system. In the end, the building required a higher initial investment but offset this with savings on operating costs.

These economic forces are reflected in the regulatory arena. Voluntary and mandatory environmental guidelines developed at the local, national, and international levels are increasingly applicable to building design and construction. Environmental regulations can present economic and administrative headaches when approached from a business-as-usual standpoint. Conversely, green building materials and methods can make compliance much, much easier.

Altruism, however, is the most frequently cited reason to use green building materials, and we would be remiss to exclude it. As custodians of the built environment, daily decisions we make with respect to product selection have a ripple effect on the natural environment that merits a significant level of professional care. Selection of products used in buildings impacts the Earth directly and indirectly. The building industry is a major consumer of raw materials. Obviously, the type and quantity of raw materials that are extracted and how they are processed constitute the direct impact. Which materials are selected also affects how the building occupants (and, often the community in general) use the building. By obligating occupants, neighbors, and the community to use buildings in certain ways, the selection of building materials constitutes the indirect impact. If, for example, a building uses a membrane roofing system, the installation is likely to involve the release of solvents in the air. If the membrane is black, it is likely to have a negative impact on the energy demands of the building and of the adjacent structures due to the *albedo* (the reflected heat that raises temperatures in the microclimate). If it is a single-ply membrane system, it is likely to be fabricated entirely from synthetic chemicals and virgin materials rather than recycled materials. Single-ply systems, especially adhered systems, make future disassembly and recycling unfeasible.

Altruism is certainly the most laudable reason to use green building products. Self-interest, however, is generally the most compelling. Using green building materials can satisfy some very self-interested motives: deflection of liability, economic gain, and simple regulatory compliance. Self-interested motives beautifully illustrate the relative worth of an ounce of prevention and a pound of cure.

Liability Issues

The Americans with Disabilities Act (ADA) of 1990 ushered in, among other changes, a new term—*biochemically handicapped*—that is not specifically cited in Title III of the ADA (the part that addresses building design). Title III prohibits discrimination on the basis of disability by public entities. *Biochemically handicapped* describes individuals diagnosed with multiple chemical sensitivity (MCS). Such individuals are acutely affected to varying degrees by chemicals commonly found in building products. They suffer headaches, nausea, rashes, and potentially life-threatening asthmatic attacks. Remember the boy in the bubble? He now has recourse under the ADA, as do all of us. But that recourse is still relatively nebulous. ADA case law presents an interesting phenomenon. While hundreds of cases involving MCS have been filed, few, if any, have gone to trial. Apparently, no building owner or material manufacturer wants to test this far-reaching document relative to responsibilities for environmental hazards. No one wants to risk the potential public liability. No one wants to set the precedent on the books. Nevertheless, various agencies and jurisdictions have recognized MCS as a handicap under certain circumstances. Although the Department of Justice (DOJ) declined to state categorically that environmental illness (also known as MCS) was a disability, it recognized that sometimes an individual's respiratory or neurological functioning is so severely affected that he or she satisfies the requirements to be considered disabled under the ADA.[2] In other words, determination of whether or not MCS is a disability is made on a case-by-case basis.

The single greatest culprit in triggering multiple chemical sensitivity reactions—and subsequent ADA filings—is poor IAQ, often referred to as *sick building syndrome*. According to the World Health Organization (WHO), as many as 30 percent of buildings exhibit some kind of sick building syndrome problem. The EPA has stated that the health risks associated with breathing indoor air are 2 to 5 times the risks of breathing outdoor air. The

EPA places poor IAQ fourth on the list of high cancer risks, with 3,500 to 6,000 deaths per year attributable to indoor air pollution. According to the National Institute for Occupational Safety and Health (NIOSH), the relative causes of indoor air pollution are as follows:

53 percent inadequate ventilation

15 percent indoor contaminants

19 percent outdoor contaminants

13 percent unknown

Poor IAQ is expensive; estimates range from tens of thousands to billions of dollars annually in employee sick leave, earnings, and productivity losses. There may also be significant costs associated with IAQ issues for those who find themselves part of a growing body of IAQ legislative case history. Examples of IAQ case law include:[3]

- *Bloomquist v. Wapello County, 500 N.W.2d 1 (Iowa 1993).* Plaintiffs sued employers and builders for providing an unsafe work environment due to an inadequate HVAC system. The jury awarded $1 million, finding chemical exposure associated with pesticide application and inadequate ventilation. The judge set aside the verdict due to inadequate scientific basis. However, the Iowa Supreme Court reversed the judge's decision and reinstated the original verdict.

- *Flores v. Winegrad, No. 87-283 4 5 B, Harris County, District Court, Texas.* The owners and manager of apartment complexes terminated the services of a licensed pest control operator in April 1985 and used their own maintenance staff to apply termiticides. When they sprayed chlordane negligently, without notice to tenants, 311 plaintiffs brought a class action seeking compensatory and punitive damages, alleging negligence. As a test case, a number of the plaintiffs were awarded $10.5 million by the jury as a result of the exposure to the misapplied chlordane.

- *Uricam Corp. v. Partridge Investment Co., No. CJ882691, OK D.C. (Oklahoma 1988).* The owner of an asbestos-contaminated building occupied by the Oklahoma Department of Commerce sued the building's prior owner for $2.9 million, the cost of asbestos inspection, abatement, and damages. The suit was based on a breach of seller's representations and warranties. The asbestos was discovered by Department of Commerce employees. In addition to damages, the complaint sought indemnification against third-party liability. The suit was settled.

- *Bloomfield Co. v. State, 3AN-87-2082 (Alaska).* The state of Alaska moved out of a building owned by Bloomfield Company, alleging sick building syndrome. When the landlord sued the state for $1.8 million for vacating the premises, the state countersued for $1 million in moving expenses. The case was settled.

One of the main reasons that manufacturers, designers, and building owners do not want to set precedents relative to MCS and the ADA is that while IAQ may be the main culprit, it is not the only trigger for MCS reactions; it is just the tip of the proverbial iceberg.

As scientific evidence continues to accumulate, chemicals previously considered inert or relatively benign come under suspicion. As we learn more about the complex workings of our ecosystems, we begin to recognize how naïve we were not to ask more questions about the scientific wonders the chemical industry heralded. And, of course, we look for the responsible parties, those who made the materials and those who profited from them. The potential legal exposure under ADA is immense. Any building occupant (employee or guest) can file a suit alleging discrimination on the basis of a disability. However unintentional this result may have been, the ADA is perhaps one of the most powerful pieces of environmental legislation on record.

Economic Benefits

Obviously, the potential for liability has a considerable economic corollary. The use of green materials, particularly materials considered green because they are natural, organic, or nontoxic, can help reduce claims made by MCS individuals under the ADA. The costs associated with potential liability are directly proportional to the size, location, type, and function of the building, and they can be pretty hefty. Anyone caught in the situation, with the clarity of hindsight, can appreciate the wisdom of the old adage, *an ounce of prevention is worth a pound of cure*.

Similarly, it is easier and more cost-effective to prevent waste than to clean it up afterward. Waste costs money. An ounce of waste prevention is easily worth a pound of waste mitigation. While trash may be the most familiar manifestation of waste, it is not the only one. Waste exists at every stage of a product's transition from a raw material through manufacturing, transportation, and use. *Waste* refers to the unused byproducts, the excess energy or heat, and the pollution produced along the way. It encompasses everything from packaging to greenhouse gases. Waste is lost profits. It is something you have purchased but cannot sell or use. Cut the waste, and you reclaim lost profits.

By performing an eco-audit of your building design, building operations, and manufacturing process, you can identify waste and possibilities for trimming it. An eco-audit is an earth-friendly review of the materials and operations in your building conducted to identify cost-effective opportunities for: improving indoor air quality, water quality and efficiency, energy efficiency, waste minimization, and the environmental integrity of the local ecosystem. An eco-audit is not a review for compliance with environmental regulations. It is a perspective of the building as a living system. An eco-audit reviews the system to identify the input (the energy, materials, and labor required to create the product or service), the output (the product or service itself), and the byproducts (the waste products created in the process). The systems approach examines processes and relationships in addition to materials. An eco-audit is useful for planned new construction and for evaluating existing construction. Opportunities exist to improve efficiency and to green a building and its operations within all schedules and budgets.

Green products can help mitigate economic losses due to waste. Hundreds of opportunities exist in nearly every arena. Water conservation and water quality management, for example, boast numerous products and systems that can pay for themselves quickly.

Water use in the United States doubled from 1950 to 1990, increasing from 910 billion liters (200 billion gallons) per day to more than 1.8 trillion liters (400 billion gallons) per day.[4] The U.S. Geological Survey estimates that the country currently uses 408 billion gallons of water each day. Fresh water is the most precious and one of the most limited resources on our planet. The United Nations Population Fund estimates that only 2.5 percent of the water on the Earth is fresh and only about 0.5 percent is accessible ground or surface water. As the global population has grown, increasing threefold over the last 70 years, the use of freshwater resources has increased sixfold. The World Bank reported in 2001 that agriculture accounts for 70 percent of annual worldwide water use, industry for 22 percent, and household use for 8 percent.

The building industry diverts an estimated 16 percent of global fresh water annually. This estimate accounts for the quantity of water required to manufacture building materials and to construct and operate buildings. It does not reflect the impact of the building industry on the quality of water. It is entirely possible that future estimates of the percentage of available fresh water will decrease as we contaminate our limited supply.

Simply replacing a leaky faucet can save 160 liters (36 gallons) per day. Sensor-operated faucets and flush valves are classic examples of automatic controls to reduce waste. Low-flow fixtures are another way to conserve water. Homes with older fixtures use about 75 gallons of water per person per day; homes with water-saving fixtures that are now required by most plumbing codes use between 25 and 50 gallons of water per person per day.[5] The U.S. Department of Defense (DOD), in compliance with Executive Order 12902, "Energy Efficiency and Water Conservation at Federal Facilities—March 8, 1994," installed new multistage dishwashing equipment in a federal cafeteria. Multistage dishwashers reuse water from the rinse cycle to prewash dishes. The DOD installation cost $57,800 and resulted in an annual savings of 500,000 gallons of water, $2,000 in water costs, and $19,000 in labor costs. Payback was 2.7 years and is projected to save almost $500,000 over the 25-year life of the installation.[6]

Selecting indigenous plant material (xeriscaping) instead of decorative hothouse species could reduce municipal water requirements more effectively than low-flow fixtures or sensor-operated faucets. Because native plants are appropriate to the climate, they are easy to maintain. They do not need extra water or care, except perhaps during the 12-month establishment period. Buffalo grass is replacing many lawns in the prairie states. Buffalo grass requires 25 inches of water per year compared to Bermuda grass, which requires 40, Zoysia, which requires 45, and St. Augustine, which requires 50. Compare such water requirements with the average 35.45 inches annual rainfall in the Dallas–Fort Worth area[7] or the average 35.30 inches in Canton, Illinois.[8] Furthermore, not only is less water required but also less chemical fertilizers and pesticides.

Ozonation equipment also offers the dual savings of reduced water requirements and reduced chemical requirements. To this it adds energy savings. Ozone oxidizes bacteria, viruses, and other contaminants up to 3,000 times faster than chlorine, thereby reducing chemical usage up to 95 percent. With the addition of ozone as an oxidant, laundry and dishwashing machines can run at lower wash temperatures for shorter cycles. Washing time can be reduced by nearly half because the rinse cycle can be eliminated. Ozone reduces total dissolved solids, which reduces calcium and scale buildup so swimming pools need to be drained less often and equipment life is prolonged.

Where droughts are common, rainwater harvesting systems are exceptionally useful at minimizing waste. Rainwater harvesting keeps rainwater on site. It lessens the burden to municipal water facilities and decreases erosion and flooding caused by runoff from impervious surfaces. Rainwater harvesting systems gained high-profile recognition when, in January 1999, the U.S. Postal Service (USPS) opened its first green post office in Fort Worth. This facility incorporated, among other items, a rainwater harvesting system. Droughts are common in Texas; they have occurred somewhere in the state once every decade of this century.[9] Therefore, it is especially important for Texans to use water wisely. The system being tested by the USPS is helping develop a viable technology and bring it to the mainstream.

Energy-efficient products and, in some cases, water-efficient products can generate economic gains that are clearly documented on utility bills. Many utilities, recognizing that it would be cheaper for them to help finance the replacement of thousands of inefficient appliances and equipment with new, efficient units than it would be to build new plants to serve anticipated loads, offered rebates throughout the 1980s and early 1990s. The incredible success of the EPA's voluntary programs, Green Lights and Energy Star, is due, in large part, to the improvements seen by participants in their bottom lines. In the summer of 2002, the EPA began to investigate ways to enhance the market for water-efficient products as a potential program to respond to the growing demands placed on U.S. water supplies and water infrastructure systems.[10] As a result of their initial investigation, EPA conducted several stakeholder meetings during 2003 and 2004. Over 100 state and local water officials, environmental organizations, and businesses indicated their support for a water-efficient product labeling program modeled after the Energy Star program. Before computer-controlled, self-regulating heating and air conditioning systems, people built climate-appropriate buildings—buildings that caught the cool breeze on a hot summer day and allowed the sun to shine deep into the interior during the cold days of winter. This approach is called *passive solar design*, and it has a long history. In 360 B.C., Socrates wrote: ". . . in houses with a south aspect, the sun's rays penetrate into the porticoes in winter; but in summer, the path of the sun is right above the roof so that there is shade. If, then, this is the best arrangement, we should build the south side loftier to get the winter sun, and the north side lower to keep out the cold winds." Technological advances permit us to build without regard for climate. However, if we combine the efforts—build in a climate-appropriate way *and* use convenient modern technologies, we can maximize our energy efficiency. Simply locating deciduous plants on the south and west sides of a building can cool a building in summer with their shade and allow warm sunshine to penetrate the building in winter when their leaves are gone. Another simple climate appropriate consideration is albedo. Albedo can affect energy efficiency because it affects the microclimate—that is, it is a lot hotter walking across black asphalt paving than it is walking across concrete paving, and it is hotter walking across concrete paving than it is walking across grass, and it is hotter walking across grass than it is walking across shaded grass. Reductions in surrounding microclimate temperatures mean that the building air conditioning does not need to work as hard. In some urban areas, utility rates are as much as 10 percent greater than in adjacent rural areas. This is due to the albedo of the paved roads and tall buildings in urban areas.[11]

Consumer Demand and New Markets

Green products can help recapture lost profits by mitigating potential liabilities and reducing waste. Manufacturers and building owners have already learned this and are implementing efficiency upgrades in various forms. This raises the benchmark and creates a demand for the identification of other possible lost profits, other opportunities for green products.

In addition to mitigating economic losses, using green building products responds to a growing market demand for organic, nontoxic, energy-efficient, earth-friendly products across the board. Consumer interest in environmental issues has been gaining ground steadily. Health food stores and environmental mail order catalogs abound. It is rare to open a newspaper or watch television without being exposed to information about environmental damage, followed by what people are doing to fix it. How many surveys have you seen estimating the environmental surcharge people are willing to pay on gasoline, cigarettes, or energy? *The Green Consumer Guide,* published in 1988, was a best-seller. Since then, entire publishing companies have been dedicated to environmental issues. The public is hungry for green products and gravitates to green markets wherever they become available.

Mirroring consumer demand, in 1993 President Clinton issued Executive Order 12873, "Federal Acquisition, Recycling, and Waste Prevention," which directed each executive agency to "incorporate waste prevention and recycling in the agency's daily operations and work to increase and expand markets for recovered materials through greater federal government preference and demand for such products." In particular, the order required that all paper purchased by the federal government contain 20 percent post-consumer recycled content by the end of 1994, increasing to 30 percent by 1998. In 1998, Executive Order 13101, "Greening the Government Through Waste Prevention, Recycling, and Federal Acquisition," expanded the earlier directive to encompass biobased (alternative agricultural) products as well. Such presidential mandates for the U.S. federal government, perhaps the single largest contractor in the world, drive new markets. The U.S. General Services Administration (GSA), which provides the buildings and supplies for the federal government, annually negotiates $200 billion of goods and services bought from the private sector.[12] It purchases the paper, which must contain a minimum of 30 percent recycled materials, that the federal government uses. It is not surprising that paper with recycled content is now readily available and comparable in cost and quality to paper manufactured entirely from virgin trees. To assist federal customers in meeting their environmental goals, the GSA's Federal Supply Service publishes an *Environmental Products and Services Guide* containing information about thousands of products that have recycled or biobased content, conserve energy and/or water, or contain pollutants, as well as environmental services offered by GSA.

The environmental market, encouraged by the federal government, is shifting away from cleanup to pollution prevention, from Superfund activities to research and design. For years, the EPA has emphasized end-of-pipe regulations, which control pollution only after its creation. The EPA is increasingly focusing its efforts on pollution prevention. Enter the architect, the manufacturer, the landscaper, and the specifier.[13] This shift in emphasis opens up a new market for products and services. The global market for environmental technologies in 1992 was approximately 300 billion dollars and five years later an estimated 400 billion dollars.[14] *Environmental technologies* are defined as those that "advance sustainable development by reducing risk, enhancing cost effectiveness, improving process efficiency, and creating products and processes that are environmentally beneficial or benign. The word technology is intended to include hardware, software, systems, and services."[15] Both green building products and green design services are factors of the burgeoning environmental technology market.

Some of the most visible displays of this shift in federal approach are the voluntary programs for energy efficiency. For a while, the EPA and the DOE stumbled over each other trying to establish programs. Finally, in 1996 they joined to increase the product categories available under the Energy Star label. More recently, Green Lights, ClimateWise, and the labeled products program were consolidated under the Energy Star umbrella. The result is impressive. Green Lights is a voluntary program to assist conversion to more energy-efficient technologies such as T-8 lamps, electronic ballasts, occupancy sensors, daylight controls, and compact fluorescent lamps. The Energy Star program expands the concepts illustrated in the EPA Green Lights program, applying the approach to other technologies, including computers, office equipment, residential appliances, and buildings. The Energy Star Homes Program requires energy consumption 30 percent less than that allowed by the model energy code. Homes that comply are eligible for energy-efficient mortgages. In 2004 alone, the Energy Star program helped save enough energy to power 24 million homes and avoid greenhouse gas emissions equivalent to those from 20 million cars, while at the same time saving $10 billion.[16]

Regulatory Requirements

Still, regulatory requirements are in place at local, state, and federal levels that are not voluntary and that do emphasize end-of-pipe solutions. Regulatory requirements can also have significant economic effects. Ask any lobbyist. For example, compliance with environmental legislation, such as the National Pollutant Discharge Elimination System (NPDES), requirements of the Clean Water Act, or the abatement requirements of the Comprehensive Environmental Response, Compensation, and Liability Act (CERCLA or Superfund) can be expensive. Green products can mitigate the expense and help streamline compliance.

NPDES prohibits discharge of pollutants into waters of the United States unless a special permit is issued by the EPA, a state, or, where the authority is delegated, a tribal government on a Native American reservation. NPDES requirements affect permit applications, regulatory guidance, and management and treatment requirements. The Phase I Stormwater program permit application requirements address certain categories of stormwater discharges associated with industrial activity, including manufacturing facilities; construction operations disturbing five or more acres; hazardous waste treatment, storage, or disposal facilities; landfills; certain sewage treatment plants; recycling facilities; power plants; mining operations; some oil and gas operations; airports, and certain other transportation facilities. Government-owned facilities must also comply. The Phase II Stormwater program applies to smaller municipalities and is estimated to include as many as 1.1 million commercial, institutional, and retail sources, and 5,700 municipalities.[17] The Phase II program also covers small construction activities disturbing between one and five acres of land.

In many circumstances, retention ponds are required to obtain NPDES permits. However, pervious paving can often reduce or eliminate the need for retention ponds. Pervious pavement is a green building product. It includes pervious concrete and interlocking pavers that allow water to percolate through the joints of the pavers and paving forms specifically designed to support soil and grass. Most of the paving forms that are designed to support soil and grass are fabricated from recycled plastic. Use of pervious concrete paving or pervious pavers reduces stormwater runoff from solid surfacing. Pervious pavement can be up to 90 percent permeable, which means that 90 percent of the moisture that hits the paved surface will percolate through it, and 10 percent will run off.

Abatement of contaminated soil is another example of the potential for a green approach to save on regulatory requirement expenses. Ordinarily, contaminated soil is removed and mechanically or chemically treated off-site and burned or landfilled. Phytoremediation is an alternative treatment that can be as much as 50 percent less expensive than standard treatment. This innovative technology utilizes plants and trees to clean up contaminated soil and water. It is an aesthetically pleasing, solar-energy-driven, passive technique that can be used to clean up metals, pesticides, solvents, crude oil, polyaromatic hydrocarbons, and landfill leachates. Plants can break down organic pollutants that contain carbon and hydrogen. Plants can also extract (phytoaccumulate) certain metal contaminants. Nickel, zinc, and copper are the best candidates for removal by phytoextraction because they are the favorites of the approximately 400 plants known to phytoextract contaminants. The plants are harvested as necessary and either incinerated or composted to recycle the metals. Trees have long taproots that act as organic pumps/filters. Poplar trees, for example, can pull out of the ground 30 gallons of water per day. The pulling action of the roots decreases the tendency of surface pollutants to move downward toward groundwater or aquifers.

At the local level, environmental regulations take on a more regional flavor, responding to local environmental quality issues and economic concerns. Like international agreements, however, local developments can translate into national policy. Concerns about air quality originally localized in New England and California have gained federal attention. Recycling procurement policies, prevalent at the state level, are replicated in Executive Order 13101 which directs federal agencies to use recycled content materials for their supplies, everything from paper to concrete paving.

The international level can also birth national regulatory requirements. Although international agreements do not obligate the signatory nations per se, they nevertheless carry a great deal of political weight. More than 150 international environmental treaties have been adopted, most since 1970. Ultimately, many are internalized by signatory nations through national legal processes in each country. As seen in Kyoto, even when international environmental treaties are not internalized via the legislative process, they can affect a country. Nations that do not embrace global political agreements are often in an extremely unpleasant spotlight. Thus, despite their relative lack of enforcement mechanisms, international treaties can be powerful tools that affect the development of national regulations and economic strategies.

The Montreal Protocol, authored in 1987, was an international agreement to phase out substances destructive to the ozone layer. It was amended in 1990 and accepted by 93 nations agreeing to phase out five key chlorofluorocarbons (CFCs 11, 12, 113, 114, and 115), carbon tetrachloride, and nonessential uses of fire-extinguishing halons by the year 2000. It also stipulated the phaseout of Hydrochlorofluorocarbons (HCFCs) by the year 2020 and established a multilateral fund to help developing nations finance this effort. In 1990, President Bush signed the Clean Air Act Amendments, which internalized the Montreal Protocol for the United States. The Clean Air Act Amendments mandated an increase in controls for acid rain, urban smog, car emissions, toxic air pollutants, and ozone depletion. Under this law, the EPA sets limits on how much of a pollutant can be in the air anywhere in the United States. Individual states may have stronger pollution controls, but no state is allowed to have weaker pollution controls than those set for the country as a whole.[18]

Agenda 21, developed in 1992 at the Earth Summit in Rio de Janeiro, had no less ambitious a goal than to stop and reverse environmental damage to our planet and to promote sustainable development in all countries. Agenda 21 contains 40 separate areas of concern with 120 separate actions and corresponding financial requirements to address: quality of life on Earth, efficient use of 'natural resources, protection of the global commons, management of human settlements, chemicals and the management of waste, and sustainable economic growth. The U.S. Climate Change Action Plan was a partial internalization of Agenda 21. It emphasizes voluntary programs to achieve a reduction in greenhouse gases to 1990 levels by year 2000. Greenhouse gases (carbon dioxide, ozone, methane, nitrous oxide, chlorofluorocarbon, and others) act like the glass panes of a greenhouse. They allow light, infrared radiation, and some ultraviolet radiation from the sun to penetrate the atmosphere to the Earth's surface, which absorbs much of the solar energy and reflects infrared radiation. Some of the reflected radiation escapes into space, and some is trapped by the greenhouse gases and reflected back to the Earth as heat. When greenhouse gases build up in the atmosphere, more heat is trapped and reflected back to Earth, resulting in global warming. Greenhouse gases have increased significantly since the Industrial Revolution of the mid-1800s. The plan addresses both economic and environmental concerns. By improving efficiencies, the United States improves our national bottom line and prevents the pollution associated with the energy generation. The U.S. Climate Change Action Plan details 45 actions and $1.9 billion in redirected federal dollars, along with an estimated $60 billion savings by year 2000. Estimated savings include 25 percent energy savings in construction and 40 percent energy savings in building operations. The plan is implemented, in part, through EPA and DOE programs such as Energy Star and Rebuild America.

Of equal importance to international agreements are international standards. Just as numerous standards-making bodies exist at the national level, many such bodies operate at the global level. International standards developed by the International Organization for Standardization (ISO), for example, are the global corollary to national standards developed by ASTM International (formerly the American Society for Testing and Materials) (ASTM). The development of ASTM standards dealing with environmental subjects is covered in more detail in chapter 3.

International standards are emerging as extremely powerful tools when wielded by global corporate interests. The World Trade Organization's (WTO) *Agreement on Technical Barriers to Trade* requires that signatories adopt international standards as the basis for national standards. Ostensibly, this means that voluntary international standards can preempt national regulations. Consider the European Union (EU) versus the United States regarding the import of beef containing growth hormones. In 1997, the WTO ruled that member nations could not impose health standards restricting farmers' use of growth hormones in beef cattle more stringent than those recommended by CODEX Alimentarius, an international food standards agency. This ruling was a result of a U.S. government challenge of EU health standards that blocked the import into Europe of beef that had been injected with hormones. Despite EU regulations prohibiting the sale of beef containing growth hormones, the EU is now obliged under the rules of the WTO to allow the import of beef containing growth hormones. As of this writing, the EU is appealing the decision. Design consultants and building product manufacturers should learn from this example and be aware of the development of international standards for green building and green building products.

Altruism and Professional Responsibility

The costs that may be tracked on a typical assets/liabilities summary may appear significant to the bottom line of a particular project or product, but they pale in comparison to the environmental costs. It may be hard to economically justify basic it's-the-right-thing-to-do logic, but it will be impossible to continue without it, economically and otherwise.

We have only this one planet. It has the same amount of resources—water, air, minerals—that it has had since the beginning of time, yet demand for them is continually increasing. More people and higher standards of living require more and more goods. Most goods are derived from the Earth's natural resources, to be used briefly and then buried in a landfill. By the middle of the next century, the same limited amount of resources is expected to support nearly 12 billion people. We need to be extremely careful of the resources we use and how much of them we use. We must vigilantly ask and answer these questions:

What are we using?

How well are we using it?

Furthermore, our limited resources are not spread out evenly. There are centers of biodiversity. *Biodiversity,* or *biological diversity,* refers to the variety of plant and animal species and the ecological communities in which they live. Scientists have discovered that each species on Earth originated in only one location. Pecans and sunflowers, for example, are believed to have originated in the Oklahoma area. From there, they spread across the earth. Because they originated in Oklahoma, however, the greatest variety of pecan and sunflower types are still found in this area. We rely on biodiversity, the different characteristics of different species, for medical, agricultural, and industrial advances. When we remove all existing vegetation during the construction process, even if we landscape with native vegetation" afterward, we destroy a portion of the biodiversity of the area forever.

We also contribute to the destruction of the Earth's biodiversity when we rely on a single species. Most lumber products, for example, are derived from an extremely limited number of species. Codes, standards, and industry structural tables are limited to a handful of species, such as southern yellow pine. Reliance on a single species or a limited number of species promotes *monoculture,* the antithesis of biodiversity. It was, in part, monoculture that devastated Ireland in the Great Potato Famine of the mid-1800s. At the time, the Irish relied almost entirely on a single species of potato. When it failed, thousands died of starvation.

Some techno-enthusiasts have argued that a little DDT would have put an end to the potato famine in a hurry. In the short term, that may have been true. But the next generation of Irish would have been much worse off. How much simpler to plant several species of potato to benefit from nature's resiliency in the vast gene pool! How much healthier for us and for the planet to eat potatoes that survive blight without poison! The DDT solution overlooks a basic law of nature, the *conservation of matter*. Everything cycles. *Everything.* Everything moves from physical reservoirs to biological reservoirs and back again. In the summer, the carbon dioxide we exhale may be utilized by the leaf of the tree, which will fall to the ground in autumn, decompose under the winter snow, and nourish our vegetable garden next spring. *Everything cycles.*

By specifying green products—products that are nontoxic, have recycled contents, and are themselves easily recyclable—we can make it safer and easier to cycle materials responsibly and eliminate waste. Waste costs money. It pollutes the planet and consolidates the Earth's resources in singularly useless pits around the world. Most landfill pits are hygienically isolated and rigorously compressed such that the contents are not exposed to oxygen or water and, consequently, do not readily decompose. Assuming a site that promotes decomposition, however, decomposition time for plastic is one million years; for paper, one month; for glass, over one million years; for apples, three to four weeks; and for aluminum, 200 to 500 years.[19]

Societal costs can be significant. A tiny island about 2,000 miles from the nearest continent was "discovered" on Easter day in 1722—Easter Island. It was barren, a biological wasteland except for grasses and insects—and the statues. You have probably seen the statues, approximately 200 mammoth stone sentries, some more than 30 feet tall and weighing over 80 tons. These statues were a scientific and historic mystery for years. Now, based on analysis of ancient pollen stratified on Easter Island, we know a little more about the statues and the people who made them. Around A.D. 400, Easter Island was a subtropical paradise, rich in biodiversity, with abundant plant life and animal life. The most common tree was the Easter Island palm, which grew more than 80 feet tall and was ideal for carving into canoes and equipment for erecting statues. The island also produced the toromiro tree, similar to mesquite, that was good for fuel; and the hauhau tree, from which could be obtained a strong fiber ideal for making rope.[20]

We now know that the inhabitants of Easter Island developed a highly organized social structure of approximately 2,000 people. We also know that they exploited their resources to the extreme—to their own extinction. These people are gone. They paid the highest price for their environmental mistakes.

Of course, we have made a few mistakes of our own. Each has had significant societal costs. Here are some recent examples:

- *Love Canal, New York (1978).* Attributing high rates of illness and birth defects to highly toxic chemicals dumped at the site from 1942 to 1953, New York State forced the evacuation of 740 families from the area. In 1980, the site became the first federal environmental disaster area.

- *Bhopal, India (December 3, 1984).* A chemical accident at a Union Carbide pesticide plant resulted in approximately 10,000 deaths and 200,000 to 500,000 injuries.

- *Chernobyl, Russia (April 25–26, 1986).* By far the worst single disaster in the world's nuclear power industry, the meltdown at the Chernobyl nuclear power plant resulted in at least 50,000 deaths and radiation levels that ten years later were reported to be 40 to 800 rads in the affected area (average normal background radiation is seven rads; 12 rads is considered dangerously high and requires protective gear to avoid exposure).

- *Prince William Sound, Alaska (March 24, 1989).* An Exxon supertanker grounded on Bligh Reef and spilled more than 11 million gallons of oil into Prince William Sound. Environmental damage is still being quantified and, unfortunately, debated.

These mistakes did not happen on isolated islands. Radiation, pollution, and chemical spills do not recognize geographical or political boundaries. They are not contained by mountains or oceans. These mistakes affect the global commons, the resources we all share. It should be no surprise, then, that we also share their economic impact. It costs each of us when the environment and our health and welfare are jeopardized. A 1984 WHO Committee report suggested that up to 30 percent of new and remodeled buildings have poor IAQ.[21] Poor IAQ, according to the EPA, costs Americans $1.5 billion in medical bills and tens of billions in lost productivity annually. Up to 10 percent of urban electric demand is spent cooling buildings to compensate for heat gain due to a concentration of buildings, traffic, and dark paved surfaces.[22]

A growing number of statistics quantify societal costs that, historically, were not quantified, nor were they even recognized. If you are susceptible to poor IAQ that can be 100 times worse than poor outdoor air quality, your head may ache, your energy level may diminish, and you may become physically ill—perhaps even suffering long-term health effects. Typically, you will not trace any of these symptoms to the cause; you will merely call in sick to work until your body can rid itself of the debilitating toxins. Then you will return to your daily routine until the buildup of toxins in your system is, once again, more than you can tolerate. This susceptibility is called MCS, and it might be considered a handicap under the Americans with Disabilities Act.

Other aspects of societal costs are also beginning to be recognized. The Department of Commerce, Bureau of Economic Statistics, is developing measures of economic value for environmental assets, including renewable resources, nonrenewable resources, air quality, and water quality[23]; and, the President's Council for Sustainability, in its 1996 publication *Sustainable America: A New Consensus for Prosperity, Opportunity, and a Healthy Environment for the Future*, recommended that measurements of gross national product (GNP) be revised to incorporate environmental assets and reflect their consumption/degradation.

GNP is an extremely poor indicator of a nation's wealth and economic stability. It is deceptive. It not only fails to subtract environmental damage from a country's assets, it also generally views them as contributing to prosperity. Global warming, for example, is readily acknowledged as costly and problematic. In 1995, the United Nation's Intergovernmental Panel on Climate Change (IPCC), a group of approximately 2,500 scientists, determined that the greenhouse effect was real, and that human activity, particularly the production of greenhouse gases, was affecting global climate patterns. Furthermore, the IPCC advised that global warming would not mean an even temperature increase across the Earth. Rather, it would mean an uneven increase resulting in significant alterations to global weather patterns. The poles would warm more quickly than the equator and continents more quickly than the deep oceans. Gulfstream and wind patterns, relied on season after season, year after year, will be affected. In turn, climate regulators such as wetlands, rain forests, and oceanic plankton will be affected. Severe phenomena such as floods, hurricanes, droughts, and fires are likely to typify the changing climate. Over the last decade, the world has experienced a significant number of weather-related disasters. Under current economic systems, the costs to repair and replace damaged property, to feed the newly homeless, and to aid the injured are calculated as increasing the GNP. Money changes hands. Services and goods are provided. These are credits to the GNP. They make it appear to rise. But there is no balance to the equation, no deduction for the property and lives lost, no deduction for businesses delayed or destroyed, and no recognition of the part global warming played in the event. Hurricane Katrina, which devastated New Orleans and the Gulf coast, resulted in losses estimated at greater than $100 billion. The insurance estimates do not take into account lost lives or lost livelihoods. They do not assess the societal costs of contamination or the impacts on wildlife. They look at the lost structures. So does the building industry. Almost before Katrina had ended her fury, the building industry began a feeding frenzy in anticipation of the profits to be made in the rising demand (and corresponding increase in prices) for building materials. Because GDP still does not account for societal costs and ecosystem costs, it looks like Katrina will result in significant economic growth . . . at least on the books.

Government and academia are not alone in recognizing societal costs of environmental degradation. Industry, particularly those segments most directly affected by global warming, is also beginning to acknowledge societal costs. Hardest hit by the climate change have been agriculture, fishery, tourism, and insurance industries. The insurance industry is extremely powerful and wields a great deal of influence. It has taken notice of cause and effect. The first five years of the 2000s cost the insurance industry $57 billion in weather-related losses, compared to $17 billion for the entire previous decade.[24] Because under the current economic valuation system the insurance industry carries a disproportionately large share of the fiscal burden for societal damage to the global commons, it is particularly interested in revising the status quo. Change certainly means accepting the cause-and-effect relationship. It also means a commitment to reducing the pollution contributing to greenhouse gases, which contributes to global warming, which increases extreme weather and related disasters, which costs the insurance industry billions of dollars. It is also likely to involve new criteria for measurement and distribution of societal costs.

More often, economic equivalents are being developed that help us quantify the enormousness of damage. Wetlands, for example, play an important role in the purification of water on the planet, and their function can be equated to water treatment facilities. Of course, they simultaneously perform other services, such as incubating the majority of freshwater aquatic life. If a vandal were to enter a water treatment facility and dump toxins or fill the holding tanks for the sake of development, he or she (or it, in the case of corporations) would be arrested, jailed, and fined. By establishing comparable values for ecosystems relative to their usefulness to humans, we create the mechanisms whereby vandals destroying wetlands are similarly penalized.

Forests are critical for air purification and planetary cooling. James Lovelock, a fellow of the Royal Society, developed the Gaia theory, the theory that Earth functions as a single organism. He also developed an interesting economic equivalent for one function of the world's forests. He wrote:

> One way to value the forests as air conditioners would be to assess the annual energy cost of achieving the same amount of cooling mechanically. If the clouds made by the forests are taken to reduce the heat flux of sunlight received within their canopies by only 1 percent, then their cooling effect would require a refrigerator with a cooling power of 6 kilowatts per hectare. The energy needed, assuming complete efficiency and no capital outlay, would cost annually $1300 per hectare. . . . A hectare of cleared tropical forest is said to yield meat enough for about 1,850 beefburgers annually, meat worth at the site not more than about $40, and this only during the very few years that the land can support livestock. . . . The 5 square meters of land needed to produce enough meat for one burger has lost the world a refrigeration service worth about $65.[25]

Even this does not begin to address the value of forests as medical resources, construction products, and habitat, nor does it consider the intrinsic value of forests, the inherent worth of a living thing and its innate right to life. (Those interested in legal arguments for the inherent rights of living things should review Christopher Stone's thesis, *Should Trees Have Standing? Toward Legal Rights for Natural Objects.*[26])

More recently, an international effort reviewed and tabulated hundreds of studies to compute the value of many of the services the world's major ecosystems provide. Robert Costanza of the University of Maryland and colleagues calculated that the current economic value of the world's ecosystem services (pollination, water purification, climate regulation) is $16 to $54 trillion per year—compared to the gross world product of $28 trillion per year.[27]

Green Building Materials: An Ounce of Prevention

Buildings impact the Earth directly through their use of resources. They work directly on the quantity and quality of the Earth's resources—the amount they use and the degree to which they contaminate what they use. Buildings impact the Earth indirectly through their performance and through their effect on the performance of adjacent structures. Buildings impact the Earth indirectly through design decisions that help drive the market. If you select a green product, you make a philosophical and an economic statement. Manufacturers are listening.

Architects, as custodians of the built environment, have an opportunity and an obligation to confront these issues. Architects can have a huge impact not only on the design of the building (which can affect the people who use it) but also on the design process (which can affect the market, regulatory requirements, and accepted practices). For building industry members associated with commercial or institutional projects, the potential impact is multiplied.

Often, however, the question is not so much whether a greener, more efficient solution exists but rather how to identify and implement such a solution. The expectations of the design and construction industry tend to limit design choices to current industry standards, which are not necessarily the most efficient. They also tend to focus attention on problem solving during the construction phase rather than problem identification during the design phase, further limiting the range of possible solutions. Standard design and construction strategies often require a pound of cure. Green strategies offer an ounce of prevention.

Notes

1. Chesapeake Bay Foundation web site, www.cbf.org.

2. U.S. Department of Justice, Nondiscrimination on the Basis of Disability in State and Local Government Services Final Rule, January 26, 1992, www.usdoj.gov/crt/ada/reg2.html.

3. Joe Manko, Manko, Gold & Katcher, cited at the National Indoor Environment Conference, Baltimore, 1996.

4. Department of Energy, *Greening Federal Facilities: An Energy, Environmental, and Economic Resource Guide for Federal Facility Managers.* DOE / EE-0123, 1997, p. 89.

5. Texas Water Development Board, *The Texas Manual on Rainwater Harvesting*, 3rd ed. (Austin, Texas: 2005).

6. Department of Energy, *Greening Federal Facilities*, 59.

7. Texas Water Development Board.

8. Canton, Illinois, Chamber of Commerce, 1998.

9. Activities of the Texas Groundwater Protection Committee, Report to the 75th Legislature, 1996.

10. http://www.epa.gov/OW-OWM.html/water-efficiency/products_program.htm.

11. Environmental Protection Agency, "Cooling Our Communities: A Guidebook on Tree Planting and Light-Colored Surfacing," 22P–2001, 1992.

12. GSA 2002 Strategic Plan, www.gsa.gov.

13. Environmental Protection Agency, "Green Lights: An Enlightened Approach to Energy Efficiency and Pollution Prevention," 430-K-93-001, July 1993.

14. National Science and Technology Council, *Technology for a Sustainable Future: A Framework for Action*, 800 / ENV-6676 (Washington, D.C.: Government Printing Office).

15. Ibid.

16. www.energystar.gov.

17. Environmental Protection Agency, "Summary of Laws and Regulations," www.epa.gov/epahome/rules.html#codified.

18. Environmental Protection Agency, "Features of the 1990 Clean Air Act," www.epa.gov/epahome/rules.html#codified.

19. Miami–Dade County Department of Environmental Resources Management, Miami, Florida.

20. "Easter Island: Learning from the Past," *Environmental Building News* 4, no. 5 (September/October 1995), Brattleboro, Vermont.

21. Environmental Protection Agency, "Indoor Air Facts No. 4: Sick Building Syndrome (SBS)," rev. 1991.

22. Environmental Protection Agency, "Cooling Our Communities."

23. National Science and Technology Council, *Technology for a Sustainable Future*, 106.

24. Christopher Flavin and Odil Tunali, Worldwatch Paper 130, "Climate of Hope: New Strategies for Stabilizing the World's Atmosphere" (Washington, D.C.: Worldwatch Institute, June 1996).

25. James Lovelock, *Healing Gaia: Practical Medicine for the Planet* (New York: Harmony, 1991), 183.

26. Christopher D. Stone, *Should Trees Have Standing? Toward Legal Rights for Natural Objects* (New York: Avon, 1975).

27. Lester R. Brown, Christopher Flavin, Hilary French, et al., "State of the World 1997: A Worldwatch Institute Report on Progress Toward A Sustainable Society" (New York: W.W. Norton, 1997): 37.

CHAPTER 3

What Are Green Building Materials?

Our entire society rests upon—and is dependent upon—our water, our land, our forests, and our minerals. How we use these resources influences our health, security, economy, and well-being.

—John F. Kennedy

Green building materials are those that use the Earth's resources in an environmentally responsible way. Green building materials respect the limitations of nonrenewable resources such as coal and metal ores. They work within the pattern of nature's cycles and the interrelationships of ecosystems. Green building materials are nontoxic. They are made from recycled materials and are themselves recyclable. They are energy-efficient and water-efficient. They are green in the way they are manufactured, the way they are used, and the way they are reclaimed after use. Green building materials are those that earn high marks for resource management, impact on indoor environmental quality (IEQ), and performance (energy efficiency, water efficiency, etc.).

Ideally, we specify only those products that use a minimum amount of perpetual or renewable resources and that use them very, very well at all stages. Ideally, we understand the basic environmental principle of finite, cyclical matter and temper our every action accordingly. Some radical environmentalists do, even in the building industry.

We support this ideal and endeavor to work toward it. Nevertheless, an awful lot of progress may be made by working with people who are not yet convinced and by demonstrating that green building, especially in shades of green, is possible and painless and often profitable. Furthermore, by so doing, we can collectively raise the benchmark and make it easier to build greener and greener buildings. This book is for those who recognize the necessity of addressing environmental issues and who must cope with those who do not. It is for those who want to do the right thing but must balance ideals with tight schedules, limited budgets, and entrenched anti-green perspectives.

While people may recognize that the term *green* means "environmentally friendly," most have several misperceptions about how environmentally friendly products perform relative to the standard, more familiar products. In the building industry, it is not uncommon for the owner's initial response to the topic to sound something like this:

"Yes! Of *course,* I'm interested in protecting our environment."

"Yes, I'd like to discuss green building options."

"Yeah, so, what kind of cost are we talking about here?"

"Well . . . does it work?"

"And, um, what would this thing look like, you know, if we did go green?"

It is politically correct to express concern for the environment. Paradoxically, it is equally acceptable to express apprehension at implementing green approaches rather than standard approaches.

Information detailing environmental degradation, global warming, and chemical contamination of our earth is readily available. It is disseminated across society, from kindergarten through graduate school, on National Public Radio programs and in CNN news clips. Leading scientists, including about 2,500 scientists from the United Nation's Intergovernmental Panel on Climate Change, concur that human activity causes pollution, vanquishes species, and is linked to global warming.[1] We know that we have a problem.

However, the correlating education and support network that would enable us to respond actively and positively to the environmental warnings is only now beginning to emerge. Partial information, outdated information, and misinformation plague the successful development of green building. The majority of building owners, designers, engineers, contractors, manufacturers, and building officials are receptive to protecting the environment but are *not* receptive to using green materials to accomplish the task. The unfortunate perception is that green building materials look bad, cost a lot, and do not perform well. Understanding this perspective is essential for effectively resolving such concerns. Therefore, in order to better understand what green building materials are, we need to clarify what they are not. We need to get rid of the pervasive misperceptions about green building materials.

What Does Green Look Like?

It is important to recognize the overwhelming societal prejudice in this country against environmental aesthetics. Environmental enthusiasts often overlook this. The resistance is reflexive—a fear of being different. And more, of being odd, and perhaps a little low-class. The stereotypical image of environmentalists is that they live off the grid and build with aluminum cans, tires, and straw bales. They wear unwashed jeans and tie-dye shirts. They have long hair and shaggy beards and eat obscure vegetables.

An awful lot of imagery is associated with the term *environmental*, and it's not all pretty. Many of us are inclined to think about blue skies, lush green foliage, and clear, sparkling water. But the average businessperson and the building owner immediately think low-tech, disheveled, overgrown, uncontrolled, and unprofitable. Translation: dangerous and unwanted.

If we believe that a green material will look trashy, we tend to actually see it that way. Perception filters reality. It adjusts the objective world into subjective information, upon which we formulate decisions and behavior.

It is true that a green product can look distinctive. A photovoltaic panel, for example, is hard to miss. It is also true that aluminum cans and old tires are indeed used directly as building materials. Some people *do* live in old school buses and decorate with found items (trash). This is reuse, pure and simple—but it is *not* what we are talking about here—at least, not only that. We are considering alternative agricultural products, recycled content products, nontoxic products, and energy-efficient products—items that may obviously display an environmental ethic. On the other hand, they may look just like the much more environmentally damaging products they replace. Sustainably harvested wood may have a label on it, but otherwise it looks like wood. In fact, for decades, many products have contained recycled materials. For example, several acoustical ceiling tile lines are fabricated from recycled cellulose. Gypsum board routinely utilizes reclaimed gypsum and recycled paper. Incorporating these materials was an economic decision made by the manufacturers. They determined that the quality of their products could be maintained and the costs lowered if they used recycled content materials instead of raw materials. Previous perceptions, however, viewed such content as trash, so manufacturers did not advertise the ingredients of their products. Many are still reluctant to claim "recycled content" for fear the pendulum will swing again, placing them in the unenviable position of marketing "trash" products.

The style and palette options available for a particular green product are sometimes more limited than for its conventional counterpart. However, the limitations are not necessarily inherent to greenness but often simply the consequence of a new and growing market. There are definitely more options available today than yesterday, and yet more will be available tomorrow. It is difficult to characterize the market impact of a more limited selection because individual response varies so greatly. Some building owners balk at restrictions of any sort. They may have no desire whatsoever to install a metallic-flecked, hot pink flooring system, but they hate the idea of losing the ability to do so. In other circumstances, the limitation is received with elitist fervor. Some building owners glow at the prospect of being the first in the neighborhood to live in a straw bale house or install a rainwater harvesting system.

Decisions about aesthetic acceptability ultimately depend on personal perceptions. They require project-specific evaluation and owner-specific review. We have worked on projects where the building owner felt the proposed green options appeared much more elegant than conventional construction materials; conversely, we have worked on projects where the very same green options were aesthetically unacceptable to the client. While the menu of green styles, patterns, and colors may be less extensive than the traditional smorgasbord of options to which we are accustomed, it still offers plenty from which to choose for interior and exterior finishes and landscaping. In general, there is enough variety in the market to make it accurate to say that, aesthetically, green options are neither better nor worse than conventional design options.

Does Green Work?

Yes, of course. Prior to the Industrial Revolution, society met most of its needs with materials obtained directly from the earth and then returned those materials to the earth after their use. The concern expressed in the "Does it work?" question is that using green materials will require us to decrease our standard of living to preindustrial levels. For some strange reason, we tend to assume that human ingenuity is limited to the development of petroleum products and synthetic chemicals. Fortunately, a host of entrepreneurs is proving us wrong. New designs for photovoltaic panels have improved efficiencies. New plastics are being derived from agricultural products. Light pipes and heat film (film that becomes opaque when exposed to heat) offer new possibilities in the way we bring natural light into a building.

Perhaps the strongest evidence that green works is that so many green products and systems are gaining in the mainstream. That would be impossible if they did not perform. It would be equally impossible if the products were not cost-competitive.

Isn't Green Expensive?

The owner's question "What kind of cost are we talking about?" reveals the economic perception of green. It costs more. Builders worry about the initial cost of the different and perhaps risky green product as well as about the impact it may have on the overall value of the building investment. Economics is closely related to aesthetics. As many designers have experienced, economics often dictates aesthetics. There is, after all, a tangible economic impact involved in appearances. What is the resale value of your house? of your car? Can you get a job or a table in a nice restaurant without proper attire?

When cost is discussed relative to environmental issues, it is necessary to consider both the broader societal costs, the costs each of us bears for destruction of the global commons, and the costs directly borne by individuals under the current economic system.

The unfortunate perception of societal costs, however, is that one person does not make much difference. It is not going to matter much if I change the oil in my car and pour it down the storm drain. There is so much water in the world, and this little bit is nothing in comparison. Besides, it is cheaper for me to do it myself than to pay a mechanic, who must comply with the environmental regulations, to do it. The reality, however, is that over 30 times more motor oil is dumped by oil changes and road runoff annually than was spilled by the Exxon *Valdez* supertanker.[2]

Nevertheless, until societal costs are captured, such as with a revised GNP, and distributed proportionally, people will continue to believe that individually they cannot hurt the Earth, and they will continue to act accordingly—that is, if they think about it at all. Even with the abundant wealth in the United States, most people spend the majority of their time devoted to survival tasks: the acquisition of food, housing, and transportation. They don't have a lot of time or money for dealing with such esoteric issues as the health of the planet or community issues such as pollution prevention. We do what is easy and familiar and what costs us the least. Our personal costs are determined by comparing the initial costs and, perhaps, the operating costs (typically maintenance and energy costs) of the readily available options. We are often guilty of the same petty, daily calculations. Building owners are no different. Hard-core environmentalists may object, but if green materials and systems are to compete in the current market, they must do so on the basis of out-of-pocket costs. Happily, many can.

Simple economic comparisons show that green products are often competitive for purchase and installation—especially those that are considered green because they contain recycled materials. Back when recycled content material was called trash, many mainstream construction products, including ceiling tile, gypsum board, and steel contained recycled content materials. The manufacturers made economic decisions—the recycled material performed just as well and was cheaper than processing virgin material. Perhaps most important, however, they could depend on the source. Increasingly, legislation is making it easier and more cost-effective for manufacturers to use recycled content material as feedstock. Legislation that encourages recycling, for example, means that manufacturers are able to depend on recycled materials as a source material; they can retool their plants and redesign their procedures to incorporate recycling without the fear that recycling is simply a fad. Similarly, the elimination of economic subsidies for mining and forestry, originally enacted to encourage settlement of western lands, would decrease the discrepancy between the cost of such materials and the cost of alternative materials. As the infrastructure, legislation, and recycling programs continue to evolve, more industries can take advantage of them.

Energy-efficient products such as light fixtures and appliances must be evaluated in terms of life cycle because they generally are more expensive to purchase and sometimes to install, but less expensive to operate. Probably the single greatest reason (without getting into political discussions of subsidies to oil and mining) is that these are new products; they must bear research and development costs, and they do not have the economies of scale of the less efficient competitors. Happily, if the energy efficiency rating (EER) is good, there is a quantifiable payback.

New, alternative products and systems (or the revival of old systems) may be more expensive to purchase. New products may also be more expensive to install. Composting toilets, for example, aren't common. Although the concept is not difficult, the contractor isn't familiar with it, and it may cost you more until he is. As new markets continue to grow, however, the disparity in initial costs should decrease. As with energy-efficient products, these products are new. The debt they carry is proportionately larger than the comparable mainstream product, and they do not have the economies of scale . . . yet.

Both manufacturers and designers are changing the way they assign cost to a building and to building products. Some manufacturers are experimenting with *green leases*. Green leasing is a new and dramatic shift in the traditional perspective on leased equipment. Under a green lease, the product manufacturer is responsible for the disposition of the product at all times. Thus, when the customer no longer requires the use of the particular product or requires an updated model, the manufacturer is obligated to reclaim it and refurbish it or disassemble it for recycling as appropriate.

Green designers and building owners are developing *performance contracts*. The classic example of a performance contract is an Energy Service Performance Contract (ESPC). Overall, initial costs for green projects are often 5 to 15 percent higher than for conventional projects. The increase in cost can be minimized by redefining traditional relationships and by accurately factoring in operating costs. Design fees, which may increase to reflect the additional research and design, can be contractually linked to the operational savings experienced by the building owner. Operational savings can accrue not only from energy efficiency and maintenance procedures but also from substantial increases in worker productivity. Studies indicate that green design (improved lighting and ventilation) has a tremendously positive economic impact on worker productivity in both manufacturing and service businesses. Because labor is the greatest expense by far for most companies, even a slight increase in worker productivity can have a significant impact on the bottom line. The trick is to determine what performance will be assessed against which benchmark, and how. The federal government is strongly supportive of ESPCs. In a 1998 memorandum, "Memorandum for the Heads of Executive Departments and Agencies Subject: Cutting Greenhouse Gases Through Energy Savings," President Clinton directed federal agencies to make more extensive use of ESPCs. Along similar lines, the Department of Energy and some financial institutions are developing energy-efficient mortgages. These recognize that energy-efficient buildings have lower utility bills and thus can allow for larger mortgage payments or better terms.

Internally, many companies are adopting the principles of Design for the Environment (DFE). DFE encompasses the product concept, need, and design. Considerations include material selection, energy efficiency, possible reuse, maintainability, and design for disassembly and recycling. DFE is a prerequisite to green leasing. Green leasing necessitates a revision of administrative services. It also requires a basic redesign of products in order to allow for future disassembly and upgrade. DFE and green leasing have the potential to be cost-effective for manufacturers and customers alike because they save much of the energy and materials needed to manufacture the product from virgin materials. They are also extremely resource-efficient. Some major corporations, including Apple and Xerox, are exploring the possibilities of the twin approaches, DFE and green lease.

Perceptions

Perceptions are difficult to change. After World War II, we were surprised that Japan was producing high-quality merchandise. We are equally surprised today to find that manufacturers are producing high-quality *green* merchandise.

Suffice it to say that green may perform the task differently, but it performs it well; green can look different, but it doesn't have to; and, green can cost a whole lot more, but it can also be more cost-effective, especially long term.

Shades of Green

The response to the question "What are green building materials?" is not black and white but rather a shade of gray—or of green. That is an obstacle for the building industry. We are accustomed to specific requirements in order to establish compliance with applicable codes and with accepted standards for professional care. But standards and measurable, prescriptive requirements delineating the greenness of a product are more difficult to define. They are the topic of chapter 4, "How Does the Product Selection Process Work?"

Let us return to the fundamental benchmarks of sustainability.

What are we using?

How well are we using it?

Obviously, the responses are not simple. They involve a multi-attribute decision-making process. In computer terminology, they involve fuzzy logic. Fuzzy logic develops a response to a complex problem by breaking the problem into a series of simpler questions. As the answers to each of these simpler questions are derived, the solution to the original problem begins to take shape. In other words, you approach the problem and develop a workable solution, but you are unlikely to generate a simple yes or no response.

The challenge of assessing the relative greenness of a product is that seemingly simple questions may still produce complex answers. For example:

- *Is it hazardous?* What if one of the byproducts at one of the stages happens to be a synthetic chemical—one of more than 65,000 synthetic chemicals in commercial use that, according the EPA, National Research Council, have *not* been tested for their effect on humans?

- *Is it locally obtained?* What if one of the input materials in one of the stages happens to be obtained from a location within an endangered ecosystem, such as bauxite for aluminum, mined in the rain forest?

- *Is it recycled?* What if the input materials are obtained entirely from recycled materials? from recycled petroleum-based materials? What if the only facility equipped to recycle those petroleum-based materials is overseas? What if a product is fabricated entirely from recycled materials but the adhesive resin binder is a known carcinogen?

- *Is it energy-intensive to make?* What if the fabricating equipment is high-efficiency, non-CFC-producing, state-of-the-art equipment? What if the energy used to power the high-efficiency fabricating equipment is produced in a coal-burning utility plant?

- *Is it reusable or recyclable?* What if the product in its final stage will probably go straight to a landfill? What if it could be recycled at some point in the future. . . if the facilities or technology could be created to recycle it?

A single product may contain several materials, any one of which may possess green characteristics. Each material may involve hundreds of perpetual, renewable, and nonrenewable resources. It may use some of them well in certain stages of acquisition, manufacture, distribution, and use, and it may not use them well at all during other stages. The information is often difficult to obtain. The product representative is unlikely to know the answers to these types of questions. But good representatives will find out for you—if you ask. Many are genuinely interested. Most want to represent a high-quality product and are often in the best position to communicate to their company the quality requirements and new possibilities for meeting and exceeding those requirements.

Balancing the "good" against the "bad" is an unfortunate and, hopefully, temporary reality. Under the current scheme of standards and threat of litigation, it can become an endless pursuit. To best manage the volume of information, to assess it and render an educated, professional opinion, it is helpful to categorize the aspects of green into three categories: (1) resource management, (2) toxicity/IEQ, and (3) performance. These categories are tools to help quickly assess and compare the greenness of one product relative to another. Green building is an evolving field, and these tools are not necessarily the ones we will be recommending ten years from now. They are currently useful because we have in place ways to quantify and compare information within each of these categories.

Resource Management, Toxicity/IEQ, and Performance

Resource Management

Resource management is a common term in the environmental community, but it is misleading for people more accustomed to the business world. In business, we manage many tasks in great detail. Management hierarchies and methodologies permeate every company, no matter how small. The overriding goal of management is to improve profit. Tangentially, we may focus on maximizing efficiency, improving morale, marketing to new customers, or cutting waste—but the bottom line is the bottom line. In contrast, resource management is not concerned with profits; it is concerned with stewardship. It is not concerned with what can be extracted; it is concerned with what remains. The distinctions are important because the term *resource management* can be used intentionally to confuse the issue. For example, forest management is not necessarily forest stewardship. It might be, but the term more likely refers to the operation of the forest to generate the most timber (profits) possible. Similarly, if you were to hire a waste management firm, your waste is just as likely to go to a landfill as to a recycling center.

Resource management relative to products refers to the impact on the Earth's resources—perpetual resources (solar, wind, tidal energy), renewable resources (timber, soil, grasses), and nonrenewable resources (oil, coal, aluminum)—due to the acquisition of raw materials and the manufacturing process. It considers the impact on biodiversity and ecosystems. Common measurements include recycled content (pre- and postconsumer) and independent environmental certifications of sustainability in acquisition or manufacture. Preconsumer recycled material is material that never made it to the consumer market; it is manufacturing scrap, and most industries utilize their own scraps in some manner. Postconsumer recycled material is the challenge and the better measure of greenness. Utilization of preconsumer waste is green, but it is standard practice. It is baseline. If the product with preconsumer recycled content merely pauses in the consumer's hands en route to the landfill, then it is not a sustainable use of resources. If, on the other hand, a means for collecting the postconsumer material is available that will channel the material back to industry (ideally, back to the original manufacturer), then it is truly recycling.

When resources are managed for the benefit of the Earth and for the benefit of future generations instead of for the maximization of profit, they are considered to be *sustainably managed*. Sustainable resource management requires a perspective that is Earth-centered instead of human-centered. What are we using from the Earth? How well are we using it in terms of the consequences for the Earth, for the water, air, soil, and wildlife?

Sustainable resource management favors these imperatives: reduce, reuse, recycle, and renew. Opportunities for the first three abound in the construction industry.

One opportunity for reduction of waste is utilizing alternative agricultural products such as soy resins, cork, and straw. These products frequently depend on agricultural by-products (waste), and they are generally biodegradable. In addition, they tend to generate fewer hazardous pollutants during production than their traditional counterparts. This sort of innovative approach is the foundation of the American entrepreneurial spirit. Henry Ford, one of America's most renowned entrepreneurs, developed Model T coil cases made of wheat gluten in 1915. In 1933, he developed soybean paint and plastics. By 1935, two bushels of soybeans went into every Ford car. Ford also developed ways to power vehicles with ethanol.[3] This approach contributes doubly to the nation's economic prosperity; it not only redirects money spent on waste but also supports the development of new American industries.

Reuse is common among thrift store shoppers and families with small children. For some reason, however, it frequently escapes consideration on a construction project. Potential sites with existing buildings are often overlooked in favor of previously undeveloped sites that can be manipulated more easily and quickly. In many cases, this is a false economy. Salvage! Adapt an existing structure. Redirect existing building components from the waste stream to local community groups, vocational schools, or church groups to give them a new home and you a tax break.

Recycling encompasses not only throwing your empty soda can in the specially marked receptacle but also consciously selecting products with recycled content over products with virgin materials. That simple choice, referred to as *closing the loop*, can save natural resources, the energy to process them, and the waste associated with their production. In 1999, the United States recovered 64 million tons (27.8 percent recovery rate) of materials from the municipal solid waste stream for recycling (including composting).[4] This is an increase of 12 percent over 1990. These materials are no longer classified as waste; they are considered raw materials, feedstock for new products. Estimates for the 1997 value of recovered materials totaled approximately $3.6 billion.[5] Of this, aluminum cans represent one of the highest market values, about $1 billion. Yet, every three months, Americans discard enough aluminum to rebuild our entire airplane commercial fleet. Not only is the material valuable in itself, but recycling one aluminum can saves enough electricity to power a TV or a 100-watt light bulb for three hours.[6]

In 1996, the amount of construction and demolition debris generated was an estimated 136 million tons. Forty-three percent of the waste was generated from residential sources, while 57 percent was from nonresidential sources. Eleven million tons per year of the waste stream was generated at construction sites, while 65 million tons came from building demolitions and 60 million tons from renovations. An estimated 20 to 30 percent of building-related construction and demolition debris was recovered for processing and recycling. The most frequently recovered and recycled materials are concrete, asphalt, metals, and wood.[7]

Building products with recycled content abound. Fiberboard, millwork, and flooring may contain reclaimed wood. Toilet partitions, car stops, and decking may contain recycled plastic. Sheathing and insulation may contain recycled cellulose. Floor mats, dock bumpers, and roof walkway pads may contain recycled tires. Upholstery, carpet cushion, and insulation may contain recycled textiles. Concrete and masonry may contain fly ash or slag. Steel generally contains some percentage of recycled content.

We need to develop opportunities to renew. It is widely believed by environmentalists that we have already exceeded the carrying capacity of the Earth. If this is true, we urgently need to rebuild ecosystems, nurture endangered species, and confront global warming as quickly as possible—before the Earth does it for us. If this is not true, renewal efforts will merely improve the quality of life for all of us. Fixing a problem is always more difficult and costly than avoiding it in the first place. Nevertheless, there are cost-effective options in the building industry. For example, we can reclaim brownfields and other abandoned or underutilized property. We can help stabilize greenhouse gas levels by designing building programs that utilize urban infrastructure and encourage alternative transportation. We can help stabilize greenhouse gas levels by the simple act of planting trees. We can promote urban agriculture and develop wildlife corridors through urban areas, reinventing the classic garden cities. We can support conversion to renewable energy.

Of course, one of the many positive actions the building industry can take is to develop and use green building products.

Not much information is available about the impact on the Earth's resources attributable to a particular product. We *do* have a lot of information about what has been extracted. It is High Quality. It is Virgin Material. It is Imported. It is 100% Pure. But not about what remains. The Depletion. The Degradation. The Contamination. The Social Costs of the Global Commons. However, we do have quite a bit of information about general practices and their results. So while we may not know specifics about Brand X resilient flooring, we do know what the environmental impacts are for the acquisition and manufacture of vinyl-resilient flooring in general. An excellent source of information describing green building materials and how to define *green* can be found in the *Environmental Building News* article "Building Materials: What Makes a Product Green."[8]

There are some commonalties among the processes and impacts. Most generate *pollution*; they contaminate ecosystems. Most are guilty of *depletion*; they utilize nonrenewable resources, and they do so inefficiently. And, most cause *destruction*; they ravage ecosystems in order to get at the nonrenewable resources, or they wastefully consume renewable resources, or both.

Pollution: Raw materials for ore and stone ingredients are removed from the Earth through mining, dredging, and quarrying. Raw materials for gas and petroleum ingredients are removed from the Earth through drilling, pumping, and piping. Raw materials for cellulose ingredients are obtained by harvesting. These acquisition processes are typically responsible for soil erosion, pollutant runoff, the subsequent contamination of groundwater, and air pollution. Transportation of the raw materials to the manufacturing facilities involves trains, truck, and boats, and the accompanying fuel, roads, rails, and ports. The greater the distance, the greater the amount of pollution associated with transportation. Fuel is also required in the processing of the raw materials. Emissions from fossil-fuel-burning power plants that generate the energy that runs the manufacturing facilities include greenhouse gases (carbon dioxide, nitrogen oxides, sulfur dioxides), which contribute to global warming and acid deposition. Historically, factories have been located adjacent to natural waterways. Water is used to cool processes, to generate power, and to flush wastes. The ongoing struggles over PCBs in the Hudson River and the contamination of the Great Lakes offer classic examples. Depending on the process and environmental regulations governing the location of the facility, other hazardous substances may also be released into the air, water, and ground. The worst offenders are those who flee strict U.S. federal regulations and establish factories in less regulated areas, especially developing countries. In Mexico, such environmental abuse is so common that there is a word for the perpetrators, *maquiladoras*, or companies that have factories just across the border, exploit the local population, rape their water and soil, export finished products to the United States, and collect the vast profits that our domestic and international governing structures allow them to acquire in such an ignoble manner.

Depletion: In the acquisition of most raw materials, renewable resources and nonrenewable resources are depleted. That we have less of a particular resource is more than just a nuisance or hardship; it is a threat. Survival of any species is dependent, in part, on the size of the gene pool. Fewer genes, less adaptability. This is especially harmful at a time when we are altering the ecosystem faster than at any point in known history, and species need to be as adaptable as possible to survive. Survival of the ecosystem itself is also often threatened. A rain forest, for example, evapotranspires water into the atmosphere that deluges the adjacent vegetation. When a portion of rain forest is clear-cut, the neighboring portion is likely to suffer. Depletion all too often leads to destruction.

Destruction: Direct destruction of ecosystems during acquisition of raw materials or site preparation for construction is readily apparent. However, pollution also destroys ecosystems and habitats and the species that depend on them. The World Wildlife Federation considers the preservation of habitat a primary goal. Without appropriate habitat, the plants, animals, fish, and insects dependent on that habitat die. Many of these species are vital to the functioning of the ecosystems and, consequently, to our own survival. Insects, bats, and birds are crucial players in the web of life. They are pollinators; 80 percent of global crops and 33 percent of U.S. crops are pollinated by wild and semi-wild pollinators.[9] In addition to local habitats, migratory species depend on appropriate sources of nectar-providing plants along their annual routes. Without wildlife corridors, many pollinators are unable to survive the journey. Mining and drilling drastically alter huge tracts of land. Heat and contaminants flushed into our natural waterways destroy the aquatic balance at point of injection and for long distances downstream. Even localized disturbances (e.g., roadways, utility lines) that segregate habitat sufficiently to impede the travel of species for hunting and mating or the pollination of one patch of wildflowers with the next can devastate biodiversity and collapse ecosystems. Conversion of natural areas to so-called productive uses (e.g., the conversion of natural forests to monoculture tree farms) eliminates the necessary complexity of the forest ecosystem. By the time the temporary disruptions (sometimes lasting decades) are restored, the local ecosystems are lost, and, perhaps the larger regional ecosystems are injured beyond repair.

Toxicity/IEQ

Concern for toxicity encompasses indoor and outdoor contaminants and their impact on our health and the health of the planet. Toxicity issues include contamination of the planet and the corresponding degradation of ecosystems and biodiversity, as described in the discussion of resource management. However, because our culture still has a human-centered perspective rather than an Earth-centered perspective, the primary measurement of toxicity in the building industry is indoor environmental quality (IEQ), and within this, indoor air quality (IAQ).

IAQ may be quantified by building owners in terms of worker productivity and customer satisfaction. It is determined more technically by industrial hygienists, researchers, and governing agencies in terms of parts per million (ppm) of a substance relative to current medical opinion of the threshold levels. *Threshold levels* are the points at which risk to human health is considered to transform from negligible to unacceptable.

Logically, this category should be pretty straightforward. Avoid synthetic chemicals in all forms. If nature didn't create a compound, chances are that it can't break it down. The classic example is polystyrene, which is completely nonbiodegradable. It floats across the surf at beaches and rolls around on the side of highways. It appears isolated from nature, an enigma. However, we are learning that some of the thousands of synthetic chemicals are not quite as isolated from nature as we thought. Rather, they are absorbed up the food chain—not digested and converted but bioaccumulated. When water is contaminated with, for example, DDT, zooplankton living in it may become contaminated as well. They do not process the DDT. They cannot. Minnows eat the zooplankton, and, similarly, store the DDT in their bodies. Larger fish repeat the process. At the top of the food chain, we eat the larger fish. We digest the nutrients and bioaccumulate the DDT. Our bodies, like those of the creatures below us on the food chain, have no way to process it. DDT is not natural. So, like other contaminants, it remains in our bodies until enough of it is accumulated to shut down our reproductive capabilities, our mental capabilities, or all of our life-sustaining functions. We die.

Bioaccumulation is not restricted to ingesting toxins. What we breathe affects us. What we touch may be absorbed through our skin into our bloodstream. A friend of ours taught us this lesson the hard way. He was working on an art project—breathing and touching lots of chemicals—in a structure with poor ventilation and inoperable windows. He fell asleep amid these conditions and never woke up. He was 25 years old. IEQ, IAQ, and bioaccumulation are not typical health, safety, welfare concerns of governmental agencies that license architects, but they should be. By selecting environmentally healthy products, we can help protect the welfare of the community.

Material selection can have a significant impact on IAQ. Even though a product itself may have low volatile organic compounds (VOC) emissions, accessory products such as adhesives may emit VOCs. Also, maintenance may require or encourage the use of products containing VOCs. Similarly, if the product can function as a sink and adsorb emissions from other sources, then the original product's benign characteristics will be overwhelmed when the product is in place. All surfaces adsorb molecules of chemical substances and compounds or particles that are in the air. Adsorption is a chemical-physical bonding that may be either permanent or reversible. The degree that surfaces sorb is a function of the volatility and polarity of the chemical and of the surface area of the sink material. Generally, the rougher the surface, the more sorption is possible. Glass and stainless steel sorb relatively low quantities compared to textiles, wood, and paper. Sinks can be heavily loaded during periods of elevated concentrations, then release (reemit) the substances when the air concentration is lower.

Following are three general guidelines for assessing a product's potential for affecting a building's IAQ:

- If it outgasses, it will outgas forever, though with decreasing intensity.
- If it is a dry, packaged product, it was packaged promptly after manufacture, trapping the new smells in the packaging; these will be released when the package is opened.
- If it is a wet product, it will probably emit VOCs as it cures.

Unfortunately, toxicity/IEQ assessment is not straightforward for two reasons. First, a lot of high-performance building materials contain synthetic chemicals; second, a lot of litigation seeks compensation from those responsible for contaminating the environment (indoor and outdoor).

Many high-performance building materials derived from petroleum and synthetic chemicals have some green characteristics. High-performance glazing, such as low-emmisivity glazing, minimizes the thermal transmission through the glass, thereby improving the energy efficiency of the structure and reducing the amount of pollution generated as byproducts of electricity generation. This high-performance glazing utilizes laminated PVC interlayers and pyrolytic coatings. In place, the glass is inert, and it is potentially recyclable. However, the manufacturing process is guilty of pollution, depletion, and destruction. If we use the product, we share responsibility with the manufacturer for that pollution, depletion, and destruction of the Earth's resources. Single-ply roofing membranes are equally problematic. They offer significant improvements in performance, thereby lengthening the lifetime of the structure below. They are available in light-colored, reflective finishes for improved albedo and corresponding reductions in energy costs. They can be mechanically fastened, making the parts of the roofing systems easier to disassemble and recycle. And they allow the creation of roof gardens, which also help reduce the albedo and reduce stormwater runoff, improve carbon sinking, and contribute to wildlife corridors through urban areas. But they involve petroleum products and synthetic chemicals that nature cannot break down.

Obviously, high-performance building materials are preferable from a performance standpoint—hence the name. But they are a mixed blessing. Consequently, a lot of time is spent trying to establish acceptable compromises and, in turn, defending against litigation that argues that the compromises were breached or flawed from the beginning.

A lot of time and money is spent on defining, in legal terms, *toxic* and *hazardous*, and on demonstrating scientifically that each of the new, non-natural materials is harmless to humans and to nature.

The Toxic Substances Control Act (TSCA), 15 U.S.C. s/s 2601 et seq. (1976), was enacted by Congress to test, regulate, and screen all chemicals produced by or imported into the United States. The act, as its name implies, declares that there may be some potential harm to human health and the environment. The purpose of the act appears to be far-reaching:

§2601. Findings, policy, and intent

(a) Findings: The Congress finds that

    (1) human beings and the environment are being exposed each year to a large number of chemical substances and mixtures;

    (2) among the many chemical substances and mixtures which are constantly being developed and produced, there are some whose manufacture, processing, distribution in commerce, use, or disposal may present an unreasonable risk of injury to health or the environment; and

    (3) the effective regulation of interstate commerce in such chemical substances and mixtures also necessitates the regulation of intrastate commerce in such chemical substances and mixtures.

(b) Policy: It is the policy of the United States that

    (1) adequate data should be developed with respect to the effect of chemical substances and responsibility of those who manufacture and those who process such chemical substances and mixtures;

    (2) adequate authority should exist to regulate chemical substances and mixtures which present an unreasonable risk of injury to health or the environment, and to take action with respect to chemical substances and mixtures which are imminent hazards; and

    (3) authority over chemical substances and mixtures should be exercised in such a manner as not to impede unduly or create unnecessary economic barriers to technological innovation while fulfilling the primary purpose of this chapter to assure that such innovation and commerce in such chemical substances and mixtures do not present an unreasonable risk of injury to health or the environment.

However, in the subsequent Definitions Section, the act dramatically limits the scope outlined in the previous section by defining the term *chemical substance* to mean "any organic or inorganic substance," excluding "any pesticide (as defined in the Federal Insecticide, Fungicide, and Rodenticide Act (7 U.S.C. 136 et seq.) . . . tobacco or any tobacco product . . . [and] any source material, special nuclear material, or byproduct material (as such terms are defined in the Atomic Energy Act of 1954 (42 U.S.C. 2011 et seq.) and regulations issued under such Act) . . . ."[10] The Toxic Substances Control Act does not define the term *toxic*.

OSHA offers the following definitions.

Hazardous chemical means "any chemical which is a physical hazard or a health hazard."

Physical hazard means "a chemical for which there is *scientifically valid* evidence that it is a combustible liquid, a compressed gas, explosive, flammable, an organic peroxide, an oxidizer, pyrophoric, unstable (reactive), or water-reactive. (Emphasis added.)

Health hazard means "a chemical for which there is *statistically significant* evidence based on at least one study conducted in accordance with established scientific principles that acute or chronic health effects may occur in exposed employees." The term *health hazard*" includes chemicals which are carcinogens, toxic or highly toxic agents, reproductive toxins, irritants, corrosives, sensitizers, hepatotoxins, nephrotoxins, neurotoxins, agents which act on the hematopoietic system, and agents which damage the lungs, skin, eyes, or mucous membranes. (Emphasis added.)

Under OSHA, the chemicals considered hazardous or carcinogenic are listed in the National Toxicology Program (NTP) "Annual Report on Carcinogens"; the International Agency for Research on Cancer (IARC) "Monographs"; or 29 CFR part 1910, subpart Z, Toxic and Hazardous Substances, OSHA.

In an appendix, OSHA affirms that determining the specific hazards is difficult and complex, stating, "The goal of defining precisely, in measurable terms, every possible health effect that may occur in the workplace as a result of chemical exposures cannot realistically be accomplished." The truth is that we do not know enough about the complex working of our planet to be able to predict how our actions may affect life's intricately balanced systems. We do not know how the products we use will directly and indirectly affect our own health. Already our ignorance has resulted in some nasty surprises. A more responsible approach would be to use known nontoxic, organic, and natural products to the greatest extent possible. Potentially toxic materials, materials whose reaction in the Earth's ecosystems is not known, should not be used.

Performance

Performance considerations address the indirect environmental impacts associated with a particular product. They examine installation methods; maintenance materials, and processes; durability; energy efficiency; and the ability of the product to be recycled or reused at the end of its useful life in the building. Performance issues also include broader considerations regarding the impact of a product on the global commons, such as the albedo of the exterior finishes and the permeability of the paving. Typical measurements include energy efficiency ratings (EER) and, increasingly, worker productivity and customer satisfaction.

Energy efficiency improvements mean less energy. Less energy means less pollution. Simple.

Longer-lasting, more durable products mean less replacement. Less replacement means less total strain on our resources. Also simple.

In addition to these issues are installation considerations. Where acceptable to code, mechanical fastening is preferable from an IAQ perspective and with respect to disassembly for future reuse. Related materials, which are required for installation of a particular product, can have environmental consequences of their own. Which finishes, adhesives, caulks, or solvents are recommended by the manufacturer? How does the product cure? What, if any, waste materials are generated due to the incorporation of the product into the building?

How much packaging is associated with the product? Opportunities abound on a construction project to reduce and to reuse packaging. Negotiate with manufacturers to explore packaging options. If the design professional never asks, the manufacturer is never made aware of the need. Some, however, already understand the environmental need and economic benefits. Reuse of packaging is cost-effective for manufacturers and, consequently, their customers. Spec Mix, for example, distributes mortar mix for masonry construction in bulk packaging that it reclaims and reuses. Alcoa offers two packaging reuse programs: Pallets Plus and Pallets Only. Under the Pallets Plus program, Alcoa accepts return of pallets and packaging from its aluminum panels; under Pallets Only, a program for customers who already have a recycling method for packaging, Alcoa accepts return of its pallets. The pallets are refurbished and reused, and the customer receives a rebate.[11]

What kind of packaging is associated with the product? Plastic? Cardboard? Building product manufacturers can better position themselves in the changing market by proactively responding to packaging issues. Reduction is fairly commonplace because it makes obvious economic sense. Less money spent on packaging easily translates into more money received in profits. Reuse is beginning to generate comparable results. The type of packaging and the associated labeling remains to be explored. Certainly cardboard with recycled content and the familiar circular arrows are a step in that direction. There are developments on the horizon for greater use of starch-based plastics, not only for packing peanuts but also for vacuum wrapping. Imagine dropping a package of instant soup into hot water—package and all. Soy-based inks are preferable for printing labels. Also, if the plastic is petroleum-based, what kind? Many recycling programs distinguish between HDPE and PET, for example, just as they distinguish between colored paper and white paper. Unfortunately, most end-users cannot readily distinguish plastic type. Plastic needs to be labeled.

Tools That Help Define Green

ASTM International's Subcommittee E06.71 on Sustainability is responding to a fast-growing market demand for green building and sustainable development. This market interest is voiced by building industry professionals, manufacturers, governmental agencies, and customers. It is expressed in developed countries and developing countries. The unique forum that ASTM International offers allows often divergent perspectives to come together to develop standards that address the issues of sustainability.

Sustainability, as defined in ASTM E2114—*Standard Terminology for Sustainability Relative to the Performance of Buildings*, is "the maintenance of ecosystem components and functions for future generations." *Sustainable development* is defined as "development that meets the needs of the present without compromising the ability of future generations to meet their own needs." Sustainability has three primary considerations: environmental, economic, and social. Each of these considerations must be addressed in the development of standards.

ASTM International Subcommittee E06.71 on Sustainability addresses "the promotion of knowledge, stimulation of research, and development of standards related to the environmental performance and sustainability of building materials, building components, building systems, and buildings individually and in aggregate."

The topic of sustainability is complex. Consequently, much of the work in this subcommittee coordinates with a wide range of ASTM committees and other organizations. The Subcommittee develops standards for a range of green building products, including earthen building systems, green roofs, and environmentally preferable products.

In 2005, the first ASTM Standard for earthen building systems (adobe, rammed earth, cob, and straw bale) was released. This new standard, ASTM E2392—*Standard Guide for Design of Earthen Wall Building Systems*, is a significant advance for such systems. Earthen building systems historically have not been engineered. The first written standards for adobe were developed in the United States in the 1930s and were based on common construction practices. Only in the last 20 years have architects and engineers attempted to engineer adobe and rammed earth for use and compliance with contemporary building codes. Standards for the use of adobe were initially limited to local and state codes, predominantly in the southwestern United States. This new mainstream standard can aid in the appropriate recognition and adoption of earthen building systems materials and methods by building codes and code enforcement agencies.

Unfortunately, despite initiatives promoting green roofs, no accredited USA standards for green roofs have been formulated—as of this writing. ASTM E06.71 is currently balloting several standards that address performance metrics for green roofs.

Other standards for which ASTM Subcommittee E06.71 is responsible include:

E1971—*Standard Guide for Stewardship for the Cleaning of Commercial and Institutional Buildings*

E1991—*Standard Guide for Environmental Life Cycle Assessment (LCA) of Building Materials/Products*

E 2114—*Standard Terminology for Sustainability Relative to the Performance of Buildings*

E 2129—*Standard Practice for Data Collection for Sustainability Assessment of Building Products*

Identifying green building materials has been facilitated by the development of several new tools. ASTM International[12] has released several standards for green building, including ASTM E2114 and ASTM E2129. ASTM E2114 provides meanings and explanations of terms applicable to sustainable development, while ASTM E2129 contains a set of instructions for collecting data that can be used to assess the sustainability of building products. E2129 includes two tables in the questionnaire. The first contains questions that apply to all products; the second includes questions related to various categories of building products. ASTM also has a guide for using data for building product sustainability assessment under development.

The Subcommittee is also responsible for the *ASTM International Standards on Sustainability in Building Compendium*. This publication unites multidisciplinary standards as appropriate to the building industry. It addresses environmentally preferable products, energy efficiency, and sustainable buildings. It covers more than 100 standards related to building materials, performance of wetlands, general principles for life cycle assessment, sustainable design, construction, and operation of buildings.

Another useful tool that can help identify green building materials is the *GreenSpec®Directory*, published by BuildingGreen, Inc.[13] Containing both guideline specifications and product listings arranged according to the CSI MasterFormat™ numbering system, *GreenSpec* includes a quick summary of environmental considerations relating to products in each section. *GreenSpec*'s goal is to make it as easy as possible to locate and use green building materials. The products included in *GreenSpec* are selected by the editors based on consideration of various factors; BuildingGreen, Inc. does not accept any advertising in its publications.

At the federal level, the *Federal Guide for Green Construction Specs* is intended to assist federal building project managers in meeting various mandates as established by statute and executive order as well as EPA and DOE program recommendations, including:

The Resource Conservation and Recovery Act Authorized Comprehensive Procurement Guidelines (CPG)

The National Technology Transfer and Advancement Act/OMB Circular A-119

Greening of Government Executive Orders 13101, 13123, 13134, and 13148

DOE's Federal Energy Management Program Product Efficiency Recommendations

EPA's Waste Minimization Priority Chemicals

EPA's Indoor Environments Program Recommendations

EPA's Construction Industry Compliance Assistance Center Recommendations

The *Federal Guide for Green Construction Specs* provides model language intended to assist users in achieving green building goals as may be determined by the individual agency and project. The *Federal Guide* is *not* intended to establish a procurement policy; therefore, there is no associated enforcement mechanism.

The *Federal Guide for Green Construction Specs* should assist in lowering design costs for green buildings, as it provides preliminary materials/methods research and model construction specifications language in a readily accessible format. It should also assist in lowering construction costs for green buildings, as it provides guidance that quantifies generally expected performance requirements for green building.

The *Federal Guide for Green Construction Specs* includes a representative range of the green building materials and methods available in the market. For most materials and methods, the range reflects a spectrum of options in cost, aesthetics, and performance. Depending on project decisions, the materials and methods selected may be more, less, or equivalent (in terms of performance and cost) to the less environmentally preferable material or method that is being replaced. While it remains true for many products that the green option costs more to install and less to operate, the market continues to evolve. For example, as contractors become more familiar with construction waste management techniques and as the national infrastructure to process recyclables expands, construction waste management becomes not only cost competitive but less expensive than landfilling.

The *Federal Guide for Green Construction Specs* does not offer complete specifications. It is intended to supplement other model construction specifications and to provide guidance in developing project construction specifications. The *Federal Guide* addresses environmental aspects in support of the federal government's Environmentally Preferable Products (EPP) mandates and related programs. Other performance requirements and procedures are not included. Also, environmental performance requirements and procedures that represent conventional practices are not included. It is anticipated that new information, including new sections, will be incorporated into the publication over time.

Several states, including Massachusetts, Pennsylvania, Minnesota, North Carolina, Missouri, Washington, and California have instituted programs that encourage the purchase of EPPs, or green products. For example, the California Division of the State Architect is developing an Environmentally Preferable Products Database.[14] The project's goal is to create a free, online EPP database, in large part to support the increasing amount of school construction planned in California during the next decade. The database will serve as a resource to finding environmentally preferable building products that have been screened against a comprehensive set of environmental, health, and performance criteria. California is creating EPP criteria for approximately 20 product categories, including gypsum panels, insulation, composite panels, adhesives and sealants, paints and coatings, carpet, resilient flooring, tile and wood flooring, acoustical ceiling tile, finish wall panels (tackwall, acoustical, laminates), structural engineered wood (OSB, Glulams, etc.), furniture (desks, modular components), seating, casework (cabinetry and countertops), doors, concrete, masonry, playground surfaces, cleaning chemicals, and siding and cladding. All product categories contain information about the same key factors: scope, references, performance, hazardous chemicals, energy, recycled content, waste, indoor air quality, water, and recyclability and reuse. These criteria will be formulated into standards against which products will be screened. Products that conform to the standards will be listed in the database. Consistent with the definition of *environmentally preferable*, listing on the database is voluntary and meant to differentiate products with excellent environmental performance.

When Are Green Building Materials *Not* Green?

Not only must design professionals ask themselves which building materials are green but also, similarly, they must be cognizant of "green" building materials that are not really green.

The explosive growth of interest in green building projects and the resultant demand for green building materials has encouraged manufacturers to market to that demand. As companies try to paint their products and practices green, we have seen the word *greenwash* become part of our vocabulary. *Greenwashing* is "giving a positive public image to commonly accepted or supposedly environmentally unsound practices." The term arose in the aftermath of the Earth Summit held in Rio de Janeiro in June 1992. For example, products once advertised for their disposability are now marketed for their recyclability.

Knowing when building materials are not green requires going beyond the attributes of the product to its manufacture. You should ask whether the manufacturer has a written environmental policy, a primary point of contact, and a department that addresses environmental issues (both risk management and proactive, green building opportunities).

Greenwash (a take-off on "whitewash") refers to the superficial and unreliable dissemination of environmental hype.

As professionals in the building industry, we must police ourselves so that in the quest to achieve differentiation we do not harm but rather support the credibility of our industry. Even more critical is the knowledge that green design standards can establish important precedents. Nonconformance with these standards, exacerbated by greenwash, can result in costly legal actions down the road. If you wonder what the potential harm could be, rent the movie *Erin Brockovich.*

In 1992, in the wake of allegations of deceptive environmental marketing practices, the Federal Trade Commission (FTC) issued its *Environmental Guides,* often referred to as the *Green Guides* (revised most recently in 1998). The *Guides* indicate how the Commission will apply Section 5 of the FTC Act, which prohibits unfair or deceptive acts or practices, to environmental marketing claims.

While initially dazzled with greenwash, clients are becoming more educated on the topic and will soon demand a functional depth of knowledge from manufacturers and consultants. Those companies that have not expended the time and resources to develop this depth will not be successful in the long run. As a professional in the field, you can avoid greenwash in several ways:

1. *Do your homework.* Green design is a complex discipline difficult to grasp primarily because the body of knowledge is vast, holistic, and constantly being updated. There are no overnight experts. Certainly knowledge of LEED and similar rating systems is important. Unfortunately, *LEED* is also rapidly becoming a buzzword and a prime leverage point for greenwash. In reality, only a handful of projects across the country have achieved LEED certification. Such rating programs are continuing to evolve. As a design professional, it is not enough to attain LEED accreditation without first developing a base of sustainable design knowledge. The reality is that clients will become informed and begin to ask the difficult questions that will separate those truly committed to green design principles from those serving greenwash.

2. *Make alliances.* Green design requires a holistic view. It is not merely the selection of an energy-efficient system or accreditation in a standards program. To provide a true green design strategy requires knowledge of ecology, biology, chemistry, products, and building methods and techniques. Related knowledge of history, political science, and law is helpful too. This necessitates the expertise of many people, and few companies have the resources to provide them in-house.

3. *Market responsibly.* Greenwash is not merely unethical; it can also result in costly litigation. Marketing is the front line of risk management. To avoid future liability requires that you be careful not only of the information you communicate but also of the information you obtain from consultants and from product manufacturers. Remember CFCs and asbestos—no one knew they would be the subject of lawsuits until decades later.

Overcoming Entropy

If we discredit negative perceptions of the cost, performance, and appearance of green products, and if we educate ourselves regarding green evaluation of products relative to resource management, toxicity/IEQ, and performance, we still have one final hurdle to be overcome: entropy.

Unfortunately, we use what we know, what we used on the last project—even if it wasn't perfect. Why? Well, presumed liability for one. If a material has been in use for an extended period, even with only moderate success, the liability is known—and shared. If everyone is using it, then the standard of care a professional can reasonably be expected to take is established. If a manufacturer, designer, or contractor steps outside the circle and tries something new, the liability is entirely theirs. But so is the success.

Many times, we fall back on the familiar because we are not permitted the time required to examine all the other possibilities. The pace at which our culture approaches life is astounding. The building industry is no exception. The fast track is the norm, and we are constantly searching for ways to improve production speed—from design through construction. Does the use of green building materials slow a job? Maybe. Design time may be extended depending on the project requirements, the client's schedule, and the designer's experience with green building. Construction time may also be affected. The contractor may not be familiar with the product or special installation requirements—but then, that could be true of anything you specify. It is also conceivable that the use of a green product could facilitate permitting and approval processes for sites subject to sewer moratoriums, waste mandates, and so on.

We need to reinvent patterns and habits as drastically as we did during the Industrial Revolution—which upset the balance in the first place. Prophetically, John F. Kennedy observed our dependence on the Earth's natural resources and the necessity for stewardship. Would that we had heeded his environmental message as enthusiastically as we did his challenge to conquer space.

Notes

1. United Nations Department of Public Information, *Setting the Record Straight: Global Climate Change,* DPI / 1939 / Rev.1 October 1998.

2. EPA National Research Council, cited in *Sierra* (March/April 1999): 17.

3. http://www2.ford.com/en/vehicles/specialtyVehicles/environmental/ethanol.htm.

4. U.S. Environmental Protection Agency*, Characterization of Municipal Solid Waste in the United States: 1999 Facts and Figures.* EPA530-R-01-014. Washington, D.C., 2001. www.epa.gov/garbage/mswfinal.pdf.

5. Tellus Institute, "Estimated Value of MSW Materials Recycled in 1995." Prepared for U.S. EPA, Washington, D.C., 1997.

6. City of Houston Solid Waste Management Department, *2004–2005 Houston/Regional Recycling and Conservation Guide,* Houston, Texas, 2004. www.houstontx.gov/solidwaste/recycling/recycleguide.pdf.

7. U.S. Environmental Protection Agency, *Characterization of Building-Related Construction and Demolition Debris in the United States.* EPA530-R-98-010. Washington, D.C., 1998. www.epa.gov/.

8. *Environmental Building News* 9, no. 1 (January 2000, rev. September 2003).

9. Lester R. Brown, Christopher Flavin, Hilary French, et al., *State of the World 1997: A Worldwatch Institute Report on Progress Toward a Sustainable Society* (New York: W.W. Norton, 1997), 102.

10. OSHA § 2602. "Definitions," The Toxic Substances Control Act (TSCA), 15 U.S.C. s / s 2601 et seq., 1976.

11. AIA Committee on the Environment, *Waste Management Task Group Implications for Designers*, 1992.

12. ASTM International, 100 Barr Harbor Drive, PO Box C700, West Conshohocken, Penna. 19428-2959. www.astm.org.

13. BuildingGreen, Inc., 122 Birge Street, Suite 30, Brattleboro, Vt. 05301. www.buildinggreen.com.

14. California Division of the State Architect, Environmentally Preferable Products Database. www.eppbuildingproducts.org.

CHAPTER 4

How Does the Product Selection Process Work?

Hurt not the Earth, neither the Sea, nor the Trees. . . .

—Revelations 7:3

The product selection process is the same for green products as for standard (nongreen) products. All of the typical considerations for the quality, performance, aesthetics, and cost of a product are explored as usual. Add *green* to this list. What are the environmental impacts of the product? How will the earth, the sea, and the trees be hurt? How will they be helped?

The standard product selection process includes the following steps:

1. Identify material categories.
2. Identify building material options.
3. Gather technical information.
4. Review submitted information for completeness.
5. Evaluate materials.
6. Select and document choice.

Obviously, some basic understanding is required at each step. You must understand how a building is put together in order to identify the material categories necessary for a project. Also, you must have a working knowledge of current construction techniques in order to assess building material options and to know what technical information is necessary for proper evaluation. Concrete, for example, has different performance criteria than does waterproofing. Some considerations, such as durability and cost, are common to all material categories, but the expectations for different materials are different. A building owner may expect the roof to last 10 to 20 years with relatively little maintenance but may anticipate replacing the carpet every 5 to 7 years.

Most design professionals are unable to personally assess available material options. There are simply too many and their properties are too complex. Consequently, the building industry relies heavily on reference standards and on the expertise of consultants and trade associations to establish current standards of care for the various material options.

Green is an additional aspect to consider in the product selection process. As for other considerations, it is imperative to understand the general concept of green (see chapter 3) and to know where to obtain the current standard of care information regarding green. That is the subject of this chapter. You must know what green is in order to know what questions to ask and what technical information to request. You must know where to obtain current standard of care information to be able to verify a manufacturer's claims. The task is sometimes intimidating, but it is, in essence, no different from exploring and evaluating any other aspect of a product. If you are determining the strength of concrete, you need to know enough about the nature of concrete to ask informed questions and obtain technical information appropriate for the requirements of the particular project. You also need to know where to obtain that information and where to validate it. The *process* of inquiry is the same.

Step 1: Identify Material Categories

During the schematic design phase, general material categories are identified. The Construction Specifications Institute (CSI) MasterFormat™ lists broad categories that can be used to organize data. The 2004 edition lists 49 categories (up from 16 in the 1995 edition). These categories are organized into groups and subgroups as follows:

MasterFormat 1995		*MasterFormat 2004**	
Division 1	General Requirements	Division 01	General Requirements
		Division 02	Existing Conditions
Division 2	Site Construction	Division 31	Earthwork
		Division 32	Exterior Improvements
		Division 33	Utilities
		Division 35	Waterway and Marine Construction
Division 3	Concrete	Division 03	Concrete
Division 4	Masonry	Division 04	Masonry
Division 5	Metals	Division 05	Metals
Division 6	Wood and Plastics	Division 06	Wood, Plastics, and Composites
Division 7	Thermal and Moisture Protection	Division 07	Thermal and Moisture Protection
Division 8	Doors and Windows	Division 08	Openings
Division 9	Finishes	Division 09	Finishes

MasterFormat 1995		*MasterFormat 2004**	
Division 10	Specialties	Division 10	Specialties
Division 11	Equipment	Division 11	Equipment
		Division 42	Process Heating, Cooling, and Drying Equipment
		Division 43	Process Gas and Liquid Handling, Purification, and Storage Equipment
		Division 44	Pollution Control Equipment
		Division 45	Industry-Specific Manufacturing Equipment
Division 12	Furnishings	Division 12	Furnishings
Division 13	Special Construction	Division 13	Special Construction
		Division 25	Integrated Automation
Division 14	Conveying Systems	Division 14	Conveying Systems
		Division 34	Transportation
		Division 41	Material Processing and Handling Equipment
Division 15	Mechanical	Division 21	Fire Suppression
		Division 22	Plumbing
		Division 23	Heating, Ventilating, and Air Conditioning
Division 16	Electrical	Division 26	Electrical
		Division 27	Communications
		Division 28	Electronic Safety and Security
		Division 48	Electrical Power Generation
	No Equivalent	Division 40	Process Integration

*Note: Gaps in division numbering are to permit future expansion.

During the design development phase, many subcategories, or CSI sections, are explored. Although you may want to use masonry for the exterior walls, you may still be exploring different types of masonry—clay, concrete, or stone.

Step 2: Identify (Green) Building Material Options

In addition to the standard array of material subcategories, identify green subcategories. Adobe masonry units, rammed earth, and straw bale might be viable options for exterior masonry walls. Also, identify green options within the material subcategories. If you want to use masonry, consider clay masonry fabricated from petroleum-contaminated soil or concrete fabricated with fly ash and slag. Explore local options for natural stone and reclaimed masonry units.

Greener options are available for almost every standard conventional building material. Though few of them are listed in mainstream product references such as *Sweets*, several green building product reference books are available, and an explosion of product information is available via the Internet. Over the last five years, the number of resources has at least doubled. Following are resources listing green product manufacturers.

- American Recycling Market—Annual Directory/Reference Manual
  Recycling Data Management Corporation (RDMC)
  P.O. Box 577
  Ogdensburg, New York 13669-0577
  (800) 267-0707
  www.recyclingdata.com

  Contains over 1,000 pages with over 20,000 cross-referenced company and agency listings including scrap metals, auto dismantlers, demolition, paperstock, glass, oil, textiles, wood waste, and reference sections.

- Austin Energy Green Building Program
  City of Austin
  P.O. Box 1088
  Austin, Texas 78767
  (512) 974-2000
  www.ci.austin.tx.us/greenbuilder

  Website offers a Sustainable Building Sourcebook that explains how and why applying green building principles makes sense. Each chapter includes a list of professionals and resources. Fact sheets offer green building information in a condensed form and include various building materials.

- Bay Area Build It Green
  Alameda County Waste Management Authority and Recycling Board (ACWMA)
  777 Davis Street, Suite 100
  San Leandro, California 94577
  (510) 614-1699
  www.stopwaste.org

  Searchable database lists green products, local suppliers, and service providers that correspond with green building guidelines developed by ACWMA. A Green Building Materials Resource Guide is also available.

- Buy Recycled Business Alliance
  National Recycling Coalition, Inc.
  1325 G Street NW, Suite 1025
  Washington, D.C. 20005
  (202) 347-0450

(202) 347-0449 (fax)
www.nrc-recycle.org

A not-for-profit organization dedicated to the advancement and improvement of recycling, source reduction, composting, and reuse.

- Buyer's Guide to Recycled Products
  METRO
  600 NE Grand Avenue
  Portland, Oregon 97232-2736
  (503) 797-1700
  www.metro-region.org

  Online guide to recycled-content products in a searchable database.

- Construction Waste Management Database
  Whole Building Design Guide
  National Institute of Building Sciences (NIBS)
  1090 Vermont Avenue NW, Suite 700
  Washington, D.C. 20005
  (202) 289-7800
  (202) 289-1092 (fax)
  www.wbdg.org/ccbref/cwm.php

  This database contains information on companies that haul, collect, and process recyclable debris from construction projects. Database is searchable by state, ZIP code, or material(s) recycled.

- ECO Design Company
  1330 Rufina Circle
  Santa Fe, New Mexico 87507
  (800) 621-2591
  (505) 438-3448

  Manufacturer/distributor/catalog retailer of Bioshield paints and finishes.

- Energy Efficient Building Products
  Shelter Supply, Inc.
  151 East Cliff Road, Suite 30
  Burnsville, Minnesota 55337-1586
  (877) 207-7043
  www.sheltersupply.com

  Lists products and technologies for energy-efficient, healthy home construction. Includes an introduction describing energy problems frequently encountered in houses.

- Environment Building Products Guide
SustainableABC.com
P.O. Box 30085
Santa Barbara, California 93130
(805) 898-0079
(805) 898-9199 (fax)
www.sustainableabc.com

Lists green building materials and healthy building materials, including information on suppliers of various categories of materials.

- Environmentally Preferable Purchasing Database
U.S. Environmental Protection Agency
1200 Pennsylvania Avenue NW
Mail Code 7409-M
Washington, D.C. 20460
http://yosemite1.epa.gov/oppt/eppstand2.nsf

Searchable database lists products and services with reduced environmental impacts. Environmental information on over 600 products and services is included.

- Forest Certification Resource Center
Metafore
The Jean Vollum Natural Capital Center
721 NW Ninth Avenue, Suite 300
Portland, Oregon 97209
(503) 224-2205
www.metafore.org

Lists search tools for certified forest products, certified forests, certified businesses, and approved certifiers.

- Green Book Product and Resource Guide
Environmental Design and Construction
2401 W. Big Beaver Road, Suite 700
Troy, Michigan 48084
(248) 244-1280
(248) 362-5103 (fax)
www.edcmag.com/FILES/HTML/EDC_buyers_guide

Searchable database of products and resources by company name, city, state, or product category.

- Green Building Materials Fact Sheets
Environmental Works Community Design Center

402 Fifteenth Avenue E
Seattle, Washington 98112
(206) 329-8300
(206) 329-5494 (fax)
www.eworks.org

Fact Sheets describe environmentally friendly materials containing recycled content, materials that have energy-efficient and nonpolluting production processes, materials that are sustainably harvested, and materials that generate minimal off-gassing when installed. Each Fact Sheet provides an overview of the product and discusses raw materials, the manufacturing process, benefits, environmental impacts, health impacts, recyclability, alternatives products, list of suppliers, and a list of references/resources.

• Green Building Materials Resource Guide
City of San Francisco Environment Department
11 Grove Street
San Francisco, California 94102
(415) 355-3700
www.sfenvironment.org

Lists green building services and materials available in the Bay Area. Website also offers Fact Sheets covering various building materials.

• Green Building Materials Resource List
Contra Costa County Green Building Program
651 Pine Street, 4th Floor—North Wing
Martinez, California 94553
(925) 335-1290
(925) 335-1299 (fax)
www.cccrecycle.org/greenbuilding

Lists green products with local suppliers.

• Green Building Resource Guide (1997)
John Hermannsson, AIA, Architect
The Architectural Machine
P.O. Box 3808
Redwood City, California 94064
www.greenguide.com

A database of over 600 green building materials and products selected specifically for their usefulness to the design and building professions rather than merely their green material content. Includes a price index number, which is a factor comparing the cost of the green product shown versus the price index standard (non-green equivalent product). Available on a CD or printed reference guide.

- GreenClips
  Sustainable Design Resources
  3168 Washington Street #6
  San Francisco, California 94115
  (415) 928-7941
  www.greenclips.com

  A biweekly electronic summary of news on sustainable building design and related government and business issues. Includes information on green building materials.

- GreenSpec Product Directory
  Green Building Products: The GreenSpec Guide to Residential Building Materials
  BuildingGreen, Inc.
  122 Birge Street, Suite 30
  Brattleboro, Vermont 05301
  (802) 257-7300
  www.buildinggreen.com

  Lists more than 1,800 environmentally preferable building products with descriptions, manufacturer information, and links to additional resources. All listings are screened and written by BuildingGreen's staff. Includes guideline specifications. Organized according to CSI 1995 MasterFormat numbering system.

- Guide to Resource-Efficient Building Elements (GREBE) Online Edition
  Center for Resourceful Building Technology
  127 North Higgins, Suite 201
  Missoula, Montana 59802
  www.crbt.org

  A directory of environmentally responsible building products that lists green building materials and manufacturers in a searchable database, including information on resource-efficient design, jobsite recycling, and resource management.

- Habitat for Humanity International
  Construction and Environmental Resources Department
  121 Habitat Street
  Americus, Georgia 31709-3490
  (229) 924-6935
  www.habitat.org/env/

  Website provides information and training on a variety of construction issues such as construction management and methods, building materials, energy efficiency, healthy indoor air quality, house design and accessibility. Includes energy bulletins.

- Materials Database
  Green Resource Center

Center Street
Berkeley, California 93939
(510) 614-1699
www.greenresourcecenter.org

Searchable materials database lists green products, local suppliers, and service providers
that correspond with green building guidelines developed by ACWMA. Fact sheets explaining both what green materials are and why they are green are also available.

- Minnesota Building Materials Database
  Center for Sustainable Building Research
  College of Architecture and Landscape Architecture
  University of Minnesota
  1425 University Avenue SE
  Minneapolis, Minnesota 55455
  (612) 624-7327
  (612) 626-7424 (fax)
  www.buildingmaterials.umn.edu

A searchable database of sustainable materials, products, systems, and services for commercial and residential building construction in Minnesota. The database uses lifecycle
thinking to analyze sourcing, health, end-of-use, LCA tools, properties, and costs.

- Minnesota Recycled Products Guide
  Recycling Association of Minnesota
  P.O. Box 14497
  St. Paul, Minnesota 55114-0497
  (651) 641-4560
  (651) 641-4791 (fax)
  www.recycleminnesota.org

Lists recycled-content products made by Minnesota companies. Includes agricultural,
construction, janitorial, landscape, office, and packaging materials. Also includes buy-
recycled tips and other resources.

- Minnesota Recycled Products Directory
  Minnesota Office of Environmental Assistance
  520 Lafayette Road N, Floor 2
  St. Paul, Minnesota 55155-4100
  (800) 657-3843
  (651) 296-3417
  www.moea.state.mn.us/rpdir/index.cfm

A searchable database of recycled-content products made by Minnesota companies. Includes agricultural, construction, janitorial, landscape, office, and packaging materials.
Website also includes buy-recycled tips and other resources.

- Oikos Green Building Source
  Iris Communications, Inc.
  P.O. Box 6498
  Bend, Oregon 97708-6498
  (800) 346-0104
  (541) 317-1626
  (541) 317-1628 (fax)
  http://oikos.com ; www.irisinc.com

  Website lists green product information organized according to CSI 1995 MasterFormat classifications. Product database searchable by either product category or company name. Includes consulting services directory, classifieds, library, and bookstore.

- Real Goods Catalog
  Renewable Energy Catalog
  Real Goods
  360 Interlocken Boulevard, Suite 300,
  Broomfield, Colorado 80021
  (800) 994-4243
  (800) 508-2342 (fax)
  www.realgoods.com

  Lists energy-efficient products and technologies for the home, power generation, off-the-grid living, electric vehicles, and more.

- RecyclingMarkets.net
  Recycling Data Management Corporation (RDMC)
  P.O. Box 577
  Ogdensburg, New York 13669-0577
  (800) 267-0707
  www.recyclingmarkets.net

  Online recycling database with over 5,000 cross-referenced, certified listings of manufacturers and distributors of recycled, remanufactured, reused, and reprocessed products; over 1,000 product classifications.

- *Sustainable Design Resource Guide*, 3rd Edition
  American Institute of Architects, Denver Chapter, and
  Architects, Designers, and Planners for Social Responsibility,
      Colorado Chapter
  www.aiacolorado.org/SDRG

  Green products and materials listed in CSI 1995 MasterFormat classifications. Includes an overview of the environmental issues applicable to each CSI division as well as additional resources.

- *The Environmentally Preferable Purchasing Guide*
  Solid Waste Management Coordinating Board (SWMCB)
  Minnesota Counties of Anoka, Carver, Dakota, Hennepin, Ramsey, and Washington
  www.swmcb.org/EPPG

  Lists environmentally preferable products in over 30 product areas and includes the latest field information, details on cost, performance, and vendors.

- *The Metro Detroit Green Building Resource Directory*
  WARM Training Center
  4835 Michigan Avenue
  Detroit, Michigan 48210
  (313) 894-1030
  (313) 894-1063 (fax)
  www.warmtraining.org

  Searchable database lists building materials by category available in the Detroit area. Products listed in the Materials section have been screened for greenness based on comprehensive environmental criteria.

- *WoodWise Consumer Guide*
  Green Page Online
  Co-op America
  1612 K Street NW, Suite 600
  Washington, D.C. 20006-2810
  (800) 584-7336
  (202) 331-8166 (fax)
  www.woodwise.org
  www.greenpages.org

  Contains forest-saving ideas, tools, referrals, and an expanded resource directory listing forest-friendly wood and paper products. Green Pages Online is a directory of green businesses offering over 25,000 products from 2,000 green companies.

Step 3: Gather Technical Information

Technical information regarding the greenness of building products is much easier to obtain today than it was a few years ago. Sources include product representatives, governmental agencies, building codes, trade organizations, industry standards, material safety data sheets, green rating programs, and environmental nonprofit organizations.

Product Representatives

If you have a specific green product in mind, the primary source of information is probably the product representative. Green product representatives can be extremely helpful in explaining the greenness of their product and potential applications for it. When researching green products, recognize you may be dealing with someone who, while familiar with the product and with the environmental issues, may not be as conversant with building industry practices as you typically expect. While the product representative teaches you about environmental issues, you may need to teach the product representative about standard performance requirements such as compression testing or fire ratings. This is a beneficial exchange for both parties.

For product representatives of green materials and systems, refer to the source listing in green material options just given.

Governmental Sources

When verifying manufacturer information or researching general possibilities, the government may be one of the first sources of information about environmental issues that comes to mind. This is not a comfortable source for most industries, which too often find themselves forced to deal with paperwork of mythic proportions and tangles of red tape in department after department. And for good reason; there are countless agencies enforcing myriad, and sometimes conflicting, environmental regulations.

Nevertheless, federal, state, and local governments can be excellent sources of information about the issues and current requirements. Generally, regulatory requirements affect manufacturing facilities and procedures more than the product itself, although there are some important exceptions for the building industry. Field-applied coatings, for example, may have VOC content limitations according to their intended application.

More than specific regulations, political activity is an important indicator of environmental trends and of related economic issues. Consider the effect on the HVAC industry of the international ratification of the Montreal Protocol and the subsequent amendments to the Clean Air Act (1990), which banned the manufacture of CFCs in the United States; and consider the effect on the lighting industry of the National Energy Act (1992), which banned the manufacture of certain lamp types and mandated minimum energy standards for new construction.

It is vital for designers and manufacturers who wish to remain ahead of the pack to monitor political activity relative to a wide range of environmental issues in order to anticipate developments and take advantage of opportunities. It is also advisable to monitor funding opportunities from governmental agencies. The Department of Agriculture, for example, sponsored the Alternative Agricultural Research and Commercialization (AARC) Corporation, a wholly owned government corporation that made equity investments in private companies to commercialize nonfood uses of agricultural materials and animal byproducts. Some of the building materials AARC subsidized include Agriboard, Environ by Phenix Biocomposites, and Primeboard.[1]

If you have not yet ventured into the arenas of politics and economics, perhaps the least painful way to do so is to visit the EPA website (www.epa.gov) and download information on their voluntary partnership programs; Green Lights and Energy Star provide assistance to improve the efficiency of building lighting and energy requirements respectively. Recognizing the causal link between air quality, pollution, and energy efficiency, the EPA tried to create a Building Air Quality Alliance Program in the mid-1990s. This voluntary partnership program was designed to help building owners and operators improve IAQ. The program was specifically defunded by the 104th Congress. The EPA has developed other useful programs to address IAQ problems in schools and large buildings. The IAQ Building Evaluation and Assessment Tool (I-BEAM) is designed for use in commercial buildings. I-BEAM enables users to conduct an IAQ building audit, plan IAQ-compatible energy projects, and calculate the cost, revenue, and productivity impacts of proposed IAQ activities. Recognizing that 20 percent of the population, or nearly 55 million people, spend their days in elementary and secondary schools, the EPA also developed Indoor Air Quality (IAQ) Design Tools for Schools. The web-based IAQ Design Tools contain recommendations and tools to assist design professionals in incorporating good IAQ practices into their school designs.

Other voluntary programs also address environmental issues. For example, the Water-Wise Council of Texas has developed WaterWise Best Management Practices (BMPs) and a landscape irrigation calculator to promote water conservation practices. EPA developed the Pesticide Environmental Stewardship Program (PESP), a voluntary public-private partnership that works to reduce pesticide risk. The purpose of the PESP is to reduce pesticide risk. In addition to promoting the use of biopesticides, PESP advocates the adoption of integrated pest management (IPM) programs or practices. IPM is the coordinated use of pest and environmental information with available pest control methods to prevent unacceptable levels of pest damage by the most economical means and with the least possible hazard to people, property, and the environment.

As you enter the fray, you will find that many environmental specialists speak a language consisting almost entirely of abbreviations and acronyms. As you become greener, you will, of necessity, learn those that are most integral to your particular market(s). Many have to do with governmental agencies or policies. Following are examples; refer to the Glossary for additional terms.

- CAA
  The Clean Air Act (CAA); 42 U.S.C. s/s 7401 et seq. (1970): "The Clean Air Act is the comprehensive Federal law that regulates air emissions from area, stationary, and mobile sources. This law authorizes the U.S. Environmental Protection Agency to establish National Ambient Air Quality Standards (NAAQS) to protect public health and the environment. The goal of the Act was to set and achieve NAAQS in every state by 1975. The setting of maximum pollutant standards was coupled with directing the states to develop state implementation plans (SIPs) applicable to appropriate industrial sources in the state. The Act was amended in 1977 primarily to set new goals (dates) for achieving attainment of NAAQS, since many areas of the country had failed to meet the deadlines. The 1990 amendments to the Clean Air Act in large part were intended to meet unaddressed or insufficiently addressed problems such as acid rain, ground-level ozone, stratospheric ozone depletion, and air toxics."[2]

- CERCLA
  Comprehensive Environmental Response, Compensation, and Liability Act (CERCLA or Superfund) 42, U.S.C. s/s 9601 et seq. (1980): "Congress enacted the Comprehensive Environmental Response, Compensation, and Liability Act (CERCLA), commonly known

as Superfund, on December 11, 1980. This law created a tax on the chemical and petro-leum industries and provided broad Federal authority to respond directly to releases or threatened releases of hazardous substances that may endanger public health or the envi-ronment. Over five years, $1.6 billion was collected and the tax went to a trust fund for cleaning up abandoned or uncontrolled hazardous waste sites. CERCLA established pro-hibitions and requirements concerning closed and abandoned hazardous waste sites; pro-vided for liability of persons responsible for releases of hazardous waste at these sites; and established a trust fund to provide for cleanup when no responsible party could be identified. The law authorizes two kinds of response actions. Short-term removals where actions may be taken to address releases or threatened releases requiring prompt re-sponse. Long-term remedial response actions that permanently and significantly reduce the dangers associated with releases or threats of releases of hazardous substances that are serious, but not immediately life threatening. These actions can be conducted only at sites listed on EPA's National Priorities List (NPL). CERCLA also enabled the revision of the National Contingency Plan (NCP). The NCP provided the guidelines and proce-dures needed to respond to releases and threatened releases of hazardous substances, pol-lutants, or contaminants. The NCP also provided the NPL. CERCLA was amended by the Superfund Amendments and Reauthorization Act (SARA) on October 17, 1986."[3]

- CWA
  The Clean Water Act (CWA); 33 U.S.C. s/s 121 et seq. (1977): "The Clean Water Act is a 1977 amendment to the Federal Water Pollution Control Act of 1972, which set the basic structure for regulating discharges of pollutants to waters of the United States. The law gave EPA the authority to set effluent standards on an industry basis (technology-based) and continued the requirements to set water-quality standards for all contaminants in surface waters. The CWA makes it unlawful for any person to discharge any pollutant from a point source into navigable waters unless a permit (NPDES) is obtained under the Act. The 1977 amendments focused on toxic pollutants. In 1987, the CWA was reautho-rized and again focused on toxic substances, authorized citizen suit provisions, and funded sewage treatment plants (POTWs) under the Construction Grants Program. The CWA provides for the delegation by EPA of many permitting, administrative, and en-forcement aspects of the law to state governments. In states with the authority to imple-ment CWA programs, EPA still retains oversight responsibilities."[4]

- EPACT
  The Energy Policy Act of 1992: Increases previous regulatory requirements for conser-vation and energy efficiency for both government and the public. For federal agencies, it requires a 20 percent reduction in per-square-foot energy consumption by the year 2000 as compared to 1985 baseline.

- EPCRA
  The Emergency Planning and Community Right-to-Know Act (EPCRA); 42 U.S.C. 11011 et seq. (1986): "Emergency Planning and Community Right-to-Know Act, also known as Title III of SARA, EPCRA was enacted by Congress as the national legislation on com-

munity safety. This law was designed to help local communities protect public health, safety, and the environment from chemical hazards. To implement EPCRA, Congress required each state to appoint a State Emergency Response Commission (SERC). The SERCs were required to divide their states into Emergency Planning Districts and to name a Local Emergency Planning Committee (LEPC) for each district. Broad representation by fire fighters, health officials, government and media representatives, community groups, industrial facilities, and emergency managers ensures that all necessary elements of the planning process are represented."[5]

- ESA
  The Endangered Species Act (ESA); 7 U.S.C. 136; 16 U.S.C. 460 et seq. (1973): "The Endangered Species Act provides a program for the conservation of threatened and endangered plants and animals and the habitats in which they are found. The U.S. Fish and Wildlife Service (FWS) of the Department of the Interior maintains the list of 632 endangered species (326 are plants) and 190 threatened species (78 are plants). Species include birds, insects, fish, reptiles, mammals, crustaceans, flowers, grasses, and trees. Anyone can petition FWS to include a species on this list. The law prohibits any action, administrative or real, that results in a 'taking' of a listed species, or adversely affects habitat. Likewise, import, export, interstate, and foreign commerce of listed species are all prohibited. EPA's decision to register a pesticide is based in part on the risk of adverse effects on endangered species as well as environmental fate (how a pesticide will affect habitat)."[6]

- Executive Order 12843
  Through Executive Order 12843, Procurement Requirements and Policies for Federal Agencies for Ozone-Depleting Substances, April 21, 1993, President Clinton officially recognized the impact of ozone-depleting substances on the stratospheric ozone layer, citing the Montreal Protocol on Substances that Deplete the Ozone Layer, to which the United States is a signatory. In order to reduce the federal government's procurement and use of substances that cause stratospheric ozone depletion, the order directed federal agencies to maximize the use of safe alternatives to ozone-depleting substances, evaluate the present and future uses of ozone-depleting substances, and revise procurement practices to substitute non-ozone-depleting substances to the extent economically practicable.

- Executive Order 12873
  Through Executive Order 12873, Federal Acquisition, Recycling, and Waste Prevention, October 20, 1993, President Clinton directed each executive agency to "incorporate waste prevention and recycling in the agency's daily operations and work to increase and expand markets for recovered materials through greater Federal Government preference and demand for such products." Specifically, the order requires agencies to "consider the following factors: elimination of virgin material requirements; use of recovered materials; reuse of product; life cycle cost; recyclability; use of environmentally preferable products; waste prevention (including toxicity reduction or elimination); and ultimate disposal, as appropriate . . . for all procurements and . . . contracts." Replaced in 1998 by Executive Order 13101, which expanded the directive to encompass bio-based (alternative agricultural) products as well.

- Executive Order 13101
Executive Order 13101, Greening the Government through Waste Prevention, Recycling and Federal Acquisition, September 14, 1998, builds on and replaces the previous order (EO 12873), which gave EPA its original mandate on environmentally preferable procurement. EO 13101 requires EPA to issue new guidance to federal agencies, encourages federal agencies to conduct pilot projects based on this guidance, and incorporates bio-based products into federal EPP efforts. The EO also has requirements related to the purchase or use of paper products that contain at least 30 percent "post consumer" fiber by January 1, 1999.[7]

- NEPA
National Environmental Policy Act of 1969 (NEPA); 42 U.S.C. 4321-4347: NEPA is the basic national charter for protection of the environment. It establishes policy, sets goals, and provides means for carrying out the policy. "The purposes of this Act are: To declare a national policy which will encourage productive and enjoyable harmony between man and his environment; to promote efforts which will prevent or eliminate damage to the environment and biosphere and stimulate the health and welfare of man; to enrich the understanding of ecological systems and natural resources important to the Nation; and to establish a Council on Environmental Quality."[8]

- NPDES
National Pollutant Discharge Elimination System (NPDES), created by EPA in 1972 under the authority of Public Law 92-500, the Federal Water Pollution Control Act: ". . . intended to control discharges to the Nation's waters from industrial, commercial, and municipal point sources; these discharges presented a threat to water quality and health. Initial efforts focused on traditional pollutant discharges from industrial manufacturing processes and municipal waste water treatment plants. Later amended to become the CWA, this law provides broad authority for EPA or States (authorized by EPA) to issue NPDES permits. Specific reporting requirements are established in the permits to require monitoring and reporting of discharges. The CWA establishes two types of standards for conditions in NPDES permits: technology-based standards and water quality-based standards. These standards are used to develop effluent limitations and special conditions in NPDES permits. Numeric effluent limitations establish pollutant concentration limits for effluents at the point of discharge. Since the implementation of the CWA requirements, EPA has begun to address nontraditional sources of pollution, such as those that result from Wet Weather Flows (WWF). The NPDES program currently requires permits for point sources, but not for NPSs."[9]

- Phase I
Typically refers to an environmental site assessment. Financial interests, in particular, want to determine potential environmental concerns on a given site, as environmental regulations place responsibility for abatement and liability for contamination on *all* entities that have touched the material, including building owners, contractors, and architects.

Insurance companies and lending institutions do not want to inherit environmental debts. The primary purpose of the Phase I environmental site assessment is to observe site conditions and identify any areas of potential environmental concern. ASTM E 1527, *Standard Practice for Environmental Site Assessments: Phase I Environmental Site Assessment Process*, and ASTM E 1528, *Standard Practice for Environmental Site Assessments: Transaction Screen Process*, are alternative approaches to records review, site reconnaissance, interviews, and reports. One offers broad guidance for investigation, the other specific questionnaires. Both seek to define commercial standards for conducting environmental site assessments with respect to contaminants under CERCLA and to petroleum products—that is, to establish the practices that constitute all appropriate inquiry under CERCLA. The goal is to determine the requirements necessary for the user to claim an innocent landowner defense to CERCLA liability.

- Phase II

Typically refers to an environmental site assessment. The goal, limiting liability, is the same as for Phase I. When suspicious conditions are identified in a Phase I Site Assessment, a Phase II Site Assessment is recommended to perform more detailed analysis. ASTM E1903, *Standard Guide for Environmental Site Assessments: Phase II Environmental Site Assessment Process* was developed specifically to identify a professional standard of care for conducting a Phase II Site Assessment. It outlines customary practices relative to a range of contaminants within the scope of CERCLA, as well as petroleum products.

- RCRA

The Resource Conservation and Recovery Act (RCRA); 42 U.S.C. s/s 321 et seq. (1976): "RCRA (pronounced 'rick-rah') gave EPA the authority to control hazardous waste from the cradle to the grave. This includes the generation, transportation, treatment, storage, and disposal of hazardous waste. RCRA also set forth a framework for the management of non-hazardous wastes. The 1986 amendments to RCRA enabled EPA to address environmental problems that could result from underground tanks storing petroleum and other hazardous substances. RCRA focuses only on active and future facilities and does not address abandoned or historical sites (see CERCLA). HSWA (pronounced 'hiss-wa'), the Federal Hazardous and Solid Waste Amendments, are the 1984 amendments to RCRA that required phasing out land disposal of hazardous waste. Some of the other mandates of this strict law include increased enforcement authority for EPA, more stringent hazardous waste management standards, and a comprehensive underground storage tank program."[10]

- TSCA

The Toxic Substances Control Act (TSCA); 15 U.S.C. s/s 2601 et seq. (1976): "The Toxic Substances Control Act of 1976 was enacted by Congress to test, regulate, and screen all chemicals produced or imported into the United States. Many thousands of chemicals and their compounds are developed each year with unknown toxic or dangerous characteristics. To prevent tragic consequences, TSCA requires that any chemical that reaches the consumer marketplace be tested for possible toxic effects prior to commercial manufacture. Any existing chemical that poses health and environmental hazards is tracked and reported under TSCA. Procedures also are authorized for corrective action under TSCA in cases of cleanup of toxic materials contamination. TSCA supplements other federal statutes, including the Clean Air Act and the Toxic Release Inventory under EPCRA."[11]

The Farm Security and Rural Investment Act of 2002 (Farm Bill 2002) includes a requirement for federal agencies to develop a procurement program for bio-based products. Section 9002 of the Act requires each federal agency to give preference in their purchases (including construction materials) to items "composed of the highest percentage of biobased products practicable."[12] This Section also mandates the establishment of a voluntary program to label bio-based products as a "U.S.D.A. Certified Biobased Product." With the publication of the final rule incorporating "Guidelines for Designating Biobased Products for Federal Procurement" in February 2005, the Federal Biobased Products Preferred Procurement Program (FB4P) began the process of evaluating potential products for listing. The evaluation process will begin by determining whether products: (1) are cost competitive with non-bio-based products; (2) meet industry performance standards; and (3) are readily available on the commercial market. The FB4P has assembled a list of bio-based items that will be used for designation under the program. The list can be viewed at www.biobased.oce.usda.gov/public/categories.cfm.

The High Performance Green Buildings Act of 2004, introduced in the Senate as Bill S.2620, would, if enacted, promote the development and construction of environmentally friendly federal buildings and schools. The bill authorizes the expenditure of "$35 million over five years to support federal buildings and schools that are designed and operated to boost environmental, economic, health and productivity performance above that of conventional buildings."[13] The bill, as introduced, includes many provisions of interest to the green building practitioner such as expansion of green building research, grants to state and local education agencies for the implementation of the EPA's Tools for Schools Program, creation of an Office of High-Performance Green Buildings at GSA, and a review of the federal budget process to identify savings that can be realized by using life-cycle costs in building construction.[14]

In addition to the activity at the federal level, many states and municipalities have taken an active role in promoting green buildings. Among the notable local programs is the one introduced by New York State in May 2000. New York became the first state to offer an incentive package to developers who build environmentally sound commercial and apartment buildings. This innovative tax law, or "green building credit," is aimed at encouraging the building materials and construction industries to adopt green practices on a large scale by providing tax credits to building owners and tenants who invest in increased energy efficiency, recycled and recyclable materials, and improved indoor air quality. The credit allows builders who meet energy goals and use environmentally preferable products to claim up to $3.75 per square foot for interior work and $7.50 per square foot for exterior work against their state tax bill. To qualify for the credit, a building must be certified by a licensed architect or engineer and meet specific requirements for energy use, materials selection, indoor air quality, waste disposal, and water use. Arizona, Hawaii, Idaho, Maryland, Minnesota, Montana, Oregon, and other states are also offering tax incentives, and the trend is continuing to grow.

Building Codes

Building codes are intended to protect the health, safety, and welfare of the public. They are inherently flawed in that they must respond to changing conditions and empirical evidence after the fact. New technologies present new hazards as well as new benefits previously unimagined. We try to codify the new systems based on old understandings. Fire standards, which became the focus of attention after the great Chicago fire of 1871, were developed around our understanding of how wood burns. These test methods must be continually reviewed and revised to adapt to changing materials and expected combinations of materials. Smoke released in a wood fire is different from smoke generated in a treated wood fire and still more different from that released from plastics. Seismic regulations changed drastically after San Francisco's Bay Bridge collapsed in 1989 and the Northridge quake toppled apartment buildings in 1994. We learned a lot about security construction, and lack thereof, after the Murrah Federal Building in Oklahoma City was bombed in 1995. Federal agencies quickly revised their security design requirements and remodeled many facilities accordingly. We are still learning from the experience of the World Trade Center devastation in 2001 and Hurricane Katrina in 2005.

The limitation of hindsight is magnified in a world moving as rapidly as ours does today. Unfortunately, if the environmental experts are correct, we have already exceeded the carrying capacity of the Earth. We are already using more of the Earth's natural resources than can be replenished annually. We are already polluting and destroying ecosystems faster than the Earth can renew itself. We have already damaged the ozone layer and altered the Earth's global climate patterns. We have already irreparably lost precious species and biodiversity. But no single disaster has yet focused our attention on the need for revising building codes to protect ecosystems. When we do recognize the need and determine an appropriate response, it may be too late.

In the interim, we have the opportunity to obtain variances. Anyone who has attempted to build a structure just a little bit differently from the manner outlined by the applicable building code will appreciate the hurdles many green designers and builders face. It is not an easy proposition. Most traditional, time-tested building methods, such as adobe, rammed earth, and straw bale, are today classified as "alternative" methods. Perversely, native, indigenous materials are required to demonstrate their ability to meet structural, energy, and fire standards on a project-by-project basis—a costly proposition. It may also be difficult, as most test method standards were designed to accommodate specific materials and systems, which generally do not include straw or mud. The challenge is further intensified because most indigenous building methods are not proprietary. Therefore, no manufacturer has a stake in paying for the testing necessary to demonstrate compliance, even when appropriate test methods exist.

Happily, many jurisdictions are beginning to respond to pubic demand, and several environmental interest groups are helping to create an information and support network. The Development Center for Alternative Technologies (DCAT), a nonprofit organization dedicated to the research and development of green building codes, is working to influence the development of the International Building Code. DCAT's goal is to develop model code language for alternative indigenous, earth-friendly building materials and methods. (Refer to the appendices for contact information for DCAT and other environmental organizations.)

Straw bale construction has a well-defined network of designers, builders, and consultants. Assistance is readily available for details, mortgage financing, and code compliance. While many jurisdictions allow straw bale building under the alternative materials and methods provisions of the existing codes, some also have specific provisions for straw bale construction, including parts of Arizona (the City of Tucson, Pima County, Pinal County, the Town of Guadalupe); California (State Guidelines and several counties and municipalities); Boulder, Colorado; the state of New Mexico; and Austin, Texas.

The city of Boulder has added environmental requirements to its residential permitting process. Unlike other green building programs, such as the one in Austin, Texas, and Colorado's statewide program, Boulder's program is mandatory. Its Green Points Program applies to new residential construction and additions larger than 500 square feet. It requires building permit applicants to earn a minimum of 25 points from the city's green points list. By requiring an additional point for every 200 square feet of floor area over 2,500 square feet, it balances "excess" use of the Earth's resources with proactive environmental efforts. Items that are fairly straightforward may be self-certified; otherwise, inspection by the city is required. For example, recycled content roofing earns three points and may be self-certified by the building owner. Structural alternatives to wood earn ten points and require city inspection.

Trade Organizations and Publications

Many independent sources of technical information exist for environmental issues. The challenge is that, historically, these sources have been isolated from the channels of communication and information exchange in the building industry. Slowly, connections are being made. With these first connections, however, has come the discovery that the language and methods of communication for environmentalists and for building industry are very, very different. They differ on specifics. *FS*, to a specifier, means "federal specifications," but to an environmentalist it is likely to mean "forest service." More important, they differ on fundamentals. Environmentalists stress ideals, whereas the building industry (or any industry, for that matter) focuses on the practical. Where the two increasingly come together is on improving efficiencies—improving energy efficiency, reducing waste, improving water quality, and improving indoor air quality. Similarly, both the captains of environmentalism and the captains of industry are big-picture people who recognize the global impact of human activity.

Sources of green information are beginning to develop a cohesive and reliable network that, at certain points, overlaps the mainstream building industry information network. Professional and trade organizations dedicated to green issues and green building can be helpful. These include the U.S. Green Building Council, Electric Power Research Institute, Environmental Business Association, Institute of Scrap Recycling Industries, Urban Land Institute, and Global Environmental Management. (Contact information for these organizations and others is available in the appendices.)

Sources of green information also include specialty publishers:

- John Wiley and Sons/AIA Environmental Resource Guide: (877) 762-2974, www.wiley .com

- Island Press: (202) 232-7933, www.islandpress.org

- CRC Press/Lewis Publishers: (800) 272-7737, www.crcpress.com

- World Resources Institute: (800) 537-5487. www.wristore.org

And they also include specialty magazines and periodicals:

- *DESIGNER/builder*
  2405 Maclovia Lane
  Santa Fe, New Mexico 87505
  (505) 471-4549
  www.designerbuildermagazine.com

  Features the latest ideas in architecture and design. Includes articles on environmentally conscious building, urban design, affordable housing, environmental psychology, alternative construction materials, and on people who are pushing the limits of design and community development.

- *Eco-structure*
  1415 Highway 54 W, Suite 105
  Durham, North Carolina 27707
  (919) 402-9300
  www.eco-structure.com

  Features articles on green building projects, the latest green building products, and new technology and techniques in the green building industry.

- *Environmental Building News*
  122 Birge Street
  Brattleboro, Vermont 05301
  (802) 861-0954
  www.BuildingGreen.com

  Focuses on environmentally sustainable design and construction. Features checklists, latest news, reviews of building products, case studies, and information sources. Provides well researched, in-depth technical articles.

- *Environmental Design and Construction*
  2401 W. Big Beaver, Suite 700
  Troy, Michigan 48084
  (248) 362-3700
  www.EDCmag.com

  Covers aspects of environmentally sound building design and construction, including recycled-content materials, energy efficiency, alternative building sources, and indoor air quality.

- *Indoor Air Bulletin*
  Indoor Air Information Service, Inc.
  P.O. Box 8446
  Santa Cruz, California 95061-8446
  (831) 426-6624
  (831) 426-6522 (fax)

  Focuses on indoor air quality, but considers all aspects of indoor environment important to occupant health, comfort, and productivity.

- *Journal of Green Building*
  College Publishing
  12309 Lynwood Drive
  Glen Allen, Virginia 23059
  (800) 827-0723
  www.collegepublishing.us

  An interdisciplinary, peer-reviewed journal that seeks to advance the state of knowledge about green buildings and high-performance, sustainable facilities and infrastructure systems.

- *Solar Today*
  The American Solar Energy Society
  2400 Central Avenue, Suite G-1
  Boulder, Colorado 80301
  (303) 433-3130
  www.solartoday.org

  Features articles on solar technologies for transportation and building applications. Includes thermal systems, photovoltaics, environmental concerns, legislation, and products and services.

Industry Standards

The contractual agreements that designate professional responsibilities and corresponding liabilities depend on measurable, assignable requirements. Generally, they depend on established industry standards. Similarly, manufacturers market their products by advertising compliance with established industry standards. Either the assembly is UL rated or it is not.

Standards-developing organizations exist on many levels. trade and professional organizations set quality requirements for their own areas of expertise. Examples include the American Concrete Institute, Ceramic Tile Institute, and Architectural Woodwork Institute, and (from a green perspective) Forest Stewardship Council. Federal specifications and military standards are being slowly phased out as private-sector standards are developed to replace them. And there are national and international standards development organizations.

ASTM International is the primary standards development organization in the United States. Both ASTM International and the International Organization for Standardization (ISO) develop standards for use internationally.

ISO is a nonprofit volunteer standards development organization. It has a history of over 50 years of standards development. ISO "identifies what International Standards are required by business, government and society, develops them in partnership with the sectors that will put them to use, adopts them by transparent procedures based on national input and delivers them to be implemented worldwide."[15] ISO Standards "make up a complete offering for all three dimensions of sustainable development—economic, environmental and social."[16] The technical work of ISO is highly decentralized, carried out in a hierarchy of some 2,900 technical committees, subcommittees, and working groups. Each technical committee has subcommittees, and each subcommittee has working groups. Although the greater part of the ISO technical work is done by correspondence, on average a dozen ISO meetings take place somewhere in the world every working day. Every country is allowed a single vote. To render the vote, each nation designates a voting member body. For the United States, the voting member body is the American National Standards Institute (ANSI)—essentially a figurehead that designates (for each ISO technical committee) an entity responsible for developing the American opinion and directing the ANSI vote. Most of the entities reside in ASTM.

ASTM is a voluntary organization, created in 1898, that develops standards for everything from dishwashing liquid to concrete curing compounds. It has produced more than 12,000 standards. The 137 main committees are organized into subcommittees, and each subcommittee is divided into task groups. ASTM is designed to be a balanced organization. Voting membership of any given committee is limited to 50 percent manufacturing interests; the remainder is composed of users, government, academia, and general public. While most voting is conducted by mail, negative votes are resolved at the biannual meetings, where a simple majority rules on interpretation (including dismissal) of negative votes.

Both ASTM and ISO have several committees dedicated to environmental issues in general and to green building issues in particular. The ISO Technical Committee (TC) on Environmental Management (ISO/TC 207) covers "standardization in the field of environmental management tools and systems" with the exception of those specific topics covered under other ISO TCs. Excluded are test methods for pollutants, which are the responsibility of ISO/TC 146 (Air Quality), ISO/TC 147 (Water Quality), ISO/TC 190 (Soil Quality) and ISO/TC 43 (Acoustics); setting limit values regarding pollutants or effluents; setting environmental performance levels; and standardization of products. TC 207 works closely with ISO/TC 176 in the field of environmental systems and audits. ISO has developed several environmental performance standards, including:

- ISO 14001 Environmental Management Systems
- ISO 14004 Environmental Management Systems—General Guidelines on Principles, Systems, and Supporting Techniques
- ISO 14010 Guidelines for Environmental Auditing—General Principles on Environmental Auditing
- ISO 14011 Guidelines for Environmental Auditing—Audit Procedures—Auditing of Environmental Management Systems
- ISO 14012 Guidelines for Environmental Auditing—Qualification Criteria for Environmental Auditors

In 1997, ISO designated an ad hoc committee to investigate the international viability and necessity of standards for sustainable building. It is also intended to review the many building rating systems that have been produced in the United Kingdom, Canada, Norway, Sweden, and the United States. By unanimous agreement, the Ad Hoc Group on Sustainable Building proposed that ISO/TC 59 develop a new subcommittee—Subcommittee (TC59/SC17) on Sustainability in Building Construction, established in 2003. The new subcommittee deals with standardization in the field of sustainability of the built environment with environmental, economic, and social aspects of sustainability included as appropriate. There are four working groups with the following focus[17]:

- WG 1: General Principles and Terminology
- WG 2: Sustainability Indicators
- WG 3: Environmental Declaration of Products
- WG 4: Environmental Performance of Buildings.

The following documents are under development by the Work Groups:

- Sustainability in Building Construction—General Principles
- Sustainability in Building Construction—Sustainability Indicators—Part 1: Framework for Development of Indicators for Buildings
- Sustainability in Building Construction—Environmental Declarations of Building Products
- Sustainability in Building Construction—Framework for Methods of Assessment of Environmental Performance of Construction Works—Part 1: Buildings
- Sustainability in Building Construction—Terminology

Committees in ASTM that are addressing environmental issues include those responsible for concrete, plastic, and glass, each responding to environmental issues specific to its arena. A more detailed discussion of the work underway by the ASTM Committees can be found in Chapter 3 under the heading "Tools That Help Define Green."

Trade organizations are also beginning to publish standards and opinions relative to environmental issues specific to their arena. The American Society of Heating, Refrigerating, and Air Conditioning Engineers (ASHRAE) is a prominent example. ASHRAE has developed standards relative to indoor air quality and energy efficiency, including ASHRAE 62, Ventilation for Acceptable Indoor Air Quality; ASHRAE 90.1, Energy-Efficient Design of New Buildings Except Low-Rise Residential Buildings, which presented code language to help states meet the October 1994 federal deadline to write codes that meet or exceed the standard as per National Energy Act; and ASHRAE 100, Energy Conservation Standards for Existing Industrial, Institutional, and Commercial Buildings. In 2004, ASHRAE released updated versions of Standards 62 and 90.1. ASHRAE 62 was redesignated 62.1 to differentiate it from ASHRAE 62.2, Ventilation and Acceptable Indoor Air Quality in Low-Rise Residential Buildings. ASHRAE 90.1 underwent a major revamping to not only make it easier to use and understand but also to add new technical requirements and stringency levels. The updated standard has a new appendix that can be used to rate the energy efficiency of building designs that exceed the standard's minimum requirements. The new appendix is also useful if you are trying to achieve a LEED certification for a project. The Energy Cost Budget (ECB) method description contains a reformatted table showing the symmetry between simulations of a design building model to a budget model. ASHRAE published *GreenGuide* in 2003; this offers guidance to heating, ventilating, air conditioning, and refrigeration designers involved in green building design. It covers the entire building life cycle, from the beginning of the project through the completed structure's operation, maintenance, and eventual demolition.

Most standards and codes govern individual building products and individual buildings. They do not attempt to address the collective impact of buildings. For environmental issues, this oversight is unacceptable. The environmental impact of buildings in aggregate—as, for example, in the classic case of urban sprawl—has generated a new genre of standards, *sustainability indicators*. Indicators augment the typical array of measurement tools, particularly with respect to complex, shifting, and holistic areas such as economics and the environment. In many diverse efforts around the world, indicators are being developed to assess the environmental and economic impacts of buildings in aggregate. "Indicators are useful because they point to trends and relationships in a concise way. They provide meaning beyond the attributes directly associated with them. In this sense, they are different from primary data or statistics, providing a bridge between detailed data and interpreted information. Indicators have been used for many years and are common in planning and economics where indicators such as GDP [Gross Domestic Product], the unemployment rate, the literacy rate and the population growth rate are widely monitored."[18]

In 1987, the World Commission on Environment and Development (Brundtland Commission) called for the development of new ways to measure and assess progress toward sustainable development. Subsequently, at the Earth Summit in Rio de Janeiro in 1992, the United Nations Conference on Environment and Development (UNCED) reiterated the importance of indicators. Chapter 40 of the UNCED Agenda 21 calls for the development of indicators for sustainable development. In particular, it requests countries at the national level, international governmental agencies, and nongovernmental organizations at the international level to develop and identify such indicators.[19] Many local, national, and international efforts have attempted to respond to this need. For example, the Commission on Sustainable Development (CSD), which grew out of the Earth Summit, is working with 21 countries to test indicators (developed through the United Nations and discussed with the Expert Group on Indicators of Sustainable Development in September 1996 in Geneva) in relation to its own national priorities and interests. These countries include the Maldives, Pakistan, the Philippines, China, Ghana, South Africa, Kenya, Morocco, Austria, Belgium, United Kingdom, Germany, Finland, France, the Czech Republic, Barbados, Brazil, Bolivia, Costa Rica, Mexico, and Venezuela. The goal of the CSD is to document viable sustainability indicators for development by the year 2000. Based on voluntary national testing and expert group consultations, the CSD developed a core set of 58 indicators in 2001. The CSD indicator set and methodological description are currently undergoing revision. An updated set is expected to be released in 2006.[20]

Another important international development in sustainability indicators is the Bellagio Principles, developed in late 1996 by the International Institute for Sustainable Development with support from the Rockefeller Foundation, in Bellagio, Italy. The Bellagio Principles outline a holistic perspective with consideration for equity and disparity within the current population and between present and future generations; for the ecological conditions on which life depends; and for economic development and other nonmarket activities that contribute to human and social well-being. The Bellagio Principles cite the need for adequate scope in terms of both human and ecosystem time scales and spatial needs. Further, it requires a practical focus with openness and the capacity to adjust goals, frameworks, and indicators as new insights are gained.

An ISO standard on this topic is under consideration, which would coordinate with the work of the CSD, the International Institute for Sustainable Development, intergovernmental organizations, and nongovernmental organizations.

Material Safety Data Sheets

Much information regarding the chemical composition of a product and the corresponding precautionary recommendations is available via Material Safety Data Sheets (MSDS). MSDSs are required under the Occupational Safety and Health Administration (OSHA) Hazard Communication Standard (1910.1200) as one of the vehicles by which employers inform their employees about the hazards of the chemicals in their workplace. They are also extremely useful tools for greening a building.

MSDSs address chemicals. They do not address articles such as door hardware. They do address coatings, adhesives, sealers, and cleaning agents. While they contain highly technical data, they also include a lot of information useful in evaluating the toxicity of a product.

According to OSHA, an MSDS must include the following information (1910.1200 (g)(2)):

- Product name
- Chemical and common name(s) of all ingredients that have been determined to be health hazards or physical hazards
- Physical and chemical characteristics of the hazardous chemical, such as vapor pressure and flash point
- Physical hazards of the hazardous chemical, including the potential for fire, explosion, and reactivity
- Health hazards of the hazardous chemical
- Primary route(s) of entry
- OSHA-permissible exposure limit (threshold limit)
- Whether the chemical is listed in the National Toxicology Program (NTP) Annual Report on Carcinogens or the International Agency for Research on Cancer (IARC) Monographs, or by OSHA
- Precautions for safe handling and use
- Control measures, such as appropriate engineering controls, work practices, and personal protective equipment

- Emergency and first-aid procedures
- Date of preparation of the MSDS or the last change to it
- Name, address, and telephone number of the chemical manufacturer, importer, employer, or other responsible party preparing or distributing the MSDS

OSHA does not specify a format for MSDSs. However, the American National Standards Institute (ANSI) has developed recommendations for a standard format (ANSI Z400.1) that are commonly used. The ANSI standard is intended to promote consistency and to help convey information in a manner that is useful and understandable across education levels, from the janitor to the emergency room physician. It includes 16 sections. The first 10 address the specific requirements under OSHA; the rest identify information that OSHA does not require but that may be necessary in order to address requirements in other countries. Because the last six sections are not legal OSHA requirements, many MSDSs do not provide data for them. Nevertheless, they are of particular interest for specifiers of green building materials because they identify the impact of the chemical(s) on the Earth in addition to the impact on human health.

Following is a summary of the 16 sections of the ANSI standard MSDS format:

- Section 1
Chemical Product and Company Identification: This section indicates the name, address, and phone number of the company, manufacturer, or distributor of the chemical. Emergency contact information is included here.

- Section 2
Composition/Information on Ingredients: This section is of limited use to most building industry professionals. It identifies chemicals and their percentage content. Note that only those chemicals referenced in 29 CFR part 1910, subpart Z, OSHA Toxic and Hazardous Substances, are likely to be listed. This section may also include OSHA Permissible Exposure Limits (PEL) and American Conference of Governmental Industrial Hygienists (ACGIH) Threshold Limit Values (TLV).

- Section 3
Hazards Identification. This section says whether or not the material is considered a carcinogen and what the known potential health effects are. Note that only those chemicals referenced in the National Toxicology Program (NTP) Annual Report on Carcinogens, the International Agency for Research on Cancer (IARC) Monographs, or 29 CFR part 1910, subpart Z, OSHA Toxic and Hazardous Substances, are likely to be listed. The "Registry of Toxic Effects of Chemical Substances," published by the National Institute for Occupational Safety and Health, indicates whether a chemical has been found by NTP or IARC to be a potential carcinogen.

- Section 4
First-Aid Measures. This section is fairly self-explanatory. It should be written for untrained individuals.

- Section 5

  Firefighting Measures. This section indicates the flammability and explosivity of the product, with firefighting instructions. It also indicates potential hazardous byproducts due to combustion.

- Section 6

  Accidental Release Measures: This section describes responses to material spills, leaks, or accidental releases.

- Section 7

  Handling and Storage: This section is self-explanatory. It might include overexposure warnings and hygiene instructions.

- Section 8

  Exposure Controls/Personal Protection: This section describes the engineering controls and protective gear that reduce personal exposure. Obviously, the greater the danger, the more protective gear is required.

- Section 9

  Physical and Chemical Properties: This section may be of limited use to building industry professionals. It includes information regarding the chemical's appearance, odor, pH, physical state, vapor pressure, boiling point, vapor density, freezing/melting point, solubility in water, and specific gravity or density.

- Section 10

  Stability and Reactivity Data. This section indicates known incompatibilities with other materials and potential hazardous decomposition. The information provides an indication of the potential interactions in the ecosystem.

- Section 11

  Toxicological Information: This section includes data used to determine the hazards cited in Section 3. The information provides an indication of the potential toxicity/IEQ impacts. It may discuss acute data, carcinogenicity, reproductive effects, and target organ effects. Do not be surprised to find "No data available."

- Section 12

  Ecological Information. This section includes data regarding environmental impact in the event of an accidental release. The information provides an indication of the potential interactions in the ecosystem. Do not be surprised to find "No data available."

- Section 13

  Disposal Considerations. This section includes data regarding the proper disposal of the chemical. It may include information regarding recycling and reuse. It may indicate whether or not the product is considered hazardous waste according to EPA Hazardous

Waste Regulations 40 CFR 261. This information provides an indication of the potential interactions in the ecosystem.

- Section 14
  Transportation Information. This section includes basic shipping information, such as the hazard class. As with Section 8 for exposure control, the greater the precautions, the greater the environmental and health risks.

- Section 15
  Regulatory Information. This section includes the regulations applicable to the material. References may include federal regulations, such as TSCA or SARA, and state-specific information, such as California's Proposition 65, the Safe Drinking Water and Toxic Enforcement Act.

- Section 16
  Other Information. This section may include hazard ratings, preparation of the MSDS, and additional labeling information.

Last, although it is not part of the OSHA requirements or the ANSI format, there will be a disclaimer. Following is a sample.

The information and recommendations set forth herein are believed to be accurate. Because some of the information is derived from information provided by our suppliers, and because we have no control over the conditions of handling and use, we make no warranty, express or implied, regarding the accuracy of the data or the results to be obtained from the use thereof. The information is supplied solely for your information and consideration, and we assume no responsibility from use or reliance thereon. It is the responsibility of the user of our products to comply with all applicable federal, state, and local laws and regulations.

Labeling

We are a litigious industry in a scientific society. We like to measure, monitor, assess, and label. Green buildings and green building materials are no exception. Since the early 1990s there has been a veritable flood of green rating systems and assessment tools, each vying for public recognition and industry acceptance. Green building does, however, present a challenge to our desire to quantify and label. In order to create simple, apples-to-apples comparisons, each assessment tool inevitably must assign single numbers to complex interrelationships. Not surprisingly, each of the tools focuses on certain aspects of our web of life—and neglects others. Nevertheless, each new generation of green building rating tools offers improvements on the predecessors.

There are many examples of rating systems for green building products. The most viable offer independent third-party verification. One such third party, Green Seal, a nonprofit environmental organization, develops standards for a variety of consumer and building products. When in compliance with a Green Seal Standard, the Green Seal certification mark may appear on the packaging and on the product itself. However, when the certification mark appears on a package or product, the product or package must contain a description of the basis for certification. Another, Scientific Certification Systems, is a for-profit company that reviews specific manufacturer claims and offers endorsement for products that pass its review. In 1998, the National Institute of Standards and Technology (NIST) released Building for Environmental and Economic Sustainability (BEES), a tool for generating relative scores for building product alternatives. BEES explores environmental issues in accordance with ISO 14040 LCA methodology to weight the environmental impacts of raw materials acquisition, manufacture, transportation, installation, use, and waste management. It does not address impact on human health nor regional environmental issues. It does incorporate economic information in accordance with ASTM E917 for initial costs, replacement costs, operations costs, maintenance and repair costs, and disposal costs.

There are even more green rating programs for buildings. With the notable exception of the City of Boulder's Green Point Program, the programs are voluntary. However, by establishing minimum requirements in various categories, voluntary programs can help establish professional standards of care for the greenness of both the building as a whole and the component green materials/products/systems. Examples of green building programs include the following:

- *Austin Sustainable Building Program:* The City of Austin's Green Builder Program received a United Nations Award for Local Government Initiatives at the Earth Summit in Rio de Janeiro. The goal of the voluntary program is to influence home builders to use sustainable building practices. The program bases its rating system on the premise that a house is a single system with four major components to consider: energy, water, materials, and waste. It offers certification using a simple scale of one to four stars—the more stars, the more green features in the home. The Austin program is regional in nature. It emphasizes locally available materials and regional factors both for the particular building and for the community in general. The Austin Green Builder Program has since been expanded to commercial and institutional structures. A separate initiative, the Austin Sustainable Communities Initiative, has been launched.

- *Building Environmental Performance Assessment Criteria (BEPAC):* BEPAC was originally designed for new and existing office buildings in British Columbia, although regional variants have subsequently been developed for Ontario and Atlantic Canada. BEPAC evaluates two main categories, the base building and tenant buildout. Each category is assessed according to five criteria: ozone layer protection, environmental impact of energy use, indoor environmental quality, resource conservation, and site and transportation. Each of the criteria is assessed within a 10-point scale. BEPAC weights the points to reflect the relative importance of aspects within each criterion but not between criteria. BEPAC is no longer used, but it remains of academic interest.

- *Building Research Establishment Environmental Assessment Method (BREEAM):* BREEAM, a tool developed by the BRE in the United Kingdom in 1990, is widely used in Europe, Hong King, Singapore, Australia, New Zealand, and Canada. A version designed for use in the United States is under development. BREEAM is based on energy and environmental principles. It evaluates a building in two stages, before and after, identifying opportunities for improvement that may be implemented prior to final assessment and certification.

- *Colorado Green Building Rating Program:* The Colorado Governor's Office of Energy Conservation and the Home Builders Association (HBA) of Metro Denver developed a voluntary, statewide Green Builder Program to recognize builders who construct homes that conserve natural resources and preserve the environment. Homes built under the program's guidelines receive the designation "Built Green." In addition, the Energy Rated Homes of Colorado's (ERHC) E-Star program rates a home's energy efficiency on a 100-point scale, which translates into scores of one to five-plus stars. ERHC's Energy Improvement Mortgage can allow prospective home buyers to add cost-effective energy upgrades into a mortgage loan for payback over the life of the loan. Home energy upgrades also can be financed through an Energy Improvement Mortgage. ERHC is operated by the Colorado Housing and Finance Authority.

- *Energy Star:* Unlike most, in this rating system one does not examine the design of the building but rather evaluates the performance. An Energy Star label is earned by comparing 12 months of utility data (including energy efficiency, IAQ, thermal comfort, and lighting levels information) against an industry-established baseline. The EPA/DOE Energy Star Building program is a voluntary, performance-based benchmarking and recognition initiative. It benchmarks against current market averages. President Clinton directed federal agencies to pursue the Energy Star Building label. The Energy Star building label is still promoted through federal agencies and is available for private construction as well, and it makes available a web-based tool capable of assessing performance of a particular building against comparable averages. With certification by a licensed engineer, any qualifying building can obtain an Energy Star label.

- *Good Cents:* Utility-sponsored programs to improve energy efficiency are the oldest green building programs in the United States. The Good Cents program was developed in 1976 to encourage the construction of energy-efficient homes. To date, more than 750,000 Good Cents homes have been built across the country; 60,000 are added annually.[21]

- *Green Globes Building Environmental Assessments:* Originally developed for use in Canada, Green Globes™ is an interactive, web-based, commercial green building assessment protocol that guides the integration of green principles into a building's design. Green Globes rates seven areas: project management, site, energy, water, resources, emissions and effluents, and indoor environment.

- *Home Energy Rating Systems (HERS):* HERS was developed by the U.S. Department of Energy in accordance with the Energy Policy Act of 1992. DOE has also developed guidelines for Energy-Efficient Mortgage Programs (EEMS) and encourages utilities and the mortgage industry to adopt them. Homes are awarded an energy-efficiency rating between 0 and 100, with 100 being a home that is completely energy-self-sufficient. In 1995, the National Association of State Energy Office Officials and Energy Rated Homes of America founded the Residential Energy Services Network (RESNET) to develop a national market for HERS and EEMS.

• *Leadership in Energy and Environmental Design (LEED):* This tool, developed by the U.S. Green Building Council, designates the relative greenness of buildings. It contains certain prerequisites. The building must be asbestos-free, CFC-free, and smoking-free. It must comply with ASHRAE 90.1, ASHRAE 62, ASHRAE 55, EPACT requirements for low-flow fixtures, and EPA standards for water quality. It must contain areas that allow occupants to recycle. It must be commissioned. Any building meeting these prerequisite requirements can earn credits in a variety of ways. Final scores place buildings in a category of greenness and entitle them to be labeled a Green Building under the LEED program.

A growing international movement, the Green Building Challenge (GBC), is culling the best of each of the national efforts. If it can avoid the dilution that tends to accompany international compromises, it is likely to dominate the green building rating arena. The GBC is developing the Green Building Tool (GBTool), which uses a series of criteria with subcriteria weighted to accommodate both hard and soft data, a typical impasse for many green rating tools, and has defaults that can be modified to reflect regional priorities. This is also an asset. Most tools are averaged over a broad area and are ill equipped to adapt to local and regional environmental concerns. In 2001, management and development of GBTool was taken over by the International Initiative for a Sustainable Built Environment (iiSBE)[22]. Since then, review, modification and testing of the GBTool has continued, culminating in the current version released in 2005 (GBTool-Sep29). Plans are to continue work on the development and refinement of the GBTool over a 3-year cycle from 2005-2008.

At some level, most of these rating systems require a subjective, albeit educated and professional, opinion. This is especially true for the whole building rating programs. Pure objectivity is nearly impossible given our limited understanding of the functioning of ecosystems. We do not know the number and type of species living with us on this planet, let alone how they interact in the web of life. Except in limited applications such as energy efficiencies, informed, subjective opinion is almost unavoidable for green rating systems. Each label implies an endorsement of the rating systems and the rating entity. After arriving at reasonably acceptable rating systems, whom should we trust to assess building products and buildings themselves? The usual array of testing laboratories and governing agencies having jurisdiction does not generally possess adequate understanding of the environmental issues.

There is a new player in the construction industry that does understand environmental issues and is likely to become a critical partner in green building: nongovernmental organizations (NGOs). Long on the sidelines, accustomed to educating the public and exposing environmental abuses, environmental NGOs are now being sought by mainstream organizations for consultation on green approaches and, ultimately, to certify the greenness of the product, system, or building in question. With increasing numbers, mainstream corporations are seeking the counsel of environmental NGOs. Some do this quite publicly, such as the now famous assistance that the Environmental Defense Fund (EDF) provided to McDonald's in the wake of the public outcry against the restaurant's use of styrene. Subsequently, McDonald's not only developed less environmentally damaging paper containers for its food products but also began incorporating recycled content materials in its buildings. Furthermore, it developed and distributed free of charge a listing of the building and furnishing materials it had identified. Many reputable for-profit green consulting firms are now established. These are generally familiar with both the building industry and the environmental arena and can readily assist building owners in design and material selection. They are also equipped to assist product manufacturers in improving efficiencies and marketing green products. For certification of a product's greenness, however, independent nonprofits are the most desirable. For authenticating a product's greenness, the environmental NGO is likely to become the primary figure.

Certification

Certification—specifically, independent third-party certification—is necessary because our society long ago abandoned the so-called gentleman's agreement as an acceptable contractual arrangement. Because in our increasingly complex and litigious world it is impossible for one person to have detailed knowledge on all topics, we rely heavily on the impartial expertise of independent experts. The design and construction industry, for example, no longer relies on the innate desire of a contractor to produce quality craftsmanship or the reliability of the owner to fairly compensate a contractor. Rather, the industry relies on form contracts, legislation, building codes, and trade standards. It is natural, under this system, for an owner to expect to verify the authenticity of the sustainable aspects of sustainably harvested wood through such independent methods. Questions subsequently arise as to what constitutes *sustainability*, who verifies the parameters, what their qualifications are, and how much it costs. Enter certification.

The certifying entity and method are critical. Independent environmental organizations, long considered on the radical fringe, are quickly stepping in to fill the void. Their environmental expertise and enthusiasm for educating industry and the public can be extremely valuable assets.

Environmental NGOs have credibility due to their long history of altruistic pursuits. They are exquisitely objective. In contrast to industry organizations whose primary goals are to facilitate commerce and promote the products of their membership, environmental organizations have one purpose: to protect the environment. The goal involves complex, holistic considerations. Too often, standard organizations are demarcated into isolated specialties, unable to address holistic concerns adequately. In this arena, the NGOs are, without question, the experts. It is entirely likely that the environmental NGOs, not ASTM, ANSI, ISO, or other established groups, will lead the practical shift to new ways of thinking, new standards, and new measurements. For example, the Forest Stewardship Council (FSC), an international nonprofit organization that trains, accredits, and monitors independent, third-party certifiers for well-managed forests around the world, has gained an acceptance in the construction industry unheard-of for NGOs in previous decades. Green designers who wish to specify wood from sustainably managed sources specify that the lumber bear the FSC label. This is a harbinger of a new era and a new player in the construction industry. Certifications from environmental NGOs offer the green equivalent of the UL endorsement.

Step 4: Review Submitted Information for Completeness

While some standards for green building products do exist, they are too few—so far. Furthermore, where they do exist, they are often performance-based, not prescription-based. Consequently, the designer is left in the position of recommending products in the absence of industry-recognized acceptable minimums that we like to have to clearly designate responsibilities and liabilities. The designer is forced to render an educated, professional opinion. This is not a comfortable position for architects in a litigious society, but it is a necessary one. The codes and standards that guide our decisions today evolved via this same process of trial and error mixed with educated, professional opinion. Undeniably, environmental issues are health, safety, and welfare issues for the occupants of a given building and for the community as a whole. Eventually, we will evolve specific industry-recognized standards addressing all aspects of construction relative to environmental issues.

In some cases, such as products with recycled content, the comparison of green products to their conventional counterparts is apples to apples. It is possible to use existing standards to establish performance quality and use other certification or assessment processes to demonstrate green qualities (biodegradability, energy efficiency, nontoxicity, recycled contents).

In other cases, the comparison is apples to oranges. For products meeting a need in a new way, such as agricultural-based products and alternate energy systems, no existing appropriate performance standards may exist. The green products perform differently from their conventional counterparts, although they accomplish the purpose of the assembly. Many of these products are viable but have difficulty competing in an industry that relies heavily on independent third-party qualification. Recognizing this, new standards are being developed. Green building is a rapidly evolving industry segment. New products, systems, regulations, and standards appear with increasing frequency to meet growing consumer demand.

Although the performance of a green product may be comparable to its conventional counterpart, the problem is finding credible information to make the comparison in the first place; in this respect, green is not yet on an equal footing with conventional design and specification methods. Architects and specifiers must spend extra effort to determine not only that a product exists but also that the quality assurance information exists. It is not unusual for a new manufacturer to need some education about the type of quality assurance information required.

As time goes on, the testing data that officially documents greenness will be developed. The empirical evidence may be more difficult to come by. While some green products are simply rediscovered products we used to use, others are new and cannot cite 10 to 20 years of satisfied customers. Keep in mind that manufacturers of green products want to make a profit just like the next guy. They can't do that if you don't buy their products. You won't buy their products if those products don't perform.

Step 5: Evaluate (Green) Materials

Perhaps the most important step in the product selection process is the evaluation. In a perfect world, all the information you need is readily available and well organized so you can simply add up the scores and pick the best. Realistically, at some point, even if you haven't obtained all the information you want, the bell rings and you must make a decision. As in all matters, there is the theory . . . and then there is practice.

First, let's review the theory. Practice is nearly always altered by reality, but it is founded in theory, so it's a good place to start. In theory, the greenness of materials is determined by answering as best you can these two questions:

1. What are you using?
2. How well are you using it?

Are you using perpetual resources, renewable resources, or nonrenewable resources? How are you affecting the quality of the resource (present and future) and the cycle of the resource (rate of flow, diversion, etc.)? Consider local, regional, and global implications of choices. This is especially important for people in the United States to understand. We have money and power. What we do matters a lot, but it is amazingly difficult for the average American to grasp that. Many—most—of the negative consequences of our actions (energy inefficiency, resource mismanagement, and waste) are felt in developing countries. Not only do Americans consume a vastly disproportionate share of the Earth's limited resources, we export waste (including hazardous waste) to developing countries for "disposal" there at a nominal fee. Furthermore, corporate America may site its factories in developing countries to avoid the more stringent environmental regulations at home. The immediate damage is removed from our direct view, but it will drift back to us.

In practice, answers to the two questions will be both descriptive and quantitative. They will also have economic implications. In theory, there is a universally accepted formula—the holy grail of life-cycle assessment (LCA) methodologies—that will process all the variables and spit out the answer. The LCA concept sounds fairly straightforward: Quantify the input, the output, and the byproducts, and you will have your answer. But LCA is not simply a matter of adding and subtracting all the variables and comparing the total to some EPA-approved matrix. It is a complex, intricate, holistic approach that defies the codes and standards with which the design and construction industry is familiar. The EPA estimates that a complete LCA of a product costs $100,000.[23] That is a bargain. But how many of us have worked on a project where there was enough money and enough time to perform the kind of research necessary for a complete LCA? Even with an open checkbook and an open schedule, much of the information is hotly debated within the scientific community, let alone the political and economic communities.

Even more distressing, the solution you do manage to find often reveals an apples-to-oranges comparison of green products and standard construction products and of one green product and another. Many green products are charting new territory. The existing standards were developed over decades by the industries they support, by the industries that have a vested interest in maintaining the status quo. Their power base is founded in current valuations of resources, tax structures, and subsidies, and in the current interpretations of regulatory requirements. The coating companies in California spent a great deal of money and effort lobbying against the development of VOC regulations by the South Coast Air Quality Management District (SCAQMD). Nevertheless, each of them developed coatings with low VOCs in compliance with the applicable SCAQMD regulations. Consumers were adamantly in favor of reducing the VOC content of coatings. Similarly, alternative wood treatment, such as borates, is handicapped by the monopoly the chromated copper arsenate (CCA) industry has on standards and the inclusion of those standards in model building codes. With increasing public awareness, this, too, is likely to shift.

In practice, green design solutions are not always simple and straightforward. For example, the knee-jerk reaction to tropical wood is to avoid it so as not to devastate the rain forest. But consider that if there is no economical value to the tropical wood, and if there is tremendous financial encouragement to clear-cut to raise cattle (which there is), there is no reason to respect and protect the wood. The tropical wood needs *some* economic value in order to be venerated and protected.

Through informative, responsible evaluation, building industry professionals can help improve the process. By making green information an integral part of the design process, building industry professionals can provide a higher quality of service to their customers and better protect the health, safety, and welfare of the community.

Step 6: Select and Document Choice

Whatever you do, including avoiding making a decision, will have an impact on the environment. What you do will shape the daily reality of the people who use the building. What you design will affect energy and water usage. The building will use a great many limited natural resources. It will probably create pollution directly and indirectly.

Solving all of the problems simultaneously is as unrealistic as avoiding them. A more constructive approach is to do what you can and continue improving. Sustainability is the goal. It is difficult to define, let alone achieve, in all areas today, but we can work toward it and raise the benchmark for everyone. Following are general rules of thumb for designing, specifying, and building green:

- Maximize durability.
- Maximize energy efficiency.
- Maximize future recyclability: Mechanical fastening is preferable to adhesive/solvent welding.
- Maximize maintainability.
- Maximize recycled content: Close the loop. Collecting and recycling is not the goal. We must incorporate recycled products into the building, and, when the product's current usefulness wanes, recycle it into yet another useful product rather than send it to a landfill.
- Maximize use of local and regional materials.
- Minimize embodied energy: Promote the highest and best use of a material to avoid wasting its embodied energy. The highest and best use of a 500-year-old redwood tree is not paper pulp.
- Minimize use of hazardous natural chemicals (asbestos, lead, etc.).

• Minimize use of synthetic chemicals: Synthetic chemicals should be considered guilty until proven innocent.

That's not too difficult. Even in practice.

While the product selection process is essentially the same for both green and non-green products, the lack of green certifications and standards places a greater burden on the specifier. Similarly, because green building product information is not typically available through mainstream building industry information resources, the burden on the specifier is also increased. However, once you are familiar with environmental resources and with environmental issues, the selection process is no more difficult than for mainstream products—and it is much more satisfying.

The next step is to specify what you have selected.

Notes

1. Alternative Agricultural Research and Commercialization (AARC) Corporation, *Sourcebook 1998* (Washington, D.C.: Department of Agriculture, 1998).
2. EPA summary of laws and regulations, www.epa.gov/epahome/rules.html.
3. Ibid.
4. Ibid.
5. Ibid.
6. Ibid.
7. Ibid.
8. National Environmental Policy Act.
9. EPA, summary of laws and regulations, www.epa.gov/epahome/rules.html.
10. Ibid.
11. Ibid.
12. www.biobased.oce.usda.gov/public/index.cfm.
13. Press release, Senator Jim Jeffords (I-Vermont), July 8, 2004, http://jeffords.senate.gov/~jeffords/04/07/070804greenbldgs.html.
14. High-Performance Green Building Act, TheOrator.com, www.theorator.com/bills108/s2620.html.
15. International Organization for Standardization, *ISO in Brief: International Standards for a Sustainable World*, Geneva, Switzerland, May 2005, www.iso.org/iso/en/aboutiso/isoinbrief/isoinbrief.html.
16. Ibid.
17. www.iso.org/iso/en/stdsdevelopment/tc/tclist/TechnicalCommitteeDetailPage.TechnicalCommitteeDetail?COMMID=5595.
18. U.N. Department of Economics and Social Affairs, *Indicators of Sustainable Development (ISD) Progress from Theory to Practice*, 14 January 1998.
19. U.N. Committee on Environment and Development Agenda 21, paragraph 40.6.

20. The current version is available on the United Nations Economic and Social Development website: www.un.org/esa/sustdev/natlinfo/indicators/isdms2001/table_4.htm.

21. GoodCents Solutions, www.goodcents.com.

22. The current version is available on the International Initiative for a Sustainable Built Environment (iiSBE) website: http://greenbuilding.ca/iisbe/gbc2k5/front-2k5.htm.

23. Annual USGBC Conference, EPA presentation on Life-Cycle Assessment, NIST, Gaithersburg, Maryland, 1994.

CHAPTER 5

How Does the Product Specification Process Work?

Sometimes the specifications even work against sustainable design, as when virgin materials are specified for work that could have been done with used materials.

The Next Efficiency Revolution: Creating a Sustainable Materials Economy
—John E. Young and Aaron Sachs

Many people are involved in a construction project. The primary participants in the average construction project are the building owner, the contractor, the design professional, the product manufacturer, and the building official. Additional players include the building occupant, the fabricator, the subcontractors, and other consultants. Understanding their roles and perspectives is crucial to the successful integration of an unfamiliar building material, green or otherwise, into the project.

Design and Construction Relationships

The Building Owner

The building owner is the person or company, either public or private, whose idea the building was in the first place. The owner is also responsible for funding the construction of the project and for operating it once it is complete. The owner is the one party who enters into separate contracts with both the design professional and the contractor. This creates a third-party relationship between the design professional and the contractor. For example, during construction, certain responsibilities of the design professional, acting on the owner's behalf, are included in the owner-design professional contract. They are also included in the owner-contractor contract.

The building owner rarely cites environmental concerns as a reason for building. The reason for building is to meet a specific need of the owner. The owner also rarely cites spending money as a reason for building. Spending money is viewed as an unfortunate consequence of meeting the identified need. Another necessary evil is the time required to transform the owner's need into a building.

The building owner may be a single person, several persons, or an organization. The organization, public or private, is probably represented by several key contacts (e.g., director of construction, facilities manager, marketing/sales manager, vice president in charge of construction, etc.), who may or may not have a clear understanding of the hierarchical relationships among themselves. However, to successfully incorporate green building materials into a project, it is as important to understand the relationships between the contacts within an organization as it is to understand the relationship of the owner to other parties on the project. Finding a champion of green materials within the organization is nice; finding the *right* champion is better.

With increasing frequency, building owners are including environmental concerns in their design requirements. The design professional must recognize that this does not imply that the owner's attitude about cost or time has changed. Nevertheless, more and more Fortune 500 companies are elevating environmental responsibility to higher levels within the corporate structure. It is not unusual for the director of environmental affairs to be a vice president or board member. According to a 2004 survey of Global 500 companies by Global Environmental Management Initiative (GEMI), approximately 81 percent rated environmental, health, and safety issues among the top ten issues facing their business.[1]

The Contractor

The contractor is the entity that enters into a contract with the building owner to build the project. The contractor, in turn, subcontracts with a multitude of subcontractors and suppliers to furnish and install specific portions of the work. The contractor, however, retains responsibility for completing the project in accordance with the contract documents. For this reason, it is important that contractors incorporate provisions of their contract into the contracts with their subcontractors and suppliers.

Provisions of the contract documents that should be incorporated include submittal procedures and substitution request procedures. The subcontract or purchase order should reference the relevant drawings and specifications that pertain to the portion of the work being performed or building material being supplied.

When green building materials are included in a project, the contractor must deal with the additional demands of purchasing and installing unfamiliar materials. The contractor must ensure that the subcontractors and suppliers are aware of and follow the environmental requirements associated with these products. The contractor must also be familiar with substitution request procedures (discussed in greater detail in chapter 6).

To avoid conflicts with both the owner and the design professional, the contractor should be aware of the owner's reasons for requiring the use of green building materials on a project and understand how flexible or not the contract documents are with respect to substituting nongreen materials for green ones.

The Design Professional

The design professional, who may be either an architect or engineer, is generally the primary consultant on a building project. Based on licensing laws and training, the primary design professional on a project is usually the architect. The architect typically subcontracts portions of the work to other design professionals, such as structural engineers, landscape architects, electrical engineers, civil engineers, mechanical engineers, and others as necessary. As the primary consultant, the architect usually has the most direct contact (and, theoretically) influence on the building owner. The architect is probably also involved in construction contract administration.

Many architects are interested in environmental issues. Some are concerned. Some do not place any priority on green at all. Others are actively attempting to improve the world to the extent they can. In short, architects are like everyone else.

When the actively committed design professional and the inspired green product manufacturer meet, the synergy can be tremendous. On average, though, the architect typically experiences more frustration than usual when searching for green building materials. Similarly, the manufacturer often feels frustrated trying to market a green product. This is true primarily for two reasons: Architects have extremely limited time in which to research new materials, and green building material manufacturers often lack a working knowledge of the building industry.

Many architects do not know where to go to get information on green building materials or know how to evaluate it once they have it. For a small firm, the time involved in researching these materials is prohibitive. Further, green building materials represent a rapidly changing segment of the industry that must be constantly monitored. Although a few small firms specialize in green architecture, many do not have the time or the expertise to follow the market changes regarding green. Larger firms can support more overhead activities. The green building material manufacturer would do well to identify those firms, large or small, that have indicated a commitment to green architecture, and market their products to them.

The Product Manufacturer

Green products are developed by two types of manufacturers: established manufacturers who produce a line or lines of green building materials, and the novice manufacturer who has a good idea and wonders why the rest of the world hasn't caught on yet. The most common difficulty facing the novice manufacturer is a lack of understanding of the target industry. A lack of basic understanding of the contractual relationships among the contractor, architect, and owner means that green product representatives may not know whom to contact, when, or how to get their product used on a project. They do not know what information must be conveyed, or why. They are not familiar with the standard procedures of the typical construction contract and contract documents.

The architect is frequently in the position of both student and teacher, learning about a new product or method while instructing the product manufacturer on the prerequisite testing and applicable building codes that pertain to the materials they are providing.

It is important that the manufacturer or supplier understand the design and construction process in order to effectively operate within it. Most new manufacturers—especially those addressing environmental issues—do not understand the process. They do not know how to get into it or how to follow it and to stay in it. Thus, even though they have a great idea and a great product, they go out of business almost as quickly as they got into it.

One of the primary actions that a green material manufacturer or supplier can take is to establish an efficient method for distribution of product information and product. For example, sustainably harvested wood, almost by definition, involves many small suppliers. It would be extremely useful for the small suppliers to organize through one or two brokerage agents, such as the nonprofit certifiers with whom they are already working, to bring their products to market.

An example of how this approach can work successfully is the use of Environ material, manufactured by Phenix Biocomposites, Inc., in two Wal-Marts. "The Environ material might have been one of those missed opportunities, except that in this case the manufacturer—Phenix Biocomposites, Inc.—was responsive to . . . [the architect's needs]. As a result, over 1,000 feet of Environ is now in place in [two] of Wal-Mart's . . . environmental demonstration stores."[2]

The manufacturer realized it did not know how to enter certain markets of the construction industry. It was willing to work with design professionals to learn how to enter the market while continuing to develop its product.

"When Environ first came out, it had so many possible uses that our marketing wasn't very focused. Everyone loved the look and liked the fact that it was recycled. We had people interested in using it for sushi bowls, rifle stocks, and our marketing staff was promoting every possible use. Technical support only got the calls when tough questions came up. For example, Environ isn't meant to be used for structural purposes, but some of our early sales staff weren't clear about that."[3] What was unusual for the product manufacturer was having more people involved in research than in sales. This permitted the company to readily offer technical information as required by the design professionals involved in the project. The technical information included results from its own testing, which was based on a version of ASTM standards.

Manufacturers of new products often focus their marketing efforts on a contractor working on a specific project. That doesn't usually work well. Contractors generally base their bid on past experience, and they may be reluctant to substitute a new, unfamiliar product for a more familiar one. It is rare that this substitution will not increase the budget or affect the schedule and, therefore, rare that the contractor will use the green building material on the project.

This brings up another stumbling block. The manufacturer who has successfully marketed to the architect must be ready to deal with the parties responsible for making decisions at different stages of the project. The manufacturer must be prepared to assist the contractor during construction and, perhaps, to convince the contractor and owner to stay with a product even after it is specified.

The Building Official

The building official is the chief code officer for the location at which the project is being constructed. Because the building official's primary responsibility is to ensure the health, safety, and welfare of the building's occupants after its completion, he or she takes a conservative approach to permitting new and unfamiliar building materials into projects.

Most building codes contain provisions governing the use of nontraditional and new materials in buildings. To avoid lengthy delays in the approval of these materials, providing the building official with extensive testing reports and, where available, engineering documentation, speeds the process of getting them approved for use on a project. Providing a list of projects where the material has already been used is also beneficial.

The building official is also burdened by an ever-increasing workload that limits the amount of time available to review nontraditional and new materials. An example of how difficult it is to get approval for nontraditional and new materials is the use of straw bale in a construction project. This material, which has been around for a long time, was not an approved material under the current building code. The code authorities required extensive testing and demonstration of its abilities to function as well as more traditional building materials, even though straw bale has been used to construct homes around the United States for many years.

The Building Occupant

This may or may not be the building owner. Broadly, the occupants of public facilities, commercial buildings, and private residences are the public. They are the ones who are directly and indirectly affected by design choices made for the building. If the only area for collecting trash is the leftover space under the kitchen sink, it is doubtful that even the most well-intentioned building occupant will separate materials for recycling or composting.

All of us are affected by the Urban Heat Island effect—the rise in temperatures in urban landscapes of two to eight degrees as a result of the reflection of heat and light from solid surfaces (asphalt, concrete, etc.). The Urban Heat Island effect obligates the typical urban building occupant to use 1 to 2 percent more energy per degree rise in temperature than if the building were in a rural area or utilized alternative construction materials.[4]

The building occupant may or may not be in a position to directly influence the selection and implementation of a green building material. However, many building owners are taking note of the public's growing interest in the environment. *The Green Consumer Guide,* published in 1988, was a best-seller.[5] For three years in a row, the Times-Mirror Magazine survey, conducted by the Roper Organization, found that most Americans (66 percent) believe that environmental protection and economic development go hand in hand. When obliged to choose between the two, six out of ten Americans stated that the environment is more important; nine out of ten feel they can personally help the environment; 48 percent are willing to pay an extra 25 cents for a gallon of gasoline if the money is used to help the environment.[6]

The Fabricator

The fabricator is a company that manufactures specific assemblies or products for incorporation into a project under a contract with the contractor. The assemblies or products may be fabricated from a combination of materials. It is important that the fabricator understand not only the special requirements on green building materials but also the standards that may govern the materials used in the assembly.

The design professional should include references to the applicable standards in the contract documents. Where compliance with the standards is critical to the success of the project, the design professional should also require that a copy of the standard be maintained on the construction job site.

On a green building project, the design professional also considers the environmental impact of the manufacturing process when evaluating which products and assemblies to include. In selecting materials for the Audubon House in New York City, the Croxton Collaborative, Architects, and the National Audubon Society team "looked at criteria such as embodied energy, the overall environmental policies of manufacturers, health and safety conditions at their factories, and even social responsibility."[7]

As in their contracts with subcontractors, contractors incorporate applicable provisions of their contract with the owner into their subcontracts or purchase orders. Fabricators not only manufacture but also install. This means they must be familiar with requirements for working at the job site, such as recycling, material and trash disposal, and air quality control. A fabricator's familiarity with the environmental issues involved in the fabrication of assemblies or products on a green building project makes its selection more likely.

The Subcontractor

The subcontractor is a company or individual that enters into an agreement with the contractor to perform a specific portion of the construction contract or to supply materials for a project.

As the use of subcontractors has grown, the need to ensure that provisions of the construction contract are included in subcontracts has increased correspondingly. Subcontractors are usually selected in much the same manner as contractors, through competitive bidding. In some instances, contractors may select subcontractors based on past experience rather than purely on price.

With subcontractors performing more and more of the work on a project, it is not only contractors who must be sensitized to special requirements of projects that include green building materials. Because subcontractors compete for work through variances in labor costs and by the use of competing materials and products, they, too, must clearly understand the limitations placed on them when green building materials are specified, because acceptable alternates for green materials may not always exist.

The Consultant

Much as a contractor has subcontractors, consultants are the design professional's subcontractors. Design professionals subcontract for the services of specialists such as civil engineers, acoustical consultants, and, with growing frequency, green building consultants.

With the introduction and growth of several green building rating systems since 2000, the role of the green building consultant has taken on greater importance and become more formalized. The Austin Green Building Program requires identification of a "sustainability consultant" on its application form, while the LEED™ Green Building Rating System awards a point for using a LEED Accredited Professional on a project. Governmental requests for proposals (RFPs) and private industry solicitations regularly request green consultants as one of their requirements. Because many architecture/engineering (A/E) firms are not specifically dedicated to green building, they have to partner with or hire an independent green consultant that specializes in tracking the ever-changing spectrum of technical, political, and financial developments surrounding green buildings. Many large A/E firms have created internal green building consultancies—so-called green teams—to service their own projects. In response to the rising demand for green consultants, universities have started offering specialized degree programs in this area. The market for consultants with green expertise is expected to grow concurrently with the growth of green building programs.

Design professionals are responsible for providing their consultants with information about the project, including the owner's programmatic requirements, the special needs or requirements of the project, and conditions governing construction of the project. When the project is a green building, the design professional must relay special instructions regarding selection of green building materials, energy conservation, and waste management to the consultants so they can incorporate them into the contract documents.

The Design Team

Ideally, a green building material is designed into a building such that it can function optimally. Good communication and a focused understanding of the environmental goals for the project help the design team identify, specify, and utilize green building materials effectively.

The relationship between the architect and the manufacturer is the most important in terms of successfully implementing green building materials. They must work together. Neither can fully implement green building materials without the other. The architect relies on the manufacturer for applicable performance data, installation expertise, and product service. The manufacturer relies on the architect for product consideration at the critical first moments of design when the green product can be implemented most efficiently, economically, and successfully. Together, they can support a growing market and have the satisfaction of knowing they have done the right thing.

Green Documents: Overview

The design and construction process for most projects can appear excessively complicated, but the basic intent is pretty simple. Someone, usually the owner, wants a building; someone, usually the architect, is going to design it; and someone, usually the contractor, is going to build it. Everything after the initial decision by the owner to build a building is about communication—how the owner communicates his or her needs to the architect and how the architect communicates the design to the contractor.

Much as we may want to, we cannot issue commands from the heavens; instead, we use contracts, samples, drawings, specifications, building codes, standards, and lots of meetings. The product manufacturers or suppliers may never see any of these things, but they are there, and if the product manufacturers understand them, they will know what questions to ask, of whom, and when. They will know how best to communicate what they have to offer to the owner, architect, and contractor. The basic tools of communication in the construction process are the drawings and the specifications.

The drawings are fairly straightforward; they indicate the type, quantity, location, and dimension of materials.

The specifications are the written documents that accompany the drawings and describe what the materials are and how to install them; they also dictate the level of quality of construction expected on the project. For example, if the drawings indicate a plaster wall, the specifications describe the plaster mix, lath and paper backing, and application requirements (e.g., three coats, finishing techniques, moist cure).

As explained in chapter 4, the specifications are organized into 49 divisions. The overall purpose is to provide a standard framework for locating information. The framework does not vary from project to project or from architect to architect. It was developed after World War II by a group of government architects who sought to bring consistency to construction specifications. This led to the formation of the Construction Specifications Institute (CSI) in 1948. The building industry was becoming progressively more complex and more regulated; every architect was organizing information for building requirements in a different way, which made contractors' lives more and more difficult. In 1963, CSI introduced a standard organizational format, known as MasterFormat™. The 2004 Edition contained several major changes necessary to accommodate the increased complexity of building projects: an expansion of the number of divisions from 16 to 49, a change in the section numbering system from five to six digits, and the inclusion of subject areas that allow MasterFormat to address the entire life cycle of the building. 1995 Edition MasterFormat section numbers appear in brackets following the 2004 Edition numbers. MasterFormat is used by building material information providers, manufacturers, architects, contractors, government agencies, and building officials across the United States and Canada.

According to CSI's MasterFormat, information is located in an outline form. The 49 divisions are divided into sections, each of which contains three parts, and each part is organized according to a standardized system of articles and paragraphs. In the 49 divisions, Division 01 defines the general administrative requirements for the project, such as submittal procedures and requirements for progress meetings. Divisions 02 through 49 contain the technical specification sections, which specify the materials and installation requirements. The sections describe units of work that are identified by six-digit numbers. The section numbering system is described in MasterFormat. The first two digits of the section number represent the division number (01–49), and the last four indicate succeedingly precise units of work. The sections are organized into parts: General, Products, and Execution.

Green Specifications

Division 01

While the best response to environmental issues is comprehensive, the simplest approach is to begin at the beginning. Division 01 addresses general administrative and procedural requirements for a project. It is important to recognize that some environmental controls are already common in most contract documents. For example:

- Section 01 33 29 (01352), Sustainable Design Reporting: This section can be used to establish requirements for processing submittals related to sustainable design during the construction phase of a project.
- Section 01 35 00 (01350), Special Procedures: This section is sometimes used to address project-specific concerns such as the existence of hazardous materials on a renovation project, noise restrictions for construction near a hospital, and special environmental procedures.
- Section 01 15 00 (01500), Temporary Facilities and Controls: This section commonly includes requirements for tree and plant protection, cleaning of the site during construction, dust control, and erosion control. It may also restrict access to the site, thereby limiting the impact of construction operations. Many architects and specifiers are currently trying to see how far they can expand these environmental controls. How large is the job? What will the client accept? What will the contractor do willingly? almost willingly? Are the environmental concerns too different from standards currently employed by the industry? What is the risk if environmental concerns are implemented? if they are not implemented? One way to address these questions is to expand the controls globally in Division 01. This section can also be used to meet requirements of local, state, national, and international green building rating system credits for construction indoor air quality management.
- Section 01 74 19 (01524), Construction Waste Management and Disposal: This section, used in conjunction with Section 00 62 23, Construction Waste Diversion Form, establishes contractor requirements for construction waste management plans to comply with green building rating systems. The section can also be used to meet requirements of green building rating system credits for construction waste management.
- Section 01 78 53 (01785), Sustainable Design Closeout Documentation: This section can be used in conjunction with Section 00 62 23 and Section 00 62 34, Recycled Content of Materials Form, to establish requirements for submittal of closeout documents needed to establish compliance with green building rating system requirements.
- Section 01 81 00 (01811), Facility Performance Requirements: Under this section, topics such as sustainable design, facility environmental, and indoor air quality (IAQ) requirements are specified. This section can also be used to meet requirements of green building rating system requirements for minimum IAQ performance.
- Section 01 90 00, Life Cycle Activities: This section includes administrative and procedural requirements for commissioning facilities and incorporating commissioning requirements needed to comply with green building rating system prerequisites and credits.

Divisions 02 through 49

For Divisions 02 through 49, communication of green requirements can be improved by identifying them in separate articles under each of the three main parts. A sample of applicable articles that should be used may be found in Section 000000 (00000), Environmental Specifications Format, given in Appendix C.

Consider the specifications format when investigating product options, and record the information gathered accordingly. Refer to the sample Environmental Impact Questionnaire and the sample Indoor Air Quality Test Report included in Appendix C. These research tools organize product data to coordinate with the major articles and paragraph format in the Environmental Specifications Format.

Develop new sections as necessary. Many green building materials do not correspond to an existing section. CSI is beginning to address this growing need. In the meantime, the design professional must create broadscope and mediumscope sections appropriate to the new categories of materials, such as alternative agricultural products, plastic lumber, and constructed wetlands. It may also be necessary to create new narrowscope sections to more efficiently organize the proliferation of similar competing materials, such as fiber insulation (cellulose, fiberglass, mineral wool, cotton), rock insulation (perlite, basalt), and foam insulation (polystyrene, polyisocyanurate, polyurethane, glass, and cementitious). Some of the sections useful on green building projects include:

- Section 02 00 00 (01710), Existing Conditions: This section includes maintenance, repair, rehabilitation, replacement, restoration, and preservation of existing conditions and can be used to specify requirements needed to comply with green building rating systems for building reuse.
- Section 02 42 00, Removal and Salvage of Construction Materials: This section can be used to specify requirements for salvage of existing construction materials on the building site and to comply with green building rating systems for resource reuse.
- Section 21 08 00 (01810), Commissioning of Fire Suppression: This section includes requirements for commissioning specific to fire suppression systems and can be used to specify requirements needed to comply with green building rating system requirements.
- Section 22 08 00 (01810), Commissioning of Plumbing: This section includes requirements for commissioning specific to plumbing systems and can be used to specify requirements needed to comply with green building rating system requirements.
- Section 23 08 00 (01810), Commissioning of HVAC: This section includes requirements for commissioning specific to HVAC systems and can be used to specify requirements needed to comply with green building rating system requirements.
- Section 25 10 00 (13800), Automated Network Equipment: This section specifies equipment and systems that permit the building automation system to monitor and control building subsystems and can be used to specify requirements needed to comply with green building rating system credits.
- Section 26 08 00 (01810), Commissioning of Electrical Systems: This section includes requirements for commissioning specific to electrical systems and can be used to specify requirements needed to comply with green building rating system requirements.
- Section 32 01 00, Operation and Maintenance of Exterior Improvements: This section can be used to specify reuse of existing asphalt and concrete paving.
- Section 32 10 00 (02700), Bases, Ballasts, and Paving: This section includes requirements for recycled-content materials such as lime-fly ash-treated base courses, granu-

lated recycled-content, rubber-modified asphalt paving, recycled-rubber unit paving, and recycled-content playground protective surfacing.

- Section 32 70 00 (02670), Wetlands: This section includes requirements for both constructed wetlands and wetlands restoration and can be used to specify requirements needed to comply with green building rating system requirements.

- Section 48 14 00 (13600), Solar Energy Electrical Power Generation Equipment: This section includes requirements for solar energy collectors and can be used in conjunction with sections in Division 23 to specify a complete solar energy system to comply with green building rating system requirements for renewable energy.

- Section 48 15 00 (13600), Wind Energy Electrical Power Generation Equipment: This section includes requirements for windmills and wind energy electrical power generators and can be used to comply with green building rating system requirements for renewable energy.

- Section 48 16 00, Geothermal Energy Electrical Power Generation Equipment: This section includes requirements for heat pumps and other geothermal power-generating equipment and can be used to comply with green building rating system requirements for renewable energy.

Public Works Projects

It is important to consider the specific requirements applicable to public works projects commissioned by public agencies. Public agencies are, by definition, organizations wholly created for the welfare and benefit of the public. They are responsible for and to the public. In some ways, this means their operations have certain restrictions. It also means they have incredible opportunities. This is definitely true for green building material specifications produced by a public agency.

Public agencies have the ability to affect positive change, or compromise, on a large scale. When people joke that "you can't fight City Hall," they mean it is difficult for a private entity, a single person, to make much of a difference. But if City Hall fights, what a difference it could make! City Hall can fight for environmental improvement in several ways:

- *Education:* City Hall can issue public announcements and create promotional campaigns that educate the public and sensitize them to environmental issues. The water conservation effort during the height of the drought in California is an excellent example. It makes for a better, and more amicable, compromise in the long run if everyone is informed of the facts and the options.

- *Legislation:* Legislation establishes the framework for meaningful change. When California Assembly Bill 939, requiring a measurable reduction in the waste stream, was passed, it established the necessity to redirect waste. It indirectly created an entire new realm of opportunities—businesses to collect recyclable material, businesses to manufacture items from recyclable material, and businesses to monitor the process. Concerned citizens who would not separate glass from plastic in their garage and carry it to a plant

15 miles away could now set out separate containers in their driveway for standard, convenient pick-up.

- *Assistance:* Price preference programs and information hotlines already help fledgling groups such as minorities, women, and veterans. A little extra assistance helps the novice with a great new idea compete with big corporations and their established old ideas. This can extend to environmentally sensitive products, processes, and companies to help get them off the ground. Energy companies, for example, frequently utilize this route. They are large enough to manage it and business-oriented enough to see the cost savings.

- *Leadership:* Public agencies can take the lead and set the example for environmentally sensitive design and construction. By establishing environmental requirements for purchase orders and project specifications, public agencies can create the standard for green building material specifications. That is the primary logic behind Executive Order Number 13101 (refer to chapter 4). An excellent example of leadership by a public agency is the green program operated by the United States Postal Service (USPS), which has one of the nation's largest construction programs and recognizes the role it can play in environmental leadership. The USPS has revised its standard master specifications for all building programs to incorporate green materials and methods. This affects all of the 300 to 500 new USPS facilities constructed annually. Incorporated items include aggregate from recycled concrete and asphalt, recycled plastic wheel stops, xeriscaping, biodegradable form release agents, concrete with fly ash, alternative agricultural sheathing, fiberglass with 25 percent recycled glass, improved albedo for roofing materials, adhesives and paint with low or zero VOCs, hook/loop carpeting, recycled plastic toilet partitions, dock bumpers made from recycled tires, increased efficiency requirements for mechanical insulation, instantaneous point-of-use water heaters, preoccupancy ventilation, and increased efficiency requirements for lighting.

These innovations were carefully researched by a cross-functional team that included representation from USPS facilities, employees expected to work in the buildings, design professionals, and the contractor. They were tested and modified in response to user comments and have now been implemented in the USPS Design and Construction Program. It is anticipated that, pending the results of continued monitoring of the first green post office in Fort Worth, Texas, and feedback from users and the public, additional green materials and methods will also be incorporated.

Green building material specifications are the cornerstone for leadership on this issue. Project-specific documents are really the only forum a private entity can access directly. A large private corporation might establish a special interest scholarship fund or research and development fund, but it will never have as much effect as the assistance a public agency can provide. So, apples for apples, the contract documents are the only common ground.

Public agencies have a unique opportunity here. The documents they produce are frequently used as industry standards. Public agencies are custodians of our health and welfare; consequently, the level of care they establish is often viewed as a standard for private work.

On the other hand, public agencies have unique concerns and unique methods for addressing the concerns not typically the province of the private entity. The investment of time and money can limit private entities. Often, they simply do not have the resources, or they do not occupy new construction space for a long enough period to warrant the type of investigation and documentation public agencies can support.

This is not meant to imply that the public coffers contain unlimited funds. But part of the job of public guardians is to investigate issues that affect public health and welfare—such as environmental design, construction, and demolition.

A public agency is in a position to see the big picture. Further, while the impact of the findings may be limited to the private entity itself, were it to undertake such a program, the impact for a public agency is much broader. It can affect the long-range building program of the agency, and it can also affect leadership, education, and legislation.

Methods unique to public agencies include:

- *Monitor processes that extend beyond the construction period:* Monitor indoor air quality and energy consumption. Compare them to predicted values. Also, compare operating costs to those of similar facilities that are not environmentally sensitive. How many sick days are used? How often are the high-efficiency light bulbs replaced? The monitoring program need not be any more extensive than one morning a month spent checking the status and plotting the information on a chart. Even such a rudimentary investigation will help evaluate the effectiveness of environmental controls implemented on the particular project.

- *Carrot Programs:* Establish goals for recycled tonnage. Establish percentages for recycled content. Create a benefit or reward system for contractors when they reach the predetermined goals and percentages. Contractors are in the low-bid system. They certainly will take advantage of opportunities to make a little extra money on the job. This is an option if the agency cannot afford the time, money, or personnel to adequately research the recycling possibilities prior to issuing the contract documents. Set up a carrot program and let the contractor find the savings. Document the results and incorporate the contractor's research into your next project.

  Requirements for recycled content (either pre- or postconsumer) may be stated generically for each material in the individual specifications sections or as an overall project goal. This allows for creativity and encourages new ideas, but be extremely cautious when setting an overall goal. In large, complex programs, this is destined to produce apples-to-oranges comparisons that do not allow for equal consideration. It may be more time-consuming initially to put the requirements in the individual sections, but the efforts will probably save time and grief in the long run.

- *Ratings systems:* The intangibles that the private entity subjectively analyzes are often converted into measurable quantities by public agencies by means of rating systems. Add "environmental sensitivity" to the categories for evaluating products, architects, and contractors. Establish ratings systems that give preferential treatment to products with recycled content or to contractors/architects who have demonstrated commitment to environmentally sensitive construction.

Public agencies are not free agents, so while they offer exciting possibilities, they are also subject to some restrictions in creating contract documents:

- A private entity can negotiate with a single architect and a single contractor, determining exactly what it wants and what is affordable. A private entity represents only its own interests. It can behave subjectively, willfully—within legal boundaries—without repercussions. Public agencies represent a larger team than the standard architect-contractor-owner relationship. Public agencies represent the people, all of the people, and the range of opinions and interests those people have.

- A private entity can identify exactly which product by which manufacturer it wants in the building. Public agencies cannot show favoritism. Contract documents for public work cannot be proprietary. Different agencies interpret this rule in different ways. Some say you may specify by a single brand name but must review any and all proposed substitutions for equivalency. Some say you must list three and state "or equal." Some refuse to accept any naming of manufacturers. Further, you must be careful not to describe a particular product so specifically that, in fact, you eliminate all but the single product around which you wrote the specifications.

That said, there is no reason that environmentally friendly documents should be any different from a performance specification. Environmental quality is simply one more control to be used to govern the overall quality of any given product or material.

Ultimately, every product should be defined not only in terms of fire resistance and durability but also in terms of recycled content, toxicity, and outgassing.

Just as there is no caveat against public agencies specifying terrazzo in the lobbies of their buildings, there is no reason why they can't require that the aggregate in the terrazzo be recycled colored glass instead of aggregate from newly quarried stone.

Another restriction is that public agencies must take the "lowest responsible bidder," which generally means the lowest bidder.

- A private entity can evaluate intangibles such as attitude, experience, personality, and professionalism when engaging a contractor. Public agencies are often destined to contract with the lowest bidder. The contractors know this. You know they know this. It becomes a game of low bid/change order.

Again, there is no reason that green building material specifications should be any different from specifying for any other project. If your documents are not complete, you will never be able to add to them.

The contractor will claim an additional cost, and if the money is not in the project's budget, you won't get it. The sad thing is that, though a few years ago it was true that products containing green materials (especially recycled materials) generally cost more, they now generally cost the same or less. Include the requirements at the start, preferably in the individual specification sections and at least in the alternates specification section.

Project Examples

One company that has successfully embraced environmental stewardship through its building program is Nestlé Waters North America (Nestlé Waters). To meet the growing consumer demand for bottled water, the company added several new bottling facilities in the past five years. Beginning in 2000, Nestlé Waters committed to building its new facilities and utilizing operational practices in a manner that respects the environment today and for the future. Each new plant is approximately 400,000 to 800,000 square feet, with 50 to 1,000 acres dedicated to conservation at each site. Imagine the positive impact if *all* manufacturers dedicated conservation land in association with each of their plants?

Nestlé Waters may be more conscious than most corporations about the need for leadership in environmental stewardship. It stakes its reputation, as well as the high quality of its water beverage product, on the natural resources of the environment. Choosing to build the company's newest bottling plants according to the U.S. Green Building Council's LEED™ Green Building Rating System was completely consistent with the company's philosophy.

As of January 2005, Nestlé Waters had achieved LEED certification for one project and had attained three LEED silver ratings. According to USGBC, these are the first food manufacturing facilities in the United States to earn LEED ratings. In every case (except one, where building officials mandated connection to municipal water treatment), Nestlé Waters earned all water credits available under LEED. This means each of these industrial facilities (except where the building officials mandated otherwise) utilizes constructed wetlands to treat wastewater, avoiding the additional costly infrastructure and stresses on local municipal water treatment plants that are typical of most manufacturing facilities.

The company nevertheless determined that still more needed to be done to help protect water and watersheds. "Water Efficiency," as the title of this LEED category implies, focuses on efficiency—minimizing the potable water demand and the generation of wastewater. Building design and operations can have a tremendous impact not only on the quantity of water used but also on its quality and the healthy, sustainable functioning of the local watershed. Because humans have already degraded much of the earth's freshwater resources, the goal of sustainable use must include a commitment to the continual improvement of the quality of this precious resource. Therefore, Nestlé Waters is extending the respect and stewardship that it developed in the management of spring water for humans to drink to the broader (and related) water resources that may be affected by their facilities.

Decisions about maintaining functioning ecosystems on Nestlé Waters's sites are based on maintaining and promoting a healthy hydrologic cycle. Thus, choices of materials include consideration for their potential relationship to water resources. For example, PVC-free flooring, countertops, and wallcovering materials were utilized because their manufacture, use, and eventual disposal are considered less hazardous and less likely to contaminate water resources than conventional vinyl alternates. Similarly, Nestlé Waters is implementing a maintenance program that utilizes environmentally friendly cleaning materials and procedures. Further, the company has developed educational programs for employees and the public that emphasize the need for water stewardship and provide examples of such stewardship.

At Nestlé Waters, the commitment to environmental stewardship originates from the top. Accordingly to Jane Lazgin, with Nestlé Waters's Public Relations Department, CEO Kim Jeffery stated, "We have great enthusiasm for being at the vanguard of this movement. . . . Looking toward the future, as Nestlé Waters builds new water bottling plants, we are committing to constructing them in a manner that supports the environment, the employees who work in our facilities, and the communities in which we operate." The company has applied its significant knowledge base in water resources, watershed ecosystems, and hydraulic functioning to the task. The results provide an excellent example for corporate responsibility.

Another example of the successful integration of green design into the building design and construction process is Audubon House, the home of the National Audubon Society, located in lower Manhattan. The Audubon House project is instructive for several reasons:

- The collaborative approach to design and construction taken by the owner and the design professionals
- The holistic concept of green being an integral part of the design and construction process
- The consideration given to the effect on the environment of existing building reuse versus constructing a new building.

The project team recognized early that in order to achieve the goals they had set for the project—that is, incorporating environmental criteria, controlling construction costs, and maintaining the aesthetics and functionality of the building—they would have to work in close collaboration. "It necessitate[d] the cooperation of parties with a stake in the project, from the owner, architect, and designer on down to subcontractors."[8] It required team members to think in an entirely new way—working to complete individual tasks without losing sight of the project's goals. Working together enabled the team to select nontraditional building materials more frequently.

This team spirit extended to the contractors and subcontractors. At a reception held at the contractor's offices, the team members explained the project's goals and "pointed out to the subcontractors the competitive advantage to be gained by acquiring skills with new materials and striving for environmental performance."[9]

Equally important to the success of the project was the holistic approach to the design. "Also known as 'integrated, high-performance design,' this system relies on the cumulative effects of no-cost or low-cost design solutions, in tandem with advanced technologies, to bring about the desired level of building performance."[10] The clearest outcome of this approach was the integrated lighting design used in the building, blending the use of natural and artificial lighting to obtain a substantial savings in energy costs.

The last lesson to be learned from the Audubon House project is that the best solution to an owner's need for a new building may be renovating or reusing an existing building. This choice sent the message that instead of expending money to develop a "clean" site elsewhere, by using a holistic team approach, an existing building could be reused at the same cost, with the added benefits of using green building materials.

Beyond Selection and Specification

Once the job of selecting and specifying building materials is completed, the formidable task of ensuring that green building materials make it through the bidding process and are incorporated into the constructed building begins. Following sound procedures during this phase of the project ensures a successful green building in the end.

Notes

1. "Clear Advantage: Building Shareholder Value," *Global Environmental Management Initiative* (February 2004).

2. "Getting New Products into Buildings: An Interview with Architect and Manufacturer," *Environmental Building News* 5, no. 4 (July/August 1996): 8–9.

3. Ibid.

4. Environmental Protection Agency, *Cooling Our Communities: A Guidebook on Tree Planting and Light-Colored Surfacing* (1992), 22P–2001, pp. 5–6.

5. Connie Koenenn, "Green: New Tide in the Affairs of the Nation's Consumers," *Los Angeles Times*, 15 March 1990.

6. "America and the Environment: The Sky Isn't Falling," *Skiing* (September 1994).

7. National Audubon Society, Croxton Collaborative, Architects, *Audubon House: Building the Environmentally Responsible, Energy-Efficient* Offices (New York: John Wiley & Sons, 1994), 118.

8. Ibid., 58.

9. Ibid., 60.

10. Ibid., 53.

CHAPTER 6

How Does the Construction Process Work?

Worldwide, the building industry is beginning to recognize the shortcomings of its products and to discover that there are readily available, cost-effective remedies.

A Building Revolution: How Ecology and Health Concerns
Are Transforming Construction
—David Malin Roodman and Nicholas Lenssen

Every building construction project, green or not, goes through several phases, beginning with the planning phase and concluding with the postconstruction phase. The bidding and construction phases are where the rubber meets the road for the building's design professionals. By examining the process of bidding and construction, we can understand the actions required to ensure the successful incorporation of green building materials into a project.

The Bidding Phase

Using the construction documents prepared by the design professionals during the preceding phase, the owner solicits construction bids either by advertisement, in the case of public projects, or by invitation, in the case of private projects.

During the bidding phase, each bidder solicits bids from subcontractors for the portions of the work they are not going to perform with their own forces. The purpose of the competitive bidding process is to determine the lowest responsive and responsible bidder who will be able to construct the project with the funds the owner has available. In public projects, the owner generally must accept the lowest bid. In private projects, the owner usually selects the bidders in advance and is free to choose any of them.

Whether bids are solicited by competitive bid or negotiation, it is during the bidding phase that bidders review project specifications and drawings to determine which products and systems are included. When green building materials and systems are specified, the design professional has two important responsibilities during bidding: (1) educating bidding general contractors, subcontractors, suppliers, manufacturers' representatives, and others about green building materials and systems that may be relatively unknown to them; and (2) processing substitution requests for green building materials and systems.

Because many green building materials are manufactured by small or new companies, many bidders may not be familiar with them or do not know how to contact them. In addition to the contact information the design professional provides either in the specifications or on the drawings, the subject should be covered at the pre-bid conference. Another issue that must be dealt with at that time is the tendency on the part of contractors to use materials with which they are familiar. The fear of the new or untried is a powerful issue when the contractor is responsible for guaranteeing or warranting the entire building for a year.

The pre-bid conference, at which the design professionals, owner, and bidders are present, can be used to dispel some of these concerns. A full discussion should be conducted by the design professionals of the importance and reasons for using green building materials and systems on the project, along with a review of the materials and systems and how to contact the manufacturers. A discussion of alternates and substitution request procedures is also helpful. Bidders should be encouraged to raise questions or concerns they have about these products and systems at this time. Minutes of the pre-bid conference should be kept and distributed to all holders of bidding documents. Documenting information discussed during the conference is extremely important to prevent misunderstandings later in the project. Of course, clarifications of, revisions of, additions to, and deletions from the bidding documents should be incorporated in an addendum.

Another useful practice is to notify the manufacturers of the green building materials and systems when a building project that incorporates their products and systems is released for bidding so they can contact the bidders directly. To further encourage the dialogue between bidders and green building material and system manufacturers, the design professional can provide a list of bidders to the manufacturers.

Alternates and Substitution Requests

Alternates are typically included in bidding documents to allow the bid price to be adjusted to fall within the limits of the funds available to construct the project. Another use for alternates is to identify the cost of specific materials and systems in comparison to alternate products and systems.

When green building materials and systems are specified, alternates can be used to compare the cost of green versus nongreen. When a project's budget is limited and the owner is concerned that using green will be more costly, alternates can establish the true cost, thereby allowing the owner to base a judgment on the cost of green over the life cycle of the building.

If alternates are used, reference to them should be included in several locations in the bidding documents, including:

- Invitation to Bid/Advertisement for Bids
- Instructions to Bidders

- Bid Form
- Agreement
- Specifications

The Invitation to Bid/Advertisement for Bids document should alert bidders to the inclusion of alternates on the project. A simple statement, like that shown in Figure 6.1, may be used.

The Instructions to Bidders should explain how bidders are to prepare alternates and how the alternates will be considered in evaluating bids. Figure 6.1 includes sample provisions that may be included in the Instructions to Bidders.

The Bid Form should include a list of alternates that matches the list in Section 01230 (01 23 00)—Alternates. To avoid confusion, the order of alternates on the Bid Form should be the same as they appear in Section 01230 (01 23 00). Each alternate on the Bid Form should be followed by a blank space where the bidders fill in their price. A sample alternate is given in Figure 6.1.

If a standard form of agreement, such as AIA Document A101 or EJCDC Document 1910-9, is not used, those alternates that have been accepted by the owner must be acknowledged within the Agreement. A sample is illustrated in Figure 6.1. When one of the standard forms is used, the accepted alternates should be listed in the space provided on the Agreement form.

To complete the series of bidding documents containing information about alternates, Section 01230 (01 23 00)—Alternates should be used to identify the alternates. Unlike the Bid Form, which contains only a title for each alternate, Section 01230 (01 23 00) includes a detailed description of each. This enables bidders to prepare accurate prices for them. Each alternate should reference the applicable technical specification sections as well as the drawings. The affected technical specification sections in Divisions 2 (02) through 16 (49) should have an article in Part 1—General, which refers to the provisions for alternates (see Figure 6.1). If design professionals wish to emphasize environmental considerations, they can use a special alternate section to do so. (A sample Section 01231 (01 23 10)—Environmental Alternates is included in Appendix C.)

Alternates are used primarily to adjust the bid price prior to the signing of the agreement, whereas substitution requests are generally used by contractors, subcontractors, manufacturers, and suppliers to propose a different manufacturer, product, material, or system than that specified.

Depending on how the project requirements are written, substitutions may be requested only during the bidding phase, only during the construction phase, or during both phases.

It is important that the bidding/contract documents contain clearly defined procedures to control and manage substitution requests whenever they occur. Due to their special nature, this is especially true when green building materials and systems are specified on a project. It is fairly common to receive substitution requests to use nongreen materials instead of green building materials and systems. The inclusion of specific requirements regarding how substitution requests for green building materials and systems will be evaluated by the design professional will make the process clearer and perhaps prevent the submittal of frivolous substitution requests.

Invitation to Bid/Advertisement for Bids

[The following text should be incorporated into the Invitation to Bid/Advertisement for Bids.]

Bids shall be on a stipulated-sum basis for the lump-sum base bid, and indicate prices for alternates.

Instructions to Bidders

[The following text should be incorporated into the Instructions to Bidders.]

Alternates are described in the specifications and are listed on the Bid Form.

The price bid for each alternate will be the amount added to or deducted from the Base Bid Price if the Owner selects the alternate.

The Owner may accept alternates in any order, regardless of the order in which they are listed, and determine lowest responsive and responsible bidder based on the sum of the base bid plus any selected alternates.

Bid Form

[The following is a sample alternate format for listing on the Bid Form.]

Alternate No. 1, Erosion Control Blankets (Note: Title of alternate should be derived from description in Section 01230 (01 23 00).

(ADD) / (DEDUCT) _____ Dollars ($ _____)
                          (In words)   (In numerals)

Agreement

[The following text should be incorporated into the Agreement between the owner and the contractor.]

The Contractor shall perform all work required by the Contract Documents for the Environmental Resource Center at 2332 Green Street, Paradise City, USA, including Alternates No. 1, 3, and 5 as described in Section 01230 (01 23 00), Alternates, of the Specifications.

Section 01230/01231 (01 23 00)/(01 23 10)

[The following is a sample alternate description which can be used in building a section of alternates in Division 1 (01) of the Project Manual.]

1.5   ALTERNATE NO. 1, EROSION CONTROL BLANKETS
    A.   Furnish and install degradable, natural-fiber erosion control blankets where indicated on the Drawings and as specified in Section 02370, Slope Protection and Erosion Control (31 25 13, Erosion Controls).

Section 02370 Slope Protection and Erosion Control (31 25 13 Erosion Controls)

[The following is a sample article referencing the Division 1 (01) section on alternates, which should be incorporated into the technical specification section.]

1.5   ALTERNATES
    A.   Refer to Section [01230/01 23 00] [01231/01 23 10], Alternates/Environmental Alternates for description of work of this section affected by alternates.

FIGURE 6.1   Examples of Alternates in Bidding Documents

Substitution request provisions should appear in bidding/contract documents in much the same manner as alternates. To supplement and expand the provisions that appear in AIA Document A201, General Conditions of the Contract for Construction, and EJCDC Document 1910-8, Standard General Conditions of the Construction Contract, Section 01630 (01 25 13)—Product Substitution Procedures, should be included in the Project Manual. This section should include a standard form for use by bidders/contractors to submit substitutions. (A sample section and form is included in Appendix C.)

To facilitate evaluation of substitutions and reporting the results, a standard form, similar to the one in Figure 6.2, should be used. The form provides a structured means of comparing the properties of the specified product or systems with the properties of the proposed substitution. It includes a column for the specified product or system and as many additional columns as are required to list proposed substitutions. The rows list properties to be compared and evaluated. In addition to properties such as size and content, the list should include green properties such as volatile organic compounds (VOC), recycled content, and distance of manufacturer from job site as required to define a product's compliance with a green building rating system or its sustainable features.

The Instructions to Bidders states when substitutions are permitted before bids are received, on which form they are to be submitted, who may submit a substitution request, and how notification of approval will be given to bidders. Once a substitution request is approved by the design professional during bidding, all bidders have the opportunity to use the substitute product or system. The benefit to the project's owner is that any savings realized by using the substitute product or system will be incorporated into the bid price.

The Division 1 (01)—General Requirements section cited above, which applies during both bidding and construction, outlines procedures governing substitutions. Once the construction contract is signed, substitutions can only be submitted by the contractor. During construction, the substitution request also must indicate any changes in the contract price and time. If the substitution request is approved, a change order must be issued to incorporate these changes into the contract.

The disadvantage to permitting substitution requests during bidding and construction is that there may not be enough time to properly research the proposed substitution. The design professional should not approve a substitution request if he or she is concerned about its level of quality or ability to perform as well as the specified product. When substitution requests are proposed for green building materials and systems, the complexity and time required for review by the design professional is increased because of the properties that must be examined beyond those of nongreen materials. Because of these concerns, it is preferable to consider substitutions during the design and construction document phases of the project. In this way, the design professional can minimize the approval and use of unacceptable materials on the project.

The Construction Phase

The construction phase of the project usually begins when the bid award is made by the appropriate authority on a publicly financed project or when the contract is signed on other projects. If the contract documents require it, the contractor must submit a list of proposed

Item No.	Description	Specified Manufacturer	Substitute Manufacturer
1	Manufacturer's Name	Ceiling of Choice	Ceilings To Go
2	Product Name & Model No.	GreenTile Acoustical Panel No. XXX	JustasGreen Panel No. YYY
3	Nominal Size & Thickness	24 × 24 × 3/4 inches	24 × 24 × 3/4 inches
4	Material	Cast Mineral Fiber	Wet-formed Mineral Fiber
5	Edge Detail	Square	Square
6	Noise Reduction Coefficient (NRC)	0.7	0.65
7	Sound Transmission Class (STC)	Not Applicable	Not Applicable
8	Ceiling Attenuation Class (CAC)	35 Minimum	35
9	Light Reflectance (LR)	LR-1; Actual 0.79	LR-1; Actual 0.80
10	Surface Finish/Color	Not Specified/White	Factory-applied vinyl latex paint
11	Fire Resistance	Class A; Flame Spread-25	Class A; Flame Spread-25
12	Recycled Content Percentage	67	69
13	Recyclable	Yes	Yes
14	Reclamation Program?	Unknown	Yes
15	Sustainable Manufacturing Program	Unknown	Yes
16	Local/Regional Material?	Yes	No
17	Rapidly Renewable Material?	N/A	N/A
18	Certified Wood Material?	N/A	N/A
19			
20			

FIGURE 6.2   Product/System Sustainability Analysis

products and a schedule of submittals to the design professional, usually within 30 days after the contract is signed. In some cases, the owner may require that the list be submitted at the same time the bids are submitted.

The list of proposed products, prepared by the contractor, is reviewed by the design professional and then forwarded to the owner for approval. The submittal of the list by the contractor to the design professional is a means of confirming that only specified products or approved substitutions are used. The preparation of the list also allows contractors to confirm that their suppliers and subcontractors are following the contract document requirements. The design professional must specify which products the contractor must include on the list, as the typical project includes a substantial number of products.

When green building materials are specified on a project, the submittal and review of the list takes on added significance. The design professional must clearly express in the contract documents that substitution requests cannot be proposed through the list of proposed products. If the list contains unapproved substitutions for specified green building materials, the design professional must quickly and clearly notify the contractor that the list is not in conformance with the contract documents. The contractor must revise and resubmit the list until it is acceptable to the design professional and the owner.

Once the list is found acceptable, the design professional distributes the approved list to the contractor, owner, and consultants. The contractor is responsible for distribution of the approved list to subcontractors and suppliers. The approved list serves as a checklist throughout the construction of the project to ensure that only specified green building materials and approved substitutions are incorporated into the completed building.

A schedule of submittals is another useful tool for the design professional to use to monitor the flow of information and tasks during the early stages of construction. The schedule of submittals is usually submitted in conjunction with the construction progress schedule. The design professional should review the schedule to confirm that the contractor has included all of the submittals required by the technical specification sections. Because the contractor must take into consideration many factors when preparing the schedule, the design professional should verify that the submittals are not scheduled simultaneously; that submittals for materials in an assembly are submitted together; and that the contractor has allowed adequate time prior to the need for materials on the project for preparation of submittals, review by the design professionals, and resubmittal in the event that the submittal is not acceptable the first time. The design professional should encourage the contractor to allow more time for submittals for green building materials due to the possibility that submittal information may be more difficult to obtain.

As mentioned earlier, many manufacturers of green building materials are either new or small or both and may require more time to assemble a submittal. With this understanding, the contractor and design professional can easily accommodate the green building material manufacturer's submittal time schedule.

The Submittal Process

Once the list of submittals is reviewed and approved, the contractor begins the submittal process. Submittals may include shop drawings, product data, samples, manufacturer's installation instructions, test reports, manufacturer's certificates, material safety data sheets, and other information as required by the individual technical specification sections.

The standard general conditions, either AIA Document A201 or EJCDC 1910-8, require that the contractor obtain the approval of the design professional for submittals required by the contract documents prior to ordering or incorporating those materials into the work.

The review and approval of submittals is an important part of the design professional's contract administration phase services. During the submittal review process, the design professional must be alert for unauthorized substitutions for specified materials. The design professional must also carefully compare the submittal to the requirements of the corresponding technical specification section to ensure it includes: (1) all of the submittal documentation required; and (2) sufficient technical information to compare the submittal to the specification.

Green building material specification sections often contain requirements for special submittals such as toxicity test reports, data about material and recycled content, and installation environmental considerations. Because these submittals are not normally required for nongreen building materials, the contractor and the design professional must pay particular attention to these special requirements to ensure their timely submittal, review, and approval.

On projects that include the requirement for a preconstruction conference, a portion of the agenda should be set aside to review the substitution request process (if the contract documents permit such requests during construction) and the submittal process. Special submittals required for green building materials should be reviewed and clarified to avoid confusion regarding the requirements. It would also be appropriate at this conference to review the design professional's responsibilities regarding verification that materials delivered to the job site and installed in the project are those specified and submitted.

The contractor should clearly understand his or her responsibility for reviewing the submittal prior to forwarding it to the design professional and must ensure that the subcontractors and suppliers are knowledgeable of their responsibilities as well. The contractor should not forward incomplete or incorrect submittals to the design professional. The design professional, in turn, should refuse to review any submittal that does not comply with the specifications.

All members of the construction team should familiarize themselves with the provisions of the Division 1 (01) section that covers submittals prior to beginning the submittal process. This will shorten the time required for review and increase the likelihood that the design professional will approve the submittal the first time around.

Construction Administration Activities

The standard contract between the owner and the design professional requires that the design professional observe the work during construction. This is done periodically to keep the owner informed about the progress and quality of the work and to prevent defects and deficiencies. The observation is not meant to be exhaustive or to make the design professional responsible for the means and methods of construction, which is contractually the responsibility of the contractor.

The design professional's periodic visits to the job site help improve coordination between design and construction, improve communications between the design professional and contractor, and ensure conformance of the work to the contract documents. The design professional's responsibilities are normally coordinated with the general conditions of the contract for construction. To avoid conflicts, this is important to verify when nonstandard documents are used, as the design professional and contractor are not in contract with each other. The design professional's contract with the owner typically defines not only his or her role during construction but also how often he or she will visit the job site to observe. In some instances, the owner may hire the design professional to make more frequent visits to the job site or assign a part- or full-time individual on the job site when the project scope or complexity requires it.

Although the design professional is not required to make an exhaustive review of the work during periodic visits to the job site, it is beneficial to the project if he or she pays special attention to the incorporation of green building materials into the work, for two reasons: first, to verify that the specified materials are being used, and second, to verify that the manufacturer's installation instructions are being followed by the contractor. As mentioned earlier, this is important because of the relative unfamiliarity of contractors with these green building materials.

The design professional can also facilitate the participation of the green building material manufacturer in the construction process because of the relationship established during the design phase of the project. As a result, questions or concerns that arise during construction can be dealt with quickly and with the least disruption to the schedule.

Certification Activities

As discussed in chapter 5, each participant in the green building process has certain responsibilities. These responsibilities do not end with the start of construction. During the construction phase of a project, many important activities must be performed to ensure compliance with green building rating system requirements.

While in some cases the design professional has in-house capability to perform the activities associated with the certification process during construction, most design professionals choose to hire a green building consultant instead.

Chief among the activities that must be performed to ensure compliance during construction are:

Reviewing documentation

Monitoring compliance

Commissioning

Reviewing Documentation

As part of the submittal process described earlier, the green building project requires additional submittals not normally associated with the administration of a building project. Review of these submittals is usually performed by the design professional. The submittals can include tracking the origin of materials (extraction, harvesting, fabrication), photographs of the indoor air quality ventilation protection, and construction waste management plans and documentation.

To facilitate tracking of the status of compliance with individual credits of a rating system, the design professional or green building consultant should set up a notebook or file system that organizes the documentation by credit for use at completion of the project. This documentation can be combined with a credit status report form that can be distributed to the contractor, owner, and other interested parties as the construction progresses (see Figure 6.3).

**Western Connecticut State University
New Science Building
LEED® Green Building Rating System
Certification Status Report**

Credit Category: Indoor Environmental Quality

Prerequisite 1: Minimum IAQ Performance:

Requirement: Meet the minimum requirements of ASHRAE 62-1999 using the Ventilation Rate Procedure.

Submittals: LEED Letter Template, signed by the mechanical engineer or responsible party, declaring that the project is fully compliant with ASHRAE 62-1999 and all published Addenda and describing the procedure employed in the IAQ analysis (Ventilation Rate Procedure).

Status: Certification Letter from mechanical engineer stating compliance is on file.

Credit 3.1: Construction IAQ Management Plan: During Construction

Requirements: Develop and implement an Indoor Air Quality (IAQ) Management Plan for the construction and preoccupancy phases of the building as follows:

- During construction meet or exceed the recommended Design Approaches of the Sheet Metal and Air Conditioning National Contractors Association (SMACNA) IAQ Guidelines for Occupied Buildings under Construction, 1995, Chapter 3.

- Protect stored on-site or installed absorptive materials from moisture damage.

- If air handlers must be used during construction, filtration media with a Minimum Efficiency Reporting Value (MERV) of eight must be used at each return air grill, as determined by ASHRAE 52.2-1999.

- Replace all filtration media immediately prior to occupancy. Filtration media shall have a Minimum Efficiency Reporting Value (MERV) of 13, as determined by ASHRAE 52.2-1999 for media installed at the end of construction.

Submittals:

☐ LEED Letter Template, signed by the general contractor or responsible party, declaring that a Construction IAQ Management Plan has been developed and implemented, and listing each air filter used during construction and at the end of construction. Include the MERV value, manufacturer name and model number.

AND EITHER

FIGURE 6.3   Sample LEED Status Report

☐ Provide 18 photographs—six photographs taken on three different occasions during construction—along with identification of the SMACNA approach featured by each photograph, in order to show consistent adherence to the credit requirements.

OR

☐ Declare the five Design Approaches of SMACNA IAQ Guidelines for Occupied Buildings under Construction, 1995, Chapter 3, which were used during building construction. Include a brief description of some of the important design approaches employed.

Status: Need copy of Construction IAQ Management Plan, as accepted by Contractor, in order to prepare LEED Letter Template. Need photographs documenting compliance with SMACNA requirements.

Credit 3.2: Construction IAQ Management Plan: Before Occupancy

Requirements: Develop and implement an Indoor Air Quality (IAQ) Management Plan for preoccupancy phase as follows:

- After construction ends and prior to occupancy conduct a minimum two-week building flush-out with new Minimum Efficiency Reporting Value (MERV) 13 filtration media at 100% outside air. After the flush-out, replace the filtration media with new MERV 13 filtration media, except the filters solely processing outside air.

OR

- Conduct a baseline indoor air quality testing procedure consistent with the United States Environmental Protection Agency's current *Protocol for Environmental Requirements, Baseline IAQ and Materials, for the Research Triangle Park Campus, Section 01445*.

Submittals:

☐ LEED Letter Template signed by the architect, general contractor, or responsible party, describing the building flush-out procedures and dates.

OR

☐ LEED Letter Template, signed by the architect or responsible party, declaring that the referenced standard's IAQ testing protocol has been followed. Include a copy of the testing results.

Status: Need copy of Construction IAQ Management Plan, as accepted by Contractor, to verify that plan includes provision for preoccupancy building flush-out. Under this approach, indoor air quality testing procedure described above will *not* be required.

Monitor Compliance

The key to achieving certification after completion of construction is monitoring construction as it progresses. Monitoring is usually conducted by a green building consultant unless the design professional specializes in green building. During construction, the consultant oversees implementation of credits at the job site, conducts rating system credit review meetings with contractors and subcontractors at the job site, and records the work in progress as it relates to rating system credits. Not many guidelines exist for monitoring compliance during construction, but an effort is being made to fill the void. The Partnership for Achieving Construction Excellence at Pennsylvania State University in conjunction with the Pentagon Renovation and Construction Program Office has published the *Field Guide for Sustainable Construction*. The *Guide* provides "education and guidance for construction field workers, supervisors, and managers on construction methods and practices," with a goal of ensuring that sustainable requirements are attained on projects during construction.[1] Monitoring compliance, however, is just part of the process of commissioning of the project.

Commissioning

Commissioning is the process of ensuring that the owner's programmatic intent is carried out in both the design and construction of the project. The commissioning process is usually facilitated by an independent commissioning consultant or agent hired by the owner. Commissioning is usually provided as an additional service to the owner and is not a typical requirement.

The commissioning process starts with the development of a commissioning plan. The plan is created during the design process and concludes after the construction phase is complete.

During construction, the commissioning consultant reviews submittals for commissioned equipment, monitors installation of equipment at the job site, attends meetings with the contractor and subcontractors, makes sure all building systems are functioning at design performance levels and that the owner's designated personnel are trained to operate and maintain the building, makes sure adequate documentation for the building's materials and systems is provided, and reports observed deficiencies and variances in the construction to the owner, contractor, and design professionals. Members of the design team also receive and review the commissioning report and documentation assembled during project closeout procedures.

The Construction Phase as the Successful End to the Project

Many design professionals, after investing a great deal of their energy and talent in the design and specification of a building project using green building materials, are disappointed when the materials are changed during the bidding and construction phases without their agreement. By putting an equal amount of effort and care into the bidding and construction phases of the project, the design professional can ensure that the green building materials they selected and worked so hard to include in their project will actually be incorporated in it. By working to make the contractor's job of using relatively unknown materials easier, the design professional can serve both the owner's needs and those of the environment.

Notes

1. The Partnership for Achieving Construction Excellence, *Field Guide for Sustainable Construction*, Pennsylvania State University, June 2004.

CHAPTER 7

Green Building Materials and Green Building Programs

Because many buildings stand for at least 50–100 years—and some last for centuries—it is essential to get them right the first time.

State of the World 2004

Prior chapters have discussed the reasons you should use green building materials and how to select and specify them. A driving force behind the growth in availability of green building materials is the growth in the number of green building programs, smart growth initiatives, and related sustainable development legislation.

Green building programs come in a variety of shapes and sizes. They are local, regional, national, and international. They are holistic, addressing a range of environmental concerns; and, they are issue-specific, focusing on a single environmental aspect. They are checklist style, accessible by the general user; and they are life cycle assessment style, necessitating a certain level of expertise. They are comprehensive, providing a one-size-fits-all approach to all building projects; and, they are sector-specific, providing a more tailored approach for buildings of a certain type.

Regardless of the shape or size, they tend to share many of the same environmental goals—stewardship of energy, water, materials, site/landscape and IEQ. Most green building rating programs outline objectives or intent as categorized according to these environmental goals. Most suggest a variety of ways to accomplish their stated objectives . . . but, they do not usually state THE way. Environmental issues are complex and interrelated. Thus, if any program were to specify THE way, it would be immediately suspect. Some flexibility is inherent in the concept.

As the market has matured, more and more consensus-based standards have been created (through ASTM, ISO, ASHRAE, FSC, SFI, etc.) that provide a firmer foundation for green building rating programs. Certainly, mainstream industry is familiar with the use of standards for other performance requirements—structural, fire-resistance, fade-resistance, etc. Incorporating standards allows the green building rating programs to more objectively implement their goals. It allows them to better communicate their design intent. It provides for better consistency in application. And it helps to integrate the administrative processes for green building programs into mainstream procedures. Today, most green building rating programs reference a variety of green product and system standards. An understanding of the requirements of these programs will help the design professional deal more successfully with them and make the job of selecting and specifying green building materials much easier.

While by no means comprehensive, the following lists are a sampling of the numerous programs created to further the efforts of cities, states, and countries that wish to have a more sustainable future.

Local Programs

Alameda County, California: The Green Building in Alameda County Program[1] covers home remodeling, new home construction, and multifamily housing. For construction of commercial and civic buildings, the program recommends the use of the LEED™ Rating System. The program includes a Green Points rating tool to evaluate how green a home is. The Materials Database[2] lists products, suppliers and service providers that correspond to the program's Green Building Guidelines. The Materials Database is searchable by category, Green Building Guidelines, or keyword. The Green Points rating tool offers credits for materials with recycled content, materials that are recyclable, alternate lumber products, sustainable materials, and energy-efficient products.

Atlanta, Georgia: The EarthCraft House™ Green Building Program,[3] developed by the Southface Energy Institute with the assistance of government and construction industry leaders, is a program of the Greater Atlanta Home Builders Association. It focuses on new homes, renovations, communities, multifamily housing, and affordable housing. This voluntary program encourages the construction of healthy, comfortable homes that reduce energy consumption and protect the environment. It encourages the use of resource-efficient building materials such as recycled and natural content materials and advanced products, as well as materials that exhibit durability. On the commercial side, the Atlanta Regional Chapter USGBC, a partnership between Southface and the U.S. Green Building Council, encourages acceptance of LEED™ certification as the regional standard for sustainable communities and buildings.

Austin, Texas: The Austin Energy Green Building Program[4], the oldest local green building program in the United States, was founded in 1992. Its goal is to produce better, environmentally sound homes and workplaces. The program covers residential, commercial, multifamily, and municipal projects. Its *Sustainable Building Sourcebook* encourages the use of building materials manufactured from byproducts of another process, that avoid landfill disposal of materials through reuse or recycling, that minimize the embodied energy required to convert the product from raw material to finished product, that are rapidly renewable, recyclable, or have recycled content, that contain reused or salvaged materials, and that contain minimal or no volatile organic compounds (VOCs). The program's Sustainable Building Guidelines include a guide in CSI format for use by design professionals to incorporate sustainability directly into their project specifications. In 2005, Austin adopted new laws modeled after the USGBC's LEED™ certification criteria mandating that commercial buildings meet the Green Building Program requirements.

Boulder, Colorado: Boulder's Office of Environmental Affairs sponsors the Green Points Building Program,[5] which applies to all new residential construction as well as additions and remodeling projects larger than 500 square feet. The program encourages the use of cost-effective and sustainable remodeling and building methods. Applicants earn points by selecting green building measures in order to receive a building permit. The program offers points for recycling of construction debris, use of reclaimed lumber, use of materials with recycled content, use of engineered lumber products, use of energy-efficient materials, and use of low-VOC paint products. Commercial building projects are encouraged to use the USGBC's LEED™ Rating System.

Chula Vista, California: Chula Vista's voluntary GreenStar Building Efficiency Program[6] offers builders and developers of residential projects the opportunity to meet the energy requirements of three building efficiency programs. The program also can be used to meet the city's requirements for air quality improvements. By encouraging the use of more energy-efficient windows and improved construction, residences are built to be 15 percent more energy efficient than those that adhere to California's Title 24 energy code.

Denver, Colorado: Created by the Home Builder's Association of Metropolitan Denver, the Governor's Office of Energy Management and Conservation, Xcel Energy, and E-Star Colorado in 1995, the Built Green® Colorado Program[7] is the largest in the nation, with members across the state. The voluntary program encourages homebuilders to use products, practices, and technologies that will provide greater energy efficiency and reduce pollution, provide healthier indoor air, reduce water usage, preserve natural resources, and improve durability and reduce maintenance. The Built Green Checklist includes several Material Resource Efficiency categories covering foundation, framing, subfloor, roofing, insulation, windows and doors, exterior wall finishes, interior finish floor, cabinetry and trim, materials reduction and reuse, and waste reduction and recycling. For example, in the Foundation category, the Checklist offers points for using concrete containing a minimum of 15 percent western coal fly ash. In the Framing category, the Checklist awards points for the use of reinforced cementitious foam-formed walls (insulated concrete forms, or ICF).

Frisco, Texas: Frisco's Green Building Program[8] includes a commercial green building program, a public facility initiative, and a residential green building program. The commercial program gathers data for all non-single-family developments of greater than 10,000 square feet, while the public facilities initiative seeks to make public buildings more environmentally friendly. The residential program mandates the EPA's Energy Star™ requirements as the minimum building standard for new homes. The residential program also mandates water conservation, indoor air quality, and waste recycling standards for buildings constructed under the program. In 2004, Frisco embarked on a one-year commercial building evaluation period using the LEED™ Checklist prepared by a LEED™ accredited professional. The purpose of the evaluation is to determine the feasibility of adopting a mandatory commercial green building program. The public facilities initiative commits the city to using the LEED™ Rating System on future public buildings, with the goal of having all new municipal buildings attain a silver certification.

Grand Rapids, Michigan: The Home and Building Association of Greater Grand Rapids sponsors a Green Built Certified Program[9] that encourages the construction of new homes, apartments, townhouses, and condominiums that use materials and resources more efficiently and seek to get the most value out of the new homes being built today without more regulation. This voluntary program also promotes the use of new green building products such as reengineered lumber and recycled-content materials. The program recognizes new methods of dealing with old problems such as more efficient framing techniques and conservation techniques to increase recycling and thereby reduce hauling and tipping fees for construction waste. It is an outgrowth of efforts by the National Association of Home Builders (NAHB) to raise awareness on the part of their members of the economic and environmental benefits of green building.

Hudson Valley, New York: The Builders Association of the Hudson Valley, with funding from the New York State Energy Research and Development Authority (NYSERDA) and assistance from the NAHB Research Center, is developing a green building program that will apply to residential construction and renovation. Much like similar programs in Austin and Denver, the Hudson Valley program will include the use of resource-efficient materials and environmentally friendly construction practices. The program will be the first of its kind in New York State.

Kansas City, Missouri: The voluntary Build Green Program[10] was developed by the Home Builders Association of Greater Kansas City to encourage a comprehensive approach to home building. The program offers participant builders four levels of achievement: platinum, gold, silver, and bronze. Participants must be members of the Build Green Council. Builders register each home they want to be designated as Built Green. This designation does not confer any certification or approval on the builders themselves or other homes they build. Each level of the program includes a checklist for the builder to complete, indicating the steps they have taken to achieve the level of greenness indicated. The checklist contains these categories: site, energy, material, indoor air quality, and recycling. The Material Guidelines include the use of one material with minimum 50 percent recycled content; engineered building products such as beams, joists, and headers; framing lumber certified by the Forest Stewardship Council (FSC), alternative building systems such as structural insulated panels (SIPs) or straw bale; certified green content siding; gypsum board with recycled content; recycled-content attic insulation; natural material (domestic cotton or wool) or recycled-content carpet; and Borate (ACQ) -treated lumber products in moisture-sensitive areas.

Portland, Oregon: Portland's Office of Sustainable Development manages the G/Rated Program,[11] which includes both residential and commercial building components. On the commercial side, the Portland LEED™ Program (PDX LEED™) is the first supplemental guide to the USGBC's LEED™ standards in the country. The supplement adds Portland's erosion control, stormwater management, and energy regulations to the LEED™ standards. It also includes a series of preapproved innovation credits to reflect the city's goals for mixed-use development, construction waste management, alternative transportation, and stormwater management. Last, it gathers local building and zoning code regulations and relevant green building resources into a centralized location. Because the program is a supplement to the national LEED™ standards, it retains all of the material requirements of that program. The residential program includes materials guidelines similar to other residential programs such as fly ash concrete, insulated concrete forms, engineered lumber, advanced framing, SIPs, FSC certified wood, reclaimed lumber, alternative and regional materials, and interior finish materials with low VOCs.

Santa Barbara County, California: In 2001, the Sustainability Project, a nonprofit organization, prepared *Green Building Guidelines*[12] for Santa Barbara County. While the county does not have an official set of guidelines for green or sustainable design, the *Guidelines* are a good resource for design professionals seeking to build green there. The *Guidelines* include a section on green building material options that offers guidance on evaluating materials for environmental impacts as well as a series of specific guidelines for various materials. Materials covered include concrete foundations, block walls, wood structure, structural wall sheathing, roofing, exterior siding, windows, doors, insulation, plaster and gypsum board, paints, millwork and cabinetry, fabrics, window- and wallcoverings, hard flooring, and floor covering. Each of the material guidelines offers choices for the design professional as well as sources of additional information and related topics that can be found elsewhere in the *Guidelines.*

San Francisco, California: San Francisco's Department of Environment offers several resources of interest to the design professional. In addition to a program covering less toxic pest management, the city also offers a Green Building Program.[13] Among the resources the city offers as part of the program is a *Green Building Resource Guide* that assists interested parties in locating green building materials and services in the Bay Area. Materials listed in the *Guide* include wood products, cabinets and countertops, composite wood decking, insulation, siding and roofing, caulking and sealants, doors, adhesives, flooring, and paints and coatings. San Francisco also has a *Green Building Compliance Guide* that applies to municipal buildings in San Francisco. The *Guide* was developed as a resource for design professionals working on city building projects. Because city code requires that new municipal buildings and renovation projects of 5,000 square feet and over meet the requirements of the LEED™ Program Silver Certification Level, it also explains how to apply LEED™ in San Francisco.

Scottsdale, Arizona: Scottsdale's Green Building Program[14] rates building projects in several categories: site use, energy, indoor air quality, building materials, solid waste, and water. The program encourages the use of environmentally responsible materials and offers guidelines to selecting materials that are durable and appropriate for the city's desert climate, are manufactured locally to limit embodied energy, are recyclable, contain recycled content, and have low embodied energy. In addition, the program encourages the avoidance of materials that unduly deplete limited natural resources, are made from toxic or hazardous constituents, or generate pollution during manufacturing or use. The program uses a point rating system to qualify projects.

Seattle, Washington: The City's *Implement*[15] sustainable building tool includes integrated design tools and best practice information sorted by project type. This web-based program leads the user through several steps that assist the user in designing a green building. Once a building type is selected, the user is presented with various tools to select from including: an energy matrix, water matrix, best practices, case studies, links, and tips on how LEED™ applies to the building type. The City adopted the LEED™ Rating System at a Silver level as the standard for all city-owned buildings and facilities of over 5000 sq ft of occupied space. The City has also created the Seattle Supplements to the LEED™ program that focus on local resources, contacts and requirements.

The Master Builders Association of King and Snohomish Counties developed *Seattle Area Built Green*™[16] as a non-profit, residential building program whose goal is to provide homeowners with environmentally friendly homes. The program is similar to other Built Green™ in other areas of the country. The program uses a checklist and third party verification to certify homes.

State Programs

California: In December 2004, the governor signed Executive Order S-20-04 regarding green buildings. It establishes the state's priority for energy and resource-efficient high-performance buildings. It sets a goal of reducing energy use in state-owned buildings by 20 percent by 2015 and encourages commercial sector buildings to set the same goal. The order also directs compliance with the Green Building Action Plan,[17] which covers public buildings, including state buildings and schools, as well as commercial and institutional buildings. The plan requires all existing state buildings over 50,000 square feet meet LEED-EB standards by no later than 2015 to the maximum extent cost-effective. The plan also requires that all new state buildings and major renovation projects of 10,000 square feet or larger and subject to Title 24 be designed and constructed to a LEED-NC Silver Level or higher. On behalf of the California Energy Commission, the Ernest Orlando Lawrence Berkeley National laboratory is preparing a report on California and national benchmarking methods for high-performance commercial building systems. This report will assist the state in fashioning a program for commercial buildings.

There is also the *California Green Builder Program (CGB)*[18], sponsored by the Building Industry Institute, which certifies both builders and residential developments. The Program includes the following components: higher energy efficiency standards, outdoor air quality improvements, resource savings and waste diversion, and water conservation. The builder completes a worksheet consisting of four sections covering these components for each home plan in a community (subdivision) and submits the completed worksheet online. The CBG sends an inspector to the project site to inspect the first unit of each floor plan who in turn submits a completed inspection report to the HERS Provider. Once reviews are complete and verification of compliance with Program requirements are made, a California Green Builder Project Certificate is issued. The builder can then display a CGB Logo and designate the project as a California Green Builder subdivision or community.

Colorado: See listing for Denver, above, for information on the joint program of the city of Denver and the state of Colorado.

Hawaii: Sponsored by the Building Industry Association-Hawaii, the Hawaii BuiltGreen™ Home Program[19] is modeled after the NAHB Model Green Home Building Program. The program's goals are to certify buildings that incorporate green features, including energy and water conservation, materials efficiency, site ecosystem protection, and improved indoor air quality and human safety; to globally market and brand the concept of green building and the benefits it provides to owners and the environment; and to provide educational and marketing tools for industry professionals. The program features a Home Builder Self-Certification Checklist that, upon completion, can qualify a project for a Hawaii BuiltGreen Star Rating™. There are three levels of ratings. A project must achieve an increasing number of points in order to attain a higher-level rating. The Checklist is broken into several sections: protecting the site's features and functions, energy performance and comfort, health and indoor air quality, durability and materials conservation, and environmentally friendly home operations. The section on durability and materials conservation addresses design choices, termite details, framing, foundation, sub-floor, windows and doors, insulation, interior walls, finish floor, cabinetry and trim, roof, exterior finish, outdoor features, and job site operations. To use the checklist, the builder checks off features included on a project and totals the points in each section.

Illinois: In May 2005, the Illinois state legislature passed SB0250, which amends the Capital Development Board Act and requires the Board to "initiate a series of training workshops across the State to increase awareness and understanding of green building techniques and green building rating systems."[20] In addition, the Board "is to identify no less than three construction projects to serve as case studies for achieving certification using nationally recognized and accepted green building guidelines, standards, or systems approved by the State."[21] Although the original version of the bill included references to the LEED™ Green Building Rating System, as passed, the bill does not mention any specific rating system. The Board is required to report its findings to the Legislature no later than December 31, 2008. The bill also requires the Board to "establish a Green Building Advisory Committee to assist . . . in determining guidelines for which State construction and major renovation projects should be developed to green building standards."[22] Further, it requires that the guidelines take into account the size and type of buildings, financing considerations, and other criteria as appropriate.

Iowa: The state's *Sustainable Design Initiative* which was initiated in 1999, encourages sustainable design in state-owned facilities. In the mid 1990s, the State Department of Natural Resources (DNR) working with the Department of Administrative Services and project architects established "Sustainable Development Principles" as part of the Iowa Capitol Complex Master Plan. The concepts that are addressed in the Plan include: sustainable site planning, energy efficiency, water safeguarding, materials and resources conservation, indoor air quality, solid waste reduction, and environmental quality. DNR is also developing "Green Buyers Guides." The Guides "define products in the overview and then make recommendations based on a number of environmental issues." [23] Each product guide includes an overview, recommendations for consumer purchasing, recommendations for specifying, a discussion of environmental issues, a list of manufacturers, and additional links. The state also has a "Sustainable Design Guide" that covers sustainable design principles. DNR evaluated several rating systems and chose the LEED™ Green Building Rating System as the one "that best represented the identified criteria." [24]

Maryland: The state's Environmental Design Program[25] seeks to advance the application of economically sound and environmentally sensitive building and site design techniques. It provides information and on-site technical assistance to identify, implement, and evaluate actions to enhance and restore natural resources in and around developed environments. The program also includes information on site design and watersheds, energy, water and resources, indoor environmental quality, sustainable materials and construction, recycling and deconstruction, and operations and maintenance. The section entitled "Sustainable Materials and Construction" covers construction, natural home construction, flooring, roofing, and lumber. In addition to recommendations on steps that can be taken to use sustainable materials on projects, the section includes references that lead to more in-depth information on the topics listed. The recommendations deal with certified wood products, recycled flooring materials, environmentally friendly insulation, advanced building materials such as SIPs, and using materials obtained from a reuse center to cut back on the amount of new materials used on a project.

Michigan: Under Executive Directive No. 2005-4, entitled "Energy Efficiency in State Facilities and Operations"[26] and issued by the governor in April 2005, Michigan will establish an energy-efficiency savings target for all state buildings with the goal of attaining a 10-percent reduction in energy use by December 31, 2008, and a 20-percent reduction in grid-based energy purchases by December 31, 2015, when compared to energy use and purchases as of the year ending September 30, 2002. The state requires that all state-supported capital outlay projects, whether for state departments or agencies, universities, or community colleges, costing over $1 million must use the LEED™ Green Building Rating System in their design and construction. The directive requires that all new construction and major renovation projects of state-owned facilities, including all capital outlay projects, score a minimum of 26 points on the LEED™ Rating System. It also requires that the LEED™ Rating System be applied to state-leased facilities to the extent feasible.

Nevada: In June 2005, the governor signed a bill that creates new incentives and standards for green building in the state. A part of Assembly Bill 3 requires that most state-funded public buildings meet the minimum requirements of the USGBC's LEED™ Green Building Rating System Silver level or an equivalent standard. The law also requires that the state select two state-owned buildings to serve as demonstration projects for LEED™ certification. In addition the law provides that any privately constructed buildings that meet the standard will earn a tax credit and the products and materials used in the building will be exempt from state sales tax. The bill also requires the adoption of guidelines for the use of resource-efficient materials.

New York: Through the New York State Energy Research and Development Authority[27] (also known as NYSERDA), the state provides green building services to building design teams. These services include computer modeling, design charrette coordination, assistance in obtaining LEED™ certification, New York State Green Buildings Tax Credit assistance, green materials recommendations, and commissioning and life-cycle costing analysis. They apply to new and rehabilitated commercial, industrial, and institutional buildings. Beginning in 1996, "NYSERDA has given more than $3.9 million in federal and state funds to provide assistance for projects affecting more than 22 million square feet of building space"[28] in New York State. The state supports the use of the LEED™ Rating System. In the area of green materials, New York's Green Building Program seeks to improve indoor air quality through the use of low-emitting materials. In addition, Executive Order No. 111, issued on June 10, 2001, directs state agencies, authorities, and other affected entities to be more energy efficient and environmentally aware.

North Carolina: The state is in the process of creating a statewide green building program known as the NC HealthyBuilt Homes Program[29]. Checklist guidelines were developed by a task force of green building experts from around the state and organized by the North Carolina Solar Center. The program offers participants four rating levels they can attain for their project, starting with "certified" at the low end and "gold certified" at the high end. It covers the following areas: site, water, building envelope energy opportunities, comfort systems energy opportunities, appliances and renewables energy opportunities, indoor air quality, and materials. Similar to other residential green building programs, the materials section of the checklist awards points for the use of fly ash in concrete, recycled concrete or glass cullet for aggregate, use of non-solvent-based damp proofing, wood from third-party certified sustainably harvested sources, recycled-content or HCFC-free rigid foam insulation, regionally obtained salvaged materials, natural cork or 100 percent recycled or recovered content underlayment, natural fiber carpet or linoleum, and paints or finishes with recycled content.

Oregon: The state, through Oregon Housing and Community Services (OHCS), promotes green building practices in the residential marketplace and encourages the use of recycled building materials in multifamily projects. To further green building awareness, OHCS published the *Green Building Source Guide*[30] in 2002. This guide goes beyond the typical green building guideline manual by offering links to other guidebooks as well as program descriptions, product directories, and technical and educational material from other sources. The *Guide* includes a listing of green products and technology websites as well.

Pennsylvania: The state claims to have the most LEED™ Certified buildings in the country (although California and Oregon might take issue). Pennsylvania's *Guidelines for Creating High-Performance Green Buildings*, available through the Governor's Green Governmental Council (GGGC)[31], defines *high-performance green building* under the guidelines. Such a building includes materials that have taken into account the life-cycle costs of its manufacture, operation, maintenance, and disposal; uses resources efficiently; maximizes use of local building materials; and incorporates products that minimize waste in their production or disposal. The *Guidelines* section dealing with materials includes guidance on the selection of materials based not only on first cost but also on life-cycle costs. The section also recommends the use of recycled building materials and environmentally friendly materials.

Vermont: The Vermont Builds Greener (VBG)[32] Program is a residential program that differs from others in that it does not exclusively depend on representatives of the building industry for its source. The program, an initiative of Building for Social Responsibility (BSR), certifies residential buildings constructed to sustainable criteria, including siting and land use, building design, quality and durability, energy use, resource impacts, occupant health and indoor air quality, and keeping it green occupant education and Operation & Management (O&M). The "Quality/Durability" category awards points for choosing quality materials and details for minimum maintenance requirement, while the "Resource Impacts" category awards points for using resource-efficient and environmentally responsible materials or local or regional materials; reducing, reusing, and recycling waste materials during construction; encouraging diversion of waste during occupancy; and water efficiency. The "Occupant Health/Indoor Air Quality" category awards points for minimizing sources of pollutants, including using urea formaldehyde-free interior panel products, flooring materials that do not contain petroleum-based products, and low-VOC adhesives.

Washington: During the 2005 regular session, the Washington state legislature passed Substitute SB5509[33] relating to high-performance green buildings. The legislation requires that state-funded buildings, including offices, schools, universities, and justice facilities be built according to the U.S. Green Building Council's LEED™ Green Building Program and attain a minimum Silver Level rating. The bill applies to any new construction of more than 5,000 square feet and any remodeling project that exceeds 5,000 square feet when the cost is greater than 50 percent of the assessed value. State-funded affordable housing projects must adopt a system for measuring building performance as well. The bill further requires that school projects be designed and constructed to the LEED™ Silver Level or the state's sustainable school design protocol standards. It includes a unique section that indemnifies members of the design and construction team if a project fails to meet the LEED™ Silver Rating standard "as long as a good faith effort was made to achieve the LEED™ standard set for the project."[34]

Wisconsin: The state's residential green building program, Green Built Home™,[35] is a voluntary program that reviews and certifies homes that meet sustainable building and energy standards. The program was initiated by the Madison Area Builders Association in cooperation with other builders' associations, utilities, and organizations that promote green building. To qualify, a home must earn a minimum of 60 points by meeting the specified criteria. Each home that is certified receives a GreenGuide Label that provides the home buyer with information on the number of points earned from the program's checklist. The checklist section that deals with materials selection covers exterior, below grade, structural frame, envelope, insulation, roof, subfloor, finish floor, and doors, cabinetry, and trim. Program requirements in this section are similar to those of the residential programs discussed elsewhere in this chapter.

U.S. Governmental Agency Programs

Environmental Protection Agency (EPA): Many EPA programs advocate green product design and manufacturing. "One of EPA's strategic goals is to improve environmental protection and encourage government, business, and the public to conserve natural resources by adopting pollution prevention strategies and sustainable practices."[36] Through its Greening EPA Program,[37] the EPA is seeking to walk its talk. The agency has a goal of making its facilities, both old and new, serve as models for a healthy workplace with minimal environmental impacts. EPA is committed to design, construct, operate, and maintain its buildings in a sustainable manner. Because EPA leases most of its major office buildings, it works to improve the environmental performance of these facilities through green lease specifications and riders. EPA also requires that all major new building construction projects achieve at least a LEED™ Silver certification. The EPA also encourages the use of environmentally friendly building materials through its Environmentally Preferable Purchasing Program.[38]

General Services Administration (GSA): The GSA, the nation's largest landlord, has long supported green buildings and has embraced the USGBC's LEED™ Green Building Rating System. The GSA's Public Building Service has an environmental goal of eliminating "all damage to the environment resulting from its operations."[39] Working in collaboration with the Sustainable Design and Energy Programs, the Environmental Program is working toward this goal. The GSA, through the Sustainable Design Program, "is committed to incorporating principles of sustainable design and energy efficiency into all of its building projects."[40] The GSA uses the LEED™ Rating System as a goal in design criteria to help apply principles of sustainable design and development to its facilities projects. "Since fiscal year 2000, GSA has mandated that all of its new construction and major modernization projects attain, at minimum, a LEED™ Certified rating, while striving for LEED™ Silver."[41] Beginning in fiscal year 2003, all new GSA building projects must meet criteria for basic LEED™ certification. By mid-2005, 6 GSA projects had been LEED™ certified.

National Park Service (NPS): The NPS, the agency responsible for maintaining and operating the nation's park system, through the Denver Service Center (DSC) maintains the Service's *Guiding Principles of Sustainable Design*[42]. The *Guiding Principles* chapter on building design includes a section on environmentally sensitive building materials. This section discusses the concept of a cradle-to-grave analysis of building materials to assist in their selection for a project. The primary selection priority is materials found in nature. The secondary priority is materials made from recycled products, and the tertiary priority is man-made materials with varying degrees of environmental impact. In the past, the DSC did not use sustainable design criteria to evaluate design contracts.

Currently, all solicitations issued by DSC stress the importance of integrated and co-ordinated designs, as well as sustainable design practices, by using these as specific evaluation criteria.

Sustainable Project Rating Tool (SPiRiT)[43]: Beginning in Fiscal Year (FY) 2002, projects were required to adopt sustainable principles to guide their development. The SPiRiT Program "provides guidance to support the consideration of sustainable design and de-velopment principles in Army installation planning decisions and infrastructure proj-ects."[44] SPiRiT was developed by the U.S. Army Engineer Research and Development Center (ERDC) for the Corps of Engineers. SPiRiT is based on the USGBC's LEED™ Green Building Rating System Version 2.0. Beginning in FY2006 all Army military construction projects are required to achieve a SPiRiT Gold rating.

National (U.S.) Programs

Energy Star®: The Energy Star[45] program is a voluntary government and industry partner-ship that seeks to make it easy for businesses and consumers to save money and protect the environment. It is administered by the EPA in conjunction with the Department of Energy (DOE). The labeling program was launched in 1992 to identify energy-efficient products. In 1996, the label was expanded to include new homes, commercial and in-stitutional buildings, residential heating and cooling equipment, major appliances, of-fice equipment, lighting, and consumer electronics. The Energy Star® Program for Buildings awards a plaque to buildings that achieve a rating of 75 or higher and have been professionally verified to meet current indoor environmental standards. By using the program's benchmarking tool, a building's performance on a scale of 1 to 100 rel-ative to similar buildings nationwide is obtained. Building types that are eligible, rep-resenting over 50 percent of U.S. commercial floor space, include:

- Offices (general offices, financial centers, bank branches, and courthouses)
- K–12 schools
- Hospitals (acute care and children's)
- Hotels and motels
- Medical offices
- Supermarkets
- Residence halls
- Warehouses (refrigerated and nonrefrigerated)

Building for Environmental and Economic Sustainability (BEES): The BEES[46] software fa-cilitates selection of cost-effective, environmentally preferable building products. The software was developed by the National Institute of Standards and Technology's (NIST) Building and Fire Research Laboratory with support from the EPA's Environ-mentally Preferable Purchasing Program. Designed for use by designers, builders, and product manufacturers, the software includes actual environmental and economic performance data for almost 200 building products. "BEES measures the environmental performance of building products by using the life-cycle assessment approach specified in ISO 14000 standards.[47] BEES is available for downloading at no charge from the NIST website.

Good Cents: Utility-sponsored programs to improve energy efficiency are the oldest green building programs in the United States. The Good Cents program was developed in 1976 to encourage the construction of energy-efficient homes. To date, more than 750,000 Good Cents homes have been built across the country with another 60,000 added annually.[48]

Green Globes-Building Environmental Assessments[49]: Developed by the Green Building Initiative originally for use in Canada, Green Globes™ is an interactive, web-based, commercial green building assessment protocol that guides the integration of green principles into a building's design. Green Globes rates seven areas: project management, site, energy, water, resources, emissions and effluents, and indoor environment. Green Globes rates a project's sustainability by awarding "Green Globes" for levels of point achievement, much like the USGBC's LEED™ Program. The Program assesses a project's level of achievement at three points during the design and construction process, at the end of schematic design, at the end of construction documents, and at the completion of construction. The rating award is not made until a project has completed the third check and it has been verified.

Home Energy Ratings Systems (HERS) Ratings: "A HERS rating is an evaluation of the energy efficiency of a home, compared to a computer-simulated reference house of identical size and shape as the rated home that meets minimum requirements of the Model Energy Code (MEC). The HERS rating results in a score between 0 and 100, with the reference house assigned a score of 80. From this point, each 5 percent reduction in energy usage (compared to the reference house) results in a one-point increase in the HERS score. Thus, an Energy Star qualified new home, required to be significantly more energy-efficient than the reference house, must achieve a HERS score of at least 86."[50] Third-party raters conduct the evaluation. The evaluation process includes an analysis of a home's construction plans and an on-site inspection of the home. Local HERS programs exist throughout the country.

Leadership in Energy and Environmental Design Green Building Rating System[51] *(LEED™):* LEED is the U.S. Green Building Council's voluntary, consensus-based national standard for developing high-performance, sustainable buildings. LEED rating systems are currently available or under development for new commercial construction and major renovations (NC), existing building operations (EB), commercial interiors (CI), core and shell projects (CS), homes (H), and neighborhood developments (ND). LEED provides a complete framework for assessing building performance and meeting sustainability goals. Based on well-founded scientific standards, LEED emphasizes state-of-the-art strategies for sustainable site development, water savings, energy efficiency, materials selection, and indoor environmental quality. LEED recognizes achievements and promotes expertise in green building through a comprehensive system offering project certification, professional accreditation, training, and practical resources. The rating system includes a materials and resources category offering credits for using recycled-content materials, local and regional materials, rapidly renewable materials, and certified wood. The indoor environmental quality category requires the use of low-emitting materials.

National Programs (Other Countries)

Australia: The Green Star Environmental Rating System for Buildings[52] was created to set a standard of measurement for green buildings in Australia. The rating system is a voluntary national program that evaluates the environmental performance of buildings. Green Star Rating Systems have been developed for office design, office as built, office interiors, and office asset. Each of the rating systems includes the following categories: management, indoor environmental quality, energy, transport, water, materials, land use, site selection and ecology, and emissions. Each category contains credits awarded based on achieving the required level in the building. Credits in the materials category are awarded for providing storage for recycling waste, reuse of façade, reuse of structure, shell, and core, recycled content of concrete, recycled content of steel, PVC minimization, and use of sustainable timber.

Canada: Building Environmental Performance Assessment Criteria (BEPAC) was originally designed for new and existing office buildings in British Columbia, although regional variants have subsequently been developed for Ontario and Atlantic Canada. BEPAC evaluates two main categories, the base building and tenant buildout. Each category is assessed according to five criteria: ozone layer protection, environmental impact of energy use, indoor environmental quality, resource conservation, and site and transportation. Each of the criteria is assessed within a 10-point scale. BEPAC weights the points to reflect the relative importance of aspects within each of the criteria, but not between criteria. BEPAC is no longer used, but remains of academic interest.

The Calgary Region Home Builders Association offers builders a voluntary program called Built Green™ Alberta[53]. The program was launched in October 2003 and is modeled after the R-2000 training program and the EnerGuide for New Houses program administered by Natural Resources Canada. The focus of the program is on: energy efficiency, indoor air quality, resource use (including waste management), and overall environmental impact. The program mirrors the requirements of other builder programs both in Canada and the United States. To qualify for a bronze, silver or gold level rating, the builder completes a checklist, provides the required documentation, and submits the completed package for verification.

The Canada Green Building Council offers a version of the USGBC's LEED™ Green Building Rating System. The *LEED® Canada-NC Version 1.0 for New Construction and Major Renovations*[54] is derived from the US version of LEED™. The Canadian version provides a set of equivalent Canadian LEED prerequisite and credit requirements and references to relevant Canadian standards and resource materials. It also provides a starting point for any jurisdiction in Canada that wishes to further refine the rating system for their area.

China: The National Resource Defense Council (NRDC), through its China Clean Energy Project,[55] has been working with the Chinese government to minimize the environmental impact of its building program. NRDC has worked to develop energy efficiency standards for residential buildings, provide assistance on national energy standards for government and commercial buildings, and translate and adapt the LEED™ Green Building Rating System for application in China. NRDC is also working with several Chinese municipalities to develop green building programs. The China Clean Energy Program,[56] in partnership with NRDC, is working on developing energy-efficient building codes and equipment standards, green building standards and documents, and green Olympics.

Hong Kong: The HK-BEAM Society created the *Hong Kong Building Environmental Assessment Method*[57], a voluntary system to measure, improve, and label the environmental performance of buildings. The system has been used on 100 buildings to date. The system applies to both new and existing buildings. In the category of materials topics such as: the efficient use of materials (building reuse, modular and standardized design, off-site fabrication, adaptability and deconstruction, and envelope durability), selection of materials (rapidly renewable, sustainable forest, recycled, ozone depleting), and waste management (demolition and construction waste, waste recycling facilities, and waste management).

Japan: The Japan Sustainable Building Consortium (JSBC) is developing the *Comprehensive Assessment System for Building Environmental Efficiency (CASBEE)*[58]. The system is a cooperative development of academic, industrial, and governmental agencies. The system's assessment tools include a pre-design assessment tool, a Design for Environment (DfE) tool, an eco-labeling tool, and a sustainable operation and renovation tool.

Korea: The Green Building Council Korea[59] has released a *Green Building Rating System* (GBRS) to measure the environmental performance of buildings. The System applies a whole building perspective over a building's life cycle. The System is based on the Green Building Challenge assessment framework. Criteria evaluated by the System includes: resource consumption, environmental loadings, quality of indoor environmental air quality, longevity, process, and contextual factors.

International Programs

ATHENA™ Environmental Impact Estimator: Created by the Canada-based ATHENA™ Sustainable Materials Institute[60], this LCA software tool assesses the environmental implications of industrial, institutional, office, and both multi-unit and single family residential designs throughout their life cycle. Where relevant, it also distinguishes between owner-occupied and rental facilities. A companion LCI Database Reports CD contains a series of life cycle inventory (LCI) and related reports that support the software.

The Building Research Establishment Environmental Assessment Method (BREEAM)[61]: This Building Research Establishment (BRE) Program was created over a decade ago in England to assess the environmental performance of both new and existing buildings. BREEAM is a tool that allows the owners, users and designers of buildings to review and improve environmental performance throughout the life of a building. BREEAM assesses performance of buildings in the areas of: management, energy use, health and well-being, pollution, transport, land use, ecology, materials, and water. Credits are awarded in each area based upon performance. Buildings are rated: Pass, Good, Very Good, and Excellent. BREEAM can be applied to: offices, homes (Eco-Homes), industrial units, retail units, and schools. BRE also publishes *The Green Guide to Specification* that provides a method of easily assessing the environmental performance of over 250 construction specifications. The *Guide* also includes an explanation of the background of green procurement, life cycle analysis and environmental issues.

Eco-Quantum[62]: Developed by IVAM Environmental Research, W/E, and Prisman in the Netherlands, this LCA tool makes it possible to select the most attractive measures for a design from an environmental point of view. It also compares the environmental performance of various measures concerning energy-saving installations, water-saving techniques, material choice, design and location.

Green Building Challenge (GBC): The GBC is an "international collaborative effort to develop a building environmental assessment tool that displays and addresses controversial aspects of building performance and from which the participating countries can selectively draw ideas to either incorporate into or modify their own tools."[63] Over 20 countries have participated in the development of the assessment tool (known as GBTool). The 2005 version permits comparisons with the LEED and Green Globes programs. Categories include site selection, project planning and development, energy and resource consumption, environmental loadings, indoor environmental quality, functionality and controllability of building systems, long-term performance, and social and economic aspects.

The Swan Ecolabel[64]: This program covers products in Denmark, Finland, Iceland, Norway, and Sweden. Items that display the Swan label have taken into consideration the product's impact on the environment from raw material to disposal, met criteria regarding quality and performance, and offer features that are at least as good as other similar products.

While this chapter just touches on the growing number of green building programs available at the local, state, national, and international levels, the variety is intended to give the design professional a good grounding in the differences among such programs. The future will certainly witness continuing growth in the number and sophistication of programs that will help define and encourage green building materials and buildings.

Notes

1. http://www.stopwaste.org/home/index.asp?page=7.
2. http://build-green.org/guide/content.cfm.

3. www.southface.org/web/earthcraft_house/ech_main.

4. www.ci.austin.tx.us/greenbuilder.

5. http://www.ci.boulder.co.us/environmentalaffairs/green_points/.

6. www.chulavistaca.gov.

7. www.builtgreen.org.

8. www.ci.frisco.tx.us/planning_dev/greenbuilding/index.html.

9. www.hbaggr.com/about_issues_green.htm.

10. www.buildgreenkc.com/.

11. www.green-rated.org.

12. www.sustainabilityproject.org.

13. www.sfenvironment.com.

14. www.ScottsdaleAZ.gov/greenbuilding.

15. www2.ci.seattle.wa.us/Implement.

16. www.builtgreen.net.

17. www.energy.ca.gov/greenbuilding.

18. www.cagreenbuilder.org.

19. www.hawaiibuiltgreen.com.

20. www.ilga.gov/legislation/BillStatus.

21. Ibid.

22. Ibid.

23. www.sustainableiowa.org/green.html.

24. www.sustainableiowa.org/guide.html.

25. www.dnr.state.md.us/ed/.

26. www.michigan.gov.

27. www.nyserda.org/programs/Green_Buildings/default.asp.

28. Ibid.

29. www.ncsc.ncsu.edu/programs/North_Carolina_HealthyBuilt_Homes_Program.cfm.

30. www.ohcs.oregon.gov/OHCS/DO_GreenBuilding.shtml.

31. www.gggc.state.pa.us.

32. www.vermontbuildsgreener.org.

33. www.leg.wa.gov/pub/billinfo/2005-06/Htm/Bills/Senate.

34. Ibid.

35. www.greenbuilthome.org/builder/index.php.

36. www.epa.gov.

37. www.epa.gov/greeningepa/index.html.

38. www.epa.gov/oppt/epp/.

39. www.gsa.gov.

40. Ibid.

41. General Services Administration. *GSA LEED® Applications Guide*, February 2005, p.1, www.wbdg.org/references/ccbdoc.php?i=298.

42. www.nps.gov/dsc/d_publications/d_1_gpsd.htm.

43. www.cecer.army.mil/SustDesign/SPiRiT.cfm.

44. Ibid.

45. www.energystar.gov.

46. www.bfrl.nist.gov/oac/software/bees.html.

47. Ibid.

48. GoodCents Solutions home page; www.goodcents.com.

49. www.greenglobes.com.

50. www.energystar.gov/index.cfm?c=new_homes.hm_verification.

51. www.usgbc.org.

52. www.gbcaus.org.

53. www.builtgreenalberta.com/home.htm.

54. www.cagbc.org/building_rating_systems/leed_rating_system.

55. www.nrdc.org/air/energy/china/greenbuilding.asp.

56. www.chinacleanenergy.org/greenbuilding.asp.

57. www.hk-beam.org.hk/general/home.php.

58. www.ibec.or.jp/CASBEE/english/CASBEE-E.htm.

59. www.gbc-korea.co/kr/eng-3.asp.

60. www.athenasmi.ca/index.html.

61. www.breeam.org.

62. www.ivambv.uva.nl/uk/index.htm.

63. http://greenbuilding.ca/iisbe/gbc2k5/gbc2k5-start.htm.

64. www.svanen.nu/Eng/about/arbete.asp.

CHAPTER 8

Conclusion

The Congress, recognizing the profound impact of man's activity on the inter-relations of all components of the natural environment, particularly the profound influences of population growth, high-density urbanization, industrial expansion, resource exploitation, and new and expanding technological advances, and recognizing further the critical importance of restoring and maintaining environmental quality to the overall welfare and development of man, declares that it is the continuing policy of the Federal Government, in cooperation with State and local governments, and other concerned public and private organizations, to use all practicable means and measures, including financial and technical assistance, in a manner calculated to foster and promote the general welfare, to create and maintain conditions under which man and nature can exist in productive harmony, and fulfill the social, economic, and other requirements of present and future generations of Americans.

—The National Environmental Policy Act[1]

The first generation of green building projects was not particularly representative of the majority of the building industry. Some projects involved high-end facilities (private residences or high-end services) that had accompanying high-end budgets. Other projects were sponsored and subsidized by interested nonprofit groups or governmental agencies and had flexible schedules and even more flexible allowances. Then there were the projects developed by people who live off the grid and built their own residences rather cheaply, and without benefit of a building inspector, using old tires, bottles, straw bales, wind or solar power, and various unique collectibles.

More recent projects have brought environmental issues—and possible solutions—within reach of mainstream design and construction. They introduce green building products that are affordable, functional, and beautiful. They clearly demarcate a new direction in architecture.

History of Green Building Materials

Out of necessity, building design by early civilizations was heavily influenced by natural elements. Structures were oriented toward available daylight and desirable breezes. Roofs were pitched to shed water. Walls were thickened to insulate against the cold. Consequently, buildings in hot, arid regions looked distinctly different from those in cold, wet climates.

Material selection was limited to regionally available natural resources, and the use of materials was molded by regional climate patterns. Depending on the prevalent eco-system, building materials included thatch, adobe, sod, straw, stone, timber, brick, wattle and daub (the precursor to lath and plaster), and fabric. Homes were constructed on raised platforms in warm, wet, flood-prone areas of the tropics. Homes were constructed from collapsible frames and lightweight breathable fabric (that swelled when wet to shed water) by desert nomads. Northern regions consistently produced thicker, denser walls to defend against the cold. In every location, people built their own buildings with materials they acquired locally.

Ironically, today, indigenous building materials, materials that evolved in harmony with the land and the people over hundreds of years, are deemed "alternative" materials. Where there are exceptions, such as stone and wood, it is largely because commercial interests privatized the acquisition of natural resources and promoted the market value of that resource. Natural materials are largely unrecognized in building codes. Alternative materials are, by their nature, nontoxic. Most comply with basic performance requirements for fire resistance. Most can be detailed to meet seismic and lateral load requirements as well. Still, "original" building materials are considered "alternative." They have been replaced with modern building products, synthetic materials, and composites.

Modern civilization's mastery of an array of scientific principles has enabled us to create artificial environments unimaginable in previous eras. A flick of the thermostat provides almost instantaneous comfort. Point-of-use water heaters provide a seemingly endless supply of hot water. Appliances in the kitchen offer relentless convenience. With the push of a button or turn of a dial, we adapt the parameters of our built environment to suit the whim of the moment. Our buildings reflect these new technology-driven expectations. As a result, an office building in New York is likely to resemble one in New Mexico. Worse, a company can design a prototype (a fast food restaurant or retail space) and build it almost anywhere with little modification. Twentieth-century architecture is much more homogenous than that of any previous period. Differences in building design and choice of building material that were once due to the influence of nature's elements are now primarily factors of aesthetics and budget.

The turning point was the dawn of the Industrial Revolution, epitomized architecturally by the Crystal Palace in the mid-nineteenth century. The Crystal Palace was a grand vision constructed with new materials in repetitive, standardized sizes. Today, it is a staple in history of architecture courses, lauded and immortalized over the years. Few histories tell the rest of the story, however. Unfortunately, the difference in thermal expansion between the glass and the metal frame was ill-considered, the glass sheets were prone to popping out, and the building leaked like a sieve. The analogy is plain. Society embraced the promises of the Industrial Revolution as it did the image of the Crystal Palace—and it tolerated similar oversights. It failed to acknowledge the new problems that accompanied the new solutions. Nothing is free. There are always trade-offs, whether we recognize them or not.

The Industrial Revolution ushered in a fabulously exciting time of new and improved products for buildings—steel, sheet glass, reinforced concrete, elevators, and curtain walls. It thrived on standardization and mass production, which helped make all these technological wonders affordable to an eager public. It permitted the construction of taller buildings. It allowed construction at a faster pace than ever before. More and bigger and "better" buildings changed the fabric of our cities. Many of the deplorably polluted conditions of older cities were improved. Indoor plumbing alone can be credited with mitigating many of the diseases pervasive in urban areas. But it was a trade. This we failed to realize. The new technologies replaced older forms of pollution with new ones. While we no longer fear treading in deposits left by horses, we have no way of avoiding the air pollution caused by some 500 million motorized vehicles on the road today. The sooty fog caused by coal combustion has been replaced by ozone (smog) and worse. Fires, always a hazard for dense urban areas, may be relatively less frequent due to improvements in building materials and systems, but they now present the added component of toxic smoke from the burning of myriad plastics and synthetic chemicals.

The Industrial Revolution was followed closely by a Scientific Revolution. Post–World War II society expects technological marvels in daily life that even the pioneers of the Industrial Revolution did not envision. The Scientific Revolution heralded a period of chemical discovery that paralleled the physical discovery of the Industrial Revolution. It fostered new attitudes toward materials, dissecting matter into atoms, neutrons, and quarks. The building industry witnessed mass production of new products from previously unknown substances. We now take for granted the benefits of stain-resistant carpet and fiber-optic communications. As did our forebears, we overlook the new problems that accompany the new solutions, the wonder materials. We are just beginning to acknowledge these new problems—the toxins, carcinogens, and mutagens. We are gaining a better, fuller perspective of the impact on our natural resources and on urban congestion and quality of life.

Both the Industrial Revolution and the Scientific Revolution altered the business of building as well. The process of building came to mirror the process of standardized manufacturing. We design to standard sizes with standard products, tested and qualified by industry-recognized standards and contracted on standard industry-recognized forms. The craftsman era is largely gone. Where it survives, it is extremely expensive. In many ways, this makes innovation more difficult than it was before the Industrial Revolution. Innovation requires a certain freedom from prescriptive standards in order to find better ways to meet basic performance requirements. Innovation is exactly what we need to solve the problems overlooked by the Industrial and Scientific Revolutions. That is exactly what green building is: the recognition of the benefits as well as the problems presented by these revolutions. It combines the affordability and convenience of standardization with the quality and thoughtfulness of craftsmanship.

Our society has developed many conveniences and made many improvements in quality of life. However, wisdom from history should not be discarded. The benefits associated with designing buildings in response to nature have been largely forgotten over the years. Green building design and green building products are rediscovering these benefits. A building design that takes climatic conditions into consideration requires less energy to operate while providing improved lighting, indoor air quality, and healthier places to live and work.

The Future of Green Building Materials

The architecture of the Industrial Revolution and the Scientific Revolution expresses the values and worldviews of society at that time. Future revolutions are likely to affect the building industry just as profoundly. New fields of scientific investigation such as holographic philosophy, virtual reality, and chaos theory may alter our perspective dramatically—and so our building. The information revolution of the computer age might alter our working relationships and daily interactions and the corresponding need for certain types of buildings. Space exploration may birth new technologies, new needs, and new worldviews. Collapsing economies and dwindling natural resources may salute an energy revolution, affecting building design and promoting new markets for renewable energy products.

The design of buildings individually and collectively (urban design) reflects our culture, our consistently shifting attitudes about issues beyond the simple need for shelter. It also reflects real and significant economic and environmental factors. Traditionally, economic and environmental issues have been isolated from each other. More and more, we are coming to understand how closely linked they are. Any one of the possible future revolutions just cited will have social, economic and environmental components. The difference from previous eras, however, is that we are more likely to recognize them as they occur.

Current trends that may evolve or contribute to the next revolution include (in no particular order): China, terrorism, nanotechnology, and the widening gap between the world's rich and poor.

Clearly, all markets, including the building industry, are dominated by the prospect of China's impacts. Some organizations salivate at the thought of the shear number of people acquiring disposable income and providing new markets to serve. Others see nothing but environmental doom for the planet as another two billion plus people start consuming. These observations are overly simplistic and imagine China's impacts in Western terms. The Chinese culture is quite different from Western culture, especially American culture. For example, Chinese are grounded in tradition. They have a long, respected history and tend to view events that happened generations ago as currently relevant. Americans rarely remember events from the previous administration and pride themselves on a rampantly carpe diem approach to life. The result is that political and economic decisions that China embraces will likely have relevance and meaning from a Chinese perspective that Americans may not understand. The size and determination of China is such that a lack of American understanding may result in a radical shift in global superpowers. Indeed, the demographics of global commerce may alter such that Mandarin (the primary language of nearly a quarter of the world's population) becomes a fundamental prerequisite for success. Chinese culture may establish the global mean.

In the midst of the evolution of shifting global superpowers is the specter of terrorism. Individuals, groups of individuals, and 'rogue' nations have become political and economic wild cards. In the USA, Homeland Security is center stage and will be for the foreseeable future. Security issues are pervasive. The U.S. federal government sponsors a website providing information to the public (www.ready.gov), municipalities struggle with disaster preparedness protocols and simulation exercises, and corporations look at options for decentralization and redundancy of critical support services. Suddenly, alternative energy and utilities are being reexamined not for their environmental benefits, but for the possible security benefits that they may offer.

One of the hottest technology topics today is nanotechnology, the science and technology of controlling matter at the nanoscale—the scale of a billionth of a meter—1/100,000 the width of a human hair, or 10 times the diameter of a hydrogen atom. A billionth of a meter is called a nanometer. Already, nanoscale zinc oxides are used in sunscreen lotions and scratch-resistant glass. Nanoscale fibers are used in stain-resistant fabrics. Digital camera displays, high resolution printer inks, and high-capacity computer hard drives have benefited from nanoscience and nanoengineering. Demand for domestic nanomaterials in 2002 has been estimated at $200 million and is projected to grow an astonishing 33 percent a year; the National Science Foundation has estimated that nanotechnology applications may be valued at more than $1 trillion in the global economy by 2015.

The potential impacts on the market extend to nearly every conceivable product and service. For example, the solution to looming water scarcity, one of the world's leading environmental problems, may be found in nanotechnology.[2] The Nanotechnology Clean Water Initiative is applying nanotechnology to water management. The Israeli National Nanotechnology Initiative (INNI) has invested about $150 million in nanotechnology with an annual operating budget of around $25 million. The first fruits of the initiative are expected to come from three areas: pure membrane technology, integration of energy and membrane components and development of nanosensors. French utility company Generale Des Eaux has also developed its own nanofiltration technology in collaboration with Dow Chemical subsidiary Filmtec. One significant application of nanotechnology in water filtration is its ability to obviate the need for large industrial-size purification plants. Argonide Corporation, a Miami-based group that produces aluminum oxide nanofibers, has developed a filtration system for NASA, which will enable large amounts of water to be filtered without the need for large high-pressure pumps.

Unfortunately, another prominent trend is the increasing gap between rich and poor. This gap is widening both globally and nationally and indicates increasing political and economic instability. The USA does not fare well in the global comparisons. While the average workday in the USA has increased, other industrialized countries have experienced a decrease. Furthermore, the relative purchasing power of the U.S. dollar is decreasing. The average American citizen is working harder and earning less in real dollars.

The economic disparity between rich and poor may generate a variety of repercussions—depending upon the interplay of other variables. Political upheaval is one possibility. This may be localized. Given the globalization of society, a local event could trigger a severe domino effect. Because our economic structure has transformed, many things previously unimaginable are quite possible. Where we once had the centuries-old, secretive but well established, bank driven model (wherein banks are the primary source of finance and central banking systems the primary control mechanism) we now have a relatively new and unpredictable market driven model (wherein non-bank mechanisms, such as stocks, mortgage houses, credit companies, and investment brokers provide a plethora of funding sources and central banking systems control only the banking processes). Individual consumers can directly invest on credit obtained without benefit of a bank. More importantly, they can invest, based on real time, readily accessible information. Never before in human history has society been in such a position. The financial herd can raise companies larger than many countries; and, they can crush them in the blink of an eye. Individual investors can—and do—demand that companies alter behavior to be more socially and environmentally correct. This has become so common that it has earned a title, "shareholder activism." Thus, one possible result of the widening gap between rich and poor is a focused shareholder activism that forces corporations towards a more benevolent behavior. Shareholder activism often mandates corporate responsibilities that, in other circumstances, might have been assumed by the government either through regulatory controls or welfare benefits.

Recent Developments (Follow-up on Our Predictions for the Future of Green Building Materials in the First Edition)

In the First Edition, we focused on the trend towards a new field of accounting called *environmental accounting*, supported by many economists and politicians, including former Vice President Al Gore. Basically, environmental accounting revises the financial systems in this country, (taxes, prices, GNP evaluations, etc.) to reflect the value of forests, minerals, clean air and water, erosion of soils, and so forth. The theory requires a complete restructuring of global economic systems. Obviously, without a magic wand, such a wholesale restructuring is unlikely. Nevertheless, piecemeal applications of environmental accounting are becoming more numerous. These are already directly affecting the building industry in the sun rights, sewer rights, and pollution rights instituted at the local levels in cities such as New York, Houston, and Los Angeles.

Broader examples have indirect, but ultimately more significant, effects on the building industry. Following are the examples of broader applications of environmental accounting we presented in the First Edition with commentary as to their current status:

- *Elimination of federal subsidies to forestry, mining, and agricultural industries:* Historically, such subsidies were enacted to encourage the claiming and taming of Wild West lands. The federal government wanted to assist pioneers and support industry that attracted settlers into the wilderness, effectively bringing it under the national umbrella. However, long past the accomplishment of the goal, such subsidies remain entrenched. Consequently, taxpayers fund the roads that logging companies now use to burrow into our dwindling natural forests and the federal government contracts to sell timber below market rate to the mainstream timber industry. Many taxpayers are outraged for purely economic reasons. Add to their voices those of environmentalists, and politicians are taking notice. The topic of forest subsidies surfaces fairly regularly. Obviously, if such subsidies were reduced or removed, many sectors of the building industry would be affected.

  Current status: This remains an important and vigorously contentious topic. It is epitomized in the debate over drilling in the Alaskan Wildlife National Refuge (ANWR). Despite an overtly pro-drilling executive branch, the federal government has yet to open ANWR. The Energy Policy Act of 2005 (Public Law 109-58) which was signed into law in August 2005 excluded the provision from the original bill that permitted drilling for oil in the ANWR.[3] In July 2005, the Stop ExxonMobil Alliance[4] launched an unprecedented push to improve the corporate practices of two of the world's largest oil companies, Exxon and Mobil, which were allowed to merge in 1999 to form a corporate behemoth with unprecedented power and government influence. The Alliance consists of many of America's leading environmental, human rights, pro-democracy and social justice organizations. The specific actions the group is promoting include: boycotting ExxonMobil products, shareholder activism (Alliance members are bringing key human rights and environment resolutions before company shareholders in 2005. These resolutions call on corporate management to take specific steps to improve ExxonMobil's terrible record. Most educational institutions have large investment funds with shares in ExxonMobil. So does TIAA-CREF, the investment manager with which many faculty and staff members have their pension funds), and encouraging employees to stop working for the company. They have successfully publicized a laundry list of corporate ills, focusing on the fact that ExxonMobil is the only oil company remaining in Arctic Power, the single-issue group lobbying to open the ANWR to drilling.

- *BTU tax:* The taxation of energy—and, more particularly, the pollution it spawns—is also a recurring political subject. Many countries tax energy. Gasoline, for example, is consistently cheaper in the United States than anywhere else in the world due, in part, to the fact that other countries levy a considerable tax on it. If in the United States gasoline were taxed commensurate with the cost for pollution cleanup, the ripple effect would permeate all industries, including the building industry.

  Current Status: This is not a strong contender at the federal level although an increasing number of state and local governments are looking at "sin" taxes.

- *Raw materials tax:* This is an ideal discussed by environmentalists and economists more than politicians. A raw materials tax is conceived as a deterrent to consuming the Earth's resources. Not only is forestry subsidized in the United States, but the value of the land is not seen to diminish once the forest is harvested. A raw materials tax would invest the forest with a measurable value in and of itself.

  Current Status: This remains an academic possibility.

- *Pollution tax:* Like a raw materials tax, a pollution tax works on the principle of taxing that which is undesirable versus that which is desirable (such as earnings). Generally, pollution taxation is proposed as a combination of penalties and incentives. For example, in a given industry sector as determined by existing IRS designations, a median pollution level for each measurable pollutant would be established. Those who exceeded the median would pay a tax (a penalty), and those who emitted less than the median would receive a bonus. If the bonus were derived from the penalties, the taxation would essentially pay for itself, and continuous improvement would be encouraged as industry members vied among themselves to reduce pollution, thereby lowering the median.

  Current Status: This is not a strong contender at the federal level although an increasing number of state and local governments are looking at "sin" taxes.

- *Trading credits:* Examples of trading credits are already emerging in both the private and pubic arenas. When items such as solar access, sewer rights, wetlands, and trash are assigned a limit, they immediately gain financial value. In the late 1980s, Houston was so overbuilt that it did not have sufficient wastewater treatment facilities to handle new construction. The city implemented a system of sewer rights, where properties were assigned an allowable number of water closets based on the square footage of the property. By virtue of the limitation, the sewer rights became valuable, tradable commodities. The EPA has developed guidance for the establishment and use of wetland mitigation banks. "Land owners needing to 'mitigate' or compensate for authorized impacts to wetlands associated with development activities may have the option of purchasing credits from an approved mitigation bank rather than restoring or creating wetlands on or near the development site."[5] There are approximately 100 mitigation banks in 34 states, including the first private entrepreneurial banks.

Current Status: Despite the lack of a national, political commitment to Kyoto, there is a national, economic response. The Chicago Climate Exchange® (CCX®)[6] was opened to the public in 2001. Its development bears all the hallmarks of a capitalist tradition responding to the market drivers. In this case, those market drivers are public concerns regarding climate change and the environment. The CCX is a greenhouse gas emission reduction and trading program for emission sources and offset projects in the United States, Canada, and Mexico. Continuous electronic trading of greenhouse gas emission allowances and offsets began on December 12, 2003 and will continue through 2006 as a pilot program.

- *Full disclosure of corporate environmental impact:* This significant issue for many corporations tends to be driven more by economic vectors than by political debate. In environmental arenas, it is referred to as *transparency*. It is one thing to state that one is operating in an environmentally friendly manner, but it is quite another to document it. As ISO 14000 standards, which have the support of the World Trade Organization, become more prevalent, stakeholders are starting to ask for verification and documentation of environmental stewardship. A growing number of investment funds advertise themselves as "socially" or "environmentally" responsible, and purport to use social and environmental screens to build their portfolios. Stockholders are asking questions and demanding answers.

Current Status: Increased shareholder activism is leveraging not only the targeted companies, but also non-targeted companies that experience a 'ripple' effect from shareholder demands in the USA and internationally. This trend towards greater environmental risk management and demand for transparency is also evident in Europe with REACH *(Registration, Evaluation and Authorisation of CHemicals)*. In October 2003, the European Commission adopted a proposal for a new EU regulatory framework for chemicals. REACH.[7] The *Registration* requirement of REACH compels manufacturers and importers to submit information to a central database on hazard, exposure, and risk on 30,000 new and existing substances that are produced or imported in yearly quantities exceeding one metric ton. *Evaluation* requires regulators to assess risks for 5,000 substances that are produced or imported in yearly quantities exceeding 100 tons, and also for substances in lower quantities if they are "of concern." The recently established European

Chemicals Agency will then determine if further testing is needed. *Authorization* applies to substances of "very high concern," for which specific permission would be required for certain uses. Approximately 1400, or 5 percent, of registered substances will be subject to authorization. REACH is applicable not only to the 30,000 specifically referenced chemicals, but also to the downstream products, which are widely used by consumers and business of all sorts that contain these chemicals.[8]

- *Green leases:* Green leasing of building products offers a potentially profitable new merchandising approach. It represents stronger, more lasting business relationships, and provides the groundwork for better environmental stewardship by all parties.

  Current Status: Take-back programs, a variant of green leasing, are becoming more common for a variety of products including: equipment, carpet, ceiling tiles, and various plastic products. Under take-back programs, the product manufacturer "takes back" used products, scrap material and/or packaging associated with its product. Many take-back programs provide a commitment to reclaim the product, refurbish it for reuse, and/or disassemble it for recycling as appropriate.

- *Revised GNP:* The Department of Commerce, Bureau of Economic Statistics; is developing measures of economic value of environmental assets, such as renewable resources, nonrenewable resources, air quality, and water quality.[9]

  Current Status: This remains an academic possibility.

Green Building Material Response to Changing Conditions

Current and continuing market effects of green considerations on products encompass packaging, labeling, sourcing, processing, and, of course, development of new products. Reducing, reusing, and recycling packaging is one of the low-hanging fruit options that most competitive manufacturers have already embraced.

- *Alternative packaging:* Alternative packaging, such as starch-based pellets and wraps, is likely to become more prevalent.

- *Labeling:* Labeling of both product and packaging is in the process of becoming more sophisticated and more common. At one time, the ubiquitous arrows-chasing-arrows symbol for recycling was the banal attempt of manufacturers to support recycling. Now, many indicate the type of plastic used in order to facilitate the sorting of feedstock for efficient recycling. Furthermore, under the auspices of the Federal Trade Commission, environmental information given on labels is becoming more substantial. *Greenwashing,* the superficial and unreliable endorsement of green issues, is becoming less and less frequent. And, because so much good information is becoming available, where greenwashing does occur, it tends to be readily apparent and not likely to fool consumers. Green information presented in labels may include certification of nontoxic content, organic content, recycled content (pre/post), life-cycle impact, and recycling classification of both product and packaging.

- *Alternative feedstock:* The sources of feedstock for manufacturing once heralded virgin materials; now they are equally proud of recycled content. The infrastructure that delivers recycled material to manufacturing facilities is growing. Similarly, the support of biobased alternative agricultural products is growing. The first biobased items for federal procurement were designated in 2005 under the Federal Biobased Products Preferred Procurement Program.[10]

- *Manufacturing processes:* New technologies for improved energy efficiency and cleaner process are gaining ground environmentally and economically. Low-emission microwave finishing, for example, can allow a fabricator to minimize the energy required in the coating process and reduce the waste heat generated. Cleaner operations lower regulatory and insurance costs. The Design for the Environment (DFE) approach, combined with green leasing, is also likely to play a role in manufacturing processes of the future.

- *New products:* Perhaps the most noticeable change is the growing availability of new, greener products. Such products include a wide variety of alternate energy systems and a renaissance in agricultural products. Solar-powered roofing shingles, waterless urinals, soy-based adhesives and plastics, bamboo flooring, and strawboard sheathing panels offer an ideal response to the federal commitment "to create and maintain conditions under which man and nature can exist in productive harmony, and fulfill the social, economic, and other requirements of present and future generations of Americans."[11]

Recommendations

The range of green building products that are currently available has grown exponentially in response to the growth in green building rating systems on the local, state, national, and international levels. They offer a range of aesthetic options. They perform well. They are cost-competitive. Many mainstream manufacturers have jumped on the bandwagon in response to the growth in demand and the realization that green building materials are not a fad that is soon going to fade away. It is not only *possible* to incorporate green building products into our design and construction practices; it is *imperative*.

It is our sincere and earnest hope that this book contributes to the redevelopment of our economic and political infrastructure in the support of sustainable approaches to green building. By promoting the use of green building products, we better serve our clients and the public. We provide a more efficient, less toxic building that respects the health, safety, and welfare of the building occupants and the community in general. And we help change the business of building in a positive way, one that helps to safeguard the "the social, economic, and other requirements of present and future generations of Americans."[12]

Notes

1. Section 101 [42 USC § 4331], Title 1, National Environmental Policy Act.
2. LONDON, November 18, 2003—Uri Sagman, Canadian scientist/entrepreneur, founds Nanotechnology Clean Water Initiative.

3. For an overview of the Act go to http://en.wikipedia.org/wiki/Energy_Policy_Act_of_2005#Provisions_in_the_original_bill_that_were_not_in_the_Act.

4. www.stopexxonmobil.org/campaign_info.html.

5. www.epa.gov/owow/wetlands/facts/fact16.html.

6. www.chicagoclimatex.com/.

7. http://europa.eu.int/comm/environment/chemicals/reach.htm.

8. For additional information on REACH and trends related to responsible chemicals management in Europe and the US, refer to:

   WWF European Policy office www.panda.org/epo/toxics

   Lowell Center for Sustainable Production www.chemicalspolicy.org

   European Environmental Bureau www.eeb.org/activities/chemicals/main.htm

   Clean Production Action www.cleanproduction.org

   European Commission www.europa.eu.int/comm/environment/index_en.htm

9. National Science and Technology Council, *Technology for a Sustainable Future: A Framework for Action* (Washington, D.C.: Government Printing Office, 1994), 800/ENV-6676.

10. www.biobased.oce.usda.gov.

11. Section 101 [42USC . . .]

12. Ibid.

Appendix A

Sources of Further Information

To assist readers in learning more, this appendix lists sources of additional information about green building materials and green buildings.

Alliance for Sustainability (AFS)
1521 University Avenue SE
Minneapolis, MN 55414
(612) 331-1099; fax (612) 379-1527
email: iasa@mtn.org; www.afs.nonprofitoffice
    .com/index.asp

The mission of the Alliance is to bring about personal, organizational, and planetary sustainability through support of projects that are ecologically sound, economically viable, socially just, and humane. The Alliance for Sustainability is a Minnesota-based, tax-deductible nonprofit supporting model sustainability projects on the local, national, and international levels.

Resources: *Manna* (e-Newsletter)

Alliance to Save Energy
1200 Eighteenth Street NW, Suite 900
Washington, DC 20036
(202) 857-0666; fax (202) 331-9588
email: info@ase.org; www.ase.org

The Alliance focuses on improving energy efficiency in new and existing buildings. It promotes energy-efficient housing through energy rating systems, assesses the effects of federal and state fiscal policies, and identifies energy-efficient products and services nationwide.

Resources: *Energy Efficiency Resource Directory: A Guide to Utility Programs; Energy Innovations*

American Council for an Energy-Efficient Economy (ACEEE)
1001 Connecticut Avenue NW, Suite 801
Washington, DC 20036
(202) 429-8873; fax (202) 429-2248
email: info@aceee.org; www.aceee.org

ACEEE explores the links between energy efficiency, economic prosperity, a cleaner environment, and other aspects of national and global concern. It conducts technical and policy assessments, advises governments and utilities, works collaboratively with businesses, and organizes conferences.

Resources: *Commercial Building Performance Resources* (website)

American Environmental Health Foundation (AEHF)

8345 Walnut Hill Lane, Suite 225
Dallas, TX 75231
(214) 361-9515
email: aehf@aehf.com; www.aehf.com

AEHF was founded in 1975 to research chemical sensitivity and to educate the public about it. The Foundation Store carries almost 1,500 environmentally safe products for the home and office. These products are designed for both the chemically sensitive individual and the environmentally aware person.

Resources: Catalog of environmentally safe products; articles on chemical sensitivity, indoor and outdoor air quality, and organic gardening

American Institute of Architects (AIA)

1735 New York Avenue NW
Washington, DC 20006
(202) 626-7300; fax (202) 626-7547
email: infocentral@aia.org; www.aia.org

The AIA's Committee on the Environment (COTE) works to sustain and improve the environment by advancing and disseminating environmental knowledge and values and by advocating the best design practices to integrate built and natural systems to the profession, industry, and public.

Resources: *AIA Environmental Resource Guide*

American Local Power Project

4281 Piedmont Avenue
Oakland, California 94611
(510) 451-1727
www.local.org

This project, a proponent of accelerated green power development, has worked for years to design and win enactment of public purchasing and financing essential to making acceleration of green power both possible and economically feasible. Local Power assists municipal, county, and state agencies in finding alternative energy providers and using decentralized solar power and other technologies to stabilize their community's energy costs, reduce exposure to grid power volatility, and clean up their air.

American Nature Study Society (ANSS)

RR2, Box 1010
Dingman's Ferry, PA 18328
(717) 828-9692; fax (717) 828-9695
email: anssonline@aol.com;
   http://hometown.aol.com/anssonline

ANSS is the oldest environmental education organization in the United States. It disseminates environmental information via its journal and newsletter.

Resources: *Nature Study* (journal); *The American Nature Study Society Newsletter*

American Rivers

1025 Vermont Avenue NW, Suite 720
Washington, DC 20005
(202) 347-7550; fax (202) 347-9240
email: amrivers@amrivers.org;
   www.amrivers.org

American Rivers works toward achieving healthy rivers, abundant fish and wildlife, and thriving river communities. Emphasis is on water quality, water scarcity, and sprawl solutions.

Resources: Toolkits on a variety of subjects; publications on subjects such as sprawl, community watersheds, and clean water

American Solar Energy Society, Inc. (ASES)

2400 Central Avenue, Suite A
Boulder, CO 80301
(303) 443-3130; fax (303) 443-3212
email: ASES@ASES.org; www.ases.org

ASES is a national organization dedicated to advancing the use of solar energy for the benefit of U.S. citizens and the global environment. ASES promotes the widespread near- and long-term use of solar energy.

Resources: *Solar Today* (magazine); *Sunbeam* (online newsletter); *ASES Reports*

Architects, Designers, and Planners for Social Responsibility (ADPSR)

P.O. Box 9126
Berkeley, CA 94709-0126
(415) 974-1306
email: forum@adpsr.org; www.adpsr.org

ADPSR works for peace, environmental protection, ecological building, social justice, and the development of healthy communities.

Resources: New Village Press books; *Architectural Resource Guide (ARG)* by Northern California Chapter

Associated Air Balance Council (AABC)

1518 K Street NW, Suite 503
Washington, DC 20005
(202) 737-0202; fax (202) 638-4833
email: info@aabcdirect.com;
www.aabchq.com

AABC is a professional organization for consultants and contractors in the HVAC and mechanical professions that works to promote state-of-the-art TAB procedures and services through technical papers and other publications such as the AABC National Standards, the industry's first comprehensive standards for field measurement and instrumentation.

Resources: *TAB Journal; TAB Specifications;* commissioning guidelines; sample specifications

Association for the Environmental Health of Soils (AEHS)

150 Fearing Street
Amherst, MA 01002
(413) 549-5170; fax (413) 549-0579
email: info@AEHS.com; www.aehs.com

AEHS is a clearinghouse for technical and regulatory information on soil issues, including chemistry, geology, hydrogeology, engineering, modeling, toxicology, regulatory science, and the law.

Resources: *Soil and Sediment Contamination* (journal); *International Journal of Phytoremediation*

Alliance of Foam Packaging Recyclers (AFPR)

1298 Cronson Boulevard, Suite 201
Crofton, MD 21114
(410) 451-8340; fax (410) 451-8343
email: info@epspackaging.com;
www.epspackaging.org

Formed in 1991 by over 80 companies representing every major manufacturer of EPS protective foam packaging, their raw material suppliers and equipment manufacturers work to facilitate EPS recycling between EPS manufacturers. The Alliance has more than 200 plant locations nationwide to serve as central collection points and help produce foam packaging made with recycled content. Emphasis is on encouraging the reuse of loose-fill foam packaging and the recycling and reprocessing of molded foam packaging.

ASID Sustainable Design Information Center

608 Massachusetts Avenue NE
Washington, DC 20002-6006
(202) 546-3480
www.asid.org/asid2/resource/sustainable.asp

This website offers general information on sustainability and green design and multiple links to resources available online. The Sustainable Design Council, composed of seven professional members, supervises this section of the website and oversees the ASID sustainable design strategic initiative.

Association for Efficient Environmental Energy Systems (AEEES)

P.O. Box 598
Davis, CA 95617
(530) 750-0135; fax: (530) 750-0137
email: info@aeees.org; www.aeees.org

AEEES is a nonprofit educational organization that works to bring geothermal heat pump use into the West Coast region of the United States. AEEES also supports the growth of other energy-efficient building technologies.

Resources: Publications, news articles, and videos

Athena Sustainable Materials Institute
email: info@athenaSMI.ca;
www.athenasmi.ca

The Institute works to facilitate the use of LCA in green building rating and assessment systems such as LEED and Green Globes. Researches the development, verification and updating of databases supporting environmental impact estimator software.

Resources: Environmental impact estimator; product life cycle inventory studies

Best Practices Benchmarking for Energy Efficiency Programs
Kenneth James, Ph.D., PG&E Project
Manager
(415) 973-0246
email: bestpractices@qcworld.com;
www.eebestpractices.com/index.asp

The project works to develop and communicate excellent practices nationwide in order to enhance the design, implementation, and evaluation of energy efficiency programs. The project uses a benchmarking methodology to identify best practices for a wide variety of program types.

Resources: *Best Practices Program Area Reports*

Bioenergy Information Network
Bioenergy Feedstock Development Program
(BFDP)
Environmental Sciences Division
Oak Ridge National Laboratory
P.O. Box 2008, MS-6422
Oak Ridge, TN 37837-6422
(865) 574-7818; fax: (865) 574-7287
email: bfdp@ornl.gov;
http://bioenergy.ornl.gov/

This DOE-funded project organizes renewable energy outreach activities, focusing on domestic production, recovery, and conversion of energy crops (fast-growing trees and grasses) and residues to economically priced, environmentally beneficial fuels and power generation.

Biomass Program
Energy Efficiency and Renewable Energy
U.S. Department of Energy
1000 Independence Avenue SW, EE-2E,
5H-021
Washington, DC 20585
www.eere.energy.gov/biomass/

The DOE Office of the Biomass Program (OBP) partners with U.S. industry to foster research and development on advanced technologies that will transform the abundant biomass resources of the United States into clean, affordable, and domestically produced biofuels, biopower, and high-value bioproducts. The Biomass Program is the combination of several previously separate programs: the Biofuels Program, the Biopower Program, and the biomass-related elements of research formerly sponsored by the Office of Industrial Technologies (OIT).

Resources: Biomass document database; Biomass project fact sheets

Bonneville Environmental Foundation (BFE)
133 SW Second Avenue, Suite 410
Portland, OR 97204
(866) 233-8247; fax: (503) 248-1908
email: info@b-e-f.org; www.b-e-f.org

The Foundation supports watershed restoration programs and the development of new sources of renewable energy. BEF markets green power products to public utilities, businesses, government agencies, and individuals.

Resources: *Quarterly electronic newsletter, Carbon Calculator*

BSI Americas
BSI Management Systems
12110 Sunset Hills Road
Reston, VA 20190-5902

(800) 862-4977; fax: (703) 435-7979
email: inquiry@bsiamericas.com;
www.bsiamericas.com

BSI is a third-party agency that offers ISO 14001 registration.

Resources: *International Environmental Systems Update;* guidance documents about ISO 14001

BuildingGreen, Inc.

122 Birge Street, Suite 30
Brattleboro, VT 05301
(802) 257-7300; fax: (802) 257-7304
email: info@buildinggreen.com;
www.buildinggreen.com

This organization provides articles, reviews, and news on energy-efficient, resource-efficient, and healthy building practices and products.

Resources: *Environmental Building News (EBN); GreenSpec Directory; Green Building Products Directory; Green Building Advisor* (CD-ROM)

Business for Social Responsibility (BSR)

111 Sutter Street, 12th Floor
San Francisco, CA 94104
(415) 984-3200; fax (415) 984-3201
www.bsr.org

BSR is a global organization that helps member companies achieve success in ways that respect ethical values, people, communities, and the environment. BSR provides information, tools, training, and advisory services to make corporate social responsibility an integral part of business operations and strategies. A nonprofit organization, BSR promotes cross-sector collaboration and contributes to global efforts to advance the field of corporate social responsibility. Environmental programs utilized by BSR members include green design, green product design, waste reduction, and energy efficiency.

Resources: *Environmental Issue Briefs*

Buy Recycled Business Alliance (MRBA)

1325 G Street NW, Suite 1025
Washington, DC 20005
email: info@brba-epp.org; www.brba-epp.org

The Alliance encourages appropriate business strategies for green products and services by providing education, tools, mentoring, and leadership by example. Emphasis is on green purchasing program, green building programs, recycled content materials, and green packaging.

Resources: *Green Library*

Canadian Institute of Chartered Accountants

277 Wellington Street W
Toronto ON M5V 3H2
Canada
(416) 977-3222; fax: (416) 977-8585
www.cica.ca/index.cfm

This group prepared the Environmental Performance and Shareholder Value Creation Survey, which identified a number of opportunities for companies in all industries to implement more effective environmental performance measurement and management systems that support long-term shareholder value creation.

Center for Economic and Environmental Partnership (CEEP)

(718) 863-4156

CEEP funds and sponsors programs promoting development of an effective and competitive environmental industry in New York State and advances development of sound environmental business policies and programs in New York State and elsewhere. Emphasis is on high-performance buildings; alternative, distributed, and renewable nergy (ADRE); and solid waste and recycling (SWR).

Center for Maximum Potential Building Systems, Inc. (CMPBS)

8604 FM 969
Austin, TX 78724

(512) 928-4786; fax (512) 926-4418
email: center@cmpbs.org; www.cmpbs.org

CMPBS works with public entities, professional organizations, community groups, universities, and individuals to develop sustainable building policies and practices that cover individual buildings to entire regions.

Resources: Reports and compendia

Center for Plant Conservation
Missouri Botanical Garden
P.O. Box 299
St. Louis, MO 63166-0299
(314) 577-9450; fax (314) 577-9465
email: CPC@MOBOT.org;
    www.centerforplantconservation.org

The Center focuses on conserving rare and endangered native plants through research, cultivation, and education at botanical gardens and arboreta in the United States. Emphasis is on five priority regions: Hawaii, Florida, California, Texas, and Puerto Rico.

Resources: *Ex Situ Plant Conservation; Plant Conservation Directory; Genetics and Conservation of Rare Plants*

Center for Resourceful Building
   Technology (CRBT)
127 Higgins, Suite 201
Missoula, MT 59802
email: crbt@ncat.org; www.crbt.org

CRBT is dedicated to promoting environmentally responsible practices in construction. It works to serve as both catalyst and facilitator in encouraging building technologies that realize a sustainable and efficient use of resources. CRBT identifies and promotes building products and methods that do more with less.

Resources: *Guide to Resource Efficient Building Elements* (online)

Center for Health, Environment,
   and Justice
PO Box 6806
Falls Church, VA 22040

(703) 237-2249; fax (703) 237-8389
email: chej@chej.org; www.chej.org

CHEJ assists communities in combating environmental threats. Emphasis is on a contaminated sites campaign, including convicting the EPA for child abuse for not cleaning up these sites.

Resources: Campaign reports

Certified Forest Products Council
   (CFPC)
14780 SW Osprey Drive, Suite 285
Beaverton, OR 97007-8424
(503) 590-6600; fax (503) 590-6655
www.certifiedwood.org.

CFPC is a nonprofit, voluntary business initiative committed to promoting responsible forest product buying practices throughout North America in an effort to improve forest management practices worldwide. Emphasis is on the purchase, use, and sale of third-party, independently certified forest products.

Resources: *Certified Forest Products* (searchable database)

Chemical Injury Information Network
   (CIIN)
PO Box 301
White Sulphur Springs, MT 59645
(406) 547-2255; fax (406) 547-3455
www.ciin.org

CIIN is a support and advocacy organization dealing with multiple chemical sensitivities (MCS). It is run by the chemically injured for the benefit of the chemically injured and focuses primarily on education, credible research into MCS, and the empowerment of the chemically injured.

Resources: *Our Toxic Times; Environmental Directory; Nontoxic Buying Guide*

City Bikes
2501 Champlain Street NW
Washington, DC 20009
(202) 265-1564; fax (202) 462-7020
www.citybikes.com

City Bikes supports local, regional, and national bicycle and other nonmotorized transportation advocacy groups and events, maintains a comprehensive recycling program, and provides support for cycling awareness and safety programs for children.

Clean Water Action

4455 Connecticut NW, Suite A300
Washington, DC 20008
(202) 895-0420; fax (202) 895-0430
www.cleanwateraction.org

This national citizens' organization works for clean, safe, and affordable water and to prevent health-threatening pollution, create environmentally safe jobs and businesses, and empower people to make democracy work. Emphasis is on citizen organizing and education.

Resources: *Clean Water Action News;* fact sheets and reports

Climate, Community, and Biodiversity Alliance (CCBA)

c/o Center for Environmental Leadership in
  Business
1919 M Street NW, Suite 600
Washington, DC 20036
(202) 912-1438; fax (202) 912-1047
email: info@climatestandards.org;
  www.climate-standards.org

CCBA is a global alliance promoting integrated solutions to land management. It designs triple-benefit voluntary standards to identify land management projects that simultaneously minimize climate change, support sustainable development, and combat loss of biodiversity.

Resources: Project design standards

Cohousing Association of the United States c/o WHDC

4676 Broadway, 2nd Floor
Boulder, CO 80304
(314) 754-5828
www.cohousing.org

The Cohousing Association of the United States (Coho/US) is dedicated to promoting and encouraging the cohousing concept, supporting both individuals and groups in creating communities, providing assistance to completed groups for improving their systems for living together in community, and creating networking opportunities for those involved or interested in cohousing.

Resources: *Cohousing* (magazine); *Cohousing* (e-zine)

Collaborative for High-Performance Schools (CHPS)

(877) 642-CHPS
email: info@chps.net; www.chps.net

The Collaborative facilitates the design of high-performance schools—that is, environments that are not only energy efficient but also healthy, comfortable, well lit, and containing the amenities needed for a quality education by providing information to school districts and designers.

Resources: *Low-Emitting Materials Products List; Best Practices Manual; Materials Specification;* fact sheets on commissioning, IAQ, and acoustics

Construction Industry Compliance Association (CICA)

National Center for Manufacturing Services
3025 Boardwalk
Ann Arbor, MI 48108-3230
(800) 222-6267; fax (734) 995-4004
www.CICAcenter.org

CICA is a source for plain-language explanations of environmental rules for the construction industry. This information is provided free by the National Center for Manufacturing Sciences with the assistance of: Associated General Contractors of America and National Association of Home Builders. Emphasis is on laws in the areas of: stormwater, C&D debris, hazardous/toxic waste, air, wetlands, endangered species, green buildings, and safety and health.

Construction Materials Recycling Association (CMRA)

(630) 585-7530; fax (630) 585-7593
email: info@cdrecycling.org;
  www.cdrecycling.org

CMRA is devoted exclusively to the needs of the rapidly expanding North American construction waste and demolition debris processing and recycling industry. It promotes the acceptance and use of recycled construction materials, including concrete, asphalt, wood, and gypsum.

Consumer Product Safety Commission (CPSC)

4330 East-West Highway
Bethesda, Maryland 20814-4408
(800) 638-CPSC; fax (301) 504-0124
email: info@cpsc.gov; www.cpsc.gov

The CPSC is charged with protecting the public from unreasonable risks of serious injury or death from more than 15,000 types of consumer products under the agency's jurisdiction. It is committed to protecting consumers and families from products that pose fire, electrical, chemical, or mechanical hazard or can injure children, and it issues product safety alerts and recalls.

Resources: Publications on a wide variety of consumer safety issues

Cool Roof Rating Council (CRRC)

1738 Excelsior Avenue
Oakland, CA 94602
(866) 465-2523; fax (510) 482-4421
email: info@coolroofs.org; www.coolroofs.org

CRRC provides building code bodies, energy service providers, architects and specifiers, property owners and community planners with accurate radiative property data on roof surfaces that may improve the energy efficiency of buildings while positively impacting the environment. CRRC administers a strict rating program under which companies can label various roof surface products with radiative property values.

Resources: *Rated Products Directory*

Co-op America

1612 K Street NW, Suite 600
Washington, DC 20006
(800) 58-GREEN; (202) 872-5307; fax (202) 331-8166
email: info@coopamerica.org;
  www.coopamerica.org

Co-op America provides economic strategies, organizing power, and practical tools for businesses and individuals addressing social and environmental problems. It focuses on educating and empowering people and businesses to make significant improvements through the economic system.

Resources: *National Green Pages; Co-op America Quarterly; Financial Planning Handbook*

Conservation International

1919 M Street NW, Suite 600
Washington, DC 20036
(800) 406-2306; fax (202) 887-0193
www.conservation.org

Conservation International focuses on the conservation of ecosystems and the preservation of biological diversity. It emphasizes working with partner organizations and locals in tropical and temperate countries to develop and implement ecosystem conservation projects.

Resources: *Conservation Frontlines; eNews Update*

Council on Economic Priorities (CEP)

30 Irving Place
New York, NY 10003
(800) 729-4237; fax (212) 420-0988
email: tknowlton@cepnyc.org;
  www.cepnyc.org

CEP evaluates and encourages corporate social and environmental responsibility. It has established the Corporate Environmental Data Clearinghouse, which profiles the environmental performance of hundreds of companies.

Resources: *Shopping for a Better World*

Defenders of Wildlife

1130 Seventeenth Street NW
Washington, DC 20036
(800) 989-8981; fax (202) 682-1331
email: info@defenders.org;
    www.defenders.org

Defenders of Wildlife protects native wild
animals and plants in their natural communities. Programs focus on what scientists consider two of the most serious environmental
threats to the planet: the accelerating rate of
extinction of species and the associated loss of
biological diversity, and habitat alteration and
destruction.

Resources: *Defenders* (quarterly magazine); electronic newsletters; reports

Design for the Environment

Industrial Research Assistance Program
National Research Council of Canada
Building M55, Montreal Road
Ottawa, Ontario K1A OR6
Canada
(613) 993-5326; fax (613) 952-1086;
email: Jim.Rollefson@nrc-cnrc.gc.ca;
    http://dfe-sce.nrc-cnrc.gc.ca/home_e.html

Design for Environment (DfE) is the sys-
tematic integration of environmental considerations into product and process design. It provides an organized structure into which
companies can integrate most features of sustainable development, e.g., eco-efficiency,
pollution prevention, and clean production.
DfE focuses on seven strategies to develop
products that incorporate environmental considerations: new concept development, physical optimization, material use optimization,
production optimization, distribution optimization, impact reduction during use, and
end-of-life systems optimization.

Resources: *Design for the Environment
Guide*

Designing and Building Healthy Places

Centers for Disease Control and Prevention
    (CDC)
1600 Clifton Road
Atlanta, GA 30333
(404) 639-3311
email: ncehinfo@cdc.org;
    www.cdc.gov/healthyplaces

CDC studies the interaction between people
and their environments, natural as well as
human-made, as they relate to public health.
Emphasis is on health issues related to land use.

Development Center for Appropriate Technology (DCAT)

P.O. Box 27513
Tucson, AZ 85726-7513
(520) 624-6628; fax (520) 798-3701
www.dcat.net

DCAT works to enhance the health of the
planet and communities by promoting a shift
to sustainable construction and development
through leadership, strategic relationships, and
education. DCAT's primary program is called
Building Sustainability into the Codes. It explores approaches to creating a sustainable
context for building codes, working with national regulatory and green building organizations.

Earth Island Institute

300 Broadway, Suite 28
San Francisco, CA 94133-3312
(415) 788-3666; fax (415) 788-7324
www.earthisland.org

The Institute develops innovative projects
for the conservation, preservation, and restoration of the global environment. Earth Island's
Project Network consists of more than 30
projects worldwide, education and activist
campaigns, to address many of the most pressing social and environmental issues.

Resources: *Earth Island Journal; Island-
Wire;* multimedia and videos

Earth 911

730 East Helm, Building D
Scottsdale, AZ 85260
(800) CLEANUP; fax (480) 889-2660
email: education@earth911.org;
    www.earth911.org/master.asp

This organization works to empower the public with community-specific resources for improving quality of life. It is a public-private partnership that effectuates prevention ideals and offers community-specific information about recycling centers, green shopping, energy conservation, household hazardous waste, kids/environmental information, and composting, among other topics.
Resources: Electronic newsletter

Earthwatch Institute
3 Clock Tower Place, Suite 100, Box 75
Maynard, MA 01754
(800) 776-0188; fax (978) 461-2332
www.earthwatch.org

Earthwatch Institute engages people worldwide in scientific field research and education to promote the understanding and action necessary for a sustainable environment. It accomplishes this through three primary objectives: education, research, and conservation.
Resources: *Off the Beaten Path* (newsletter)

Ecospecifier
Centre for Design at RMIT
GPO Box 2476V
Melbourne, Victoria, 3001
Australia
61 7 3348 4177; fax 61 3 9639 3412
email: info@ecospecifier.org;
www.ecospecifier.org

Ecospecifier is a guide to eco-preferable products and materials for the construction industry, specifically targeted at the needs of decision makers and specifiers. It responds to the need for greater clarity about what is and is not green, for the desire to specify products that will lead to better indoor air quality and well-being, and for the growing body of public- and private-sector clients who want to save energy and water and to use sustainable resources.
Resources: *Environmentally Preferable Products* (database); technical guides

Energy Crossroads
email: EETDwebmaster@lbl.gov;
http://eetd.lbl.gov/EnergyCrossroads

This is Lawrence Berkeley National Laboratory's contribution to organizing a wide array of pointers to energy-efficient resources on the Internet.
Resources: Links to nearly 700 websites

Energy Efficient Building Association (EEBA)
10740 Lyndale Avenue S, Suite 10W
Bloomington, MN 55420-5615
(952) 881-1098; fax (952) 881-3048
email: info@eeba.org; www.eeba.org

EEBA promotes awareness, education, and development of energy-efficient, environmentally responsible buildings and communities.
Resources: *Builder Guides; Houses That Work*

Energy Efficiency and Renewable Energy Program
Oak Ridge National Laboratory (ORNL)
P.O. Box 2008
Oak Ridge, TN 37831-6186
(865) 576-8176; fax (865) 576-7572
email: eere@ornl.gov;
www.ornl.gov/sci/eere/

ORNL's Energy Efficiency and Renewable Energy Program develops sustainable energy technologies that foster a cleaner environment, a stronger economy, and a more secure future for the nation. The program conducts research in distributed energy, buildings, weatherization, federal energy management, and renewables.

Energy Ideas Clearinghouse
Washington State University Extension
Energy Program
P.O. Box 43165
Olympia, WA 98504-3165
(360) 956-2237
email: info@energyideas.org;
www.energyideas.org

Established in 1990, the Energy Ideas Clearinghouse provides the most comprehensive, technical resource that Pacific Northwest business, industry, government and utilities can use to implement energy technologies and practices.

Resources: Energy newsbriefs; electronic mailing lists

Energy Outreach Center (EOC)
Climate Solutions
610 Fourth Avenue E
Olympia, WA 98501-1113
(360) 352-1763; fax (360) 943-4977
email: info@climatesolutions.org;
    www.climatesolutions.org

The EOC provides information to the public about home energy conservation and renewable energy. Emphasis is on home energy analysis service, residential heat loss calculations, classes and workshops, information center, newsletters, and research.

Resources: Downloadable fact sheets

Energy Star Programs
U.S. Environmental Protection Agency
Climate Protection Partnerships Division
1200 Pennsylvania Avenue NW, MS-6202J
Washington, DC 20460
(888) STAR-YES
www.energystar.gov

Energy Star is a government-backed program helping businesses and individuals protect the environment through superior energy efficiency. Energy Star includes the Green Lights program.

Resources: Product specifications; product and manufacturer lists

Environmental Careers Organization (ECO)
30 Winter Street
Boston, MA 02108
(617) 426-4375; fax (617) 423-0998
www.eco.org

ECO's mission is to protect and enhance the environment through the development of diverse leaders, the promotion of careers, and the inspiration of individual action. ECO accomplishes this through internships, career advice, publications and research. Founded in 1972, ECO has placed more than 8,450 college and graduate students and recent graduates in environmental internships in the public, private, and nonprofit sectors. ECO is a leader in workforce diversity and mentorship, sponsoring 1,850 associates from over 200 colleges through its groundbreaking diversity initiative, which began in 1992.

Resources: *The ECO Guide to Careers That Make a Difference: Environmental Work for a Sustainable Future; The Complete Guide to Environmental Careers in the 21st Century; Increasing Diversity in the Environmental Field: The Report from the National Roundtable on Diversity in the Environment*

Environmental Construction Outfitters of New York
901 East One Hundred Thirty-fourth Street
Bronx, NY 10454
(800) 238-5008; fax (718) 742-5140
email: info@environmentaldepot.com;
    www.environmentaldepot.com

Environmental Construction Outfitters provides environmentally friendly products for both home and office use to the developer, architect, designer, contractor, and homeowner.

Resources: Information about environmental issues

Environmental Council of Concrete Organizations (ECCO)
5420 Old Orchard Road
Skokie, IL 60077-1083
email: jzuchman@ecco.org; www.ecco.org

ECCO communicates the environmental aspects of using concrete products on behalf of its members.

Resources: Searchable reference library; ECCO bulletins

Environmental Defense
257 Park Avenue S
New York, NY 10010

(212) 505-2100; fax (212) 505-2375
www.environmentaldefense.org

Through its program areas, Environmental Defense brings together experts in science, law, and economics to tackle complex environmental issues and develop sound solutions. Emphasis is on urgent issues such as climate and air, ecosystem restoration, environmental health, living cities, and health.

Resources: Fact sheets on environmental topics

Environmental Law Institute (ELI)

2000 L Street NW, Suite 620
Washington, DC 20036
(202) 939-3800; fax (202) 328-3868
email: law@eli.org; www2.eli.org/index/cfm

ELI provides information services, training courses and seminars, research programs, and policy recommendations to environmental professionals in government, industry, the private bar, public interest groups, and academia.

Resources: Publications catalog offering monographs, deskbooks, and reports; *The Environmental Forum, The Environmental Law Reporter, National Wetlands Newslette*r

Environmental Product Declarations (EPD)

The Swedish Environmental Management
   Council
Vasagatan 15-17
SE-111 20 Stockholm
Sweden
46(0)8 700 66 91
email: info@miljostyrning.se;
   www.environdec.com

EPDs provide science-based, verified, and comparable environmental information for various products and services to support continuous improvements based on flexible in-company product development processes. Developed by the Swedish Environmental Management Council, EPDs are applicable worldwide for all interested companies and organizations. Currently, companies and organizations in seven countries have partici-

pated in the creation of EPDs in various stages. The intent of an EPD is to provide a basis for fair comparison of environmental performance of products.

Resources: Searchable database of EPDs

Environmental Sustainability Index (ESI)

Center for International Earth Science
   Information Network (CIESIN)
Columbia University
P.O. Box 1000, 61 Route 9W
Palisades, NY 10964
(845) 365-8988; (845) 365-8922
email: ciesin.info@ciesin.columbia.edu;
   www.ciesin.columbia.edu/indicators/esi
The Yale Center for Environmental Law and
   Policy
205 Prospect Street
New Haven, CT 06511
(203) 432-3123; (203) 432-6597
email: esi@yale.edu; www.yale.edu/esi

The ESI is a composite index tracking a diverse set of socioeconomic, environmental, and institutional indicators that characterize and influence environmental sustainability at the national scale. An environmental performance index focusing on assessing key environmental policy outcomes using trend analysis and performance targets is under development.

Resources: *2005 Environmental Sustainability Index; Environmental Performance Index*

Environmental Yellow Pages (EYP)

P.O. Box 771375
Coral Springs, FL 33077
(800) 451-1458; fax (954) 970-447
www.enviroyellowpages.com

EYP provides information on the latest education, reference, health, environmental products, and professional services in the environmental industry for consumers and professionals worldwide. Coverage includes environmental bids, employment, and environmental services.

Resources: Searchable online database; hardcopy directories available in California,

Delaware, Florida, Georgia, New Jersey, New York, Pennsylvania, and Texas

Enviroene
EPA Office of Research and Development
www.epa.gov/envirosense/

This portion of the EPA's website is a repository for pollution prevention, compliance assurance, and enforcement information and databases.

Resources: *Solvent Substitution Data System; Contacts, Resources, and Vendors;* and *Technical R&D Case Studies*

FacilitiesNet
email: facilitiesnet@tradepress.com;
www.facilitiesnet.com

This website is sponsored by Autodesk, Inc., BASF Corp., BOMI Institute, Butler Mfg., Marvin Windows and Doors, and Mpulse Maintenance Software. It provides several energy-related links for products, organizations, state-specific lists of power organizations, legislative updates, and other energy information.

Resources: *Buyer's Guide; Building Operating Management* (magazine)

Forest Certification Resource Center
Metafore
721 NW Ninth Avenue, Suite 300
Portland, OR 97209
(503) 224-2205; fax (503) 224-2216
email: info@metafore.org;
www.certifiedwood.org

This website allows searches for certified products, certified forests, and approved certifiers. It also permits comparison of certification systems and confirmation of certification status, and provides information on forest certification.

Forest Stewardship Council—U.S. (FSC-US)
1155 Thirtieth Street NW, Suite 300
Washington, DC 20007
(202) 342-0413; fax (202) 342-6589

email: info@fscus.org; www.fscus.org

FSC sets forth principles, criteria, and standards that span economic, social, and environmental concerns for guiding forest management toward sustainable outcomes. Emphasis is on standards for forest management.

Friends of the Earth (FOE)
1717 Massachusetts Avenue NW, Suite 500
Washington, DC 20036-2002
(877) 843-8687; fax (202) 783-0444
email: foe@foe.org; www.foe.org

This advocacy group focuses on ozone depletion, agricultural biotechnology, toxic chemical safety, groundwater protection, nuclear weapons production wastes, tropical deforestation, and international projects.

Resources: *Friends of the Earth* (quarterly newsmagazine)

Global Environment Management Initiative (GEMI)
One Thomas Circle NW, 2nd Floor
Washington, DC 20005
(202) 296-7449; fax (202) 296-7442
email: info@gemi.org; www.gemi.org

GEMI is an organization of leading companies dedicated to fostering global environmental, health, and safety (EHS) excellence through the sharing of tools and information. Through the collaborative efforts of its members, GEMI also promotes a worldwide business ethic for EHS management and sustainable development through example and leadership.

Resources: *Clear Advantage: Building Shareholder Value/Environment: Value to the Investor; Exploring Pathways to a Sustainable Enterprise: SD Planner*™

Global Network of Environment and Technology (GNET)
Global Environment and Technology Foundation
2900 South Quincy Street, Suite 410
Arlington, VA 22003
(703) 379-2713; fax (703) 820-6168

email: gnet@getf.org; www.gnet.org

GNET contains information resources on environmental news, innovative environmental technologies, government environmental technology programs, contracting opportunities, market assessments, market information, current events, and other material of interest to the environmental technology community. It uses communications and state-of-the-art technology to bring together the information, resources, and people that shape the environment and technology marketplace.

Resources: *Technology Developer's Resource Guide (TDRG); GNET Direct e-Newsletter*

Global Village: The Institute for Appropriate Technology

89 Schoolhouse Ridge Road
P.O. Box 90
Summertown, TN 38483-0090
(931) 964-4324; fax (931) 964-2200
email: ecovillage@thefarm.org; www.i4at.org

Global Village is a nonprofit organization founded for the purpose of researching promising new technologies that can benefit humanity in environmentally friendly ways. The philosophy of the Institute is that emerging technologies that link the world together are not ethically neutral but often have long-term implications for viability of natural systems, human rights, and our common future.

Resources: Online reports covering topics including buildings, solar devices, and water systems

Government Institutes Division, ABS Consulting

16800 Greenspoint Park Drive, Suite 300 S
Houston, TX 77060-2329
(800) 769-1199; fax (281) 673-2931
email: giinfo@govinst.com ;
    www.govinst.com

Government Institutes provides continuing education and practical information to help businesses and individuals meet the unique challenges of new regulations, international standards, and technologies.

Resources: Practical books and references, including all of the U.S. Code of Federal Regulations (CFRs), in print, electronic, and online versions; federal register notification service

The Green Building Initiative (GBI)

222 SW Columbia Street, Suite 1800
Portland, Oregon 97201
(877) GBI-GBI1; fax (503) 961-8991
email: info@thegbi.org; www.thegbi.org

The GBI is a nonprofit organization supported by a broad cross-section of groups and individuals interested in promoting energy-efficient and environmentally sustainable practices in residential and commercial construction. Working closely with the National Association of Home Builders (NAHB) and local home builder associations (HBAs), the GBI provides information on green building approaches that, in addition to being environmentally progressive, are practical and affordable; Web-based support such as model guidelines; case studies and online technical assistance; promotional and marketing support for local green building programs; educational seminars for builders and other stakeholders in the building industry; and market research regarding evolving consumer trends and attitudes.

Resources: *Green Globes Assessment Tool*

GreenClips Sustainable Building Design News

Sustainable Design Resources
3168 Washington Street #6
San Francisco, CA 94115
(415) 928-7941
www.greenclips.com

GreenClips is a summary of news on sustainable building design and related government and business issues published every two weeks by email.

Green Corps

44 Winter Street, 4th Floor
Boston, MA 02108
(617) 426-8506; fax: (617) 292-8057
email: info@greencorps.org;
    www.greencorps.org

Green Corps teaches the next generation of environmental leaders the strategies and skills needed to win tomorrow's environmental battles while providing critical field support for today's pressing environmental problems.

Green-e Program, Center for Resource Solutions
P.O. Box 29512, Presidio Building 97,
  Arguello Boulevard
San Francisco, CA 94129
(888) 634-7336; fax: (415) 561-2105
email: webmaster@green-e.org; www.green-e.org

Green-e provides an easy way for consumers to quickly identify environmentally superior electricity products in competitive markets. Green-e certifies renewable electricity products that meet the environmental and consumer protection standards established by the Program.

Resources: *Green-e Dictionary; Green-e Renewable Energy Certification Program*

Green Globes Building Environmental Assessments
email: info@greenglobes.com;
  www.greenglobes.com

Green Globes™, originally developed for use in Canada, is an interactive, Web-based, commercial green building assessment protocol that guides the integration of green principles into a building's design. Green Globes™ rates seven areas: project management, site, energy, water, resources, emissions and effluents, and indoor environment.

Resources: Online building self-assessment tool; user guides; case studies

Green Lights/Energy Star Buildings Programs
U.S. Environmental Protection Agency
401 M Street SW, 6202J
Washington, DC 20460
(202) 775-6650; fax (202) 775-6680
www.energystar.gov;
  www.epa.gov/greenlights.html

Managed by the Atmospheric Pollution Prevention Division of the EPA, the Green Lights and Energy Star Buildings programs seek to work cooperatively with companies, governments, and other institutions to encourage the use of energy-efficient lighting and other building technologies, including air conditioning and air distribution systems.
Resources: Several publications

Greenpeace USA
702 H Street NW, Suite 300
Washington, DC 20001
(800) 326-0959; fax (202) 462-4507
email: info@wdc.greenpeace.org;
  www.greenpeaceusa.org

Greenpeace is an independent campaigning organization that uses nonviolent direct action and creative communication to expose global environmental problems and to promote solutions that are essential to a green and peaceful future. Emphasis is on campaigns to save ancient forests, stop global warming, expose toxic pollutants, protect the oceans, eliminate the threat of genetic engineering, and end the nuclear age.

Resources: Reports on forests, global warming and energy, toxics, and other topics

Green Products
221 East Rocbaar Drive
Romeoville, IL 60446
(877) 474-7481; fax (815) 407-0906
email: info@greenproducts.net;
  www.greenproducts.net

Green Products works to bring biobased product innovations from the fields of the farm to the lab and, ultimately, to a building. Emphasis is on developing products for roofing, masonry, and metal.

Green Roofs for Healthy Cities
177 Danforth Avenue, Suite 304
Toronto, Ontario M4K 1N2
Canada
(416) 971-4494; fax (416) 971-9844
www.greenroofs.org

GRHC works to create a market for green roof products and services in cities throughout North America. It collects and publishes technical data on green roof performance, project, and policy developments.

Resources: *Green Roof Infrastructure Monitor* (semiannual publication); *Green Roof Infrastructure Journal* (quarterly publication)

Green Seal

1001 Connecticut Avenue NW, Suite 827
Washington, DC 20036-5525
(202) 872-6400; fax (202) 872-4324
email: greenseal@greenseal.org;
    www.greenseal.org

Green Seal is a nonprofit organization dedicated to protecting the environment by promoting the manufacture and sale of environmentally responsible consumer products (including doors, windows, and appliances). It develops environmental standards and awards a Green Seal of Approval to products that cause less harm to the environment than the conventional products they replace.

Resources: Several publications, including standards for environmental consumer products. The website defines standards for environmentally responsible products and provides general information on health concerns, energy efficiency, and so on. A list of products with Green Seal certifications is also provided.

Green Tags, Bonneville Environmental Foundation

133 SW Second Avenue, Suite 410
Portland, OR 97204
(866) 233-8247; fax (503) 248-1908
email: information@b-e-f.org ;
    www.greentagsusa.org/GreenTags/
    index.cfm

The Green Tags program encourages the purchase of wind and other forms of renewable energy as a substitute for traditional power. Buying Green Tags has the same effect as buying green power. Both replace fossil fuel generators with clean renewables, and both have exactly the same environmental benefits.

Resources: *Green Tags Mailing List*

GreenWare Environmental Systems, Inc.

145 King Street E, Suite 200
Toronto, Ontario, M5C 2Y8
Canada
(800) 474-0627; fax (416) 367-2653
www.greenware.ca

GreenWare is a provider of environmental software and professional services to companies and governments worldwide. Their expertise in environmental management systems and auditing, environmental science and technology, business management and environmental regulation, coupled with technical strengths in information technology, allows them to create powerful software applications for implementing comprehensive environmental management, auditing, and reporting information systems.

Resources: Software: ISO 14000 EMS Series, Perform Series, GreenWare Auditor, GreenWare Environmental Information System (EIS)

Greenwire

www.eenews.net/Greenwire.php

Greenwire provides comprehensive daily coverage of environmental and energy politics and policy by subscription.

Healthy Building Network (HBN)

Institute for Local Self-Reliance
927 Fifteenth Street NW, 4th Floor
Washington, DC 20005
(202) 898-1610; fax (202) 898-1612
email: info@healthybuilding.net;
    www.healthybuilding.net

The Healthy Building Network prioritizes green building strategies that are closely linked to the goals of the environmental health movement. HBN brings the perspectives of people directly affected by the source, production, use, and disposal of building materials to green building professionals: architects, planners, designers, specifiers, builders, and manufacturers. HBN identifies common interests, advocates careful material selection as a means of improving the quality of life throughout the material lifecycle, and coordinates coalitions and campaigns to accelerate the transition to healthier building materials.

Resources: Biweekly email newsletter

Human Dimensions of Urban Forestry and Urban Greening

Center for Urban Horticulture, College of
Forest Resources
University of Washington, Box 354115
Seattle, WA 98195-4115
(206) 543-8616; fax (206) 685-2692
email: kwolfe@u.washington.edu;
www.cfr.washington.edu/
research.envmind/

This project researches peoples' perceptions of and behaviors with respect to nature in cities. Areas of research include nature and consumer environments, trees and transportation, civic ecology, and urban forestry and human benefits.

Resources: Fact sheets, professional publications, and scholarly publications

The Institute for Earth Education

Cedar Cove
Greenville, WV 24945
(304) 832-6404; fax (304) 832-6077
email: IEE1@aol.com;
www.eartheducation.org

The Institute is a nonprofit, volunteer organization made up of an international network of individuals and member organizations that develops and disseminates educational programs to promote harmony with the Earth. Emphasis is on Earth education program development and support for teachers and leaders.

Resources: *The Earth Education Sourcebook*

Institute for Local Self-Reliance (ILSR)

927 Fifteenth Street NW, 4th Floor
Washington, DC 20005

(202) 898-1610
email: info@ilsr.org; www.ilsr.org

ILSR works with nonprofit organizations, businesses, and government toward self-reliance through resource management. It offers technical assistance, organizes conferences, conducts research, analyzes public policy issues, and disseminates information.

Resources: Numerous publications

Institute of Scrap Recycling Industries, Inc. (ISRI)

1325 G Street NW, Suite 1000
Washington, DC 20005-3104
(202) 737-1770; fax (202) 626-0900
email: isri@isri.org; www.isri.org

This trade association represents processors, brokers, and consumers of scrap commodities, including metals, paper, plastics, glass, and textiles, as well as suppliers of equipment and services to the industry.

Resources: *SCRAP* (bimonthly magazine)

International Institute for Bau-Biologie and Ecology (IBE)

1401A Cleveland Street
Clearwater, FL 33755
(727) 461-4371; fax (727) 441-4373
www.buildingbiology.net

The Institute focuses on the education of the building industry and the public regarding healthy houses. Emphasis is on electromagnetic radiation and the offgassing of building materials.

International Institute for Sustainable Development (IISD)

161 Portage Avenue E, 6th Floor
Winnipeg, Manitoba R3B OY4
Canada
(204) 958-7700; fax (204) 958-7710
email: info@iisd.org; www.iisd.org

IISD promotes sustainable development in decision making within government, business, and the daily lives of individuals. Emphasis is on policy research, international trade, business strategy, and national budgets.

Resources: Publications

Interstate Renewable Energy Council (IREC)

P.O. Box 1156
Latham, NY 12110-1156
(518) 458-6059; fax (518) 458-6059
email: info@irecusa.org; www.ireusa.org

The IREC's mission is to accelerate the sustainable utilization of renewable energy sources and technologies in and through state and local government and community activities. IREC's programs include the Going Solar/PV4You Program, Connecting to the Grid Project, the Schools Going Solar Information Clearinghouse, Community Outreach, Small Wind Energy News, and Annual Renewable Energy Recognition Awards.

Resources: Database of State Incentives for Renewable Energy (DSIRE); *Small Wind Energy* (newsletter); Schools Going Solar (database)

Investor Responsibility Research Center (IRRC)

1350 Connecticut Avenue NW, Suite 700
Washington, DC 20036-1702
(202) 833-0700; fax (202) 833-3555
www.irrc.org

IRRC is the leading source of high-quality, impartial information on corporate governance and social responsibility. Founded in 1972, IRRC provides proxy research and analysis, benchmarking products, and proxy voting services to more than 500 institutional investors, corporations, law firms, foundations, academics, and organizations.

Journal of Industrial Ecology

MIT Press Journals
Five Cambridge Center
Cambridge, MA 02142-1407
(617) 253-2889; fax (617) 258-6779
http://mitpress.mit.edu/catalog/item/
default.asp?id=32&ttype=4

An international, peer-reviewed, multidisciplinary quarterly designed to foster both understanding and practice in the emerging field of industrial ecology. The journal addresses a series of related topics: material and energy flows studies ("industrial metabolism"); dematerialization and decarbonization; life cycle planning, design and assessment; design for the environment; extended producer responsibility ("product stewardship"); eco-industrial parks ("industrial symbiosis"); product-oriented environmental policy; and eco-efficiency.

Keep America Beautiful, Inc. (KAB)

1010 Washington Boulevard
Stamford, CT 06901
(203) 323-8987; fax (203) 325-9199
email: info@kab.org; www.kab.org

KAB is dedicated to litter and graffiti prevention, beautification, waste minimization, and community improvement. It is a national organization with 540 local affiliates in 41 states, including 21 official statewide affiliates.

Lady Bird Johnson Wildflower Center

4801 Lacrosse Avenue
Austin, TX 78739
(512) 292-4100; fax (512) 292-4627
www.wildflower.org

The Center is dedicated to native plants. Their vision for the future is to preserve and restore the natural beauty and biological richness of North America by inspiring people to love the land. They encourage people to think differently about the plants around them. They want people to understand the role of native plants in a healthy ecosystem, to value the beauty and health of the natural landscape that defines their heritage, and to take action to protect, conserve, and restore the natural landscapes of North America.

Resources: *Native Plants* (quarterly magazine); *The Wildflower Wire* (monthly email newsletter)

The Land Institute

2440 East Water Well Road
Salina, KS 67401
(785) 823-5376; fax (785) 823-8728
email: theland@landinstitute.org ;
www.landinstitute.org

The Institute has worked for over 20 years on the problem of agriculture. Its purpose is to develop an agricultural system with the ecological stability of the prairie and a grain yield comparable to that of annual crops. The Institute is working to establish Natural Systems Agriculture as a new paradigm for food production, where nature is mimicked rather than subdued and ignored.

Resources: Publications

Land Trust Alliance (LTA)
1331 H Street NW, Suite 400
Washington, DC 20005-4734
(202) 638-4725; fax (202) 638-4730
email: lta@lta.org; www.lta.org

The Alliance provides technical assistance for land trusts and other land conservation professionals, fosters public policies supportive of land conservation, and builds public awareness of land trusts and their goals.

Resources: *Exchange* (quarterly); *Searchable Online Directory of Land Trusts*

League of Conservation Voters (LCV)
1920 L Street NW, Suite 800
Washington, DC 20036
(202) 785-8683; fax (202) 835-0491
www.lcv.org

The League is a national, nonpartisan organization that seeks to have pro-environmental issues better represented in the U.S. Congress. Emphasis is on endorsing and supporting candidates for election to the U.S. House and Senate.

Resources: *LCV Insider* (electronic newsletter)

Million Solar Roofs Initiative
Solar Energy Technologies Program
www.millionroofs.org

The Initiative is a unique public-private partnership aimed at overcoming barriers to market entry for selected solar technologies. The goal of the Initiative is practical and market-driven: to facilitate the sale and installation of one million solar roofs by 2010. Eli-

gible technologies include photovoltaics (PV), solar water heating, transpired solar collectors, solar space heating and cooling, and pool heating.

The National Arbor Day Foundation
100 Arbor Avenue
Nebraska City, NE 68410
(888) 448-7337; fax (402) 474-0820
www.arborday.org

The Foundation is dedicated to tree planting and environmental stewardship. Emphasis is on community programs such as Trees for America and the National Arbor Day Program.

Resources: *Arbor Day*

National Association of Conservation Districts (NACD)
509 Capitol Court NE
Washington, DC 20002-4946
(202) 547-6223; fax (202) 547-6450
www.nacdnet.org

The Association promotes conservation, management, and orderly development of the natural resources of the United States

Resources: *Forestry Notes; Buffer Notes*

National Association of Regulatory Utility Commissioners (NARUC)
1101 Vermont NW, Suite 200
Washington, DC 20005
(202) 898-2200; fax (202) 898-2213
email: admin@naruc.org; www.naruc.org

The Association provides links to state public utility commissions and other industry and association sites. It also features news items on regulatory issues.

National Audubon Society
700 Broadway
New York, NY 10003
(212) 979-3000; fax (212) 979-3188
www.audubon.org

The Society focuses on protecting wildlife and its habitats through research, lobbying, litigation, and citizen action. Emphasis is on ancient forests, wetlands, endangered species, Arctic National Wildlife Refuge, Platte River, the Everglades, and the Adirondack Park.

Resources: *Audubon* (magazine)

The National Coalition Against the Misuse of Pesticides

701 E Street SE, Suite 200
Washington, DC 20003
(202) 543-5450; fax (202) 543-4791
email: info@beyondpesticides.org;
   www.ncamp.org

The Coalition focuses on pesticide safety and the adoption of alternative pest management strategies that reduce or eliminate dependency on toxic chemicals. Emphasis is on effecting a change through local action and providing assistance to individuals and community organizations.

Resources: Several publications

National Energy Information Center (EIC)

EI 30, 1000 Independence Avenue SW
Washington, DC 20585
(202) 586-8800; fax (202) 586-0727
email: infoctr@eia.doe.gov; www.eia.doe.gov

EIC is an office within the Energy Information Administration (EIA), responsible for the dissemination of information related to all types of energy sources. The EIA, created by Congress in 1977, is a statistical agency of the U.S. Department of Energy. The Center provides policy-independent data, forecasts, and analyses to promote sound policy making, efficient markets, and public understanding regarding energy and its interaction with the economy and the environment.

Resources: Several publications

National Environmental Balancing Bureau (NEBB)

8575 Grovemont Circle
Gaithersburg, MD 20877
(301) 977-3698; fax (301) 977-9589
www.nebb.org

NEBB is a professional organization of consultants and contractors in the HVAC and mechanical profession. Many provide commissioning services.

Resources: Several publications

National Ground Water Association (NGWA)

601 Dempsey Road
Westerville, OH 43081-8978
(800) 551-7379, (614) 898-7791; fax (614) 898-7786
email: ngwa@ngwa.org; www.ngwa.org

NGWA is a nonprofit international professional society for the groundwater industry. It provides leadership and guidance for sound, scientific, and economic management of underground resources.

Resources: *Water Well Journal; Ground Water Monitoring and Remediation; Ground Water*

National Lead Information Center (NLIC)

422 South Clinton Avenue
Rochester, NY 14620
(800) 424-LEAD, fax: (585) 232-3111
www.epa.gov/lead/nlic.htm

The NLIC provides the general public and professionals with information about lead hazards and their prevention.

Resources: Several online publications

National Pesticide Information Network (NPTN)

Oregon State University
333 Weniger Hall
Corvallis, OR 97331-6502
(800) 858-PEST; fax (541) 737-0761
email: npic@ace.orst.edu;
   http://npic.orst.edu/index.html

The Network provides information about pesticides and how to recognize and respond to poisonings.

Resources: *Pesticide Fact Sheets* (available on website)

National Pollution Prevention Roundtable (NPPR)

11 Dupont Circle NW, Suite 201
Washington, DC 20036
(202) 299-9701; fax (202) 299-9704
www.p2.org

The NPPR is the largest membership organization in the United States devoted solely to pollution prevention (P2). NPPR acts as a window on the P2 community. Its mission is to provide a national forum for promoting the development, implementation, and evaluation of efforts to avoid, eliminate, or reduce pollution at the source (i.e., source reduction instead of traditional end-of pipe methods). NPPR's members include the country's preeminent P2 experts from regional resource centers, state and local government programs, small business assistance networks, nonprofit groups, industry associations, and federal agencies.

Resources: *Yellow Pages* (a directory of national, regional, state, and local pollution prevention programs)

The National Safety Council's Environmental Health Center (EHC)

1025 Connecticut Avenue NW, Suite 1200
Washington, DC 20036
(800) 505-2270; fax (202) 293-0032
www.nsc.org/ehc.htm

The EHC fosters improved public understanding of significant health risks and challenges facing modern society. Topics include air quality, climate change, hazardous chemicals, solid waste, and water.

Resources: Several online publications

National Solid Wastes Management Association (NSWMA)

4301 Connecticut Avenue NW, Suite 300
Washington, DC 20008-2304
(202) 244-4700; fax (202) 364-3792
email: membership@nswma.org;
www.nswma.org

NSWMA is a trade association representing for-profit companies in North America that provide solid, hazardous, and medical waste collection, recycling and disposal services, and companies that provide professional and consulting services to the waste services industry.

Resources: *Waste Age* (monthly magazine); *Waste News* (biweekly newspaper and Web publication)

National Trust for Historic Preservation

1785 Massachusetts Avenue NW
Washington, DC 20036-2117
(800) 944-6847; fax (202) 588-6038
www.nationaltrust.org

The Trust fosters an appreciation of the diverse character and meaning of the U.S. cultural heritage and preserves and revitalizes the livability of communities by saving America's historic environments. The Trust is a privately funded nonprofit organization that provides leadership, education, advocacy, and resources to save diverse historic places and revitalize communities.

Resources: *Historic Preservation* (bimonthly magazine); *Preservation Law Reporter* (legal quarterly); *Forum Journal* (bimonthly journal); *Preservation Atlas, National Trust Newsletter; Preservation Policy* Newsletter; books and brochures

National Wildlife Federation (NWF)

11100 Wildlife Center Drive
Reston, VA 20190-5362
(800) 822-9919; fax (703) 790-4040
www.nwf.org

The NWF promotes conservation, responsible use of natural resources, and protection of the global environment. It distributes education materials, sponsors nature programs, lobbies Congress, and litigates environmental disputes. Emphasis is on endangered species, forests, wetlands and water resources, grazing and mining reform, biotechnology, toxic pollution sunsetting, and backyard habitat programs.

Resources: *National Wildlife* (bimonthly magazine); *Wildlife Online* (monthly e-newsletter)

Native Seeds/SEARCH

526 North Fourth Avenue
Tucson, AZ 85705-8450
(520) 622-5561; fax (520) 622-5591
www.nativeseeds.org

Native Seeds/SEARCH is a nonprofit conservation organization that works to conserve, distribute, and document the adapted and diverse varieties of agricultural seed, their wild relatives, and the role these seeds play in cultures of the American Southwest and northwest Mexico.

Resources: *Native Seed/SEARCH Seed Listing; Seedhead News* (quarterly newsletter)

Natural Resources Defense Council (NRDC)

40 West Twentieth Street
New York, NY 10011
(212) 727-2700; fax (212) 727-1773
email: nrdcinfo@nrdc.org; www.nrdc.org

This organization protects U.S. natural resources through legal action, scientific research, and citizen education. Emphasis is on energy policy and nuclear safety, air and water pollution, urban transportation issues, pesticides and toxic substances, forest protection, global warming, and the international environment.

Resources: *Unearth* (quarterly magazine); *Nature's Voice* (bimonthly bulletin); *NRDC Reports*; email bulletins

The Natural Step (TNS)

50 Osgood Place, Penthouse
San Francisco, CA 94105
(415) 318-8170; fax (415) 999-0928
email: tns@naturalstep.org;
    www.naturalstep.org

TNS is an educational organization that uses consensus building to help guide businesses, communities, governmental agencies, and individuals toward sustainability.

Resources: *The Natural Step for Communities*; case studies, other publications

The Nature Conservancy

4245 North Fairfax Drive, Suite 100
Arlington, VA 22203-1606
(703) 841-5300; fax (703) 841-1283
email: comment@tnc.org; www.tnc.org

This organization works to conserve plants, animals, and natural communities that represent the diversity of life on Earth by protecting the habitats they need to survive. It manages a system of more than 1,300 nature sanctuaries in all 50 states. Emphasis is on demonstrating that biodiversity protection can also accommodate human economic and cultural needs.

Resources: *Nature Conservancy* (magazine); *Great Places* (e-newsletter)

New Buildings Institute

P.O. Box 653
142 East Jewett Boulevard
White Salmon, WA 98672
(509) 493-4468; fax (509) 493-4078
email: info@newbuildings.org;
    www.newbuildings.org

The Institute promotes energy efficiency in buildings through policy development, research, guidelines, and codes.

Resources: *Advanced Lighting Guidelines; Skylight and Light Well Photometrics*; reports

New Rules Project, Institute for Local Self-Reliance

1313 Fifth Street SE
Minneapolis, MN 55414
(612) 379-3815; fax (612) 379-3920
email: bailey@ilsr.org; www.newrules.org

This organization works to establish new rules at the local level to build community by supporting humanly scaled politics and economics and to begin viewing communities and regions as places that nurture active and informed citizens. Topics covered include the environment and energy.

Resources: Reports and publications

Northeast Recycling Council (NERC)

139 Main Street, Suite 401
Brattleboro, VT 05301
(802) 254-3636; fax (802) 254-5870
email: info@nerc.org; www.nerc.org/

NERC provides information on regional
recycling issues and state programs.

Resources: *Environmental Benefits Calculator; NERC Email Bulletin*

Northeast Sustainable Energy Association (NESEA)

50 Miles Street
Greenfield, MA 01301
(413) 774-6051; fax (413) 774-6053
email: nesea@nesea.org; www.nesea.org

NESEA promotes energy efficiency, sustainable energy design, and the use of renewable energy. It sponsors annual conferences on green building. NESEA offices are in the Northeast Sustainability Center, an evolving project that will serve as a renewable energy design model.

Resources: *Northeast Sun* (quarterly magazine); *Sustainable Yellow Pages*

Nuclear Information and Resource Service (NIRS)

1424 Sixteenth Street NW, Suite 404
Washington, DC 20036
(202) 328-0002; fax (202) 462-2183
email: nirsnet@nirs.org ; www.nirs.org

NIRS serves as a networking information clearinghouse for environmental activists concerned with nuclear power and waste issues. Emphasis is on challenging radioactive waste policy; publication of energy audit manual for towns and universities; and preventing new nuclear reactors.

Resources: *The Nuclear Monitor* (monthly newsletter); fact sheets

The Ocean Conservancy

1725 DeSales Street NW, Suite 600
Washington, DC 20036
(800) 519-1541
email: info@oceanconservancy.org;
www.oceanconservancy.org

The Ocean Conservancy promotes healthy and diverse ocean ecosystems and opposes practices that threaten ocean life and human life. Through research, education, and science-based advocacy, the conservancy informs, inspires, and empowers people to speak and act on behalf of the oceans.

Resources: Monthly eNewsletter; *Blue Planet* (quarterly magazine)

Oikos Green Building Source

Published by Iris Communications, Inc.
P.O. Box 6498
Bend, OR 97708-6498
(541) 317-1626; fax (541) 317-1628
email: info@oikos.com; http://oikos.com

This website is dedicated to sustainable and energy-efficient construction.

Resources: *Energy Source Builder* (newsletter); searchable green product database

Penn State Lean and Green Initiative

Department of Architectural Engineering
104 Engineering Unit A
University Park, PA 16802
(814) 865-6394; fax (814) 863-4789
email: aegeneral@engr.psu.edu;
www.engr.psu.edu/leanandgreen/

The Initiative develops high-performance processes for high-performance building projects. Its goal is to incorporate the waste elimination principles of lean production into the project processes of green projects to create high-performance processes.

Resources: *Field Guide for Sustainable Construction*

Photovoltaic Systems Research and Development Program

Sandia National Laboratories
P.O. Box 5800, Mail Stop 0753
Albuquerque, NM 87185-0753
(505) 844-1548
email: pvsac@sandia.gov; www.sandia.gov

The Program works with the U.S. photo-voltaic industry, the U.S. Department of Energy, the National Renewable Energy Laboratory, other government agencies, and international organizations to increase the worldwide use of photovoltaic power systems by reducing cost, improving reliability, increasing performance, removing barriers, and growing markets.

Resources: Photo database; system design tools; various publications

Physicians for Social Responsibility
1875 Connecticut Avenue, Suite 1012
Washington, DC 20009
(202) 667-4260; fax (202) 667-4201
email: psrnatl@psr.org; www.psr.org

PSR is committed to eliminating weapons of mass destruction, preserving a sustainable environment, and reducing violence and its causes. It uses its members' expertise and professional leadership influence within the medical community and strong links to policymakers to address threats to human welfare and survival. PSR is the U.S. affiliate of International Physicians for the Prevention of Nuclear War, a network of physicians in over 80 countries. They work to protect people from environmental health hazards; to shift government spending priorities away from wasteful military expenditures; to educate the medical community, public, policy makers, and the media about the human costs of unnecessary military spending and the environmental crisis; to research the health effects of environmental degradation; and to promote international cooperation and local community action.

Resources: *PSR Reports* (members-only newsletter); *Environment and Health Activist* (newsletter)

Plants for Clean Air Council (PCAC)
3458 Godspeed Road
Davidsonville, MD 21035
email: zone10@zone10.com;
www.zone10.com

The Council provides information about the use of plants in removing toxins from indoor air.

Population Action International (PAI)
1300 Nineteenth Street NW, 2nd Floor
Washington, DC 20036
(202) 557-3400; fax (202) 728-4177
email: pai@popact.org;
www.populationaction.org

PAI promotes public awareness, population growth reduction programs, and voluntary access to family planning services. Emphasis is on the relationship between population and environmental degradation.

Resources: Several publications

Population Connection (formerly Zero Population Growth)
1400 Sixteenth Street, Suite 320
Washington, DC 20037
(202) 293-4800; fax (202) 293-9211
email: info@populationconnection.org;
www.populationconnection.org

Population Connection supports efforts to create a sustainable society, both in the United States and worldwide, that integrates an awareness of the central role population plays in meeting this objective. Specifically, for the United States, these include efforts to conserve energy and natural resources and improve efficiency, eliminate the "disposable society" lifestyle, and use the best possible technology to protect the natural and human environment.

Resources: Fact sheets; factoids; *The Reporter* (quarterly magazine)

President's Council on Sustainable Development (PCSD)
http://clinton2.nara.org/PCSD

This legacy site contains information developed by the PCSD during the 1990s on sustainable development. Site provides information on sustainable development and governmental policy in the United States.

Resources: Various publications

Product Stewardship Institute (PSI)

University of Massachusetts, Lowell
Kitson Hall, Room 200
One University Avenue
Lowell, MA 01854
(978) 934-4855; fax (978) 934-3037
email: doris@productstewardship.us;
   www.productstewardship.us

PSI is a national organization affiliated
with the Lowell Center for Sustainable Production at the University of Massachusetts.
PSI works with state and local government
agencies to partner with manufacturers, retail-
ers, environmental groups, federal agencies,
and other key stakeholders to reduce the
health and environmental impacts of consumer products. PSI takes a product stewardship approach to solving waste management
problems by encouraging product design
changes and mediating stakeholder dialogs.

Public Citizen

1600 Twentieth Street NW
Washington, DC 20009
(202) 588-1000
www.publiccitizen.org

Public Citizen fights for clean, safe, and
sustainable energy sources and for strong
health, safety, and environmental protections.
Resources: *Renewable Energy Sourcebook: A Primer for Action*

Public Employees for Environmental Responsibility (PEER)

2001 S Street NW, Suite 570
Washington, DC 20009
(202) 265-7337; (202) 265-4192
email: info@peer.org; www.peer.org

PEER is a national nonprofit alliance of
local, state, and federal scientists, law enforcement officers, land managers, and other
professionals dedicated to upholding environmental laws and values. Emphasis is on monitoring natural resource management agencies
and informing the administration, Congress,
state officials, media, and the public about
substantive environmental issues.

Resources: *White Papers; PEEReview*
(quarterly newsletter); agency surveys

Rails-to-Trails Conservancy (RTC)

1100 Seventeenth Street NW, 10th Floor
Washington, DC 20036
(202) 331-9696; fax (202) 331-9680
email: RTCMail@Transact.org;
   www.railtrails.org

The Conservancy seeks to convert thousands of miles of abandoned railroad corridors to public trails for walking, bicycling,
horseback riding, cross-country skiing,
wildlife habitat, and nature appreciation. Emphasis is on linking major metropolitan areas
via rail-trails.
Resources: *Rails-to-Trails Magazine* (quarterly); other publications

Rainforest Action Network (RAN)

221 Pine Street, 5th Floor
San Francisco, CA 94104
(415) 398-4404; fax (415) 398-2732
email: rainforest@ran.org; www.ran.org

The Network campaigns for forests, their
inhabitants, and the natural systems that sustain life by transforming the global marketplace through grassroots organizing, education, and nonviolent direct action. Emphasis is
on protecting old-growth forests from logging.
Resources: *Guide to Tree-Free, Recycled,
and Certified Papers; Cut Waste, Not Trees:
A Wood Use Reduction Guide*

Rainforest Alliance

665 Broadway, Suite 500
New York, NY 10012
(212) 677-1900; fax (212) 677-2187
email: canopy@ra.org; www.rainforest-
   alliance.org

The Alliance promotes the conservation of
the world's tropical forests by developing
sound alternatives to the activities that cause
tropical deforestation. It also provides public
education for conservation. Emphasis is on
Smart Wood certification, medicinal plant
projects, and non-timber forest products.

Resources: *The Canopy* (quarterly magazine for members); *Eco-Exchange; Rainforest Matters* (email newsletter); *RA Perspectives*

Reef Relief, Inc.
P.O. Box 430
Key West, FL 33041
(305) 294-3100; fax (305) 293-9515
email: info@reefrelief.org; www.reefrelief.org

Reef Relief preserves and protects living coral reef ecosystems of the Florida Keys. Emphasis is on educating the public and policy makers to achieve conservation, protection, and restoration of the coral reefs.

Resources: *Reef Line* (quarterly newsletter)

Renew America
1200 Eighteenth Street NW, Suite 1100
Washington, DC 20036
(202) 721-1545; fax (202) 467-5780
email: renewamerica@counterpart.org;
   solstice.crest.org/environment/
   renew_america

This organization seeks to renew community spirit in the United States through environmental success. Emphasis is on identification, verification, and promotion of successful environmental programs in 20 categories ranging from air pollution reduction to wildlife conservation.

Resources: *Environmental Success Index* (annual publication)

Resources for Global Sustainability
P.O. Box 3665
Cary, NC 27519-3665
(800) 724-1857; fax (919) 363-9841
email: rgs@environmentalgrants.com;
   www.environmentalgrants.com

This organization focuses on disseminating information on funding to the environmental community. It also maintains a large database on environmental grants.

Resources: *Environmental Grantmaking Foundations* (biennial report)

Rocky Mountain Institute (RMI)
1739 Snowmass Creek Road
Snowmass, CO 81654-9199
(970) 927-3851; fax (927) 927-3420
www.rmi.org

RMI's Green Development Services program researches environmentally and economically feasible opportunities for the building industry.

Resources: *RMI Solutions Newsletter*; other publications

Save the Dunes Council, Inc.
444 Barker Road
Michigan City, IN 46360
(219) 879-3937; fax (219) 872-4875
email: std@savedunes.org;
   www.savedunes.org

The Council works to protect the Indiana dunes for public use and enjoyment by promoting the control of air, water, and waste pollution. Emphasis is on erosion and policy issues affecting the Indiana Lake Michigan shoreline, wetlands preservation, and groundwater protection.

Resources: Newsletter

Savory Center for Holistic Management
1010 Tijeras NW
Albuquerque, NM 87102
(505) 842-5252; fax (505) 843-7900
email: savorycenter@holisticmanagement.org;
   www.holisticmanagement.org

The Center seeks to restore deteriorating landscapes and the lives of the people dependent on them using practical, low-cost solutions. It focuses on cooperation and sustainable results. It influences the conversations, views, and policies of government agencies, business leaders, agricultural producers, and environmental groups by means of cutting-edge ideas.

Resources: *The Complete Holistic Management Planning and Monitoring Guide; In Practice Journal*

Scenic America

1634 I Street NW, Suite 510
Washington, DC 20006
(202) 638-0550; fax (202) 638-3171
email: scenic@scenic.org; www.scenic.org

This organization works to preserve the scenic quality of America's communities and countryside. It provides information and technical assistance on scenic byways, tree preservation, economics of aesthetic regulation, and billboard and sign control.

Resources: *Viewpoints* (quarterly online newsletter); technical bulletins; *Facts for Action;* case studies

Scientific Certification Systems, Inc. (SCS)

2000 Powell Street, Suite 1350
Emeryville, CA 94608
(510) 452-8000; fax (510) 452-8001
www.scscertified.com

SCS is a for-profit, third-party certification organization that evaluates and certifies environmental claims made by manufacturers. Manufacturers may include the SCS label on their products. SCS does not release proprietary information but does share the standards and processes used for evaluation. For example, the Forest Stewardship Council principles are used for the SCS Forestry Program.

Resources: Environmental Claims Program List of Certified Products and Claims; Forestry Management Program information

Sierra Club

85 Second Street, 2nd Floor
San Francisco, CA 94105-3441
(415) 977-5500; fax (415) 977-5799
email: information@sierraclub.org;
    www.sierraclub.org

The Sierra Club protects the wild places of the Earth and promotes the responsible use of ecosystems and resources by educating the public. Emphasis is on old-growth forest protection, global warming, wilderness/national

parks protection, toxic waste regulations, and international development lending.

Resources: *Sierra* (magazine); *Sierra Club Newsletter*

Smart Growth Network (SGN)

International City/County Management
    Association
777 North Capitol Street NE, Suite 500
Washington, DC 20002
(202) 962-3623
email: smartgrowth@icma.org;
    www.smartgrowth.org

The SGN works to encourage development that serves the economy, the community, and the environment. It raises public awareness of how growth can improve community quality of life; promotes smart growth best practices; develops and shares information, innovative policies, tools, and ideas; and cultivates strategies to address barriers to and advance opportunities for smart growth.

Resources: *Green Guide for Health Care™;* case studies; reports

Soil and Water Conservation Society

945 SW Ankeny Road
Ankeny, IA 50021-9764
(515) 289-2331; fax (515) 289-1227
email: swcs@swcs.org; www.swcs.org

The Society promotes the conservation of soil, water, and related natural resources.

Resources: *The Journal of Soil and Water Conservation; Conservogram* (monthly e-newsletter); *Advocacy Publications*

SolarSmart Roof Alliance

515 King Street, Suite 420
Alexandria, VA 22314
(703) 684-5020; fax (703) 684-6048
email: trideout@epdmroofs.org;
    www.solarsmartroof.org

The Alliance is an organization of roofing service and roofing product trade associations committed to providing credible information about the environmental, performance, and

economic issues associated with sustainable
and reflective roofing systems.

Resources: Position papers

South Coast Air Quality Management District (AQMD)

21865 East Copley Drive
Diamond Bar, CA 91765
(800) CUT-SMOG
www.aqmd.gov

This organization provides public information, governing board agenda, minutes and
committee agendas, rules and regulations,
business assistance.

Resources: *AQMD Rules and Regulations;
Rule 1168 "Adhesive and Sealant Applications"*

Southwest Network for Environmental and Economic Justice (SNEEJ)

P.O. Box 7399
Albuquerque, NM 87194
(505) 242-0416; fax (505) 242-5609
email: eva@sneej.org; www.sneej.org

The Network supports the direct link between economic and environmental issues. It
brings together activists and grassroots organizations to address social, racial, and economic
injustices.

Resources: E-newsletter; corridor map;
reports

Steel Recycling Institute (SRI)

680 Andersen Drive
Pittsburgh, PA 15220-2700
(412) 922-2772; fax (412) 922-3213
email: sri@recycle-steel.org;
www.recycle-steel.org

SRI educates the solid waste industry, government, businesses, and, ultimately, consumers about the benefits of steel's recycling
cycle. Emphasis is on recycling construction
materials and LEED certification.

Resources: Fact sheets; educational resources; Steel Recycling database

The Student Conservation Association, Inc. (SCA)

P.O. Box 550
Charlestown, NH 03603-0550
(603) 543-1700; fax (603) 543-1828
www.sca-inc.org

The SCA provides educational opportunities for volunteers to assist with the stewardship of public lands and natural resources.
Emphasis is on encouraging youth (particularly minorities and women) to pursue
careers in conservation and resource
management.

Resources: *e-Volunteer* (monthly magazine)

Sustainable ABC

P.O. Box 30085
Santa Barbara, CA 93130
(805) 898-9660; fax (805) 898-9199
www.sustainableabc.com

This website is devoted to exploring the
relationship between ecology and sustainability. It works to educate the public and design
professionals about sustainable construction,
architecture, and environmental protection.

Resources: *Green and Healthy Building
Materials Online Product Directory;* newsletter

Sustainable Building Industry Council (SBIC)

1112 Sixteenth Street NW, Suite 240
Washington, DC 20036
(202) 628-7400; fax (202) 393-5043
email: sbic@sbicouncil.org; www.psic.org

SBIC is an independent, nonprofit organization whose mission is to advance the
design, affordability, energy performance,
and environmental soundness of U.S.
buildings.

Resources: *Green Building Guidelines:
Meeting the Demand for Low-Energy,
Resource-Efficient Homes; High-Performance
School Buildings Resource and Strategy
Guide;* Energy-10 Software

Sustainable Forestry Board (SFB)

1800 North Kent Street, Suite 1120
Arlington, VA 22209
(703) 797-2506
email: contact@aboutsfb.org;
www.aboutsfb.org

The SFB was chartered as an independent body in July 2000 to oversee development and continuous improvement of the Sustainable Forestry Initiative, associated certification processes and procedures, and program quality control mechanisms. In January 2002, the SFB filed articles of incorporation to become a separate entity and obtained 501(c)3 non-profit status. The new entity is called the Sustainable Forestry Board, Inc.

Resources: Certification audit reports; Sustainable Forestry Initiative (SFI) Standard

Thomas Legislative Information on the Internet

The Library of Congress
101 Independence Avenue SE
Washington, DC 20540
(202) 707-5000
email: Thomas@loc.gov;
http://thomas.loc.gov/

This searchable database, established in 1995, stores bill text, *Congressional Record* text, bill summaries and status, *Congressional Record* index, the Constitution, and public laws by number.

TreePeople

12601 Mulholland Drive
Beverly Hills, CA 90210
(818) 753-4600; fax (818) 753-4635

TreePeople's mission reaches far beyond the simple act of planting a tree. K-12 education programs raise environmental awareness, also enrich academic lessons, and teach potent life skills. Forestry programs restore watersheds and fragile habitats, heal inner-city communities, bring neighbors together, establish cool and green campuses, and address serious urban issues such as water and energy conservation, flood prevention, and storm-water pollution. The T.R.E.E.S. project works to change the nation's approach to urban watershed management, motivating other cities to adopt best management practices.

Resources: *Seedling News* (quarterly newsletter); other publications

Triangle J Council of Governments

4307 Emperor Boulevard, Suite 200
P.O. Box 12276
Research Triangle Park, NC 27709
(919) 549-0551; fax (919) 549-9390
email: tjcog@tjcog.org; www.tjcog.dst.nc.us

The organization works to meet the region's needs in a wide range of areas, from land-use planning, economic development, and emergency medical services support to environmental protection, programs for the aging, and information services. It is also a leader in construction and demolition waste reduction efforts and has published *Waste-Spec*, a manual to help architects and engineers specify waste reduction and recycling measures before construction projects begin.

Resources: *WasteSpec;* North Carolina Green Building Technology (NC GBT) database, *High-Performance Guidelines: Triangle Region Public Facilities*

Tropical Forest Foundation (TFF)

2121 Eisenhower Avenue, Suite 200
Alexandria, VA 22314
(703) 518-8834; fax (703) 518-8974
email: tff@igc.org;
www.tropicalforestfoundation.org

The Foundation is a nonprofit, educational institution dedicated to the conservation of tropical forests through sustainable forestry. TFF is widely recognized for establishing demonstration models and training schools to show the advantages and teach the principles of sustainable forest management and reduced-impact logging.

Resources: *TFF News;* TFF species bulletins; CITES list of tropical species

The Trust for Public Land (TPL)

116 New Montgomery Street, 4th Floor
San Francisco, CA 94105
(415) 495-4014; fax (415) 495-4103
email: info@tpl.org; www.tpl.org

TPL assists public agencies and communities in acquiring and protecting land of recreational, ecological, and cultural value for the public. Specializing in urban open space, TPL provides education and assistance for non-profit land acquisition processes.

Resources: *Land and People* (magazine); *TPL Near You* (email newsletter); *Landlink* (newsletter)

Union of Concerned Scientists (UCS)

2 Brattle Square
Cambridge, MA 02238-9105
(617) 547-5552; fax (617) 864-9405
email: ucs@ucsusa.org ; www.ucsusa.org

UCS investigates renewable energy options, the impacts of global warming, the risks of genetically engineered crops, and related topics.

Resources: *Catalyst* (quarterly magazine); *Earthwise* (quarterly newsletter); *Greentips* (monthly email newsletter)

United Nations Development Programme (UNDP)

One United Nations Plaza
New York, NY 10017
(212) 906-5000; fax: (212) 906-5364
www.undp.org

UNDP helps countries build and share solutions to the challenges of democratic governance, poverty reduction, crisis prevention and recovery, energy and environment, and HIV/AIDS. UNDP's Energy and Environment Practice works in six priority areas: frameworks and strategies for sustainable development, effective water governance, access to sustainable energy services, sustainable land management to combat desertification and land degradation, conservation and sustainable use of biodiversity, and national/sectoral policy and planning to control emissions of ODS and POPs.

Resources: Reports and publications

United Nations Division for Sustainable Development

Department of Economic and Social Affairs
2 United Nations Plaza, Room DC2-2220
New York, NY 10017
(212) 963-2803; fax (212) 963-4260
www.un.org/esa/sustdev

The Division for Sustainable Development provides leadership and is an authoritative source of expertise within the United Nations system on sustainable development. It promotes sustainable development as the substantive secretariat to the UN Commission on Sustainable Development (CSD) and through technical cooperation and capacity building at international, regional, and national levels. The context for the Division's work is the implementation of Agenda 21, the Johannesburg Plan of Implementation, and the Barbados Programme of Action for Sustainable Development of Small Island Developing States. The Division includes the Commission on Sustainable Development.

Resources: Reports and discussion papers; newsletters

United Nations Environment Programme (UNEP)

Regional Office for North America
1707 H Street NW, Suite 300
Washington, DC 20006
(202) 785-0465; fax (202) 785-2096
www.rona.unep.org

UNEP is the environmental agency of the United Nations. It helps develop and coordinate environmental policies at the municipal, national, regional, and international levels by working with scientific agencies, the private and public sectors, nongovernmental organizations, legal institutions, and others. The North American office works with the governments and civil society organizations of Canada and the United States to promote effective responses to international environmental challenges and to foster cooperation on environmental issues between North America and the broader international community.

Resources: *Our Planet* (magazine); *Annual Report of the Executive Director*; regional and specialized newsletters

United Nations Population Fund (UNFPA)

220 East Forty-second Street
New York, NY 210017
(212) 297-5000; fax (212) 557-6416
www.unfpa.org

UNFPA assists developing countries with population problems and plays a leading role in the UN system in promoting population programs. Changes in the structure, distribution, and size of populations are interlinked with all facets of sustainable development. Thus, UNFPA works to advance sustainable development.

Resources: *State of World Population* (annual report); *Dispatches* (newsletter); reports and studies

U.S. Department of Commerce (DOC)

National Technical Information Service (NTIS)
Technology Administration
5285 Port Royal Road
Springfield, VA 22161
(703) 605-6000, fax: (703) 487-4650
email: info@ntis.gov; www.ntis.gov

The DOC is the federal government's central source for the sale of scientific, technical, engineering, and related business information produced by or for the U.S. government.

Resources: Numerous

U.S. Department of Energy (DOE)

Smart Communities Network
Office of Energy Efficiency and Renewable Energy
Central Regional Support Office
1617 Cole Boulevard
Golden, CO 80401-3393

(303) 275-4826; fax (303) 275-4830
email: ee@ee.doe.gov;
www.sustainable.doe.gov

The DOE provides information and services pertaining to how communities can adopt a sustainable development program. Topics include green buildings, green development, land-use planning, community energy, sustainable business, resource efficient air, water, and materials, and transportation.

Resources: Email newsletter; *Toolkit of Sustainable Development Decision Support Tools*

U.S. Department of Energy (DOE) Energy Efficiency and Renewable Energy Information Portal

Mail Stop EE-1
Washington, DC 20585
(202) 586-9220
www.eere.energy.gov/

The EERE Information Portal is a gateway to hundreds of websites and thousands of online documents on energy efficiency and renewable energy.

Resources: Numerous

U.S. Department of Energy (DOE) Energy Information Administration National Energy Information Center

EI-30, 1000 Independence Avenue SW
Washington, DC 20585
(202) 586-8800
email: infoctr@eia.doe.gov; www.eia.doe.gov

The Center provides information on DOE programs and distributes fact sheets and publications on energy resources, consumption, imports, exports, and related economic and statistical information.

Resources: Numerous; e-mail newsletters

U.S. Department of Energy (DOE) National Renewable Energy Laboratory (NREL)

Central Regional Support Office
1617 Cole Boulevard
Golden, CO 80401-3393

(303) 275-3000; fax (303) 275-4053
www.nrel.gov

NREL is a leading laboratory for research
and development of renewable energy and energy efficiency technologies. Major programs
include advanced vehicle technologies and
fuels, basic energy science, biomass, building
technologies, electric infrastructure systems,
energy analysis, geothermal energy, hydrogen
and fuel cells, and solar and wind energy.

Resources: Publications; *NEON* (weekly
email service); PIX (photograph library); renewable resources maps and data

U.S. Environmental Protection Agency (EPA)
Asbestos Abatement/Management Ombudsman
Central Regional Support Office
Mail Code 123QC
1617 Cole Boulevard
Golden, CO 80401-3393
(800) 368-5888; fax: (202) 566-2848
www.epa.gov

This office provides the public sector, including individual citizens and community
services, information on handling, abatement,
and management of asbestos in schools, workplaces, and homes.

U.S. Environmental Protection Agency (EPA)
Hotlines and Clearinghouses
Ariel Rios Building
1200 Pennsylvania Avenue NW
Washington, DC 20460-0003
(202) 272-0167
www.epa.gov/epahome/hotline.htm

This organization maintains an alphabet-
ized list of EPA hotlines and clearinghouses.

U.S. Environmental Protection Agency (EPA)
Indoor Air Quality Information Clearinghouse (IAQINFO)
P.O. Box 37133
Washington, DC 20013-7133

(800) 438-4318; fax (703) 356-5386
email: iaqinfo@aol.com;
  www.epa.gov/iedweb00/iaginfo.html

These information specialists provide information, referrals, publications, and database
searches on indoor air quality. Areas covered
include pollutants and sources, health effects,
control methods, commercial building operations and maintenance, standards and guidelines, and federal and state legislation. The
clearinghouse also provides information on
constructing and maintaining homes and buildings to minimize indoor air quality problems.

U.S. Environmental Protection Agency (EPA)
Municipal Solid Waste (MSW)
National Service Center for Environmental
  Publications (NSCEP)
P.O. Box 42419
Cincinnati, OH 45242-2419
(800) 490-9198; fax: (513) 489-8695
www.epa.gov/epaoswer/osw/publicat.htm

NSCEP provides statistics on waste generation, international material recycling rates,
source reduction, and composting, all available
on disk. It also offers state-by-state statistics on
recycling rates, programs, and contacts.

U.S. Environmental Protection Agency (EPA)
Office of Ground Water and Drinking Water (OGWDW)
Ariel Rios Building
1200 Pennsylvania Avenue NW
Washington, DC 20460-0003
(202) 564-3750; fax (202) 564-3752
www.epa.gov/safewater

This office works with states, tribes, and
partners to protect public health by ensuring
safe drinking water and protecting groundwater.

U.S. Environmental Protection Agency (EPA)
Office of Science and Technology (OST)
Ariel Rios Building

1200 Pennsylvania Avenue NW
Washington, DC 20460-0003 (4301T)
(202) 566-0430
email: Ost.Comments@epa.gov;
   www.epa.gov/ost

OST develops sound, scientifically defensible standards, criteria, advisories, guidelines, limitations, and standards guidelines for water quality and industrial water pollution.

U.S. Environmental Protection Agency (EPA)
Office of Solid Waste and Emergency Response
Ariel Rios Building
1200 Pennsylvania Avenue NW
Washington, DC 20460-0003
(800) 424-9346
www.epa.gov/swerrims

This office develops guidelines and standards for land disposal of hazardous wastes and underground storage tanks.

U.S. Environmental Protection Agency (EPA)
Office of Wastewater Management (OWM)
Ariel Rios Building
1200 Pennsylvania Avenue NW
Washington, DC 20460 (4204M)
(202) 260-5850
email: comments.web@epa.gov;
   www.epa.gov/owm

OWM oversees a range of programs contributing to the well-being of the nation's waters and watersheds. Through its programs and initiatives, OWM promotes compliance with the requirements of the Federal Water Pollution Control Act. It works in partnership with EPA regions, states, and tribes to regulate discharges into surface waters such as wetlands, lakes, rivers, estuaries, bays, and oceans. Specifically, OWM focuses on the control of water collected in discrete conveyances (also called point sources), including pipes, ditches, and sanitary or storm sewers.

Resources: Publications on biosolids, pollution prevention and control, pretreatment, stormwater and combined sewer overflows, treatment, water conservation and efficiency, and water quality and standards

U.S. Environmental Protection Agency (EPA)
Office of Wetlands, Oceans, and Watersheds (OWOW)
Ariel Rios Building
1200 Pennsylvania Avenue NW
Washington, DC 20460 (4501T)
(202) 566-1300
email: ow-owow-internet-
   comments@epa.gov;
   www.epa.gov/owowtr1

OWOW and its partners work together on a watershed basis to protect the nation's water resources.

Resources: Databases, data systems, mapping, and water quality models; numerous publications

U.S. Environmental Protection Agency (EPA)
Safe Drinking Water Hotline
Ariel Rios Building
1200 Pennsylvania Avenue NW
Washington, DC 20460 (4606M)
(800) 426-4791; fax (202) 564-3753
www.epa.gov/safewater/hotline/index.html

The hotline provides the general public, regulators, medical and water professionals, academia, and media with information about drinking water and groundwater programs authorized under the Safe Drinking Water Act. Topics covered include local drinking water quality, drinking water standards, public drinking water systems, source water protection, large-capacity residential septic systems, commercial, and industrial septic systems, injection wells, and drainage wells.

Resources: *Water Lines* (monthly hotline activity report); drinking water data and databases; reports

EPA Regional Offices

Each of the EPA's 10 regional offices listed below is responsible within its states for the execution of the Agency's programs. The regional offices offer a library of local resources, superfund records, environmental laws and regulations, and regional data about toxic chemicals.

**U.S. Environmental Protection Agency
EPA Region 1 (New England)**
John F. Kennedy Federal Building
One Congress Street, Suite 1100
Boston, MA 02203-2023
(888) 372-7341; (617) 918-1111; fax: (617) 918-0101
www.epa.gov/region1
Region 1 includes Connecticut, Maine, Massachusetts, New Hampshire, Rhode Island, Vermont, and ten tribal nations.

**U.S. Environmental Protection Agency
EPA Region 2**
290 Broadway
New York, NY 10007-1866
(212) 637-1866
www.epa.gov/region2
Region 2 includes New Jersey, New York, Puerto Rico, U.S. Virgin Islands, and seven tribal nations.

**U.S. Environmental Protection Agency
EPA Region 3 (Mid-Atlantic)**
1650 Arch Street
Philadelphia, PA 19103-2029
(800) 438-2474; (215) 814-5000
www.epa.gov/region3
Region 3 includes Delaware, District of Columbia, Maryland, Pennsylvania, Virginia, and West Virginia.

**U.S. Environmental Protection Agency
EPA Region 4 (Southeast)**
Sam Nunn Atlanta Federal Center
61 Forsyth Street SW
Atlanta, GA 30303-3104
(404) 562-9900; fax: (404) 562-8174
www.epa.gov/region4
Region 4 includes Alabama, Florida, Georgia, Kentucky, Mississippi, North Carolina, South Carolina, and Tennessee.

**U.S. Environmental Protection Agency
EPA Region 5**
77 West Jackson Boulevard
Chicago, IL 60604-3507
(312) 353-2000
www.epa.gov/region5
Region 5 includes Illinois, Indiana, Michigan, Minnesota, Ohio, Wisconsin, and 35 tribes.

**U.S. Environmental Protection Agency
EPA Region 6 (South Central)**
1445 Ross Avenue, Suite 1200
Dallas, TX 75202-2733
(214) 665-6444
www.epa.gov/region6
Region 6 includes Arkansas, Louisiana, New Mexico, Oklahoma, Texas, and 66 tribes.

**U.S. Environmental Protection Agency
EPA Region 7**
901 North Fifth Street
Kansas City, KS 66101
(913) 551-7003
www.epa.gov/region7
Region 7 includes Iowa, Kansas, Missouri, Nebraska, and seven tribal nations.

**U.S. Environmental Protection Agency
EPA Region 8 (Mountains and Plains)**
999 Eighteenth Street, Suite 300
Denver, CO 80202-2466
(303) 312-6312
www.epa.gov/region8
Region 8 includes Colorado, Montana, North Dakota, South Dakota, Utah, Wyoming, and 27 tribal nations.

**U.S. Environmental Protection Agency
EPA Region 9 (Pacific Southwest)**
75 Hawthorne Street
San Francisco, CA 94105
(415) 947-8000
www.epa.gov/region9

Region 9 includes Arizona, California, Hawaii, Nevada, The Pacific Islands, and over 140 tribal nations.

U.S. Environmental Protection Agency EPA Region 10 (Pacific Northwest)
1200 Sixth Avenue
Seattle, WA 98101
(206) 553-1200
www.epa.gov/region10

Region 10 includes Alaska, Idaho, Oregon, and Washington.

U.S. Green Building Council (USGBC)
1015 Eighteenth Street, Suite 508
Washington, DC 20036
(202) 828-7422; fax (202) 828-5110
email: info@usgbc.org; www.usgbc.org

The Council is the nation's foremost coalition of leaders from across the building industry working to promote buildings that are environmentally responsible, profitable, and healthy places to live and work.

Resources: Leadership in Energy and Environmental Design (LEED) Green Building Rating System; conferences; reports

U.S. Office of Science and Technology Policy (OSTP)
Executive Office of the President
Washington, DC 20502
(202) 456-66130; fax: (202) 456-6027
email: info@ostp.gov; www.ostp.gov

OSTP serves as a source of scientific and technological analysis and judgment for the President with respect to major policies, plans, and programs of the federal government.

Urban Ecology, Inc.
414 Thirteenth Street, Suite 500
Oakland, CA 94612
(510) 251-6330; fax: (510) 251-2117

Urban Ecology is an international organization dedicated to creating sustainable cities through use of ecology principles in urban planning and development. Emphasis is on land use planning, transportation, restoration, international education, and eco-city research.

Resources: *The Urban Ecologist* (quarterly newsletter); *Blueprint for a Sustainable Bay Area*

Vanderbilt University Center for Environmental Management Studies (VCEMS)
401 Twenty-first Avenue S
Nashville, TN 37203
(615) 322-8004; fax: (615) 343-7177
email: vcems@vanderbilt.edu;
    www.vanderbilt.edu/VCEMS/index.html

VCEMS promotes and develops alliances among industry, government, and academia to study the relationship of environmental policy to business management and operations. The Center is a Vanderbilt University systemwide initiative jointly led by the School of Engineering, the Owen Graduate School of Management, and the Law School. Center activities are interdisciplinary and focus on environmental business, management, and technology.

Webdirectory
The Environmental Directory
email: info@webdirectory.com;
    www.webdirectory.com

The Directory is created and maintained by a group of people dedicated to helping others keep in touch and informed on the World Wide Web. With thousands of sites, it is the largest exclusively environmental organization directory on the Web and includes sites from over 100 countries.

The Wilderness Society
1615 M Street NW
Washington, DC 20036
(800) THE-WILD, (202) 833-2300; fax (202) 429-3959
email: tws@tws.org; www.tws.org

The Society works to protect wildlands and wildlife. Emphasis is on the Arctic Wildlife Refuge, national forest policy, national parks, endangered species protection, and economics of public land use.

Resources: *WILDALERT NEWS; WILDALERTS; Wilderness Report; Wilderness Year* (quarterly magazine)

The Wildlife Society
5410 Grosvenor Lane, Suite 200
Bethesda, MD 20814-2144
(301) 897-9770; fax (301) 530-2471
email: tws@wildlife.org; www.wildlife.org

The Society is dedicated to conserving wildlife productivity and diversity through resource management. Emphasis is on education for wildlife managers.
Resources: *Wildlife Society Bulletin* (quarterly publication); *The Journal of Wildlife Management* (quarterly publication); *The Wildlifer* (bimonthly newsletter)

WoodWise Program
Co-op America
1612 K Street, Suite 600
Washington, DC 20006
(800) 58-GREEN
email: info@woodwise.org;
      www.woodwise.org

This program works to preserve forests by reducing demand for wood products and promoting sustainable alternatives.
Resources: *WoodWise Guide*

World Health Organization (WHO)
Programme on Indoor Air Pollution
Avenue Appia 20
1211 Geneva 27
Switzerland
(+41 22) 791 21 11; fax: (41 22) 791 3111
email: phedoc@who.int;
      www.who.int/indoorair/en/

The Programme works to combat the substantial and growing burden of disease and high levels of indoor air pollution caused by cooking and heating with solid fuels.
Resources: Publications, fact sheets, and databases on air pollution

World Resources Institute
10 G Street NE, Suite 800

Washington, DC 20002
(202) 729-7600; fax (202) 729-7610
email: swilson@wri.org; www.wri.org

The Institute helps governments, the private sector, nonprofit organizations, and others address human needs and economic growth while preserving natural resources. Emphasis is on forests, biodiversity, economics, technology, climate, energy, pollution, education, and governance.
Resources: Several publications

World Society for the Protection of Animals (WSPA)
34 Deloss Street
Framingham, MA 01702
(508) 879-8350; fax (508) 620-0786
email: wspa@wspausa.com;
      www.wspa.org.uk

The Society is an international animal protection/wildlife conservation organization. Emphasis is on enacting animal protection legislation, disaster relief program to aid animal victims of disasters, animal spectacles, education, and less developed countries.
Resources: *WSPA Newsletter*

Worldwatch Institute
1776 Massachusetts Avenue NW
Washington, DC 20036-1904
(202) 452-1999; fax (202) 296-7365
email: worldwatch@worldwatch.org;
www.worldwatch.org

Worldwatch is an environmental research institute. Emphasis is on interdependence of the world economy and its environmental support systems.
Resources: *State of the World* (annual report); *WorldWatch* (magazine); *The WorldWatch Papers; Vital Signs* (annual report)

World Wildlife Fund (WWF)
1250 Twenty-fourth Street NW, Suite 500
Washington, DC 20037
(202) 293-4800; fax (202) 293-9211
www.worldwildlife.org

The WWF seeks to preserve endangered wildlife and wildlands by encouraging sustainable development. Emphasis is on conservation of tropical rain forests and preserving biological diversity.

Resources: Publications

University Education Programs

This category includes education programs with a sustainable focus to assist those considering entering a career in sustainable design or construction. The list is not exhaustive but offers a brief overview of available programs for further investigation by the reader.

Architecture Degrees with Sustainable Emphasis

The Wallace Research Group
P.O. Box 50128
Bellevue, WA 98015
(425) 637-9049
email: info@wallaceresearch.net;
   www.wallaceresearch.net/educationNorth America.html

The Wallace Research Group provides an online listing of international architecture and building environment degree programs that emphasize sustainable, environmental, or green design courses.

Resources: Alphabetic listing by U.S. State or Canadian Province

Ball State University Major in Environmental Design

Department of Architecture
AB 402
Ball State University
Muncie, IN 47306
(765) 285-1900; fax (765) 285-1765
email: cap@bsu.edu;
   www.bsu.edu/cap/curriculum/undergrad/En_Arch.html

The University offers a bachelor of science or bachelor of arts with an undergraduate major in environmental design for students interested in alternative careers in design, construction, and related fields.

Boston Architectural Center

320 Newbury Street
Boston, MA 02115
(617) 262-5000; fax (617) 585-0121
email: ce@the-bac.edu; www.the-bac.edu/index.cfm?pageID=122

The Center offers a certificate in sustainable design. The program prepares practitioners to design spaces in harmony with the environment. The sustainable design certificate may be earned at either the undergraduate or graduate level. Students seeking a graduate certificate must have a prior bachelor's degree and take the required courses (excluding the elective) at the graduate level. The sustainable design certificate program is now available entirely online in partnership with Building-Green, Inc.

The Ecosa Institute

212B South Marina Street
Prescott, AZ 86303
(928) 541-1002; fax (928) 776-8086
email: info@ecosainstitute.org;
   www.ecosainstitute.org

This educational institute provides undergraduate and graduate design students with a detailed understanding of the impact of design on the environment and exposes them to alternative strategies for reducing that impact. Ecosa also offers programs for architecture instructors.

Minneapolis College of Art and Design (MCAD)

2501 Stevens Avenue
Minneapolis, MN 55404
(800) 874-MCAD
email: online@mcad.edu;
   http://online.mcad.edu

MCAD offers a sustainable design online certificate. The online program covers topics from theoretical underpinnings to practical design techniques. Individual classes are also available on topics such as: systems thinking and life cycle analysis; principles of sustainable design applied to graphic design, packaging, and product design; green marketing; international standards; and green design innovation.

San Francisco Institute of Architecture (SFIA)

1366 Mission Street
San Francisco, CA 94501
(510) 523-5174; fax (510) 523-5175
email: SFIA@aol.com;
    www.sfia.net/EcoDes.asp

The Institute offers a master of ecological design degree program with options for students with architecture degrees, degrees in other fields, or work experience. The Institute also offers distance learning courses in ecological design, planning, and construction.

University of California at Berkeley

Building Science Program
http://arch.edu/resources/bldgsci/building_science.htm

This program is dedicated to the energy efficiency and environmental quality of buildings. It offers bachelors, masters, and doctoral degrees as well as research opportunities.

The University of Texas at Austin

School of Architecture
1 University Station, Mail Stop B7500
Austin, TX 78712-0222
(512) 471-1922; fax (512) 471-0716
http://web.austin.utexas.edu/architecture/
    academic/architecture/grad/climate.html

The Graduate Architecture program offers a masters of architecture with a specialization in sustainable design. The program studies the relationship between the built and natural environments. The expanded program focuses on three areas of interest: natural systems, buildings systems, and cultural systems.

Appendix B

Summary of Environmental Issues in CSI MasterFormat™ Organization

To assist readers in asking appropriate questions regarding the greenness of a material, this appendix lists issues relative to resource management, toxicity/IEQ, and performance according to CSI MasterFormat sections.

This summary was developed by theGreenTeam, Inc., and is the result of its ongoing work with building owners, building product manufacturers, green building trade and professional organizations, standards development organizations, and environmental organizations to develop sustainable building. This summary is intended to be a guide for researching environmental issues relative to building products. No warranty is made as to the completeness or accuracy of information contained herein. References to manufacturers do not represent a guaranty, warranty, or endorsement thereof.

The summary of information is tabulated to correspond with the product summary in *The Green Home Product Guide,* coauthored by Dru Meadows and Charles E. Bell, founders of theGreenTeam, Inc.

theGreenTeam, Inc.
2 West Sixth Street, Suite 304
Tulsa, OK 74119
(918) 295-TEAM
fax: (918) 295-8322
email: dmeadows@thegreenteaminc.com
www.thegreenteaminc.com

Understanding the Listings

Section and Division numbers and titles that follow are based on the 1995 Edition of CSI's MasterFormat™. Section and Division numbers and titles that appear in brackets (__) are based on the 2004 Edition of MasterFormat™.

DIVISION 1 (01)—GENERAL REQUIREMENTS

01100 (01 10 00)	SUMMARY: Identify owner's environmental goals and requirements, including energy efficiency, resource management, and specific project issues. Also, clearly indicate a team approach to addressing environmental issues.
01200 (01 20 00)	PRICE AND PAYMENT PROCEDURES: If submittal of updated Summary of Solid Waste Management and Environmental Protection Plan is required with Application for Payment, coordinate with Section 01351 (01 74 19).
01231 (01 23 10)	ENVIRONMENTAL ALTERNATES: Identify options for green products. Use of this section will allow the owner to compare financial and practical viability of green product options for a particular project.
01300 (01 30 00)	ADMINISTRATIVE REQUIREMENTS: Require contractor to designate an on-site party responsible for instructing workers and overseeing the environmental goals for the project.
01310 (01 31 00)	PROJECT MANAGEMENT AND COORDINATION: Coordinate with Section 01354 (01 35 43) for project quality control, coordination, and construction meetings. Review environmental procedures and status of Solid Waste Management and Environmental Protection Plan at each construction meeting.
01320 (01 32 00)	CONSTRUCTION PROGRESS DOCUMENTATION: Coordinate with Section 01351 (01 74 19) and Section 01200 (01 20 00) for periodic submittal of updated Summary of Solid Waste Management and Environmental Protection Plan. Where violation of environmental procedures requirements will irreversibly damage the site, identify requirements for documentation of progress at specific intervals. Documentation may also be useful for educational purposes.
01330 (01 33 00)	SUBMITTAL PROCEDURES: Clarify need for submission of material safety data sheets (MSDSs). Often, owners and architects incorporate a blanket request for MSDSs in response to environmental issues. While this may be appropriate, remember that interpreting chemical profile and test results requires understanding the health effects of exposure to the emitted chemicals, which is beyond the professional expertise of most architects; furthermore, adequate information is not available for most chemicals.
(01 33 29)	SUSTAINABLE DESIGN REPORTING: This section includes requirements for submittals needed to demonstrate compliance with requirements of a green building rating system. Identify special submittals related to sustainable features of the design. This section is a new title in MasterFormat™ 2004.
01351 (01 74 19)	WASTE MANAGEMENT (CONSTRUCTION WASTE MANAGEMENT AND DISPOSAL): This section includes requirements for waste management. This section represents data quality objectives and waste management consistent with ASTM D5792, Standard Practice for Generation of Environmental Data Related to Waste Management Activities: Development of Data Quality Objectives, for typical commercial construction. This section does not address environmental remediation, abatement, regulatory requirements, or requirements for environmental impact statements/reports.

01352 (01 57 19.11)   INDOOR AIR QUALITY (IAQ) MANAGEMENT: This section includes requirements for IAQ management during construction. Coordinate with requirements of other sections; verify that products and installation methods specified in other sections are environmentally appropriate. This Section may include procedures for testing baseline IAQ. Baseline IAQ requirements specify maximum indoor pollutant concentrations for acceptance of the facility. This Section may include requirements for Independent Materials Testing of specific materials anticipated to have measurable impact on IAQ.

01353 (01 57 19.12)   NOISE AND ACOUSTIC MANAGEMENT: This section includes requirements for noise management during construction. Refer to ASTM E1433, Standard Guide for Selection of Standards on Environmental Acoustics, for an overview of the ASTM standards relative to environmental acoustics.

01354 (01 35 43)   ENVIRONMENTAL MANAGEMENT (ENVIRONMENTAL PROCEDURES): This section includes requirements for environmental management during construction operations. It emphasizes an integrated team approach to address environmental issues. This section does not address environmental remediation, abatement, regulatory requirements, or requirements for environmental impact statements/reports. Coordinate with requirements for other sections; verify that products and installation methods specified in other sections are environmentally appropriate. Refer to sample section in Appendix C.

01400 (01 40 00)   QUALITY REQUIREMENTS: Include information required for conformance to regulatory requirements such as energy codes and National Pollutant Discharge Elimination System (NPDES). Coordinate with Section 01351 (01 74 19).

01500 (01 50 00)   TEMPORARY FACILITIES AND CONTROLS: Coordinate with Sections 01351 (01 74 19) and 01354 (01 35 43) for temporary heating, cooling, and ventilating and progress cleaning and waste removal.

01600 (01 60 00)   PRODUCT REQUIREMENTS: This section addresses requirements for delivery, storage, and handling. Sometimes, it also specifies general requirements for materials and equipment identified as new. If you are specifying new materials made from recycled materials, that is acceptable. However, if you wish to allow reused materials, such as brick or millwork, edit your specifications accordingly.

01630 (01 25 13)   PRODUCT SUBSTITUTION PROCEDURES: Specify that substitutions may be considered when the contractor becomes aware of a product or procedure that is more environmentally sensitive.

01740 (01 74 13)   CLEANING (PROGRESS CLEANING): Require nontoxic cleaning materials and procedures. Coordinate with Section 01351 (01 74 19). Alternatives to more toxic commercial cleaning agents include vinegar, citrus, borax, cornstarch, and baking soda.

- Abrasive cleaners: Substitute 1/2 lemon dipped in borax.
- Ammonia: Substitute vinegar, salt, and water mixture, or baking soda and water.

- Disinfectants: Substitute 1/2 cup borax in 1 gallon water.

- Drain cleaners: Substitute 1/4 cup baking soda and 1/4 cup vinegar in boiling water.

- Upholstery cleaners: Substitute dry cornstarch.

01780 (01 78 00)   CLOSEOUT SUBMITTALS: Require submittal of Final Summary of Solid Waste Management, as specified in Section 01351 (01 74 19). Also, for government projects, require submittal of Resource Conservation and Recovery Act Project Summary, as specified in Section 01351 (01 74 19). Require submittal of certifications and test data where appropriate. Several manufacturers have obtained independent certifications from Green Seal or Scientific Certification Systems. Sustainably harvested wood products may be labeled under the FSC principles. Refer to Section 06100 (06 10 00), Rough Carpentry. Emissions testing has not been conducted for most products. Industries that have begun testing include paint manufacturers, carpet manufacturers, office furnishing manufacturers, floor covering adhesive manufacturers, and composite wood manufacturers. Verify that manufacturers have obtained the services of qualified health scientists to determine that their products are suitable for the intended use.

(01 78 53)   SUSTAINABLE DESIGN CLOSEOUT DOCUMENTATION: Identify requirements for closeout documentation related to sustainable design to comply with green building rating systems. This section is a new title in MasterFormat™ 2004.

(01 90 00)   LIFE CYCLE ACTIVITIES: Indicate requirements for commissioning of a building's substructure, shell components, or interiors. This section is a new title in MasterFormat™ 2004.

01810 (01 91 00)   COMMISSIONING: Indicate requirements for commissioning of facilities and facility systems to verify compliance with design, including optimum energy-efficient operations.

01820 (01 79 00)   DEMONSTRATION AND TRAINING: Require education for owner's personnel regarding both facility systems and the green materials in the building. Because the green items may be different from the systems and materials with which the owner's personnel are familiar, education about the environmental qualities as well as the operation and maintenance requirements may be necessary.

01830 (01 78 23)   OPERATION AND MAINTENANCE: Require maintenance instructions for specified products with attention to indoor air quality impacts of the recommended maintenance procedures and materials. Coordinate with Section 01820 (01 79 00). Also identify maintenance contracts and green leases. Green leasing is a new and dramatic shift in the traditional perspective of leased equipment. Under a green lease, the product manufacturer is responsible for the disposition of the product at all times. Thus, when the customer no longer requires the use of the particular product or requires an updated model, the manufacturer would be obligated to reclaim it and refurbish it or disassemble it for recycling as appropriate. Coordinate with the appropriate technical section(s).

DIVISION 2—SITE CONSTRUCTION

(DIVISIONS 31–33—EARTHWORK, EXTERIOR IMPROVEMENTS, AND UTILITIES)

The 2004 Edition of MasterFormat relocated the subject matter in Division 2 to multiple divisions to permit expanded coverage of the topic and permit future expansion.

02055 (31 05 13)   SOILS (SOILS FOR EARTHWORK)

Resource Management: Implement mulching and composting programs where appropriate to the project's scale and duration. Coordinate with Section 01354 (01 35 43), Environmental Procedures, and Section 02230 (31 10 00), Site Clearing. Soil amendment can be made from recycled scrap gypsum; coordinate with Section 09250 (09 29 00), Gypsum Board.

Toxicity/IEQ: Coordinate with Section 01354 (01 35 43), Environmental Procedures, to stockpile topsoil and to protect existing soils. Where soil tests indicate existing contamination, consider in situ treatment via phytoremediation instead of bioremediation and landfilling. Phytoremediation is an innovative technology that utilizes plants and trees to clean up contaminated soil and water. It is an aesthetically pleasing, solar-energy-driven, passive technique that can be used to clean up metals, pesticides, solvents, crude oil, polyaromatic hydrocarbons, and landfill leachates. Plants can break down (degrade) organic pollutants (those that contain carbon and hydrogen). Plants can also extract (phytoaccumulate) certain metal contaminants (nickel, zinc, and copper are the best candidates for removal by phytoextraction because they are the favorites of the approximately 400 known plants); the plants are harvested as necessary and either incinerated or composted to recycle the metals. Trees have longer taproots and can act as organic pumps/filters. Poplar trees, for example, pull out of the ground 30 gallons of water per day. The pulling action of the roots decreases the tendency of surface pollutants to move downward toward groundwater/aquifers.

Performance: Traditional consideration focuses on bearing capacity and the amendments required for the selected landscaping elements. Environmental issues for performance should examine the potential to renew the soil, avoid erosion, and minimize stormwater runoff. Compost, for example, can improve the quality of both sandy soil and clay soil by improving the ability of the soil to percolate and to hold water. By breaking up clay soil and by congealing sandy soil, compost aids the healthy root growth of plants as well as contributing to their nutritional needs. Similarly, the appropriate selection of plants can help rebuild the local ecosystem, including the soil.

02060 (31 05 16)   AGGREGATE (AGGREGATES FOR EARTHWORK)

Resource Management: Aggregate fabricated from 100 percent recycled rubble or concrete is available. Due to the mass of the material and the corresponding energy/cost to transport, specify locally available sources. Fill material fabricated from 100 percent recycled tires is available.

Toxicity/IEQ: Toxicity is often a concern when utilizing recycled materials for aggregate, especially old tires. Tests are being performed by the University of Maine on the effect of tire chips on drinking water for chips placed both above and below the water table. To date, the accumulation of metals appears to be below secondary drinking water standards; some volatile and semivolatile organic compounds have been detected for tire chips located below the water table.

Performance: Recycled porcelain, concrete, or stone may be expected to perform comparably to standard gravel/stone aggregate. Tire chips, 1-inch to 2-inch chips of waste steel and glass belted tires, have a low unit weight of 40 to 60 pcf versus the typical 125 pcf unit weight of gravel. Therefore, tire chips perform well where compressible, lightweight, stable fill is required, such as for retaining walls or for embankment construction where there is slope stability or excessive settlement caused by weak foundation soils and/ or the weight of the embankment. Tire chips also insulate about eight times better than gravel in reducing frost penetration. The permeability of tire chips is greater than most gravel aggregate.

02220 (02 41 13)   SITE DEMOLITION (SELECTIVE SITE DEMOLITION)

Resource Management: Collect, recycle, reuse, and dispose of demolished materials, as specified in Section 01354 (01 35 43), Environmental Procedures, and as approved by the owner in the Solid Waste Management and Environmental Protection Plan.

Toxicity/IEQ: Coordinate with applicable regulations regarding detection and abatement of hazardous materials.

Performance: Thoughtful and considered disassembly, as opposed to wholesale demolition, will produce more usable reusables and will help prevent damage to items scheduled to remain.

02230 (31 10 00)   SITE CLEARING

Resource Management: Protect natural resources; collect, recycle, reuse, and dispose of demolished materials, as specified in Section 01354 (01 35 43), Environmental Procedures, and as approved by the owner in the Solid Waste Management and Environmental Protection Plan. Identify organic debris that is free of disease, pest infestation, and chemical contamination and that is suitable for recycling on-site. Chip and compost suitable organic debris for use on-site. Stockpile where indicated on drawings or directed by the owner. Coordinate with mulch/compost requirements of Section 02900 (32 90 00), Planting, and Section 02055 (31 05 13), Soils (Soils for Earthwork).

Toxicity/IEQ: Coordinate with Section 02055 (31 05 13), Soils (Soils for Earthwork), for phytoremediation of existing contaminated soils. Avoid composting diseased vegetation and animal waste (from carnivorous animals) in situ. Because the operations of commercial composting facilities are monitored and controlled to maintain the high temperatures required in the thermophyllic phase of composting (the thermophyllic phase of the average residential composting pile is only four to seven days and relies on thermophyllic bacteria that function at 1048 to 1708 F and that are extremely efficient at processing compostables) commercial composting can accept diseased vegetation and, in many cases, all types of animal waste. However, composting in situ is not generally so well controlled. If temperatures in the pile do not get hot enough to kill the undesirable organisms, those organisms can reinfest new vegetation when the compost is applied.

Performance: This section typically specifies removal of vegetation from the site, including stripping of sod and soil, in preparation for construction and landscaping. Where vegetation must be removed, coordinate with Section 01354 (01 35 43), Environmental Procedures, to avoid loss of topsoil and contamination of waterways. Minimize site-clearing activities and identify indigenous vegetation to be protected in situ or relocated. Plants that are native and indigenous to the site will not only help to preserve biodiversity, but will perform better than most imported plants.

02340 (31 32 00)   SOIL STABILIZATION

Resource Management: Specify natural clay binders. Also, consider using fly ash to partially replace cement.

Toxicity/IEQ: Soil stabilization involves the addition and integration of foreign material in and on soil in order to strengthen the soil material for the intended construction. Consider the possible impact of such foreign materials on the ground water. Avoid asphalt soil stabilization methods and synthetic geotextile stabilization methods.

Performance: Performance is comparable for green methods and standard methods.

02360 (31 31 00)   SOIL TREATMENT

Resource Management: For soil treatment options, resource management issues closely parallel toxicity issues. The more environmentally friendly alternative to canvassing the construction site with poison is to investigate, evaluate, and adjust the local ecosystem such that the undesirable creatures are not attracted to materials and areas in which they are unwanted. For example, tree limbs or vegetation that touch the exterior walls or roof provide excellent transportation for unwanted wood-boring insects. Rather than spraying the yard, consider relocating and/or trimming plants. For alternative termite control, consider designing a sand barrier around perimeter of the foundation. Because termites live in moist underground colonies and travel upward into buildings only to feed on the wood, they build shelter tubes above ground where they would be exposed to the outside air, which would dry them out and kill them. Termites are very capable of digging through soil, but they are unable to dig through soil of certain grain size. Grains of size 1.6 to 2.5 mm particle size range (mesh 12 to 8) are too large for them to move, and the interstitial space is too small for them to move between the grains.

Toxicity/IEQ: This section typically specifies pesticides and herbicides to control unwanted vegetation, rodents, and insects. Avoid poisonous soil treatment. Utilize the least toxic treatment possible. Borates, for example, are less environmentally damaging than dioxins. Utilize alternative control methods where possible. For example, consider spot applications of gin/soap/vinegar (refer to organic gardening sources for additional recipes). For more pervasive unwanted vegetation, consider importing goats. Goats will eat just about anything and can leave a site bare and ready for tilling and re-planting.

Performance: Alternative designs such as the termite sand barrier require certain preventative maintenance on the part of the building owner, such as keeping vegetation and dead leaves away from the building. Verify that the owner understands the maintenance involved and is willing to perform such maintenance. When used in combination with a termite flashing shield, a metal flashing between the sill plate and the foundation wall, the sand barrier can be extremely effective. If the termites do find an alternate route up the foundation to the wood sill plate, their shelter tube must extend around the angled drip of the flashing, easily exposing their location for spot chemical treatment. The sand barrier system has been approved by the City of Honolulu building code, but other municipalities may require a variance.

02370 (31 25 00)   **EROSION AND SEDIMENTATION CONTROL**

Resource Management: Specify recycled content and natural fiber erosion control blankets. Avoid solid surfacing for erosion control.

Toxicity/IEQ: Consider the impact of foreign substances such as synthetic chemicals in geotextiles on the ecosystems and groundwater. Refer to Section 02340 (31 32 00), Soil Stabilization.

Performance: By specifying plant materials in lieu of slope paving, erosion problems can be addressed without contributing to problems associated with stormwater runoff and flash flooding. Plants utilized for erosion control along drainage channels can form wildlife corridors that help preserve the biodiversity of the area. Coordinate with Section 02900 (32 90 00), Planting. Coordinate with Section 02055 (31 05 13), Soils (Soils for Earthwork), for improving performance of existing soils as a significant component of the local ecosystem.

02500 (33 00 00)   **UTILITY SERVICES (UTILITIES)**

Resource Management: Utility services include water, gas, sewerage, electrical power, and communication services brought to the building. Obviously, the preference is for the appropriate use of renewable resources such as wind or solar energy collected in situ, rainwater collection systems, and constructed wetlands for wastewater treatment. However, buildings that efficiently utilize common infrastructure may also be considered to be green. Many large complexes and even some urban areas are designed to take advantage of economies of scale via central utilities plants. For example, buildings may tap into a central supply of hot water and chilled water to provide heating and cooling.

The routing of services across a site may impact local resources. Consider options for connecting to the infrastructure that preserve existing trees and minimize impact on the local ecosystem, even if it means adding a couple of feet to the service line.

In lieu of storm sewerage, consider minimizing the footprint of the structure and utilizing permeable paving. For permeable paving, refer to Section 02795 (32 12 43), Porous Pavement (Porous Flexible Paving).

Toxicity/IEQ: Water quality is a growing concern in the United States. Most water treatment facilities are attempting to cope with industrial pollutants for which they were not originally designed. Also, many areas have grown so quickly that they have surpassed the capacity of the treatment facilities that serve them. Some municipalities have had to issue moratoriums on new construction based on water treatment capacity. All sources of drinking water contain some contaminants. Because water is the universal solvent, many materials are easily dissolved upon contact. The EPA has issued drinking water standards, or *maximum contaminant levels* (MCLs) for more than 80 contaminants, including benzene (paint, plastic), 1,2-dichloroethane (paints), trichloroethylene (textiles, adhesives), vinyl chloride (PVC pipe), antimony (fire retardants, solder), barium (pigments, epoxy sealants), cadmium (galvanized pipe, paints), chromium (pigments), cyanide (steel, plastics), pentachlorophenol (wood preservatives), phthalate (PVC and other plastics), xylenes (paints), and lead (plumbing, solder, faucets). The EPA generally sets MCLs at levels that will limit an individual's risk of cancer from that contaminant to between 1 in 10,000 and 1 in 1,000,000 over a lifetime. In 1996, 4,151 systems of the nation's approximately 55,000 community water systems, or 7 percent, reported one or more MCL violations, and 681 systems (less than 2 percent) reported violations of treatment technique standards.

Electromagnetic radiation is a growing concern relative to electric utility supply and electrically operated products. There is some evidence linking EM fields surrounding power lines to certain cancers. Refer to Section 16050 (26 05 00), Basic Electrical Materials and Methods (Common Work Results for Electrical).

Performance: Design choices for material selection, systems selection, and general layout of building will greatly impact efficiencies and are addressed under other Sections. The performance of renewable energy systems is improving daily; refer to Section 13600, Solar and Wind Energy Equipment (48 14 00, Solar Energy Electrical Power Generation Equipment) (48 15 00, Wind Energy Electrical Power Generation Equipment). Because of the state of flux in energy distribution systems, communication technologies, and urban approaches to water and waste management, perhaps the greatest performance issue for utility services is flexibility. Ideally, the building owner should be able to easily access, monitor, and, potentially, convert utility services as more efficient and environmentally friendly options are made available. The axiom of design for disassembly and reuse is particularly relevant to the work of this section.

02660 (33 47 00)   PONDS AND RESERVOIRS

Resource Management: This section includes not only decorative ponds and retention basins but also leaching pits (simple biofiltration and graywater filtration systems).

Toxicity/IEQ: It is imperative to understand the local ecosystem, the local climate, and the local drainage patterns before installing a pond. Water in decorative ponds and detention basins may become stagnant and breed mosquitoes. Conversely, when appropriately designed and managed, it may contribute to the health of the local habitat as well as perform the decorative and practical functions for which it was intended.

Pond liners are typically fabricated from synthetic chemicals and petroleum-based products. Consider using natural expanding clay soils where possible.

Graywater filtration systems rely primarily on mechanical processes to treat water. Water is filtered through carbon, sand, rock, and so on. Water can be treated to advanced secondary standards.

Performance: Performance is comparable for green methods and standard methods.

02670 (32 71 00)

CONSTRUCTED WETLANDS

Resource Management: Constructed wetlands address the management of the Earth's freshwater resources. They attempt to address water quality issues with a broad view of the hydrologic cycle that involves less embodied energy in the facility and less chemicals in the water. Because they utilize natural systems to process wastewater, they also contribute to carbon sinking and may contribute to local habitats and wildlife corridors.

The amount of land required for constructed wetlands varies depending on the desired level of treatment and the complexity of the system. Simple exterior wetland systems require 10 to 20 times more square footage than greenhouse systems.

Toxicity/IEQ: Constructed wetlands treat water both mechanically and biologically, not chemically. Water can be treated to advanced tertiary standards and can process metals, fats, greases, oils, gasoline, and some industrial toxins. The Federal Clean Water Act regulates water quality. Regional, state, and local governing agencies adopt their own standards to regulate water treatment. Minimum general standards for wastewater treatment are secondary wastewater, $BOD_5 < 30$ mg/l and TSS < 30 mg/l; advanced secondary wastewater, $BOD_5 < 15$ mg/l and TSS , 30 mg/l; advanced tertiary wastewater, $BOD_5 < 10$ mg/l and TSS < 15 mg/l; pathogen removal required for beneficial public use, fecal coliform, 200/100 ml.

Performance: A constructed wetland is a system engineered and constructed for treatment of graywater, blackwater, and/or stormwater to levels that meet federal, state, and local discharge requirements. They can be interior (greenhouse wetlands) or exterior. Constructed wetlands may serve individual facilities or whole municipalities. They can process metals, fats, greases, oils, gasoline, and some industrial toxins. They also produce usable byproducts such as nursery and water garden plants, compost, and methane gas.

Constructed wetlands may also produce potable water; however, local regulatory requirements for monitoring and acceptance of water treated by constructed wetlands may be challenging. Nevertheless, hundreds of constructed wetlands, 25 to 30 of which are sophisticated designs, currently are operational in the United States.

Maintenance requirements vary with size—approximately 1/2 hour per day for 5,000 gpd system to monitor computers and to trim and harvest plants and organisms. Blackwater treatment systems generally require a licensed wastewater operator.

02700 (32 10 00)   BASES, BALLASTS, PAVEMENTS, AND APPURTENANCES
(BASES, BALLASTS, AND PAVING)

Resource Management: Unless otherwise required in applicable state highway specifications, specify base course aggregate fabricated from minimum 30 percent recycled rubble or concrete and asphalt cement fabricated from minimum 15 percent recycled content asphalt. Refer to 02060, Aggregate (31 05 16, Aggregates for Earthwork) for information on aggregate containing recycled tires.

Wheel stops made from 100 percent recycled plastic are available; refer to Section 06500 (06 50 00), Structural Plastics.

Toxicity/IEQ: Refer to 02060, Aggregate (31 05 16, Aggregates for Earthwork), for information on aggregate containing recycled tires. Refer to Section 06500 (06 50 00), Structural Plastics, for information on plastic lumber.

Performance: Due to stormwater runoff and albedo, pervious paving is preferable to solid surfacing. Refer to Section 02795, Porous Paving (32 12 43, Porous Flexible Paving). Where impervious paving is used, concrete paving is preferable to asphalt paving because of better albedo and maintenance requirements.

The U.S. Green Building Council's green building rating system (LEED) recommends an albedo of less than 0.4 for paved surfaces.

Refer to 02060, Aggregate (31 05 16, Aggregates for Earthwork), for information on aggregate containing recycled tires.

Refer to Section 06500 (06 50 00), Structural Plastics, for information on plastic lumber.

02795 (32 12 43)   POROUS PAVEMENT (POROUS FLEXIBLE PAVING)

Resource Management: Pervious pavement includes interlocking pavers that allow water to percolate through the joints between the pavers and paving forms specifically designed to support soil and grass. Most of the paving forms that are designed to support soil and grass are fabricated from recycled plastic.

Toxicity/IEQ: It has been theorized that pervious pavement, especially pervious pavers designed to grow grass, provide biofiltration similar to graywater systems.

Performance: Specify pervious concrete paving or pervious pavers to minimize stormwater runoff from solid surfacing. Both are subject to failure under heavy loads. Contact product manufacturers for maximum load on pervious paving, and contact the Florida Concrete Paving Association for information regarding pervious concrete paving.

Pervious pavement can be up to 90 percent permeable; that is, under certain conditions, 90 percent of the moisture that hits the paved surface will percolate through the paved surface or evaporate and 10 percent will run off.

02800 (32 30 00)   SITE IMPROVEMENTS AND AMENITIES (SITE IMPROVEMENTS)

Resource Management: Specify site amenities (planters, benches, waste receptacles, bicycle racks, play field equipment, fencing, etc.) manufactured from sustainably harvested wood, 100 percent postconsumer recycled plastic lumber, and recycled metals.

Toxicity/IEQ: Where possible, specify untreated, naturally rot-resistant heartwood such as redwood, western cedar, cypress, elm, black locust, or chestnut in order to avoid chemicals in treated wood. Many South American species, such as cuchi and pau lope, are also naturally rot-resistant. Untreated cuchi wood has been used for more than 100 years as railroad ties in the tropical climate of South America. Refer to Section 06500 (06 50 00), Structural Plastics, for information on plastic lumber.

Performance: Performance is comparable for green methods and standard methods; however, maintenance requirements for plastic lumber will generally be significantly less than painted amenities. Refer to Section 06500 (06 50 00), Structural Plastics, for information on plastic lumber.

02900 (32 90 00)   PLANTING

Resource Management: Specify plants based on a xeriscaping approach, preferably one that utilizes indigenous plants appropriate to the local ecosystems. Where possible, specify appropriate companion planting, seasonal mixes, and habitat vegetation. Companion planting is an art practiced by most gardeners that takes advantage of complementary relationships between some plants, such as carrots and tomatoes or parsley and roses. Seasonal mixes utilize plants that thrive at various times of the year. Seasonal mixes are closely related to providing habitat vegetation. Many birds, animals, and insects, especially migratory creatures, depend on certain plants flowering or seeding at specific times of the year and in certain regions.

Wood fiber mulch manufactured from 100 percent postconsumer paper content and yard trimming composts are available in most areas. Mulch can be made from recycled site debris. Coordinate with Section 01354 (01 35 43), Environmental Procedures, and Section 02230 (31 10 00), Site Clearing. Soil amendment can be made from recycled scrap gypsum; coordinate with Section 09250 (09 29 00), Gypsum Board. Waste gypsum board should be pulverized and spread evenly over the entire site area. Do not deposit it in areas that lack adequate drainage. Verify appropriate application rates with a landscaping consultant. Studies conducted through the Gypsum Association indicate that application rates may be as high as 22 tons per acre. However, in some areas, there may be regulatory restrictions on the disposal of construction waste on-site, and a variance may be required.

Toxicity/IEQ: Specify an integrated pest management approach to plant establishment. Integrated pest management, according to the U.S. Department of Agriculture, Agricultural Research Service, is the judicious use and integration of various pest control tactics of the associated environment of the pest in ways that complement and facilitate the biological and other natural controls of pests to meet economic, public health, and environmental goals. Specify use of native beneficial insects. Specify use of appropriate companion plants, such as those with natural pyrethrums. Minimize chemical pesticides and fertilizers; where chemicals are required, specify the least toxic. Specify organic matter to support establishment of indigenous plants. Specify organic mulch products. Use inorganic materials such as sand or gypsum to improve workability and drainage of soil as appropriate to indigenous plants.

Performance: Xeriscaping utilizes indigenous plants and low-maintenance plants that are tolerant of the site's existing soils and climate without supplemental irrigation or fertilization once established. Native plants perform better than imported species and require less maintenance. Where plants are imported to a region, it is advisable to monitor sufficiently to determine the relative invasiveness of the imported species. Exotic plants, or plants not indigenous to a region, can blend into the local ecosystem, but they can also overrun it, suffocating indigenous plants and crippling habitats.

DIVISION 3 (03)—CONCRETE

03100 (03 10 00)   CONCRETE FORMS AND ACCESSORIES (CONCRETE FORMING AND ACCESSORIES)

Resource Management: This section includes both permanent and temporary forms for structural and architectural cast-in-place concrete. Resource-efficient options for permanent formwork include earth forms and insulated, stackable forms made of minimum 10 percent recycled polystyrene pellets and cement. Temporary forms (metal pan forms, wood forms, and corrugated paper forms) are generally reusable and easily recyclable. Most typically contain recycled contents. Specify reclaimed wood or sustainably harvested wood for wood forms. Refer to Section 06100 (06 10 00), Rough Carpentry, for information on sustainably harvested wood.

Toxicity/IEQ: There are 100 percent biodegradable, zero-VOC form release agents available.

Performance: Permanent insulating formwork conserves energy. Reuse temporary forms to the greatest extent possible. Coordinate with Section 01351 (01 74 19) for reuse and recycling of spent formwork.

03200 (03 20 00)   CONCRETE REINFORCEMENT (CONCRETE REINFORCING)

Resource Management: Chairs and bolsters fabricated from recycled plastic are available. Fibrous reinforcement fabricated from recycled plastic is available. Steel reinforcement typically contains recycled steel. Refer to Section 05100 (05 10 00), Structural Metal Framing, for information regarding the impact of mining and smelting on the Earth's resources and for discussion of recycled content in the steel industry. Steel reinforcing containing 100 percent remelt steel is available.

Toxicity/IEQ: Refer to Section 06500 (06 50 00), Structural Plastics, for information on plastic products. Refer to Section 05100 (05 10 00), Structural Metal Framing, for information on steel products.

Performance: Performance is comparable for green methods and standard methods. Steel reinforcing may be easily separated with magnets from concrete aggregate during recycling operations. Separation of plastic from concrete aggregate may require water to float plastic shards.

03300 (03 30 00)   CAST-IN-PLACE CONCRETE

Resource Management: Mining raw materials (aggregate and components of Portland cement: lime, oxides of calcium silicon, aluminum, and iron) produces soil erosion, pollutant runoff, and habitat loss. Materials for concrete manufacture are found throughout the United States, yet localized depletion of these resources may occur. Where pozzolanic cement is specified, natural pozzolans such as diatomaceous earths, volcanic ash, and pumicites may be used. Fly ash, a pozzolan created as a byproduct of coal combustion, may be used as a substitute for a maximum of 20 percent of Portland cement. Specify 20 percent fly ash or 30 percent ground granulated blast furnace slag content in cement and concrete as per ASTM standards (for cement: ASTM C 595, ASTM C 150, AASHTO M 240; for concrete: ASTM C 618, ASTM C 311, ASTM C 989, AASHTO M 302, ACI 266.R1). The production of concrete is extremely energy-intensive. Equipment required for mining, processing, mixing, and pouring at the site burn fossil fuel and generate pollution.

Toxicity/IEQ: The production of Portland cement generates large volumes of CO_2, a significant greenhouse gas, and dust. Some facilities have reduced their CO_2 production through energy efficiency improvements and through increased use of waste lime (instead of converting limestone to lime). Approximately 50 percent of the kilns in North America use hazardous waste as fuel. There is significant controversy over the burning of waste materials (tires, MSW, and hazardous materials) in cement kilns. The EPA and the Cement Kiln Recycling Coalition are addressing citizen concerns.

Concrete is relatively inert once cured. Admixtures, curing compounds, and sealers may emit VOCs, especially during the curing process. Specify water-based, zero- or low-VOC additives, sealers, and coatings. Verify that the curing compound is compatible with the specified floor sealer or finish. Specify temporary ventilation during placing and curing for interior work. Comply with applicable regulations and with South Coast Air Quality Management District regulations.

Hazardous materials may be encapsulated by being mixed with or embedded in nonporous, durable concrete. However, consider future disassembly and possible options for recycling concrete that has encapsulated hazardous materials.

Performance: Coordinate with Section 01351 (01 74 19) for reuse and pollution prevention. Return excess concrete to supplier and minimize water used to wash equipment. Concrete admixtures are now available that retard the setting of concrete so effectively that a partial load can be brought back to the ready-mix plant for one or two days, then reactivated for use. Cured waste concrete may be crushed and reused as fill or as a base course for pavement. It can also be used as aggregate in concrete manufacturing. Cured waste concrete still possesses an active cement ingredient that reduces the required virgin cement in recovered content mixes by 3 to 10 percent. Despite the recycling potential for concrete, most concrete waste in the United States (approximately 67 percent by weight, 53 percent by volume) is landfilled.

Performance in place is comparable for green methods and standard methods. Concrete construction provides thermal mass and durable construction.

03400 (03 40 00)   PRECAST CONCRETE

Resource Management: Plant fabrication handles raw materials and byproducts at a single location that allows greater efficiency and better pollution prevention than job-site fabrication. Architectural items (planters, birdbaths, bollards) fabricated from lightweight and recycled content aggregates are available. The quantity and type of recycled materials vary from manufacturer to manufacturer, and include cellulose, fiberglass, polystyrene, and rubber.

Autoclaved aerated concrete (AAC) is a type of lightweight precast concrete prevalent in Europe, Asia, and the Middle East. It recently became available through manufacturing facilities in the United States. It is made with Portland cement, silica sand or fly ash, lime, water, and aluminum powder or paste. The aluminum reacts with the products of hydration to release millions of tiny hydrogen gas bubbles that expand the mix to approximately five times the normal volume. When set, the AAC is cut into blocks or slabs and steam-cured in an autoclave. There is also a growing array of precast panel/CMU substitute products; refer to Section 04700, Simulated Masonry (04 70 00, Manufactured Masonry).

Toxicity/IEQ: Refer to Section 03300 (03 30 00), Cast-in-Place Concrete. AAC uses less Portland cement by volume than cast-in-place concrete and traditional precast concrete. When fully cured, AAC forms microscopic crystals of the mineral tobormorite, a form of calcium silicate hydrate.

Performance: AAC is significantly lighter (about one-fifth the weight of traditional concrete) than normal concrete and can be formed into blocks or panels. AAC has the structural, fire-resistive, and acoustic properties of concrete, yet it is lightweight and can be cut with a saw much like a wood product. Coordinate with structural requirements of project. AAC is thermally efficient and considered to be more dimensionally stable than standard concrete.

DIVISION 4 (04)—MASONRY

04050 (04 05 00)   BASIC MASONRY MATERIALS AND METHODS (COMMON WORK RESULTS FOR MASONRY)

Resource Management: Refer to Section 03300 (03 30 00), Cast-in-Place Concrete, for information regarding Portland cement.

Toxicity/IEQ: Refer to Section 03300 (03 30 00), Cast-in-Place Concrete, for information regarding Portland cement.

VOCs may be emitted due to additives, sealers, and coatings. Water-based, low-VOC additives, sealers, and coatings are available. Specify temporary ventilation for interior work.

Performance: Performance is comparable for green methods and standard methods.

04210 (04 21 00)   CLAY MASONRY UNITS (CLAY UNIT MASONRY)

Resource Management: Mining of clay, shale, soil, sand, limestone, and metal ores produces soil erosion, pollutant runoff, and habitat loss. Manufacturing waste is typically recycled in new units. Salvaged units are available in many communities. Brick firing produces fluorine and chlorine emissions. Select locally produced masonry units when available to minimize the environmental impact due to transportation of heavy material.

Toxicity/IEQ: Clay masonry is considered to be relatively inert. Because oil is commonly added (and burned away) during the production of brick, the manufacturer can use oil-contaminated soil that is free from hazardous contaminates. Although radon has been associated with certain soils, bricks do not produce abnormal exposure to radon gas, except in rare situations.

Performance: Performance is comparable for green methods and standard methods. Traditional masonry construction provides thermal mass and durable construction. Masonry is reusable and easily recyclable.

04220 (04 22 00)   CONCRETE MASONRY UNITS (CONCRETE UNIT MASONRY)

Resource Management: Mining of clay, shale, soil, sand, limestone, and metal ores produces soil erosion, pollutant runoff, and habitat loss. Manufacturing waste is typically recycled in new units. Salvaged units are available in many communities. Industrial waste byproducts (air-cooled slag, cinders or bottom ash, ground waste glass and concrete, granulated slag and expanded slag) can be used for aggregate in concrete blocks although documenting this is often difficult. Refer to Section 03300 (03 30 00), Cast-in-Place Concrete, for information regarding use of fly ash and slag in concrete materials. Combustion emissions from mineral process, limestone calcining, and cement kiln operation include carbon dioxide and dust, and may include hazardous materials depending on waste burned in cement kilns. Select locally produced masonry units when available to minimize the environmental impact due to transportation of heavy material.

Toxicity/IEQ: Concrete masonry is considered to be relatively inert. The EPA has reported various aromatic and halogenated hydrocarbon emissions from concrete masonry units, ranging from 0.06 to 0.39 $\mu g/m^2$ per hour. Polystyrene foam insulation emissions include aromatic hydrocarbon emissions of 20 $\mu g/m^2$ per hour. Refer to Section 03300 (03 30 00), Cast-in-Place Concrete, for information regarding Portland cement.

Performance: Performance is comparable for green methods and standard methods. Traditional masonry construction provides thermal mass and durable construction. Masonry construction, when roughly textured, ribbed, or fluted, can help reduce noise by dispersing sound waves. Consider interlocking concrete masonry units for landscape retaining walls; interlocking concrete masonry units do not require mortar and are easy to disassemble and reuse. Masonry is reusable and easily recyclable. Autoclaved aerated (cellular) concrete is available; refer to Section 03400 (03 40 00), Precast Concrete.

04290 (04 24 00)   ADOBE MASONRY UNITS (ADOBE UNIT MASONRY)

Resource Management: Adobe blocks are made from local clays/soils and dried in the sun, avoiding associated pollution of standard masonry manufacture. Primary ingredients include adobe soil and water. Adobe soils are principally from alluvial deposits and are acquired primarily as a byproduct of sand and gravel mining. Straw is sometimes added to prevent cracking.

Moisture disintegrates adobe; therefore, adobe is protected with cement plaster and overhangs. Also, adobe may be stabilized with asphalt emulsion. Asphalt emulsion is made by combining asphalt, a byproduct of crude oil distillation, with water and proprietary surfactants.

Toxicity/IEQ: Only limited VOC outgassing is associated with asphalt emulsion.

Performance: Adobe construction provides thermal mass. Sizes and shapes of adobe blocks vary, and include structural bricks, face brick, and tiles. Adobe construction is suitable for a wide range of climates (not just American Southwest), including extremely cold and extremely wet. Performance may vary in accordance with the type of soil materials available locally. An unstabilized adobe wall without protection from rain erodes at a rate of approximately one inch per 20 years in the American Southwest. Demolished adobe can disintegrate and return to the soil. Adobe is an indigenous construction technique; refer to Section 06700 (06 90 00), Alternative Agricultural Products. Adobe construction dates back to the walls of Jericho, around 8300 B.C.

Cob wall construction uses material similar to adobe (earth mixed with sand and straw) but requires no forming. The word *cob* comes from the early English building technique of using earth (mixed with sand and straw) to form organic shapes, or cobs, of the material, which is then placed to form walls. The cobs require no cement or mortar. The thick walls are sculpted, many times in curves with arches for doors and windows.

04295 (04 29 50)   RAMMED EARTH (*not a standard CSI Section*)

Resource Management: Rammed earth is a compacted mixture of earth, other soil materials, and Portland cement.

Toxicity/IEQ: Rammed earth construction is natural and nontoxic. It is frequently left unfinished on the interior. Refer to Section 03300 (03 30 00), Cast-in-Place Concrete, for information regarding Portland cement.

Performance: Lifts of the soil material are rammed within formwork, which is constructed on-site and removed after walls have undergone adequate curing. Tampers compact approximately 8 inches depth of mix into 4 inches depth in each layer. The walls are characterized by strata of mixture indicating the construction technique. Walls (both interior and exterior) may be left exposed or plastered. Like adobe, rammed earth structures perform best in sunny climates, although they can withstand water. Rammed earth is an indigenous construction technique; refer to Section 06700 (06 90 00), Alternative Agricultural Products. The Great Wall of China, constructed around 200 B.C., is made of rammed earth. Currently, approximately 15 percent of France's population resides in rammed earth structures. Rammed earth construction provides thermal mass and is water- and fire-resistant.

Traditional rammed earth construction is not appropriate where subject to seismic loads. To comply with building codes in California, rammed earth construction has been used as infill for a post-and-beam structure, and has been pneumatically sprayed (similar to gunite) over reinforcing anchored to a concrete foundation.

04400 (04 40 00)   STONE (STONE ASSEMBLIES)

Resource Management: Quarrying stone produces soil erosion, pollution runoff, and loss of habitat. In some instances, quarry sites have been restored to approximate previous condition. From 15 percent to 90 percent of the stone can be wasted during the quarrying process due to chipping, trimming, and inferior materials. Most such waste is disposed of as fill at the quarry site or used for base aggregate in local road construction. Stone is available in this country and abroad. Use of local stone reduces transportation impacts.

Toxicity/IEQ: Toxicity/IEQ is comparable for green methods and standard methods. Radon may be a consideration in extremely rare circumstances.

Performance: Stone construction is very durable and can provide thermal mass. Stone is reusable and easily recyclable. However, excess and demolished stone is usually crushed and landfilled.

04700 (04 70 00)   SIMULATED MASONRY (MANUFACTURED MASONRY)

Resource Management: Alternative masonry products are available in block, plank, and panel form. Depending on the manufacturer, components may include cement, wood fibers, straw, recycled plastic, and expanded polystyrene foam beads.

Toxicity/IEQ: Like concrete masonry, simulated masonry is considered relatively inert. However, plastic and EPS components may outgas. Refer to Section 06500 (06 50 00), Structural Plastics.

Performance: Methods of erection are similar to standard concrete masonry units although some products feature laying without mortar joints (dry stacking). Methods of insulating are also similar to concrete masonry units. Alternative masonry products tend to be lighter than standard CMU and more thermally efficient. Efficient recycling of mixed composition materials (e.g., synthetic plastic and cellulose) is problematic at this time as the technology to separate different materials is still evolving.

DIVISION 5 (05)—METALS

05050 (05 05 00)   BASIC METAL MATERIALS AND METHODS (COMMON WORK
                    RESULTS FOR METALS)

Resource Management: Specify factory finishing rather than field coating where possible. Plant fabrication and finishing handles raw materials and byproducts at a single location, which allows greater efficiency and better pollution prevention than job-site fabrication/finishing. Specify compliance with applicable VOC regulations and, where possible, with South Coast Air Quality Management District regulations (SCAQMD) for shop-applied coatings.

Powder coating is preferable to solvent-based coating application systems. Powder coating uses an electrostatic charge to adhere colored powder to metal. The powder remaining in the electrostatic chamber is vacuumed out and reused. Consider factory finishing that utilizes mechanical process rather than chemical. Mechanical processes such as abrasive blasting, grinding, buffing, and polishing do not generate as much hazardous waste as chemical and electrical processes.

Avoid electroplated coatings wherever possible. When electroplating is necessary, select one of the available replacement technologies listed by the U.S. EPA. The EPA has identified as toxic and/or polluting cadmium plating materials, chromium plating materials, cyanide-based electroplating, and copper/formaldehyde-based electroless copper solutions. Available replacement technologies include the following: noncyanide copper plating, metal stripping, and zinc plating; ion vapor deposition (IVD); physical vapor deposition (PVD); chromium-free substitutes for selected immersion processes; metal spray coating; and trivalent chromium plating for decorative applications. Zinc smelting for galvanizing generates toxic metals waste.

Green Seal recommends that anticorrosive paint contain less than 250 g/l VOCs, less than 1.0 percent aromatic compounds by weight, and be free of the following compounds: halomethanes, methyl chloride; chlorinated ethanes, 1,1,1-trichloroethane; aromatic solvents, benzene, toluene (methyl benzene), ethylbenzene; chlorinated ethylenes-vinyl chloride; polynuclear aromatics—naphthalene; chlorobenzenes—1,2-dichlorobenzene; phthalate esters—di (2-ethylhexyl) phthalate; butyl benzyl phthalate; di-n-butyl phthalate; di-n-octyl phthalate; diethyl phthalate; dimethyl phthalate; miscellaneous semivolatile organics—isophorone; metals and their compounds —antimony; cadmium; hexavalent chromium; lead; mercury; preservatives —formaldehyde; ketones—methyl ethyl ketone; methyl isobutyl ketone; and miscellaneous VOCs—acrolein; acrylonitrile.

Toxicity/IEQ: Factory-applied finishes emit considerably fewer VOCs in situ than field-applied coatings because the primary outgassing occurs at the plant under controlled conditions.

Performance: Performance is comparable for green methods and standard methods. Powder coating is susceptible to damage due to field welding.

05100 (05 10 00) STRUCTURAL METAL FRAMING

Resource Management: Mining raw materials (iron, limestone, coal) produces soil erosion, pollutant runoff, and habitat loss. Ore refinement produces heat and combustion emissions and requires significant amounts of water. Primary environmental concerns in the galvanizing process are related to the rinsing of the fabricated item, which contaminates the wastewater with metals and toxic chemicals. Supply of some of the raw materials (nickel, chromium, and manganese) is very limited. Production of new steel from recycled steel requires 39 percent of the energy required to process steel from virgin material. Traditional manufacturing procedures for processing steel include refining molten iron in either a basic oxygen furnace, an open-hearth furnace, or an electric-arc furnace. A new procedure, not readily available in the United States, is direct steelmaking that eliminates the iron ore agglomeration, cokemaking, ironmaking, and basic oxygen furnace and open-hearth furnace; it also eliminates much of the associated pollution and energy inefficiencies.

Toxicity/IEQ: Steel does not outgas; however, the protective coat of oil found on some steel framing may irritate sensitive individuals if not removed prior to installation.

Performance: Where feasible, use bolted connections to allow for disassembly and reuse. Steel is easily recyclable because it can be magnetically separated from the waste stream. The overall recycling rate for the steel industry is approximately 71 percent. Recycled contents of particular products can vary greatly. Companies that manufacture their own steel for various steel fabrications can better document exact percentages in their products. Zinc can be recovered from both new and old galvanized steel products.

05500 (05 50 00)   METAL FABRICATIONS

Refer to Section 05100 (05 10 00), Structural Metal Framing, for information regarding steel. Refer to Section 05700, Ornamental Metal (05 70 00, Decorative Metal), for information regarding other metals.

05700 (05 70 00)   ORNAMENTAL METAL (DECORATIVE METAL)

Resource Management: Mining raw materials produce soil erosion, pollutant runoff, and habitat loss. Ore refinement produces heat and combustion emissions and requires significant amounts of water. Metal ores are a nonrenewable resource.

Copper has been used for roofing since ancient Greece (the Parthenon in Athens had copper shingles). Approximately 50 percent of the copper used in the United States comes from scrap, which is as usable as the primary copper refined from ore. Declining ore grades has led to increasingly large mines. Ore is crushed and mixed with water and surfactants to make the minerals float to the surface. After smelting, which separates the copper from the iron, sulfur, and other minerals, the copper is refined by fire or electrolytic processes. Sulfur dioxide is produced in copper smelting.

Aluminum is subject to corrosion and must have a protective coating (anodized or duranodic finish). Although aluminum beverage containers are readily recyclable in most communities, most are recycled into new beverage containers. Most aluminum building products contain virgin material. Aluminum is fabricated from bauxite, a mineral found primarily in tropical areas. A significant factor in the clear-cutting of tropical rain forests is the desire to gain access to bauxite mines. Aluminum manufacture is water-intensive; wastewater contaminants include: aluminum, fluoride, nickel, cyanide, and antimony.

Wrought iron (iron that is fashioned or formed into intricate patterns) uses iron with a carbon content of 0.03 to 0.05 percent (ASTM A186); carbon is the ingredient that gives iron a fibrous nature and allows it to be malleable when heated. The lower the carbon content, however, the more resistant to corrosion.

Stainless steel is a family of iron-based alloys containing about 10.5 percent chromium or more and other elements such as nickel, manganese, molybdenum, sulfur, selenium, and titanium. Sixty commercial stainless steel types were originally recognized by the American Iron and Steel Institute (AISI) in three primary categories: austenitic stainless steels are chromium-nickel-manganese compositions (AISI Series 200 and 300); ferritic stainless steels are straight chromium steels (AISI Series 400) that are not hardenable by heat treatment; and martensitic stainless steels are straight-chromium (AISI Series 400) that are hardenable by heat treatment.

Toxicity/IEQ: Metal is inert and has virtually no impact on IAQ.

Performance: Performance is comparable for green methods and standard methods.

DIVISION 6 (06)—WOOD AND PLASTICS (WOOD, PLASTICS, AND COMPOSITES)

06050 (06 05 00)   BASIC WOOD AND PLASTIC MATERIALS AND METHODS (COMMON WORK RESULTS FOR WOOD, PLASTICS, AND COMPOSITES)

Resource Management: Fasteners fabricated from up to 100 percent recycled steel are available. Refer to Section 05100 (05 10 00), Structural Metal Framing, for information regarding steel. Wood products fabricated from reclaimed and remilled structural and nonstructural lumber is available.

Toxicity/IEQ: VOCs may be emitted during the curing process for adhesives and finishes.

Performance: Performance is comparable for green methods and standard methods. Structural lumber fabricated from reclaimed structural lumber generally performs better than comparable lumber available today, because most reclaimed lumber is from turn-of-the-century construction that utilized old-growth, tight-grained hardwood. Despite the demonstrated excellent structural performance, most building codes will require that such lumber/timber be regraded according to current methods.

06070 (06 05 73)   WOOD TREATMENT

Resource Management: There are hundreds of species of trees growing in the world's forests, but we tend to use only a few of them. The ones we do not use are often treated like weeds, left to rot or burned as waste. Using only a handful of tree species puts unbalanced pressure on our forest resources. Where possible, specify lesser-known species. Some species of wood are naturally resistant to decay caused by the elements or termite attack. These include black locust, black walnut, cedar, and redwood. Many South American species, such as cuchi and pau lope, are also naturally rot-resistant. Untreated cuchi wood has been used for over 100 years as railroad ties in the tropical climate of South America.

Toxicity/IEQ: There are three broad classes of wood preservatives: (1) creosote, which is generally used in railroad ties, utility poles, and pilings; (2) oil-borne preservatives, such as pentachlorophenol and copper naphthenate, generally used for utility poles, assembly area roof supports, and glulam construction; and (3) waterborne preservatives, which are the most common preservatives used in residential, commercial, and industrial construction. Waterborne preservatives include chromated copper arsenate (CCA), ammoniacal copper zinc arsenate (ACZA), ammoniacal copper arsenate (ACA), and ammoniacal copper quat (ACQ). Of these, ACQ is generally regarded as the least toxic. However, there are alternative products available that utilize borates, generally a mixture of borax and boric acid. Chlorothalonil, a mildewcide in paints and EPA-registered agricultural fungicide, may prove a viable alternative treatment. Copper napthenate, a water-insoluble copper soap of naphthenic acid—a byproduct of the petroleum refining industry—is being rediscovered and may find increased use in general construction. Borates, chlorothalonil, and copper napthenate are considered less toxic than the standard waterborne preservatives.

CCA is the most common waterborne preservative treatment. The EPA has listed the inorganic arsenical and chromium wastes (residuals, wastewater, treated wood drippage, and spent preservative) as hazardous. Wood treated with CCA may be burned only in approved incinerators, but it may be landfilled.

In use, wood preservatives are usually of fairly low volatility, but they outgas for a very long time. While their emissions rates are not large and they do not generally result in high indoor air concentrations, many of the preservatives present health hazards, including chromium and arsenic.

Performance: Wood preservatives are used to make wood resistant to fungus growth and termite attack. Most building codes require that structural wood elements in direct contact with earth, embedded in concrete/masonry that is in direct contact with earth, or exposed to moisture be treated wood. Many allow alternative, decay-resistant species.

Borate-treated wood performs well relative to protection against decay due to fungus and insects. However, at their present state of development, they do not fix well in the lumber. Consequently, they should not be used in exposed applications where the borates can leach out. Where borate treatment is used, a variance from the building department may be required. The American Wood Preservers Association (AWPA) standards are commonly cited as approved treatment methods in building codes. AWPA is in the process of revising standards to address alternate preservative treatment, such as borate. Refer to Section 02360 (31 31 00), Soil Treatment, for information regarding sand barriers to termites.

06100 (06 10 00)   ROUGH CARPENTRY

Resource Management: Wood is a renewable resource. Harvesting of wood can produce soil erosion, pollutant runoff, increased levels of atmospheric carbon dioxide, global warming, and habitat loss. Approximately 80 percent of the world's ancient forests are gone. Less than 4 percent of U.S. ancient forests remain. Forests provide many environmental benefits, including habitats, potential sources for medicines, and climatic control. Many certified sources of sustainably harvested wood are available. Note that terminology tends to vary in accordance with the program emphasis (economic interest in timber versus environmental interest in forests). For example, *sustained yield* generally refers to the production of a given quality and quantity of timber on an annual basis, but *sustainable* refers to the preservation of the ecosystem. The American Forest and Paper Association (AF&PA), a national trade association of the forest, pulp, paper, and wood products industry, has developed a program called the Sustainable Forestry Initiative that promotes environmentally responsible forest management through self-certification.

Specify lumber bearing the Forest Stewardship Council (FSC) label. The FSC is the only independent, nonprofit, nongovernmental organization that trains, accredits, and monitors independent third-party certifiers around the world. The FSC also promotes excellence in forestry management by helping to establish regional and international forest management standards.

For additional information regarding forests, tree farms, sustainably harvested wood, and non-timber products, contact the FSC or the Certified Forest Products Council. Refer to Appendix A for contact information.

Toxicity/IEQ: Toxicity/IEQ for rough carpentry framing is comparable for green methods and standard methods. Refer to Section 06050, Basic Wood and Plastic Materials and Methods (06 05 00, Common Work Results for Wood, Plastics, and Composites), for information regarding adhesives and finishes.

Performance: The quality of framing materials has decreased as the number of remaining old-growth, tight-grained trees has decreased. Old-growth trees are typically tall, with high canopies and few branches to produce knots along the thick portion of their trunks. The lumber produced from these trees produces high-grade (Architect Clear, Architect Custom Clear, Clear Heart, A Clear, and B Clear) and tight-grained pieces. Avoid these grades where possible. Also, avoid virgin lumber with grain more than 15 lines per inch, as it is likely to have come from temperate ancient forest trees. Specify least grade and grain to suit purpose. Maximize reclaimed and prefabricated lumber. Refer to Section 06170, Prefabricated Structural Wood (06 17 00, Shop-Fabricated Structural Wood).

06160 (06 16 00)   SHEATHING

Resource Management: Sheathing includes Oriented Strand Board (OSB), particleboard, chipboard, Medium Density Fiberboard (MDF) and hardboard. Refer to Section 06170, Prefabricated Structural Wood (06 17 00, Shop-Fabricated Structural Wood), for information regarding resource management of composite wood products. Alternative products such as cellulose fiberboard (recycled newsprint), honeycomb cardboard (recycled paper or alternative agricultural fibers), and straw fiberboard (agricultural waste) are available and can serve many of the same purposes as MDF and particleboard; refer to Section 06700 (06 90 00), Alternative Agricultural Products. Specify the sheathing product with the smallest component wood pieces (the most resource-efficient) that will meet performance requirements. Plywood is fabricated from layers of wood veneer and generally uses the largest component wood pieces. OSB is made from approximately 6-inch-long wood shavings oriented in different directions and bonded together with a synthetic resin. MDF uses smaller waste wood particles than OSB. Particleboard uses the smallest wood particles.

Toxicity/IEQ: Processed wood and wood waste products such as particleboard, chipboard, and hardboard often utilize formaldehyde-based resins as a binder or adhesive. Formaldehyde is considered a probable carcinogen even at low exposure levels. Interior-grade particleboard is fabricated with urea-formaldehyde; exterior-grade particleboard is fabricated with phenol resin, which is at least 10 times less toxic than urea formaldehyde. Particleboards that are formaldehyde-free are also available. Alternative binders include paraffin wax (such as some cellulosic fiberboard) and methyl diiso-cyanate (such as straw fiberboard or some MDF).

ANSI A208.1 limits formaldehyde emissions in particleboard and ANSI A208.2 limits formaldehyde emissions in MDS. Current particleboard products have 80 percent to 90 percent lower emissions than those produced roughly one decade ago.

Performance: Performance is comparable for green methods and standard methods. MDF, particleboard, and alternative agricultural sheathing products function well in nonstructural applications, such as door cores and mill-work.

06170 (06 17 00)   **PREFABRICATED STRUCTURAL WOOD (SHOP-FABRICATED STRUCTURAL WOOD)**

Resource Management: Examples of prefabricated structural wood include wood I-joists, prefabricated wood trusses, finger-jointed lumber, and composite panels. Prefabricated wood assemblies and composite wood panels are more resource-efficient than standard lumber. Prefabricated assemblies utilize sawdust, fibers, chips, and small pieces of lumber. Prefabricated wood generally contains preconsumer waste wood, although some trees are grown specifically for chipping.

Toxicity/IEQ: Adhesive binders used in prefabricated structural wood are any of several synthetic resins that pose varying degrees of human health risks.

Performance: By reducing lumber to component products and reassembling the component products in a manner that maximizes and standardizes the performance of each of the components, prefabricated structural wood can perform better with less material than conventional lumber/timber construction. Prefabricated wood is more difficult to recycle than standard lumber due to the binders.

06200 (06 20 00)   **FINISH CARPENTRY (PREFABRICATED)**

Resource Management: Refer to Section 06100 (06 10 00), Rough Carpentry, for information on wood as a renewable resource and on sustainable forestry. Sheathing materials manufactured from alternative agricultural products are available. Refer to Section 06700 (06 90 00), Alternative Agricultural Products.

Plastic laminates are composed of thin layers of paper and thermosetting resins. Two types of resins, melamine and phenol, are used. Production of melamine and phenol resins is energy-intensive and generates air and water pollutants. Melamine resin contains melamine (produced from urea) and formaldehyde (produced from methanol); phenol resin contains phenol (produced from benzene and propylene, which in turn are obtained from crude oil and natural gas) and formaldehyde.

Two types of paper, kraft (brown, unbleached) and alpha-cellulose (white, bleached), are used. Paper manufacture is energy-intensive and generates air and water pollutants, including oxygen-depleting organics and toxic chlorinated compounds such as dioxins. Paper manufacture is considered to be one of the most polluting processes in manufacturing because of the bleach (chlorine) utilized in whitening the paper. Both types of paper are typically manufactured from virgin materials.

Pigments and inks color the decorative top layer of paper (the alpha-cellulose paper). The inks may also contain toxins such as titanium dioxide and phthalocyanine blue.

Alternatives to plastic laminate countertops include ceramic tile, linoleum, and alternative agricultural products.

Toxicity/IEQ: VOCs may be emitted during the curing process for adhesives and finishes. Low- and zero-VOC adhesives are available. Low-VOC finishes for wood are available. Refer to Section 09900, Paints and Coatings (09 90 00, Painting and Coating). Plastic laminates are relatively inert after manufacture.

Performance: Plastic laminates are easy to clean and disinfect, but can scratch easily. Plastic laminates are difficult to recycle because they are a composite material with thermosetting resins.

06500 (06 50 00)   STRUCTURAL PLASTICS

Resource Management: Plastic lumber is generally fabricated from 100 percent recycled pre- and postconsumer plastics (PET or HDPE, depending on the manufacturer). It may also contain recycled cellulose.

Toxicity/IEQ: As a substitute for treated lumber, it reduces potential leaching of chemicals used in wood treatment. Refer to Section 06070 (06 05 73), Wood Treatment. Plastics are traditionally considered to be inert. Recent academic investigation, however, has indicated that plastics may not be as inert as previously believed. There is some evidence that plastic coatings commonly used to line food cans leach into the food. Once ingested, they may act as endocrine disrupters. To date, there have been no comparable studies researching the health impact of plastic building materials.

Performance: Structural plastic is perhaps a misnomer. CSI MasterFormat 1995 and 2004 Editions includes "plastic lumber and other structural plastics'" in this category. However, plastic lumber is not a substitute for structural wood members. It is formed in boards and posts and may be used for nonstructural applications such as fencing and benches. Plastic lumber is a durable, weather-resistant, and low-maintenance material. Plastic lumber is integrally colored and homogenous, and so does not require painting. It is recyclable.

One hundred percent recycled content plastic lumber may not perform well in lengths greater than 6 feet or where shear is a significant consideration (e.g., fencing, decking, and bollards). For such uses, specify plastic lumber with cellulose fiber. The cellulose fiber improves stability and resistance to screw pullout.

In 1997, ASTM International (ASTM), with significant assistance from the Plastic Lumber Trade Association, approved some of the first standards for plastic lumber: D 6108, Standard Test Method for Compressive Properties of Plastic Lumber and Shapes; D 6109, Standard Test Method for Flexural Properties of Unreinforced and reinforced Plastic Lumber; D 6111,

Standard Test Method for Bulk Density and Specific Gravity of Plastic Lumber and Shapes by Displacement; D 6112, Standard Test Method for Compressive and Flexural Creep and Creep Rupture of Plastic Lumber and Shapes; and D 6118, Standard Test Method for Mechanical Fasteners in Plastic Lumber and Shapes.

06600 (06 60 00)   PLASTIC FABRICATIONS

Resource Management: Plastic fabrications include cultured marble, glass-fiber-reinforced plastic, and plastic formed to various profiles such as trim and planters. Many plastic-formed profiles contain recycled plastic. A few manufacturers are experimenting with recycled fiberglass/plastic possibilities for consumer and building products.

Toxicity/IEQ: Refer to Section 06500 (06 50 00), Structural Plastics.

Performance: Refer to Section 06500 (06 50 00), Structural Plastics.

06700 (06 90 00)   ALTERNATIVE AGRICULTURAL PRODUCTS (*not a standard CSI Section*)

Resource Management: The number of species of plants and animals on which society depends is exceptionally small relative to the number of species available and adequate to the purpose. By promoting the use of alternative agricultural products, the building industry not only can promote less toxic, renewable-resource, carbon-sinking products but also revitalize the market interest in a variety of flora and help to preserve the Earth's biodiversity. *Alternative agricultural products* refers to a growing market segment for the building industry (and other industries) that is capitalizing on little known and underutilized species. The most obvious substitutions are alternative lumber species. Specify alternate, nonendangered/nonthreatened species. The Convention on International Trade and Endangered Species (CITES) lists wood species that are endangered or threatened. Contact the Certified Forest Products Council for information regarding alternative lumber species, their characteristics and availability. Refer to Appendix A for contact information.

Perhaps an even greater potential for developing alternative agricultural building products exists in non-timber plants. Products fabricated from wheat straw, kenaf fibers, soy resins, and bamboo are currently available. There are several sources of fiberboard fabricated from straw and recycled cellulose. There is a decorative hardboard product fabricated from recycled cellulose and soy resins. There are form-release agents for concrete, and adhesives for laminated wood products fabricated from soy resins. Several universities, including Iowa State, the University of Arkansas, and the University of Nebraska, are involved in the research and development of soy adhesives for wood. There is flooring manufactured from bamboo, a fast-growing grass that may be harvested in four years. Starch-based plastics have penetrated the consumer market and are gaining ground in packaging. There are starch-based plastics and cellulose aggregate additives in development that might drastically alter construction procedures.

The Alternative Agricultural Research and Commercialization (AARC) Corporation, which was a wholly owned government corporation of the U.S. Department of Agriculture, made equity investments in private companies to commercialize alternative agricultural products. Because the federal government had an equity position in these companies, Section 729 of the 1996 Federal Agricultural Improvement and Reform Act permitted other federal agencies to establish set-asides and preferences for AARC-funded products, thus helping improve the infrastructure and grow new, green industries. Some of the products developed with AARC assistance include Environ, by Phenix Biocomposites, Inc.; PrimeBoard, by PrimeBoard, Inc.; Bio-Form, by Leahy-Wolf Company; and Agriboard, by Agriboard Industries.

Alternative fuels and the systems that utilize them (e.g., heaters that use corn for fuel) are available. Custom systems utilizing biofuels are available across the United States.

Toxicity/IEQ: Most of the alternative agricultural products are designed to replace petroleum- and synthetic chemical–based products and were specifically developed to be environmentally friendly.

Performance: Typically, only a limited number of wood species (relative to the tremendous diversity available) have approval by governing agencies based upon their documented structural characteristics (bending strength, compression strength, etc.), and by millwork fabricators based on their physical characteristics (grain, luster, heartwood color, sapwood color, texture, odor, ease of drying, weathering, etc.) and woodworking characteristics (blunting effects, boring, carving, cutting resistance, gluing, mortising, molding, nailing, painting, planing, polishing, sanding, screwing, varnishing, veneering, etc.). Introducing alternative species for structural purposes may require a variance from the building department.

Alternative agricultural products are often based on indigenous materials. Indigenous materials include straw, wool, coconut fibers, cactus juice, leaves, ice, and sod. Most governing agencies classify indigenous construction as alternative construction. Use of alternative or indigenous building materials and methods will probably require a variance from the building department. Fortunately, obtaining such a variance is easier than it was previously, due to the groundbreaking work of the Development Center for Appropriate Technology (refer to Appendix A for contact information) to develop sustainable model building codes, and the grassroots efforts in Arizona, California, and New Mexico to incorporate straw bale construction in building codes; refer to Section 06750 (06 75 00), Straw Bale Construction.

Most alternative agricultural products perform adequately to the purpose for which they were designed. In some instances, however, the manufacturer does not have all the testing data typically used to describe performance requirements (i.e., compression, screw pull-out, etc.). Furthermore, such tests have often been specifically drafted and redrafted over the years to accommodate the petroleum- and/or synthetic chemical–based product that the alternative agricultural product is replacing. The standard test methods may not be appropriate to the new type of material. ASTM, ISO, and other standards organizations are only beginning to address this need.

06750 (06 75 00)   STRAW BALE CONSTRUCTION *(not a standard CSI Section)*

Resource Management: Straw is a renewable resource and an agricultural waste product that is typically burned, thus contributing to air pollution. Straw is often confused with hay, which is a food product; straw is the dry stems of cereal grains after the seed heads are removed.

Toxicity/IEQ: Straw is natural and nontoxic, although some people may be allergic to it. While straw bales do not represent a food source, they may provide a home for microbes, insects, and small animals, so it is important to encapsulate the bales inside and outside with Portland cement plaster.

Performance: Straw bale walls can be either load-bearing or non-load-bearing. Typically, straw bale walls are stacked bales pinned together using reinforcing bar (rebar) dowels, which are drilled or driven into the successive courses of bales.

Transverse loading testing in accordance with ASTM E 330, Test Method for Structural Performance of Exterior Windows, Curtain Walls, and Doors by Uniform Static Air Pressure Difference, resulted in a maximum deflection of 1.87" at 20 psf for unstuccoed straw bale walls, and a maximum deflection of 0.13" at 20 psf and a maximum deflection of 0.22" at 50 psf for stuccoed straw bale walls.

Fire testing in accordance with ASTM E 119, Method for Fire Tests of Building Construction and Materials, resulted in a survived flame penetration for unstuccoed straw bale wall of 34 minutes and for stuccoed straw bale walls of 120 minutes (the test discontinued at 120 minutes). The stuccoed straw bale walls survived the fire hose test with no indication of distress or failure.

The *R*-value for straw bale walls, as tested by Sandia Laboratories, is 2.67 per inch of thickness; thermal values for walls range from R-44 to R-52. Many jurisdictions allow straw bale building under the alternative materials and methods provisions of the existing codes, but some have specific provisions for straw bale construction, including parts of Arizona (the City of Tucson, Pima County, Pinal County, the Town of Guadalupe); California (state guidelines and several counties and municipalities); Boulder, Colorado; the state of New Mexico; and Austin, Texas.

DIVISION 7 (07)—THERMAL AND MOISTURE PROTECTION

07100 (07 10 00)   DAMPPROOFING AND WATERPROOFING

Resource Management: Natural materials such as bentonite clay are available (and have long been used) for waterproofing below grade. Many sheet membrane waterproofing materials contain a small percentage of recycled asphalt or rubber. Zero-VOC, clear, penetrating water repellents for masonry, concrete, and stucco are available.

Toxicity/IEQ: VOCs may be emitted during the curing process. Comply with applicable regulations regarding toxic and hazardous materials, South Coast Air Quality Management District regulations, and as specified.

Performance: Performance is comparable for green methods and standard methods.

07200 (07 20 00)   THERMAL PROTECTION

Resource Management: Mining raw materials produces soil erosion, pollutant runoff, and habitat loss. Manufacture of plastic foams may emit benzene and other known carcinogens.

Insulation made from renewable resources such as cellulose is available. Straw, wool, coconut fibers, leaves, and sod are traditional and indigenous insulation materials; refer to Section 06700 (06 90 00), Alternative Agricultural Products.

Insulation made from recycled materials such as cellulose and textiles and glass are available. Thermal batt insulation includes glass fiber (can contain 5 percent to 30 percent recycled glass), cotton insulation (can contain 95 percent postindustrial recycled fiber), mineral wool (made from slag wool, an industrial byproduct from iron ore blast furnace, and rock wool, natural material such as basalt and diabase). Sprayed insulation includes cellulose (which contains up to 75 percent postconsumer recovered paper). Loose fill insulation includes perlite, vermiculite, polystyrene beads (which may contain recycled-content polystyrene, and cellulose (which contains up to 75 percent postconsumer recovered paper). Foamed in-place insulation includes silicate foam (made from inorganic cementitious stabilizer, magnesium oxide, a catalyst, and compressed air) and polyicynene (a petrochemical-based product, with foaming agent of carbon dioxide and water). Rigid board insulation includes cellular glass foam, expanded polystyrene, extruded polystyrene, and polyurethane. Polyurethane typically uses an HCFC or an HFC blowing agent. Polyisocyanurate now uses hydrocarbon blowing agents.

The EPA's "Guideline for Procurement of Building Insulation Products Containing Recovered Materials" (40 CFR 248) recommends minimum recycled content for construction projects receiving federal funding. The EPA recommendations for insulation materials include rock wool: slag 75 percent; fiberglass: glass cullet 20 percent to 25 percent; cellulose (loose-fill and spray-on): postconsumer paper 75 percent; perlite composite board: postconsumer paper 23 percent; plastic rigid foam: (polyisocyanurate/polyurethane): recovered material 5 percent; glass fiber-reinforced: recovered material 6 percent; phenolic rigid foam: recovered material 5 percent.

Avoid insulation materials manufactured with chemical compounds that have ozone-depleting potential, such as extruded polystyrene board. Chlorofluorocarbons (CFCs) and hydrochlorofluorocarbons (HCFCs) have been widely used as blowing agents in the manufacture of insulation foams; they are known to contribute to depletion of the stratospheric ozone. CFCs have already been eliminated in the United States by Clean Air Act amendments, and HCFCs used in many plastic foams will be eliminated by 2020 or sooner. Carbon dioxide and hydrocarbon are available replacement blowing agents, and are already being used by some manufacturers.

Toxicity/IEQ: Adsorptive materials such as batt insulation may act as sinks for VOCs. Thermal and fireproof insulation materials do not necessarily need a soft, adsorptive surface; consider coating with a smooth and impermeable membrane to reduce the adsorption of VOCs. Design such that an impermeable layer is not located to create a moisture problem in the exterior envelope.

Synthetic insulations manufactured via polymerization or foaming and expansion emit VOCs that are known irritants, such as formaldehyde, xylene, and toluene. Most plastic foams release noxious and toxic chemicals when subject to intense heat or fire. The International Agency for Research on Cancer (IARC) identifies slag wool, rock wool, and fiberglass as possible carcinogens. OSHA requires warning labels and MSDSs for fiberglass material, identifying it as a "possible" carcinogen. The long, thin fibers of fibrous minerals are suspected of increasing the risk of cancer. Avoid the use of fiberglass and mineral fiber insulations in conditions that are exposed to the airstream. Fibrous glass insulation materials may contain formaldehyde-based resin binder materials. EPA classifies fiberglass as a probable carcinogen.

It is generally believed that airborne cellulose is nontoxic. However, cellulose insulation can contain chemical additives such as ammonium sulfate, boric acid, and sodium borate, for fire retardancy. The chemicals are considered to be stable under normal conditions (including typical attic conditions). Borates are considered to have low acute toxicity for mammals.

Performance: Insulation conserves energy. Avoid thermal bridging, especially with highly conductive metal framing systems. Loose-fill insulation materials can settle over time, thereby reducing their insulation value; however, loose-fill spray insulation can have an added binder to eliminate settling. Foil facing provides some resistance to air infiltration and adds radiant barrier if air space is provided in front of the foil.

07310 (07 31 00)   SHINGLES (SHINGLES AND SHAKES)

Resource Management: Mining raw materials for the manufacture of fiberglass mat, stabilizers, and surfacing granules produces soil erosion, pollutant runoff, and habitat loss. Asphalt, modifiers, and fiberglass mat binders are derived from petrochemicals. Extraction of petroleum and natural gas can generate air and water pollution. Organic felt with a recycled fiber content is available in some asphalt shingles. Shingles manufactured from 100 percent recycled plastic and cellulose are available.

Toxicity/IEQ: Asphalt base shingles contain petroleum products and will outgas, especially in warm, sunny climates. Because the material is on the exterior of the structure, there is generally little direct contamination of indoor air quality.

Performance: Provide light-colored roof surfaces to improve albedo. Asphalt shingles are recyclable, especially for paving, but the infrastructure necessary to effectively recycle them is not yet developed.

Recycled plastic shingles can have a class A fire rating, pass wind tests up to 110 mph, and be sawed and nailed like wood.

Photovoltaic shingles are available and can be specified in either Section 07 31 63, Solar Collector Shingles, or Section 13600, Solar and Wind Energy Equipment (48 14 00, Solar Energy Electrical Power Generation Equipment).

07320 (07 32 00)   ROOF TILES

Resource Management: Roof tiles may be fabricated from clay, fiber cement, concrete, or metal. Refer to Section 03300 (03 30 00), Cast-in-Place Concrete, for information regarding Portland cement. Fiber-cement roofing can include recycled-content fiber. Felt underlayment can include recycled content. Metal roofing tiles and panels can contain up to 100 percent recycled metal.

Toxicity/IEQ: Clay, concrete, fiber cement, and metal are considered inert. Because the material is on the exterior of the structure, there is generally little direct contamination of indoor air quality.

Performance: Provide light-colored roof surfaces to improve albedo. Clay, concrete, fiber cement, and metal are durable, fire- and insect-resistant, and easily disassembled. Clay, concrete, and fiber cement may be crushed and used for sub-base material or fill.

07330 (07 33 00)   ROOF COVERINGS (NATURAL ROOF COVERINGS)

Resource Management: Obviously, sod and garden roofs offer an excellent opportunity to incorporate renewable resources into the built environment. Modern systems have evolved from traditional building techniques and include membranes and drainage layers appropriate to modern building needs. Some systems are available with drainage layers manufactured from recycled plastic.

Toxicity/IEQ: Garden and sod roofing systems are not only nontoxic, they also have the capacity to improve environmental quality. Plants process carbon dioxide (carbon sinking). They can process certain types of toxins through their leaves and roots. Refer to Section 02055, Soils (31 05 13, Soils for Earthwork), for information on phytoremediation.

Performance: Garden and sod roof systems, when properly detailed and installed, can provide excellent thermal and acoustic insulation. Warranted garden roof systems have been used in Europe for decades. The plants contribute to carbon sinking and can provide wildlife corridors, urban agriculture, and recreational areas. By using water in situ, they also help minimize stormwater runoff and improve local hydrologic cycle functions. Care must be taken to design for anticipated live and dead loads.

07400 (07 40 00)   ROOFING AND SIDING PANELS

Resource Management: Can contain recycled content materials for steel, aluminum, and copper. Refer to Section 05050, Basic Metals Materials and Methods (05 05 00, Common Work Results for Metals), for information on metal finishing.

Toxicity/IEQ: Metal is considered inert. Composite panels generally utilize polystyrene insulation. Refer to Section 07200 (07 20 00), Thermal Protection, for information on polystyrene. Fiber-cement siding is also considered inert.

Performance: Provide light-colored roof surfaces to improve albedo. Composite panels that adhesively combine polystyrene and different metals are difficult to recycle. Fiber-cement siding is recyclable. Mechanical fastening aids in deconstruction for future recycling.

07500 (07 50 00)   MEMBRANE ROOFING

Resource Management: Membrane manufacturers are developing products fabricated from postconsumer materials.

Toxicity/IEQ: The cold adhesives used in adhesive application of roofing membranes are volatile chemicals that pose health and safety risks. They are combustible, harmful, or fatal if swallowed, and dangerous to inhale. Roofing adhesive that is water-based and/or low-VOC is available. Where a solvent-based adhesive is necessary, coordinate with temporary ventilation requirements in Section 01354 (01 35 43), Environmental Procedures, to close all air intakes near the work area to prevent solvent fumes from entering the building. Avoid polyvinyl chloride (PVC) membrane roofing, the most common thermoplastic membrane. Refer to Section 09651, Vinyl Flooring (09 65 00, Resilient Flooring), for information regarding PVC.

Performance: Provide light-colored roof surfaces to improve albedo (at ballasted membranes, provide light-colored ballast). ASTM has developed standards to quantify albedo. New product labels with the EPA and DOE, under the Energy Star program, indicate the solar reflective index. Use roof insulation systems as required by building location and energy calculations for building type and project requirements.

Membrane roofing is relatively durable. The average life expectancy of a coal tar built-up roof is 20 years; the average life expectancy of an asphalt built-up roof is 15 years. The average life expectancy of modified bitumen roofing is 15 years. The life expectancy of EPDM roofing is 20 years. Membrane roofing is difficult to recycle because of the variety of materials involved and because those materials are generally adhered to each other. While reuse and recycling of membrane roofing is not typical, it is possible. Mechanically fastened membranes will be easier to disassemble in the future, facilitating recycling of membrane and of substrate. Installation of a layer of sheathing between roofing insulation and roofing membrane may allow for membrane removal without damage to insulation.

07600 (07 60 00) FLASHING AND SHEET METAL

Refer to Section 05050, Basic Metals Materials and Methods (05 05 00, Common Work Results for Metals), for information on metals and metal finishing.

07800 (07 80 00) FIRE AND SMOKE PROTECTION

Resource Management: Mineral wool has a high resistance to fire and is often used as a firesafing insulation. Mineral wool includes rock wool (from expanded perlite or other mineral) and slag wool (from steel, copper, or lead mill slag). Rock wool is no longer produced in the United States. The EPA recommends that mineral wool insulation contain at least 75 percent recovered slag.

Toxicity/IEQ: Spray-on fireproofing fibers or other components may be released into indoor air. Dust problems can occur when fireproofing is drilled or otherwise penetrated. Adsorptive materials may act as sinks for VOCs.

The International Agency for Research on Cancer (IARC) identifies slag wool and rock wool as possible carcinogens. The long, thin fibers of fibrous minerals are suspected of increasing the risk of cancer. Avoid the use of fiberglass and mineral fiber insulation in conditions exposed to the airstream.

Performance: Performance is comparable for green methods and standard methods.

07900 (07 90 00)   JOINT SEALERS (JOINT PROTECTION)

Resource Management: Avoid polyvinyl chloride (PVC) based products. Refer to Section 09651, Vinyl Flooring (09 65 00, Resilient Flooring), for information regarding PVC.

Toxicity/IEQ: VOCs may be emitted during the curing process. Coordinate with temporary ventilation requirements in Section 01354 (01 35 43), Environmental Procedures. Sealants continue to outgas throughout their life. Specify sealants, particularly for interior applications, that are water-based and low-VOC. Specify that curing-type interior sealants do not contain butyl rubber, neoprene, SBR (styrene butadiene rubber), or nitride. Avoid sealants containing aromatic solvents, fibrous talc, formaldehyde, halogenated solvents, mercury, lead, cadmium, chromium, and their compounds. The following sealants are generally considered acceptable for indoor use: oleoresinous (small amounts of aliphatic hydrocarbons), acrylic emulsion latex, polysulfide (small amounts of toluene vapors), polyurethane (small amounts of xylene and other solvents), and silicone (small amounts of xylene and other solvents). The following sealants should be avoided indoors: butyl rubber (aliphatic hydrocarbons), solvent-based acrylic (xylene), neoprene (xylene), styrene butadiene rubber (various VOCs—hexane, toluene, and xylene, depending on type), and nitrile (various VOCs—hexane, toluene, and xylene, depending on type).

Closed-cell backer rods outgas when ruptured. Open-cell polyurethane backer rods are spongelike and may absorb moisture. Consider composite backer rods.

Performance: Reduces air infiltration and moisture penetration. Performance is comparable for green methods and standard methods. Verify that the proper sealant is specified for the given application. Improper selection can result in reapplication, air infiltration, and water damage.

DIVISION 8 (08)—DOORS AND WINDOWS (OPENINGS)

08050 (08 05 00)   BASIC DOOR AND WINDOW MATERIALS AND METHODS (COMMON WORK RESULTS FOR OPENINGS)

Resource Management: Refer to Division 6 (06) for information related to wood and plastic. Refer to Division 5 (05) for information related to metal.

Toxicity/IEQ: Plastics and factory coatings may outgas.

Performance: Specify window systems that are compatible with the calculated thermal loads of the building. This reduces condensation not only on the glazing and sash but also on the adjacent wall and other interior surfaces. For wood doors and windows, see comments in Division 6 (06). Provide thermal break for exterior framing systems, and weather-stripping for doors in exterior frame to reduce thermal conductivity and improve energy efficiency.

08100 (08 11 00)   METAL DOORS AND FRAMES

Resource Management: Core materials for metal doors vary widely, including fiberglass and plastic foams (polystyrene and polyurethane) for insulating doors, steel ribs, honeycomb paperboard (which often has recovered content), or a fire-resistive core (such as mineral fiber) for fire-rated doors. HFC-free, HCFC-free expanded polystyrene is the preferable insulating core; refer to Section 07200 (07 20 00), Thermal Protection, for information on blowing agents.

Where possible, specify factory finishing; refer to Section 05050, Basic Metal Materials and Methods (05 05 00, Common Work Results for Metals). Where field finishing is required, specify a high-solids, low-VOC durable coating such as a high-performance water-based acrylic paint. Avoid alkyd enamel paint, a solvent-based paint that emits large quantities of VOCs.

Toxicity/IEQ: Metal is inert and has virtually no impact on IAQ.

Performance: Specify an insulation core for exterior metal doors.

08200

WOOD AND PLASTIC DOORS (08 14 00, WOOD DOORS; 08 15 00, PLASTIC DOORS)

Resource Management: Doors fabricated from sustainably harvested wood are available. Specify doors that are certified under FSC principles. Some wood fiber composite doors have insulating cores; refer to Section 08100 (08 11 00), Metal Doors and Frames.

Toxicity/IEQ: Refer to Section 06500 (06 50 00), Structural Plastics. Refer to Section 09651, Vinyl Flooring (09 65 00, Resilient Flooring) for information regarding PVC.

Performance: Performance is comparable for green methods and standard methods. Refer to Section 08500 (08 50 00), Windows, for information regarding the National Fenestration Rating Council (NFRC) rating program.

08500 (08 50 00)

WINDOWS

Resource Management: Windows fabricated from sustainably harvested wood are available. Specify wood windows that are certified under FSC principles and/or are finger-jointed construction.

Toxicity/IEQ: Refer to Section 09651, Vinyl Flooring (09 65 00, Resilient Flooring) for information regarding PVC.

Performance: Specify low-conductivity frame, sash, and spacer materials. Wood has a high R-value. Metal conducts heat; metal frames should have a thermal break.

According to the EPA Energy Star standards for residential construction, in southern states, windows, doors, and skylights must have a U-factor of 0.75 or lower and a solar heat gain coefficient (SHGC) of 0.40 or lower; in the middle states, windows and doors must have a U-factor of 0.40 or lower and an SHGC of 0.55 or lower, and skylights must have a U-factor of 0.50 or lower and an SHGC of 0.55 or lower; and in northern states, windows and doors must have a U-factor of 0.35 or lower, and skylights must have a U-factor of 0.45 or lower.

Green Seal has developed standards for windows (GS-13) and window films (GS-14) that specify minimum requirements for energy efficiency, packaging, and labeling. The National Fenestration Rating Council (NFRC) has a rating program for a fixed set of environmental conditions and specific product sizes. While the ratings may not be directly applicable for determining seasonal energy performance, they nevertheless indicate general energy efficiency parameters. An NFRC label should include residential and non-residential values for the *U*-factor, solar heat gain coefficient, and visible light transmittance. It should also indicate the specific product descriptions such as "Model xxx Casement, low-e, argon-filled."

08600 (08 60 00)   SKYLIGHTS (ROOF WINDOWS AND SKYLIGHTS)

Resource Management: Resource management impacts are comparable for green methods and standard methods.

Toxicity/IEQ: Toxicity/IEQ is comparable for green methods and standard methods.

Performance: Daylight tubes that pipe or duct natural light into a space are available. Active tracking devices are available that follow the sun's path and maximize the amount of natural light directed through the skylight opening. Refer to Section 08500 (08 50 00), Windows, for information regarding the National Fenestration Rating Council (NFRC) rating program.

08700 (08 70 00)   HARDWARE

Refer to Section 05050, Basic Metals Materials and Methods (05 05 00, Common Work Results for Metals), for information on metals and metal finishing.

08800 (08 80 00)   GLAZING

Resource Management: Mining raw materials (sand, limestone, and soda ash) produces soil erosion, pollutant runoff, and habitat loss. Manufacturing is energy-intensive and can generate heat, air, and water pollution.

Recycled glass products are available for decorative architectural glass (stained glass and glass block).

Toxicity/IEQ: Glass is inert and has virtually no impact on IAQ. VOCs may be emitted from glazing compounds during the curing process.

Performance: Glazing technologies are improving rapidly. Control of light and heat transmittance, and the corresponding energy efficiency, is becoming much more sophisticated. At one end of the spectrum is the traditional insulated glazing. Typical, off-the-shelf energy-efficiency specifications may call for double-glazed, low-E units with coating on the second surface (inner side of outer panel) in climates below 3,000 heating degree days, and on the third surface (outer side of inner panel) for climates at or over 3,000 heating degree days. At the other end of the spectrum, however, are photovoltaic spandrel panels and films that turn increasingly translucent/opaque when exposed to heat. Refer to Section 08900, Glazed Curtain Wall (08 44 00, Curtain Wall and Glazed Assemblies).

08900 (08 44 00)   GLAZED CURTAIN WALL (CURTAIN WALL AND GLAZED ASSEMBLIES)

Resource Management: Refer to Section 08800 (08 80 00), Glazing, for information regarding glass, and refer to Section 05050, Basic Metal Materials and Methods (05 05 00, Common Work Results for Metals), for information regarding metals.

Toxicity/IEQ: Glass and metal are considered inert.

Performance: Photovoltaic curtain wall panel systems are available; refer to Section 13600, Solar and Wind Energy Equipment (48 14 00, Solar Energy Electrical Power Generation Equipment).

DIVISION 9 (09)—FINISHES

09050 (09 05 00)   BASIC FINISH MATERIALS AND METHODS (COMMON WORK RESULTS FOR FINISHES)

Resource Management: Many low-VOC, recycled-content products and alternative agricultural-content products are available for interior finishes. Refer to the individual sections for additional information.

Toxicity/IEQ: VOCs may be emitted from products, especially factory-packaged (e.g., shrink-wrapped) products, adhesives, and finishes during the curing process. Ventilate products prior to installation. Remove from packaging and ventilate in a secure, dry, well-ventilated space free from strong contaminant sources and residues. Ventilate away from other materials that may adsorb. Provide a temperature range of 60 degrees F minimum to 90 degree F maximum continuously for minimum 72 hours. Do not ventilate within limits of work unless otherwise approved by the owner. Coordinate with temporary ventilation in Section 01354 (01 35 43), Environmental Procedures.

For most applications, low- or zero-VOC adhesives are available.

Performance: Performance is comparable for green methods and standard methods for a broad range of finish materials; that is, many green products are available at the low, middle, and high end of the performance and cost spectrum, just like standard materials and methods. Performance of a particular green product to a particular standard product may vary.

09100 (09 22 00)   METAL SUPPORT ASSEMBLIES (SUPPORTS FOR PLASTER AND GYPSUM BOARD)

Resource Management: Refer to Section 05100 (05 10 00), Structural Metal Framing, for information regarding steel.

Toxicity/IEQ: Thermal bridging at steel framing in exterior walls can create cold spots in the wall that promote the growth of mold. Refer to Section 05100 (05 10 00), Structural Metal Framing, for information regarding steel.

Performance: Thermal bridging at exterior walls can negatively impact energy efficiency. Dimpled framing is being tested to determine if a dimpled leg, with less surface area in direct contact with sheathing materials, will improve performance. Proper design with sufficient insulation can address this problem as well. Refer to Section 05100 (05 10 00), Structural Metal Framing, for information regarding steel.

09210   GYPSUM PLASTER; 09220, PORTLAND CEMENT PLASTER (09 23 00, GYPSUM PLASTERING; 09 24 00, PORTLAND CEMENT PLASTERING)

Resource Management: Mining raw materials (cement rock, limestone, clay, and/or shale) produces soil erosion, pollutant runoff, and habitat loss. Plaster includes Portland cement plaster and gypsum plaster and metal lath. Refer to Section 03300 (03 30 00), Cast-in-Place Concrete, for information regarding Portland cement. Refer to Section 09250 (09 29 00), Gypsum Board, for information regarding gypsum and paper. Refer to Section 05100 (05 10 00), Structural Metal Framing, for information regarding steel.

Toxicity/IEQ: Plaster is considered inert when cured. VOCs may be emitted from plaster additives during the curing process.

Performance: Performance is comparable for green methods and standard methods.

09250 (09 29 00)   GYPSUM BOARD

Resource Management: Mining raw materials (gypsum, limestone, clay, talc, mica, and perlite) produces soil erosion, pollutant runoff, and habitat loss. Gypsum is a nonrenewable, although relatively abundant, resource. Calcining (heating at 325 to 340 degrees F to become the hemihydrate of calcium sulfate, stucco) produces significant air emissions; particulate emissions include: calcium sulfate dihydrate, calcium sulfate hemihydrate, anhydrous calcium sulfate, and gangue. Paper (cellulose) is a renewable resource. Paper manufacture is water- and energy-intensive. It generates significant air and water pollutants, including oxygen-depleting organics and toxic chlorinated compounds such as dioxins. Refer to Section 09651, Vinyl Flooring (09 65 00, Resilient Flooring), for information on dioxins as carcinogens and endocrine disrupters. According to the EPA's Toxic Release Inventory (TRI) data for 2003, the pulp and paper industry ranked fifth in U.S. industries for total discharges to land, water, and air of TRI pollutants. Most gypsum board products are manufactured with paper backing from primarily recycled paper and gypsum core containing minimum 10 percent recycled gypsum. Percentages vary depending on the manufacturing facility, and are generally increasing throughout the industry as manufacturing facilities upgrade.

Toxicity/IEQ: Additives used to produce waterproof gypsum board (greenboard) and fire-resistant gypsum board may include VOCs. The paper backing may contain chemicals from previous uses (most paper backing contains recycled materials) and additives or chemicals used in the production of the paper itself. VOCs may be emitted from taping compounds and finishes during the curing process. VOC emissions from gypsum board can be minimized in the final building when gypsum installation is properly sequenced (i.e., installed prior to installation of potential sinks) and encapsulated (painted or coated). Coordinate with temporary ventilation in Section 01354 (01 35 43), Environmental Procedures. Joint cement and texture compounds formulated with inert fillers and natural binders are available.

Performance: Performance is comparable for green methods and standard methods. Scrap gypsum can be recycled on-site as soil amendment; coordinate with Section 02900 (32 90 00), Planting, to identify requirements for gypsum soil amendment. Also, placing small scraps in interior wall cavities can add thermal mass and sound insulation.

09300 (09 30 00)   TILE (TILING)

Resource Management: Mining raw materials (clay, silica, talc, feldspar, and limestone) for tile produces soil erosion, pollutant runoff, and habitat loss. Clay and sand are nonrenewable, although relatively abundant, resources. Adhesives for setting tile and for latex mortar and grout are typically derived from petrochemicals. Standard Portland cement mortar is composed of Portland cement, sand, and water; refer to Section 03300 (03 30 00), Cast-in-Place Concrete, for information regarding Portland cement. Pigments include a variety of crystalline materials obtained from the calcining of oxides of metals such as cobalt, nickel, aluminum, and chromium.

Manufacturing of ceramic tile is energy-intensive; however, there have been some energy efficiency improvements in firing techniques in recent years. Manufacture generates significant particulate emissions. Most manufacturers reclaim their fired scrap materials.

Tile containing recycled glass is available; generally, the recycled glass is preconsumer, industry waste such as windshield glass and waste from light bulb manufacture. Tile containing feldspar tailings, a byproduct of the feldspar refining process, is available.

Toxicity/IEQ: Tile (ceramic and quarry) is inert, and cementitious mortar and grout is considered inert when cured. VOCs may be emitted from self-leveling cements and adhesives during the curing process. Avoid mortars, grout, and adhesives containing petroleum or plastic additives. Additives in latex formulations may include styrene butadiene rubber, acrylic resin, polyvinyl acetate, and ethylene vinyl acetate.

Performance: Tile is extremely durable and requires little maintenance. Performance is comparable for green methods and standard methods.

09400 (09 66 00)   TERRAZZO (TERRAZZO FLOORING)

Resource Management: Terrazzo flooring was originally developed as a byproduct of Italian mosaic artwork. As mosaic artists chipped marble tessera for their mosaic pieces, the marble and lime mortar tailings that fell to the floor were swept out on the terrace, where they were trampled into the surface. Soon, such flooring was common on Italian terraces—hence, *terrazza*. Today, the chips are generally not byproducts but are specifically mined. Mining raw materials (marble, granite, quartzite, quartz, silica pebbles, sand, and components of Portland cement) produces soil erosion, pollutant runoff, and habitat loss. Underground mining of crushed stone is becoming more common due to increased environmental and economic benefits. In underground (room-and-pillar) mining, there is less overburden to be removed, and operations can continue all year long. Components of resins, primers and sealers are typically derived from petrochemicals. Refer to Section 03300 (03 30 00), Cast-in-Place Concrete, for information regarding Portland cement.

Terrazzo aggregate can contain recycled glass stone and glass aggregate.

Toxicity/IEQ: When cured, terrazzo is fairly inert. VOCs may be emitted from plastic matrix during the curing process and from sealers during curing and periodic maintenance. Coordinate with temporary ventilation in Section 01354 (01 35 43), Environmental Procedures, especially where epoxy terrazzo systems are used. Waterborne acrylic sealers are available for most applications. Avoid epoxy sealers except where chemical or stain resistance is required. Avoid polyvinyl divider strips; refer to Section 09651, Vinyl Flooring (09 65 00, Resilient Flooring), for information on PVC.

Performance: Performance is comparable for green methods and standard methods. Terrazzo with glass aggregate has an apparent depth and luminescence that can be very beautiful. An alternative to sealing Portland cement terrazzo is to clean with a neutral cleaner/water solution. After several cleanings, the residue of cleaner on the floor makes it buffable. After approximately two months, the floor finish has a patina that requires less maintenance.

09510 (09 51 00)   ACOUSTICAL CEILINGS

Resource Management: The major constituents of acoustical ceiling tiles are mineral wool (fabricated from slag and rock wool), cellulose, starch (primarily from corn), clay (for fire-rated products), fiberglass, and paint. Mining raw materials produces soil erosion, pollutant runoff, and habitat loss. Manufacture of acoustic ceiling tiles does not generate much waste because scrap material is recycled back into the process. Acoustic ceiling tile manufactured from recycled cellulose is available; generally, the recycled cellulose is preconsumer industry waste. Steel framing containing recycled steel is available. Refer to Section 05100 (05 10 00), Structural Metal Framing, for information regarding steel.

Toxicity/IEQ: Paints used in ceiling tiles and panels are low-VOC water-based paints. Refer to Section 07200 (07 20 00), Thermal Protection, for information regarding slag wool, rock wool, and fiberglass as possible carcinogens. Avoid vinyl-faced ceiling tiles. PVC is used in the vinyl facing on some ceiling tiles. Refer to Section 09651, Vinyl Flooring (09 65 00, Resilient Flooring), for information regarding PVC.

Adsorptive materials may act as sinks for VOCs emitted from other sources. When the concealed spaces above suspended ceilings are used as return air plenums, both the upper and lower surfaces of the ceilings are exposed to the circulating air stream. The temperatures at the ceiling surfaces are generally among the warmest in the interior space due to the thermal stratification that normally occurs. The increased temperature results in increased emissions of VOC from the ceiling materials.

Cornstarch used as a binder can, in the presence of moisture, fuel growth of bacteria and mold.

Performance: Performance of green materials for noise reduction coefficient (NRC) standards and light reflectance is comparable to standard materials. Cellulose ceiling tiles are suitable for dry areas and moderate acoustical requirements. Where acoustical demands are higher, specify mineral fiber tiles or cellulose tiles coated with low-VOC water-based paint. Cellulose, mineral fiber, and glass fiber can absorb moisture in high humidity areas and promote microbial growth. In those areas, specify tiles with non-absorptive cores such as glass fiber reinforced polyester.

09640 (09 64 00)   WOOD FLOORING

Resource Management: Wood flooring manufactured from reclaimed lumber and from alternative species is available. Bamboo, for example, is a fast-growing grass that can be finished into beautiful hardwood flooring. Bamboo can be specified in Section 09 62 23, Bamboo Flooring. Refer to Section 06700 (06 90 00), Alternative Agricultural Products, for information on alternative species. Refer to Section 06100 (06 10 00), Rough Carpentry, for information on wood as a renewable resource and on sustainable forestry. Most stains and varnishes are derived from petrochemicals.

Toxicity/IEQ: Avoid wood floor finishes that are solvent-based polyurethanes. Water-based polyurethanes contain mostly aliphatic hydrocarbons instead of the mostly carcinogenic aromatic hydrocarbons found in solvent-based finishes. Other alternatives include waxes and citrus-based finishes.

Performance: Performance is comparable for green methods and standard methods. Bamboo has twice the stability of red oak and up to 90 percent of the hardness. Installation and maintenance is similar to a hardwood floor. Water-based polyurethanes may not perform as well as solvent-based in high-traffic areas.

09651 (09 65 00)   VINYL FLOORING (RESILIENT FLOORING)

Resource Management: Many of the components of vinyl flooring are derived from petrochemicals. Resilient flooring manufactured from 100 percent recycled PVC is available in sheet, tile, and plank.

Vinyl flooring and vinyl composite tiles (VCTs) are manufactured from a variety of hazardous chemicals and nonrenewable petroleum-based resources, including ethylene dichloride and polyvinyl chloride (PVC). Manufacture of PVC produces many highly toxic byproducts, including: dioxins, polychlorinated biphenyls (PCBs), and organochlorines. Hundreds of substances known or suspected of causing cancer and/or of disrupting our immune and reproductive systems are produced. There are two main groups of hormone-disrupting chemicals associated with PVC: dioxins (formed as a byproduct in the oxychlorination process) and phthalates (plasticisers). Phthalates are possible carcinogens. Dioxins are known carcinogens and are considered by many the most toxic man-made chemical ever. In addition, other chemicals suspected as hormone disrupters are used as additives in PVC, including organotins, cadmium, lead, and small quantities of alkyl-phenols. Dioxins are released during the manufacture of PVC and when PVC is burned or is recycled. Phthalates are released during processing of plastics, during the product's life, and even after it is disposed. Internationally, use of PVC is becoming more and more restricted. Communities in Germany, Austria, Japan, the Netherlands, Norway, Sweden, and Denmark have PVC restrictions in place. Restrictions are also in various stages of development and implementation at the national level in Spain, Switzerland, Denmark, and Sweden. The U.S. Environmental Protection Agency is currently reassessing dioxin.

Titanium dioxide (TiO_2) is a common white pigment in resilient flooring. Manufacture of titanium dioxide can produce sulfuric acid, metal sulfate, and metal chloride byproducts. According to NIOSH, titanium dioxide may cause lung fibrosis and is considered an occupational carcinogen.

Toxicity/IEQ: Vinyl flooring outgasses and, when burned, releases hydrogen chloride, metal chlorides, and dioxins. When vinyl flooring is incinerated, heavy metals remaining in the ash must be treated as hazardous waste.

Most leveling compounds contain latex or polyvinyl acetate resins, and can emit VOCs, including 4-PC. Adhesives may also be a source of VOCs. Factory-backed adhesive tiles have fewer emissions than standard wet adhesive installation. Low- and zero-VOC adhesives are available. Some styles of plastic flooring are available in loose-laid design (puzzle pieces that are tapped together with a rubber mallet) that can be installed without adhesive.

Performance: Solid vinyl flooring has a static load resistance of up to 700 psi; vinyl composition tile (VCT) has a static load resistance of up to 80 psi. Vinyl becomes brittle as it ages, and the plasticizers migrate out of the material; vinyl-resilient flooring typically has a lifespan of 8 to 15 years. Consider solid vinyl products only where chemical resistance is required. Factory-backed adhesive tiles may not perform as well as wet adhesive installation in high-traffic areas.

09652 (09 65 00)   RUBBER FLOORING (RESILIENT FLOORING)

Resource Management: Rubber floors may contain industrial and natural rubber. Industrial rubber is obtained through the polymerization of petroleum products. By varying the polymerization process, rubber with varying characteristics is produced. Natural rubber is a renewable raw material that is extracted from the sap of the tropical rubber plant (without harming the plant). Rubber flooring with 75 percent to 100 percent postconsumer recycled content is available.

Toxicity/IEQ: Rubber does not contain any PVCs, halogens (chlorine, bromine, iodine, fluorine), plasticizers, formaldehyde, or cadmium.

Performance: Rubber flooring is extremely hard-wearing and flame-retardant, and it is permanently resilient. Antistatic and chemically resistant rubber flooring is available. No waxes are required to maintain rubber floors. Fewer color and pattern options are available for rubber than are available for linoleum or vinyl. Rubber is recyclable.

09653 (09 65 16.13)   LINOLEUM FLOORING

Resource Management: Linoleum is manufactured from cork, linseed oil, wood flour, and pine resin. Ground stone and wood are added for color. Backing is typically jute or polyglass. As agricultural products, cultivation of jute, flax (linseed oil), and pine can contribute to carbon sinking; they can also result in runoff of pesticides and chemical fertilizers. Wood flour and cork flour are typically obtained from preconsumer industrial wastes. Polyglass is a combination of fiberglass and polyester fibers. The finish coat is typically a waterborne acrylic. Titanium dioxide (TiO_2) is a common white pigment in resilient flooring. Refer to Section 09651, Vinyl Flooring (09 65 00, Resilient Flooring), for information on titanium dioxide.

Manufacture generates very little waste because nearly all manufacturing waste is recycled into product.

Toxicity/IEQ: Linoleum is made predominantly from renewable resources, and while it has a distinctive odor, it emits no dangerous VOCs. Offgassing from linoleum may cause problems for persons with chemical sensitivity, especially during the first few days after installation. After a few days or weeks, the oxidation of the linseed oil decreases significantly.

Linoleum is naturally antibacterial because of the continuous oxidation of the linseed oil.

Performance: Linoleum is biodegradable and may be shredded and composted. It is very durable; linoleum flooring typically has a lifespan of 40 years (or more). Linoleum tile has a static load resistance of 700 psi; linoleum sheet has a static load resistance of 150 psi. Linoleum is water-resistant, but it must be protected from moisture from the substrate both during and after installation.

Linoleum is available in sheet or tiles.

Linoleum can be maintained with a dry maintenance system and periodic buffing; it does not require (and may be damaged by) the periodic wet maintenance and refinishing that is typical on vinyl flooring.

09654 (09 62 29) CORK FLOORING

Resource Management: Cork is a renewable resource harvested on a nine-year cycle. Some cork flooring is fabricated from bottle-cork industry waste. Manufacture involves few toxins and generates very little waste because nearly all manufacturing waste is recycled into product.

Toxicity/IEQ: Cork is naturally antibacterial.

Performance: Cork provides good soundproofing and insulation. It may be used as an underlayment for ceramic or wood floors. It may also be finished flooring itself. Cork is biodegradable and recyclable. It is very durable; cork flooring typically has a lifespan of 40 years (or more).

09680 (09 68 00) CARPET (CARPETING)

Resource Management: Wool, cotton, jute, hemp, sea-grass, and sisal rugs and carpets are available. Carpet manufactured from recycled PET (soda pop bottles) or from BASF nylon (sometimes called *6 again nylon*) is available. The BASF nylon is recyclable, and a close-the-loop infrastructure is developing within the carpeting industry, whereby manufacturers can reclaim and recycle carpeting manufactured from the BASF fiber. Previously, carpet manufacturers argued that old carpeting could not be recycled into new carpeting, and that reclaimed synthetic carpet was recycled into roadbase aggregate and fill. Carpet pads manufactured from recycled textiles and waste carpets are available.

Toxicity/IEQ: Synthetic carpet fiber, backing, pad, adhesive, seam sealants, carpet treatment (mothproofing, antimicrobial, etc.) and floor-preparation chemicals are all potential sources of VOCs in indoor air. Carpet can contain more than 100 chemicals, including possible carcinogens. VOCs may be emitted from adhesives and from interaction of adhesive and carpet backing during the curing process. Install with tack strips (stretch-in method) over pads to avoid adhesive interaction with carpet backing. Hook-and-loop (Velcro) installation has been developed by 3M (called the TacFast system) and is available for carpeting from several mills. The carpet has a special loop backing that easily fastens and refastens to the companion hook strips adhered to the substrate. TacFast installation significantly reduces the VOCs due to adhesive carpet installation, making replacement of carpeting easier.

The Carpet and Rug Institute (CRI) addresses issues of IAQ and carpeting, and sponsors a green label program. CRI has established emission-level standards for: total volatile organic compounds (TVOCs), styrene; 4-PC (4 phenylcyclohexene), and formaldehyde. Green Seal recommends that carpets bear the CRI Indoor Air Quality Carpet Testing Program label or satisfy the State of Washington guidelines.

Carpeting also provides a sink for absorbing VOCs emitted from other sources and a home for a variety of bacteria, microbes, dust mites, and so on. Area rugs are a good alternative because they can be removed and cleaned outdoors by beating and letting the sun bake them.

Performance: Carpeting provides improved thermal and acoustic performance. Natural carpets are typically more expensive and require more care than most synthetic rugs, but they can age more beautifully.

In addition to the close-the-loop recycling programs developing in the carpet industry, a few manufacturers also have green lease programs.

09720 (09 72 00)   WALL COVERINGS

Resource Management: Cellulose (in wallpaper) is a renewable resource. Refer to Section 09250 (09 29 00), Gypsum Board, for information regarding paper. Polyvinyl chloride (in vinyl wall covering) is a significant environmental hazard. Refer to Section 09651, Vinyl Flooring (09 65 00, Resilient Flooring), for information on PVC.

Wall coverings manufactured from recycled cotton, sustainably harvested wood, and natural materials such as sisal, jute, straw, and wool are available.

Toxicity/IEQ: Fabrics, plastics, and paper wall coverings all have unique potential chemical content and emission characteristics. Avoid vinyl wall covering due to the PVC content.

VOCs may be emitted from adhesives and backings during the curing process.

Performance: Performance is comparable for green methods and standard methods.

09900 (09 90 00)   PAINTS AND COATINGS (PAINTING AND COATING)

Resource Management: Most standard paints contain some materials that are derived from petroleum products. Titanium dioxide (TiO_2) is a common white pigment in standard paint; refer to Section 09651, Vinyl Flooring (09 65 00, Resilient Flooring), for information regarding titanium dioxide. Paints manufactured from natural plant- and mineral-based finishes are available. They contain extracts from plant sources and minimally processed earth minerals, such as chalk or iron oxides. Solvents for natural paints include citrus oils and small amounts of low-odor petroleum solvents (dearomaticized isoparrafinics). Milk-based paint contains lime, milk protein, clay, and earth pigments. Recycled-content paints are available.

Toxicity/IEQ: Paint products contain a variety of VOCs incorporated as drying agents, flattening agents, mildewcides, fungicides, preservatives, and others. Harmful chemicals found in paint include methylene chloride, 1,1,1-

trichloroethane, benzene, toluene, ethylbenzene, vinyl chloride, naphthalene, 1,2-di-chlorobenzene, di(2-ethylhexyl) phthalate, butyl benzyl phthalate, di-n-butyl phthalate, di-n-octyl phthalate, diethyl phthalate, dimethyl phthalate, isoprene, antimony, cadmium, hexavalent chromium, lead, mercury, formaldehyde, methyl ethyl ketone, methyl isobutyl ketone, acrolein, acrylonitrile. These VOCs have been measured in indoor air many months after application of the paints. South Coast Air Quality Management District (SCAQMD) has adopted VOC regulations; jurisdictions outside of California, including the federal government, have begun adopting similar regulations. Low-biocide paint is available. Low- and zero-VOC paint is available for both interior and exterior paint. Even paint labeled "zero-VOC" may contain a maximum 1 gram/liter (white paint). There may be a slight increase in VOC for colored paint. Pigments can add as much as 5 percent to a paint's VOC content. Even natural paints may emit VOCs (natural VOCs), which may pose a problem for some chemically sensitive individuals.

Coordinate with temporary ventilation in Section 01354 (01 35 43), Environmental Procedures.

Performance: Milk-based paint, the most common paint prior to this century, is not appropriate for exterior use or damp conditions.

Recycled-content paints, depending on the source of reclaimed paint products, may not meet VOC regulations. Some locals are developing regulatory language that exempts recycled-content paint from VOC restrictions. Recycled-content paint may also be limited in color depending on the source of reclaimed paint products. Sources of recycled content include community hazardous waste collection programs and contractor leftovers.

The performance of low-VOC paint has improved considerably over the last several years. Specify compliance with applicable VOC regulations and SCAQMD VOC regulations, which continue to be some of the strongest VOC requirements in the country, and have contributed to the development of viable low-VOC paints. However, be careful when specifying particular VOC maximum contents relative to the type of paint and type of application. VOC regulations have been volatile themselves, and limits change frequently. Rule 1113, the SCAQMD rule covering paints and coatings, has the distinction of being one of the most amended pieces of regulations in U.S. history. As a guide, for general interior and exterior applications, use water-based latex primers and paints with no aromatic hydrocarbons and VOC content of fewer than 10 grams/liter; for applications subject to impact such as door frames, use water-based, 100 percent solids, high-performance acrylic instead of solvent-based paints; if solvent-based paint is required, use a product with a VOC content of fewer than 380 grams/liter and an aromatic hydrocarbon content less than 1 percent by weight; if epoxy paint is required, use a solvent-free, high-solids, zero-VOC epoxy.

Green Seal has developed standards for anticorrosive paints (GS-03) and for paints (GS-11); they specify minimum requirements for performance, utilizing applicable ASTM standards, VOC limitations, chemical component limitations, packaging, and labeling.

Ceramic coatings for field application over typical exterior cladding materials (masonry, stucco, wood) are also available. Ceramic coatings are low-emissivity paints that reflect radiant energy. Such coatings can generate energy savings of up to 30 percent during the cool season, and are extremely durable.

DIVISION 10—SPECIALTIES

10100 (10 11 00)   VISUAL DISPLAY BOARDS (VISUAL DISPLAY SURFACES)

Refer to Section 09654 (09 62 29), Cork Flooring, for information regarding cork.

10170 (10 21 13.19)   PLASTIC TOILET COMPARTMENTS

Resource Management: Toilet compartments with cores manufactured from minimum 50 percent recycled plastic are available.

Toxicity/IEQ: Refer to Section 06500 (06 50 00), Structural Plastics.

Performance: Plastic partitions perform as well or better than most toilet partitions. They are water-resistant, graffiti-resistant, and nonabsorbent, with plastic face sheets permanently fused to plastic core. The pilaster shoes are one-piece-molded HDPE. Wall-mounting brackets are continuous, full-height, heavy-duty plastic.

10260 (10 26 00)   WALL AND CORNER GUARDS (WALL AND DOOR PROTECTION)

Recycled plastic wall guards are available. Refer to Section 06500 (06 50 00), Structural Plastics. Sustainably harvested wood wall guards are available. Refer to Section 06100 (06 10 00), Rough Carpentry.

10270 (09 69 00)   ACCESS FLOORING

Resource Management: Access flooring is fabricated with aluminum, steel, and medium-density fiberboard parts. At least one manufacturer, Camino Modular Systems, in Ontario, Canada, is reclaiming used access flooring and refurbishing it for reuse.

Toxicity/IEQ: Medium-density fiberboard generally contains formaldehyde. The concealed space between the raised floor and the structural floor can be a source of contaminants, either gaseous or particulate. However, it can also be used for locating sophisticated personal air control systems.

Performance: Performance is comparable for green methods and standard methods.

10290 (10 81 00)   PEST CONTROL (PEST CONTROL DEVICES)

Resource Management: Integrated pest management is an environmentally sound system of controlling landscape pests. It includes well-timed nontoxic treatments and an understanding of the pest's life cycle and natural enemies. Gardeners have been using this approach for centuries. For example, carnivorous insects such as ladybugs are often used to combat aphids; and certain plant combinations promote mutual health and growth (roses and parsley or carrots and tomatoes). Some plants, such as chrysanthemums, have natural pyrethrums. Integrated pest management works with the natural cycles of the ecosystem to take advantage of nature's pest controls. This not only minimizes introduction of toxic, synthetic chemicals, but can also help renew functioning ecosystems. Proper design can also minimize the need for application of toxic chemicals. Refer to Section 02360 (31 31 00), Soil Treatment.

Toxicity/IEQ: Selection of materials, proper application, and proper scheduling of pesticide applications can reduce exposures of building occupants. Alternatives to more toxic commercial pest control agents include:

- Exterior plant insecticide: Substitute vinegar, soap, gin, and water mixture.
- Indoor plant insecticide: Substitute dishwater or bar soap and water.
- Mothballs: Substitute cedar chips and lavender flowers.

Performance: Because it addresses the problem, not just the symptom, alternative pest control can be more effective than standard chemical treatment methods. It does, however, tend to require certain preventative maintenance on the part of the building owner, such as preventing pest access to food sources. Verify that the owner understands the maintenance involved and is willing to perform such maintenance.

| 10300 (10 30 00) | FIREPLACES AND STOVES |

Resource Management: Steel utilized on stoves is recycled material. Steel stoves used for heating that are manufactured from up to 100 percent postconsumer steel are available. Although local conditions vary, combustion appliances rely on a relatively inefficient use of natural resources that generates air emissions and contributes to global warming.

Toxicity/IEQ: Combustion appliances including fireplaces and wood stoves can be sources of organic and inorganic gases and of particulate matter. Smoke particles are possible carcinogens.

Performance: Cast-iron woodstoves, gas stoves, and fireplaces may be used for space heating. Efficiencies have improved in recent years, and range from 50 percent to 90 percent.

| 10800 (10 28 00) | TOILET, BATH, AND LAUNDRY ACCESSORIES |

Resource Management: Automatic, sensor-operated hand dryers are available.

Toxicity/IEQ: Automatic hand dryers replace paper towels and eliminate their disposal and associated bacteria.

Performance: Performance is comparable for green methods and standard methods.

DIVISION 11—EQUIPMENT

| 11110 (11 23 00) | COMMERCIAL LAUNDRY AND DRY CLEANING EQUIPMENT |

Resource Management: Ozonation is an alternative method for laundry (and dishwashing) that conserves water and minimizes chemical usage. With ozone laundering, washing time can be reduced by nearly half because the rinse cycle can be eliminated.

Toxicity/IEQ: Ozone oxidizes bacteria, viruses, and other contaminants without undesirable odors or byproducts. Ozone is ph neutral, and reduces chemical usage up to 95 percent. Ozone oxidizes contaminants up to 3,000 times faster than chlorine.

Performance: With the addition of ozone as an oxidant, laundry and dishwashing machines can run at lower wash temperatures for shorter cycles. In most situations (including hotels), laundry is cleaned as effectively with ozonation as with chemical laundry methods. Ozonation reduces chemical costs, chemical storage requirements, and labor expenses. It requires weekly, rather than daily, chemical check. It prolongs life of equipment by reducing calcium and scale buildup.

11140 (11 11 00)   VEHICLE SERVICE EQUIPMENT

Resource Management: Electric charging stations and compressed natural gas (CNG) fueling stations are necessary for changing our transportation infrastructure. By utilizing alternative fuels, we can all help to reduce greenhouse gas emissions, especially one of the most significant: carbon dioxide. Carbon dioxide is a major greenhouse gas. In the upper levels of the atmosphere, carbon dioxide acts similarly to the windshield on a car, trapping heat. Atmospheric carbon dioxide concentrations are significantly greater than preindustrial levels. Much of the carbon dioxide buildup is due to automobiles, which have increased in number steadily since World War II.

Vehicle washing equipment routinely recycles water. Depending on the applicable regulatory requirements, auto service centers may reclaim tires and recycle oil.

Toxicity/IEQ: Equipment that promotes alternative fuel and recycling is always environmentally preferable and less polluting.

Performance: Specific performance evaluations are difficult, as they tend to be apples-and-oranges comparisons.

11150 (11 12 00)   PARKING CONTROL EQUIPMENT

Resource Management: Traffic control speed bumps manufactured from recycled rubber are available. Parking stops manufactured from recycled plastic are available. Refer to Section 06500 (06 50 00), Structural Plastics.

Toxicity/IEQ: Toxicity/IEQ is comparable for green products and standard products.

Performance: Performance is comparable for green methods and standard methods. Recycled rubber speed bumps often have longer life cycles than asphalt speed bumps. Recycled plastic parking stops often have longer life cycles than concrete parking stops; and, where colored stops are required, plastic outperforms concrete, as it is homogenous (including color) and does not require painting.

11160 (11 13 00)   LOADING DOCK EQUIPMENT

Resource Management: Bumpers manufactured from recycled tires are available.

Toxicity/IEQ: Toxicity/IEQ is comparable for green products and standard products.

Performance: Performance is comparable for green methods and standard methods.

11170 (11 82 00)   SOLID WASTE HANDLING EQUIPMENT

Resource Management: Reclamation and recycling options exist for almost every region for almost every material.

Toxicity/IEQ: Toxicity/IEQ is comparable for green methods and standard methods.

Performance: Composting and recycling equipment is available for commercial and residential use. Refer to Section 11450 (11 30 00), Residential Equipment. Chute systems that allow for separate collection of solid waste are available for multistory construction.

11200   WATER SUPPLY AND TREATMENT EQUIPMENT (44 40 00, WATER TREATMENT EQUIPMENT)

Resource Management: Rainwater harvesting systems are available for irrigation and potable water. The system can be as simple as a barrel under a downspout or as complex as a system with filters, settling tanks, pumps, UV radiation, and water purification treatment. Rainwater harvesting keeps rainwater on-site. It lessens the burden on municipal water facilities, and decreases erosion and flooding caused by runoff from impervious surfaces. Refer to Section 02670 (32 71 00), Constructed Wetlands, for information regarding natural treatment of water. Refer to Section 11110 (11 23 00), Commercial Laundry and Dry Cleaning Equipment, for information regarding ozonation.

Toxicity/IEQ: Chlorine is routinely added to municipal water supplies and is likely to be a required additive for water collected/treated in situ and destined for potable use. Where such additives are necessary, iodine is a less toxic alternative.

Rainwater is generally of better quality than well and municipal tap water. The exception is near industrial sites, where rainwater may be extremely acid. If you plan to use rainwater for drinking water, have it tested by a laboratory certified by the State Department of Health or the Environmental Protection Agency.

Performance: Performance is comparable for green methods and standard methods. In many instances, rain-water and water treated via constructed wetlands have tested better than the available municipal water. Rainwater is soft (hardness of zero) and can significantly reduce the quantity of detergents and soaps needed for cleaning.

11450 (11 30 00)   RESIDENTIAL EQUIPMENT

Resource Management: Several green manufacturers produce super-efficient appliances, and most standard, mainstream manufacturers now produce energy-efficient models. Current refrigerator models do not use CFC refrigerants; however, as of this writing, some still use insulation manufactured with HCFCs as blowing agents.

Some manufacturers have developed residential washers on the horizontal axis that require much less water. When used in combination with ionizing washer disks, they can significantly reduce water usage and pollution.

Toxicity/IEQ: Toxicity IEQ impact is comparable for green appliances and standard appliances. However, by virtue of their improved energy efficiency, green appliances contribute far fewer contaminants to the environment during their lifetime than do standard appliances.

Performance: Obviously, energy-efficient appliances require less energy to operate. Most perform the task for which they were designed comparably to the standard designs that they replace. Federal regulations require appliances to be labeled indicating their energy performance (a bright yellow EER—energy efficiency rating—label). As this field continues to mature, models are constantly being improved. Green Seal has developed standards for refrigerators (GS-20), clothes washers (GS-22), clothes dryers (GS-23), dishwashers (GS-24), and cooktops/ovens/ranges (GS-25), which specify minimum requirements for energy efficiency, water use, packaging, and labeling. The EPA has developed minimum energy efficiency standards for Energy Star–labeled products. EPA Energy Star categories include clothes washers, dishwashers, refrigerators, room air conditioners, televisions, VCRs, and computers.

Typically, horizontal axis washers are more efficient than top-loading, and side-by-side refrigerators are less efficient than top-bottom refrigerator/freezers.

Recycling systems are available and include under-the-counter containers to separate recyclables. They also include interior composting systems, which are generally a variation of standard garbage disposal. In some designs, the composting chute empties to an externally accessible composting bin.

11680 (11 28 00)	OFFICE EQUIPMENT

Resource Management: Office equipment historically has been available on a lease basis. The shift to green leasing has brought dramatic changes to the traditional perspective of leased equipment. Under a green lease, the product manufacturer is responsible for the disposition of the product at all times, meaning that when the customer no longer requires the use of the product or requires an updated model, the manufacturer is obligated to reclaim it and refurbish it or disassemble it for recycling, as appropriate. This approach necessitates a revision of administrative services. It also requires a basic redesign of products to allow for future disassembly and upgrade. This has the potential to be cost-effective for manufacturers and customers alike. It is also extremely resource-efficient. Some major corporations, including Apple and Xerox, are exploring the possibilities of a green lease approach.

Toxicity/IEQ: Toxicity/IEQ is comparable for green products and standard products.

Performance: The EPA has developed minimum energy efficiency standards for Energy Star–labeled products. EPA Energy Star categories include computers, copiers, facsimile machines, monitors, printers, and scanners.

DIVISION 12—FURNISHINGS

12050 (12 05 13)	FABRICS

Resource Management: Typical fabrics used in building products include: wool, worsted wool, wool and polyester blend, polyester, vinyl, modacrylic, silk and flax, nylon, and chlorofiber.

Wool, a natural fiber obtained from domesticated sheep, is valued for its absorbency, resiliency, insulation, and ability to take dye well. Wool presents some environmental concerns relative to animal husbandry, including soil erosion due to over-foraging and pesticide runoff due to the immersion treatment (for parasites on sheep).

Polyester is produced from petroleum and natural gas. Manufacture of polyester fiber generates air emissions including polymer dust, volatized residual monomer, and fiber lubricants.

A variety of dyes are used, depending on the fabric and color desired. Many fabric dyes contain petrochemicals. Dyeing fabric is water-intensive and can generate toxic pollutants.

Draperies, upholstery, and wall coverings manufactured from organically grown natural fibers with nontoxic dyes are available. Organically grown cotton in certain colors is available. Some fabrics are also available that have recycled plastic (generally PET—soda pop bottles) content. Unfortunately, this combines petroleum-based plastics and organics in a way that is difficult to separate for future recycling.

Toxicity/IEQ: Dyes and fabric treatments, such as wrinkle-free or fire-resistant, can be toxic. Chemicals used for finishes and other purposes on fabrics can be sources of VOCs. Cornstarch and tapioca are used as sizing. Copper compounds, chromium compounds, and chlorinated phenol are used to inhibit mold and mildew. Silicofluorides and chromium-fluorides, camphor, naphthalene, and paradichlorobenzene are used for mothproofing. Organic halo-genphosphorous compounds, aryl bromophosphate, triethanolamine, and trimethylol melamine are used as flame retardants.

Performance: Fabric produced from natural fiber*s*, especially when dyed with natural, nontoxic dyes, is biodegradable.

12100 (12 10 00)	ART

Resource Management: Many artists have embraced environmental ethics. Options range from lead-free, recycled-content stained glass to reclaimed, found-object sculpture to green statements beautifully expressed in traditional media.

Toxicity/IEQ: While many media can be very toxic during production, most are considered inert when cured/ complete.

Performance: Performance is comparable for green methods and standard methods.

12400 (12 40 00)	FURNISHINGS AND ACCESSORIES

Resource Management: A variety of green furniture products are available, including products manufactured from sustainably harvested wood, recycled metal, recycled plastic, alternative agricultural materials, and organically grown fibers.

Toxicity/IEQ: Fabric coverings may act as sinks for VOCs. Refer to Section 12050 (12 05 13), Fabrics.

Performance: Performance is comparable for green methods and standard methods.

12700 (12 59 00)   SYSTEMS FURNITURE

Resource Management: Several modular office furniture manufacturers have environmental lines that include reclaimed, refurbished furniture, furniture with recycled materials, and furniture with organic fibers/fabric.

Toxicity/IEQ: Fabric coverings may act as sinks for VOCs. They are constructed from various materials, often including composite wood products, insulations, and adhesives, that are all potential sources of VOC emissions. Freestanding, partial-height partitions (or panels) can interfere with the proper distribution of ventilation air. Install panels according to plans prepared in harmony with the design of the HVAC system. Raising partition bottoms above the floor may improve air flow at workstations contained within partial height panel systems.

Performance: Performance is comparable for green methods and standard methods.

12800   INTERIOR PLANTS AND PLANTERS (12 92 33, INTERIOR PLANTERS; 32 93 00, PLANTS)

Resource Management: Many recycled content planters are available. Refer to Section 06600 (06 60 00), Plastic Fabrications, and Section 06500 (06 50 00), Structural Plastics.

Toxicity/IEQ: There are potentially positive and negative impacts of plants on indoor air quality. Claims have been made that plants can remove contaminants from indoor air. The potential damage of plant materials and the associated growing media relate to elevated moisture levels and potential amplification of microbial contaminants. Where plants are used, planters should be well drained and the drainwater removed to the exterior.

Performance: Performance is comparable for green methods and standard methods.

DIVISION 13—SPECIAL CONSTRUCTION

13020 (13 42 00)   BUILDING MODULES

Resource Management: Prefabricated assemblies are more resource-efficient than field-constructed assemblies. Standardized shapes and processes mean less waste. Shop fabrication allows for environmental controls unavailable at the site, such as paint booths that can reclaim overspray.

Toxicity/IEQ: Prefabricated module units have been severely criticized for their poor IAQ. The same considerations and investigations conducted on field-constructed components should be exercised when reviewing prefabricated components.

Preengineered structures that are assembled on-site can provide the best of both worlds: minimal waste and good IAQ.

Performance: Performance is comparable for green methods and standard methods.

13080 (13 48 00)   SOUND, VIBRATION, AND SEISMIC CONTROL

Resource Management: Resource management is comparable for green methods and standard methods.

Toxicity/IEQ: Vibration transmitted through the building structure can cause occupant complaints similar to sick building syndrome complaints. Isolate mechanical equipment and other building equipment. Vibration sources can also include adjacent roadways or parking garages.

Performance: Performance is comparable for green methods and standard methods. In some cases, equipment life can be prolonged by appropriately dampening vibration.

13170 (13 17 00)   TUBS AND POOLS

Resource Management: Refer to Section 11110 (11 23 00), Commercial Laundry and Dry Cleaning Equipment, for information on ozonation.

Toxicity/IEQ: Ozonation is an alternative to chlorination. Chemical-free tub systems that utilize ozonation are available. Refer to Section 11110 (11 23 00), Commercial Laundry and Dry Cleaning Equipment, for information on ozonation.

Performance: Ozonation reduces total dissolved solids (TDS) so pools need to be drained less. Refer to Section 11110 (11 23 00), Commercial Laundry and Dry Cleaning Equipment, for information on ozonation.

13185 (13 19 00)   KENNELS AND ANIMAL SHELTERS

Resource Management: Concentrated animal feeding operations (CAFO) issues have focused public attention on the potential environmental damage from animal operations. Such damage includes destruction of native habitat, erosion, and contamination of waterways. Proper design and operations can mitigate the environmental impact. For example, by placing composting bins under cages of vegetarian animals such as birds and rabbits, the droppings can be easily composted.

Toxicity/IEQ: Improper management of kennels, animal shelters, and CAFO can produce some extremely unhealthy conditions. Select products that are easily maintained with nontoxic methods to help promote proper management. Depending on the scale of the CAFO operations, an NPDES permit may be required.

Performance: From a human perspective, performance is comparable for green methods and standard methods. From an animal perspective, green methods are likely to perform much better. Animals respond instinctively to healthy and environmentally appropriate conditions.

13400   MEASUREMENT AND CONTROL INSTRUMENTATION (40 90 00,
               INSTRUMENTATION AND CONTROL FOR PROCESS SYSTEMS)

               Resource Management: The systems specified for energy and water use in a
               building can dramatically impact both the quantity and the quality of such re-
               sources. Monitors and controls that regulate use of electricity, gas, and water
               can help improve efficiencies.

               Toxicity/IEQ: Monitoring and control equipment that maintains indoor air
               quality is available.

               Performance: Monitoring and control systems can help prolong the life of
               energy and water equipment by preventing spikes in demand and by warn-
               ing of potential problems.

13600   SOLAR AND WIND ENERGY EQUIPMENT (48 14 00, SOLAR EN-
               ERGY ELECTRICAL POWER GENERATION EQUIPMENT; 48 15 00,
               WIND ENERGY ELECTRICAL POWER GENERATION EQUIPMENT)

               Resource Management: Renewable, clean energy is, ultimately, the only en-
               vironmentally responsible option.

               Toxicity/IEQ: In many systems, battery storage is required. While there are
               well-known concerns regarding the toxic components of batteries, overall,
               the systems that utilize renewable energy sources are significantly less haz-
               ardous than our continued dependence on nonrenewable energy is to human
               health and environmental health.

               Performance: Many configurations of solar systems are available. In each,
               photovoltaic cells convert sunlight into electrical energy. Collected energy is
               usually stored in batteries and converted into AC electric for building use.
               Solar equipment is becoming more common for stand-alone items such as ex-
               terior lighting. Photovoltaic arrays can be designed to power the entire build-
               ing. These may be mounted on the roof or ground. They may also be building-
               integrated. Thin-film photovoltaic systems that laminate thin-film photovoltaic
               film to one-fourth-inch glass are available. Wires collecting the energy are con-
               cealed in the standard glass-framing system. Also, photovoltaic roof shingles,
               developed primarily in response to Japan's Solar Roof initiative, are available.
               Systems using the sun's radiant energy to heat water are available. Panels are
               mounted either on the roof or ground, and water is piped to storage.

               Wind-powered generators are available for residential and commercial
               applications. This is a rapidly changing field. Many of these systems, priced
               as luxury items only a few years ago, are today affordable.

13800   BUILDING AUTOMATION AND CONTROL (25 00 00, INTEGRATED
               AUTOMATION)

               Refer to Section 16500 (26 50 00), Lighting, for information on occupancy
               sensors.

13850   DETECTION AND ALARM (28 31 49, CARBON-MONOXIDE
               DETECTION SENSORS)

               Carbon monoxide detectors are available. These are similar in appearance
               and function to smoke detectors. Refer to Section 13400, Measurement and

Control Instrumentation (40 90 00, Instrumentation and Control for Process Systems).

DIVISION 14—CONVEYING SYSTEMS (CONVEYING EQUIPMENT)

14200 (14 20 00)   ELEVATORS

Resource Management: Refer to Division 5 (05) for information regarding metal products. Refer to the applicable Division 9 (09) section for information regarding interior finish products.

Toxicity/IEQ: Hydraulic fluids and lubricants used in elevators can cause indoor air quality problems. Isolate lubricated equipment from the circulating air or air in the shaft, and pressurize elevator lobbies relative to the shaft to minimize escaping air from the shaft. Ventilate the shaft with negative pressure.

Performance: Performance is comparable for green methods and standard methods.

14900   TRANSPORTATION (DIVISION 34—TRANSPORTATION)

Resource Management: This section (division) typically specifies cars and motorized vehicles and equipment utilized in railroads, subways, and tramways. Public transportation that helps minimize the use of individual vehicles is always environmentally preferable.

Toxicity/IEQ: Indoor environmental quality is not directly applicable for transportation equipment.

Performance: Performance is comparable for green methods and standard methods.

DIVISION 15—MECHANICAL (DIVISION 21—FIRE SUPPRESSION; DIVISION 22—PLUMBING; DIVISION 23—HEATING, VENTILATING, AND AIR CONDITIONING)

15050   BASIC MECHANICAL MATERIALS AND METHODS
(21 05 00, COMMON WORK RESULTS FOR FIRE SUPPRESSON;
22 05 00, COMMON WORK RESULTS FOR PLUMBING;
23 05 00, COMMON WORK RESULTS FOR HVAC)

Resource Management: The systems specified for energy and water use in a building can dramatically impact both the quantity and the quality of such resources. Energy-efficient and low-flow fixtures are readily available and required by code. Systems that promote more responsible use of energy and water by building occupants are also available. They range from reuse of waste heat via transfer piping to pre-use of water via handwashing basin piped into the supply side of the toilet bowl.

Toxicity/IEQ: The primary IEQ consideration for domestic water supply is water quality, which, for most buildings, is largely determined by the municipal water treatment facility. Most water treatment facilities rely on chemicals, including chlorine, to combat pathogens. Chlorine is highly reactive and readily forms chlorinated compounds, many of which are dangerous.

Chlorinated hydrocarbons, such as DDT, have been and are used as pesticides. Water filter systems for chorine are available.

Performance: The primary environmental concern for mechanical systems is performance. Even when passive design is maximized for natural lighting, solar control of heat gain, natural ventilation, and water management, active systems are still commonly used. Mechanical systems may be standalone, such as rainwater harvesting systems, constructed wetlands for wastewater management, solar power/water systems, or wind-power systems. More typically, one or more utilities are connected to the grid and may utilize high-efficiency systems. Generally, such systems are more expensive to install but pay for themselves over time. Refer to Section 11200, Water Supply and Treatment Equipment (44 40 00, Water Treatment Equipment), Section 02670 (32 71 00), Constructed Wetlands, and Section 13600, Solar and Wind Energy Equipment (48 14 00, Solar Energy Electrical Power Generation Equipment; 48 15 00, Wind Energy Electrical Power Generation Equipment), for information on these alternative technologies.

15080   MECHANICAL INSULATION (21 07 00, FIRE SUPPRESSION
             SYSTEMS INSULATION; 22 07 00, PLUMBING INSULATION;
             23 07 00, HVAC INSULATION)

Resource Management: Refer to Section 07200 (07 20 00), Thermal Protection.

Toxicity/IEQ: Refer to Section 07200 (07 20 00), Thermal Protection.
     Insulation may produce airborne fiberglass and microbial contamination. When soft, adsorptive duct linings become contaminated by particles, they can absorb up to 10 times more moisture; and moisture can contribute to microbial contaminants such us molds. Insulation for application to the outside of ductwork is preferable.

Performance: Specify minimum thickness in accordance with ASHRAE 90.1. Provide additional thickness to ensure that surface temperatures are below 100 degrees and to prevent condensation on cold surfaces.

15100   BUILDING SERVICES PIPING (21 11 00, FACILITY FIRE-
             SUPPRESSION WATER-SERVICE PIPING; 22 10 00, PLUMBING
             PIPING AND PUMPS; 23 11 00, FACILITY FUEL PIPING;
             23 20 00, HVAC PIPING AND PIPING)

Resource Management: Traditional metal piping has been largely replaced by PVC piping. Refer to Section 09651, Vinyl Flooring (09 65 00, Resilient Flooring) for information regarding manufacture of PVC.

Toxicity/IEQ: Specify traditional metal piping. Do not specify PVC piping. Refer to Section 09651, Vinyl Flooring (09 65 00, Resilient Flooring), for information regarding PVC. Several ionization options are available for preventing mineral buildup. These range from drop-in–type toilet bowl cleaners to equipment spliced into piping runs.
     Grease traps that utilize bacteria to decompose the grease are available. When the food source is exhausted, the bacteria turn on each other; therefore, the bacteria supply must be replenished each day. Natural strains of

bacteria are generally used; these have an exceptionally high capacity for digesting specific organic compounds found in grease traps.

J-drains (traps) with removable panels for easy cleaning are available. These allow cleaning without use of polluting chemicals at sinks and lavatories.

Performance: Avoiding chemical pollution during operation typically means that the building owner must understand the operating system better and be willing to expend a pound of prevention instead of ten pounds of cure. Verify that owner's operating manuals include information regarding J-drains, grease traps, and so on.

15400   PLUMBING FIXTURES AND EQUIPMENT (22 40 00, PLUMBING FIXTURES; 22 30 00, PLUMBING EQUIPMENT)

Resource Management: Specify low-flow fixtures and automatic, sensor-operated faucets and flush valves. Most standard, mainstream companies have developed low-flow lines in response to building code requirements that require water-conserving fixtures. For faucets and aerators, specify a maximum 2.5 gallons/minute when measured at a flowing water pressure of 80 pounds per square inch. For water closets, specify maximum 1.6 gallons. Avoid gravity tank type water closets. For urinals, specify maximum 1.0 gallons/flush. For showerheads, specify maximum 2.5 gallons/minute when measured at a flowing water pressure of 80 pounds per square inch.

Composting toilets are available. Composting reduces water usage and creates soil amendment. Vacuum toilet systems, traditionally associated with water conservation in marine, air, and railroad transports are also available for application in commercial/residential buildings.

Toxicity/IEQ: Composting is the biological reduction of organic wastes to humus. It is a natural process that is critical for support of all terrestrial life. Although composting manure is a traditional and extremely valuable process, manure (especially from carnivorous animals) can promote unwanted bacteria and diseases if handled improperly. Refer to Section 02055, Soils (31 05 13, Soils for Earthwork).

Performance: When low-flow fixtures were first developed, many were deemed unsatisfactory because they could not deliver the pressure Americans were used to. More recent models do not have this problem, except for extremely high-pressure demands in some high-use areas.

Green Seal has developed standards for water efficient fixtures (GS-06), which specify minimum requirements for showerheads, faucets, toilets, packaging, and labeling.

Adjust automatic sensor-operated faucets and valves in accordance with manufacturer's instructions. Comply with ASHRAE 90.1 for minimum energy efficiency.

Vacuum toilets not only reduce water consumption but also reduce piping and can eliminate need for toilet vent pipes, allowing for flexibility in design layout.

15480

DOMESTIC WATER HEATERS (22 33 00; ELECTRIC DOMESTIC WATER HEATERS; 22 34 00, FUEL-FIRED DOMESTIC WATER HEATERS)

Resource Management: Refer to Section 15050, Basic Mechanical Materials and Methods (22 05 00, Common Work Results for Plumbing).

Toxicity/IEQ: The primary IEQ consideration for domestic water supply is water quality, which, for most buildings, is largely determined by the municipal water treatment facility. Refer to Section 15050, Basic Mechanical Materials and Methods (22 05 00, Common Work Results for Plumbing).

Performance: Energy efficiency is improved over older heaters because of new heating technologies and better tank insulation. Obviously, energy-efficient appliances require less energy to operate. Most perform the task for which they were designed comparably to the standard designs they replace. Federal regulations require appliances to be labeled indicating their energy performance (a bright yellow EER—energy efficiency rating—label). This is a developing field, and models are constantly being improved.

   Instantaneous point-of-use (tankless, on-demand) electric water heaters are available for commercial and residential use. These are particularly effective when demand is located far away from domestic hot water mains.

15500

HEAT-GENERATION EQUIPMENT (23 50 00, CENTRAL HEATING EQUIPMENT)

Resource Management: Refer to Section 15050, Basic Mechanical Materials and Methods (23 05 00, Common Work Results for HVAC).

   According to the EPA, space heating and cooling in residential buildings generate 420 million tons of carbon dioxide, a significant greenhouse gas, annually. According to the Department of Energy, natural gas, used in about 55 percent of homes in the United States, is the most common heating fuel. Though it is perhaps the cleanest combustion fuel (compared with wood, oil, and coal) production and transmission of natural gas still results in emissions of methane, a greenhouse gas. Equipment that promotes conservation through high-efficiency and passive controls is a good solution to resource management concerns. Equipment that utilizes alternative, renewable, nonpolluting energy is also ideal.

   Geothermal projects can result in overuse of the commons when the ground temperature in a microclimate is raised. This can affect both the local ecosystem and the performance of the geothermal equipment that has been designed around lower expected ground temperatures.

Toxicity/IEQ: Specify sealed combustion equipment to help maintain good IAQ.

Performance: Reduce the heating demand through passive solar design. Specify high-efficiency equipment. The EPA has developed minimum energy efficiency standards for Energy Star-labeled products. EPA Energy Star categories include furnaces, boilers, air-source heat pumps, gas-fired heat pumps, geothermal heat pumps, and programmable thermostats.

Gas-fired furnaces and boilers with efficiencies of 90 percent are available. Radiant electric heating equipment is available and can be efficient and cost-effective when heating loads are small. For larger loads, consider a heat pump. Specify air-source heat pumps in moderate climates and ground-source heat pumps in cold climates.

15600   REFRIGERATION EQUIPMENT (23 60 00, CENTRAL COOLING EQUIPMENT)

Resource Management: Refer to Section 15050, Basic Mechanical Materials and Methods (23 05 00, Common Work Results for HVAC).

Most refrigerants are greenhouse gases. Furthermore, they are used in HVAC and refrigeration equipment, huge consumers of electricity the generation of which releases greenhouse gases. Alternative refrigerants include hydrofluorocarbons (HFCs), hydrochlorofluorocarbons (HCFCs), ammonia, and hydrocarbons. HCFCs still impact the ozone layer and are scheduled to be phased out early in the twenty-first century. HFCs, while not damaging to the ozone layer (and so not slated for phaseout), are significant greenhouse gases. HFCs break down into trifluoroacetic acid and other compounds that accumulate in the hydrologic cycle and are toxic to wildlife.

Toxicity/IEQ: The primary IEQ concern is leaking of refrigerants from the system. Proper installation and maintenance can help prevent the release of refrigerants into the indoor environment and the atmosphere.

Performance: As of January 1, 1996, the production of CFCs and most other Class I ozone-depleting substances was banned in the United States and in other industrialized countries. HVAC and refrigeration equipment must rely on existing stockpiles of CFCs, black market CFCs, or be converted to use one of the alternative refrigerants.

Ammonia and hydrocarbons such as propane and isobutane perform very well as refrigerants and have been used in the past. They are, however, quite flammable. The Clean Air Act and many building codes prohibit hydrocarbon refrigerants; nevertheless, several European countries are reinvestigating this technology.

15700   HEATING, VENTILATING, AND AIR CONDITIONING EQUIPMENT (23 50 00, CENTRAL HEATING EQUIPMENT; 23 60 00, CENTRAL COOLING EQUIPMENT; 23 70 00, CENTRAL HVAC EQUIPMENT)

Resource Management: Maximize passive opportunities to reduce HVAC load. Refer to Section 15050, Basic Mechanical Materials and Methods (23 05 00, Common Work Results for HVAC), and Section 15600, Refrigeration Equipment (23 60 00, Central Cooling Equipment).

Toxicity/IEQ: HVAC systems can contribute to poor IAQ by failing to provide enough ventilation to dilute indoor contaminants to acceptable levels, by spreading contaminants introduced from outside sources and by generating contaminants within the HVAC system itself. The primary contaminants from HVAC systems are microbial and particulate. Design the system to prevent water collection. Specify nonwoven cotton fabric filters, not fiberglass filters.

Performance: Comply with ASHRAE 62 for ventilation; comply with ASHRAE 52 for filtration; comply with ASHRAE 55 for thermal comfort. Maintain positive pressure within the building. Comply with ASHRAE 90.1 for minimum energy efficiency. Provide economizer for systems with fan capacity of 5,000 cfm and higher and where required by codes.

Obviously, energy-efficient systems require less energy to operate. Most perform the task for which they were designed comparably to the standard designs that they replace. Federal regulations require appliances to be labeled, indicating their energy performance (a bright yellow EER—energy efficiency rating—label). This is a developing field, and models are constantly being improved.

The EPA has developed minimum energy efficiency standards for Energy Star–labeled products. EPA Energy Star categories include furnaces, boilers, air-source heat pumps, gas-fired heat pumps, geothermal heat pumps, and programmable thermostats.

15800	AIR DISTRIBUTION (23 30 00, HVAC AIR DISTRIBUTION)

Resource Management: Refer to Section 15050, Basic Mechanical Materials and Methods (23 05 00, Common Work Results for HVAC).

Toxicity/IEQ: Locate outside air intakes away from potential sources of contamination (e.g., sources of motor vehicle emissions, building HVAC system exhausts). The air in rooms where contaminants are generated should be exhausted directly outdoors (e.g., labs, copying areas). ASHRAE Standard 62 calls for delivery of ventilation air to occupant breathing zone. Amount is contingent upon carbon dioxide levels; other contaminants must be considered separately.

Performance: Properly sizing and sealing ductwork can improve energy efficiency.

15810	DUCTS (23 31 00, HVAC DUCTS AND CASINGS)

Resource Management: Refer to Section 15050, Basic Mechanical Materials and Methods (23 05 00, Common Work Results for HVAC), and Division 5 (05).

Toxicity/IEQ: Fiberboard ductwork has been implicated in microbial contamination. Metal surfaces can be cleaned more easily without fear of damaging the surface material. VOCs may be emitted from duct sealant during the curing process. They are very exposed to the air stream, so their emissions are very important. Fibrous glass insulation materials may contain formaldehyde-based resin binder materials. Install insulation so that unfaced fiberglass and mineral fiber insulation are not in contact with the airstream.

Performance: Properly sizing and sealing ductwork can improve energy efficiency.

15900	HVAC INSTRUMENTATION AND CONTROLS (23 09 00, INSTRUMENTATION AND CONTROL FOR HVAC)

Resource Management: Refer to Section 13400 (40 90 00), Measurement and Control Instrumentation.

Toxicity/IEQ: Refer to Section 13400 (40 90 00), Measurement and Control Instrumentation.

Performance: Sensors may be used to detect airflow, contaminant concentrations, thermal properties, or moisture content of air. Humidity control can help prevent microbial growth. Steam is preferable to liquid water as source.

15950   TESTING, ADJUSTING, AND BALANCING (23 05 93, TESTING, ADJUSTING, AND BALANCING FOR HVAC)

Resource Management: Refer to Section 13400 (40 90 00), Measurement and Control Instrumentation.

Toxicity/IEQ: Testing does not usually address IEQ issues. To better address IEQ issues relative to the HVAC system, coordinate with Section 01354 (01 35 43), Environmental Procedures and Section 01810 (01 91 00), Commissioning.

Performance: Provide preoccupancy ventilation as specified in Section 01354 (01 35 43), Environmental Procedures; provide prior to final testing, adjusting, and balancing of HVAC system. Coordinate with commissioning; refer to Section 01810 (01 91 00), Commissioning.

DIVISION 16 (26)—ELECTRICAL

16050   BASIC ELECTRICAL MATERIALS AND METHODS (26 05 00, COMMON WORK RESULTS FOR ELECTRICAL)

Resource Management: Refer to Section 15050, Basic Mechanical Materials and Methods (22 05 00, Common Work Results for Plumbing; 23 05 00, Common Work Results for HVAC).

Toxicity/IEQ: Many studies have indicated an apparent link between exposure to electromagnetic fields (for example, under overhead power lines) and an increased risk of cancer. A link between electrical wiring configurations in the home and the incidence of childhood cancer has also been indicated. Most studies have concentrated on the magnetic, not the electric, component of electromagnetic fields. This is primarily because the human body is a good conductor, so the penetration of electric fields into the body itself is minimal. Magnetic fields, on the other hand, readily penetrate the body. However, recent studies have demonstrated that electromagnetic fields can attract and concentrate aerosols of all types, including known carcinogenic aerosols, natural aerosols containing the radioactive radon decay atoms of radon gas, and bacteria. The effect is primarily due to the electric, rather than the magnetic, field component.

Performance: Coordinate with Division 8 (08) and Division 15 (22 and 23) to minimize load requirements and improve energy efficiency.

16100   WIRING METHODS (26 05 00, COMMON WORK RESULTS FOR ELECTRICAL)

Resource Management: Refer to Section 15050, Basic Mechanical Materials and Methods (22 05 00, Common Work Results for Plumbing; 23 05 00, Common Work Results for HVAC).

Toxicity/IEQ: Some experimentation with twisting of wires has been done to control the generation of electromagnetic fields. Theoretically, twisting is effective not so much because it brings wires closer together, but because the actual geometry of the twisted wires makes their fields cancel. A certain number of twists per foot is optimum for a certain frequency (presumably 60 Hz for North American power wiring). Twisting is used to reduce electromagnetic interference from inverter wires. Inverters are devices that typically take low-voltage DC electricity and convert it to high-voltage AC electricity. The low-voltage side of inverters can carry very large currents and are, therefore, large generators of EMF. Twisting of wires is also commonly used inside audio electronics and computers to prevent internal interference.

Performance: Performance is comparable for green methods and standard methods.

16500 (26 50 00)   LIGHTING

Resource Management: Refer to Section 15050, Basic Mechanical Materials and Methods (22 05 00, Common Work Results for Plumbing; 23 05 00, Common Work Results for HVAC). Maximize the use of natural lighting.

Toxicity/IEQ: Currently, products are not legally permitted to be manufactured with PCBs. Lead is commonly used in solder for ballasts on HID lamps; however, many manufacturers now crimp ballasts rather than solder. Mercury is commonly used in fluorescent lamps; however, some manufacturers have developed low-mercury fluorescent lamp products containing maximum 20 ppm of mercury.

Light quality is also a consideration for IEQ. Full-spectrum lighting is preferred in all normal applications because it approximates natural daylight. Full-spectrum lamps and filters are available.

Performance: Comply with National Energy Policy Act requirements for lighting products. Energy-efficient HID, sodium, halogen, and fluorescent lamps are available. Green Seal has developed standards for compact fluorescent lamps (GS-05), which specify minimum requirements for performance, energy efficiency, mercury content, packaging, and labeling.

Occupancy sensors are available to turn lights on when a room or covered area is occupied and off when unoccupied. Passive infrared and ultrasonic operations are common. Specify with adjustable time delay for turning lights off.

Photoelectric control is available for exterior lighting. Specify that photoelectric control be completely self-contained and adjustable in NEMA 1 weatherproof enclosures with adjustable 0 to 15 minute minimum time delay to provide a dead band zone for temporary changes in daylighting. Specify automatic operation as follows:

• Daylight-only lighting level, 50 foot-candles or more: No fixtures on.
• Daylight-only lighting level less than 25 foot-candles: All fixture lamps activated.

Foot-candle lighting level readings should be measured at grade.

Full-spectrum lamps provide better light quality than conventional standard artificial lighting; full-spectrum lamps are neither more nor less energy-efficient. They generally cost more than the fluorescent and incandescent lamps they replace; however, the full-spectrum filters can be a very cost-effective compromise because they are reusable.

16530 (26 52 00)   EMERGENCY LIGHTING

Resource Management: Refer to Section 15050, Basic Mechanical Materials and Methods (22 05 00, Common Work Results for Plumbing; 23 05 00, Common Work Results for HVAC).

Toxicity/IEQ: Toxicity/IEQ is comparable for green methods and standard methods.

Performance: Light-emitting diode (LED) lighting is available and much more efficient than compact fluorescent lighting. LEDs last from 80 to 500 years. Specify LED type with maintenance-free battery backup for 120 minutes; UL listed.

Appendix C

Sample Sections and Forms

The following sample forms and specifications sections were developed by theGreenTeam, Inc., and are the result of its ongoing work with building owners, building product manufacturers, green building trade and professional organizations, standards development organizations, and environmental organizations to develop sustainable building. Sections 01351, 01611, 06100, and 10170 were developed under contract with the U.S. Environmental Protection Agency (EPA) and have been peer reviewed by governmental agencies, building industry professional organizations, and the public; these sections are part of the *Federal Green Construction Guide for Specifiers*. Containing more than 60 sections, the *Federal Green Construction Guide for Specifiers* is available on the Whole Building Design Guide website at http://fedgreenspecs.wbdg.org.

The sample forms and specifications sections are intended to be a guide for researching and implementing green building products. No warranty is made as to completeness or accuracy of information contained herein. References to manufacturers do not represent a guaranty, warranty, or endorsement thereof.

- Environmental Impact Questionnaire
- Indoor Air Quality (IAQ) Report
- Section 00000—Environmental Specifications Section Format
- Section 01231—Environmental Alternates
- Section 01351—Waste Management
- Section 01352—Indoor Air Quality (IAQ) Management
- Section 01354—Environmental Mangement
- Section 01611—Environmental Requirements for Products
- Section 06100—Rough Carpentry
- Section 10170—Plastic Toilet Compartments

theGreenTeam, Inc.
2 West Sixth Street, Suite 304
Tulsa, OK 74119
(918) 295-TEAM (8326)
www.thegreenteaminc.com

Alison Kinn Bennett
Federal Green Construction Guide for Specifiers Project Officer
US EPA Environmentally Preferable Purchasing Program
1200 Pennsylvania Avenue, NW mail code 7409M
Washington, DC 20460
(202) 564-8859; fax: (202)-564-8899
email: kinn.alison@epa.gov

The following sample specification section was developed by Ross Spiegel and is the result of his ongoing work to develop sustainable buildings. The sample specification section is intended to be a guide for researching and implementing green building products. No warranty is made to completeness or accuracy of information contained herein. References to manufacturers do not represent a guaranty, warranty, or endorsement thereof.

• Section 01630—Product Substitution Procedures

Ross Spiegel
Fletcher-Thompson, Inc.
3 Corporate Drive, Suite 500
Shelton, CT 06484-6244
(203) 225-6551; fax: (203) 225-6800
email: RSpiegel@ftae.com

SPECIFIER NOTE: THIS DOCUMENT IS INTENDED TO BE A GUIDE FOR RE-SEARCHING ENVIRONMENTAL ISSUES RELATIVE TO BUILDING PRODUCTS. IS-SUES ARE ORGANIZED UNDER THREE PRIMARY CATEGORIES: RESOURCE MAN-AGEMENT, TOXICITY, AND PERFORMANCE.
LANGUAGE IS PRESENTED FOR EXAMPLE ONLY AND NO WARRANTY IS MADE AS TO COMPLETENESS OR ACCURACY OF INFORMATION CONTAINED HEREIN.

ENVIRONMENTAL IMPACT QUESTIONNAIRE (EIQ)

I.   DIRECTIONS

   A. Complete the following questionnaire and submit for review to:

       _____

       _____

       _____

       _____

   B. Relate information concerning only one product per questionnaire.

   C. All questions may not apply to every product or manufacturer. It is not expected the manufacturer will have addressed all of the environmental concerns expressed in the EIQ.

      1. Respond to every question even if response is "not available," "not applicable," or "no."

      2. Attach additional sheets as required. Reference additional sheets to correspond with the question number.

II. IDENTIFICATION

   A. Material/Product: _____

      Brand Name: _____

      Manufacturer: _____

      What is the primary use or application for this product? _____

      _____

      _____

      _____

   B. Contact for EIQ:

      Name: _____ Title: _____

      Address: _____

      Zip Code: _____

      Telephone: _____ Fax: _____

      Date: _____

III. RESOURCE MANAGEMENT
    A. Renewable Resources:
      1. List renewable resources used as product raw materials. Provide percentage amounts in relation to complete (100%) product.

Renewable Resource	Percentage
_____	_____
_____	_____
_____	_____
_____	_____

      2. Does manufacturer obtain product raw materials or fabricate this product outside of the United States: ____Y ____N?
        a. If yes, are United States environmental standards or more strict standards followed in these countries: ____Y ____N?
        b. List countries involved.

        _____

        _____

    B. Managed Resources:
      1. Does extraction of product raw materials or fabrication of this product affect endangered specie(s): ____Y ____N?
        a. If yes, list species and describe effect, including mitigation methods for negative effects.

Endangered Species	Effect
_____	_____
_____	_____
_____	_____

      2. Products Containing Wood: Are wood materials obtained from certified sustainable forestry operations: ____Y ____N?
        a. If yes, provide name of certification organization for each wood species being used in this project.

Species	Certification Organization
_____	_____
_____	_____
_____	_____

        b. If no, state where the product resources are produced and describe forestry operations.

Product Resources	Forestry Operations
_____	_____
_____	_____
_____	_____

C. Recycled Content:

1. List recycled materials used as product raw materials; distinguish preconsumer and postconsumer materials. Provide percentage amounts in relation to complete (100%) product.

Recycled Material	% Preconsumer	% Postconsumer
_____	_____	_____
_____	_____	_____
_____	_____	_____
_____	_____	_____

D. Embodied Energy:

1. Product Transport:

a. Where are raw materials acquired? Identify state and country.

Raw Material	Source (State and Country)
_____	_____
_____	_____
_____	_____
_____	_____

b. Describe means of transporting raw materials to the manufacturing plant.

Raw Material	Transportation
_____	_____
_____	_____
_____	_____
_____	_____

c. Where is product manufactured/fabricated? Identify state and country.

_____

d. Is the product warehoused locally, regionally, or nationally? _____

e. Describe means of transporting product to distribution facilities.

_____

_____

2. Production Energy: List energy sources used in production process; indicate which are renewable energy sources (e.g. wind, solar). Provide percentage amounts in relation to complete (100%) product.

Energy Sources	Renewable		Percentage
_____	___ Y	___ N	_____
_____	___ Y	___ N	_____
_____	___ Y	___ N	_____

3. Provide an embodied energy study of the product from extraction of raw materials through production and assembly. Include an estimate for the total number of BTUs required per pound of finished products. Identify parameters for study.

_____

_____

4. Describe measures the manufacturer has taken to minimize energy usage in the production process.

_____

_____

_____

_____

E. Reuse/Recyclability/Disposal:

  1. Reuse:
     a. Can product be reused directly (in same or similar use): ____Y ____N?
     b. If yes, discuss possibility of direct reuse of the product after project demolition.

     _____

     _____

  2. Recycling:
     a. Can product be recycled: ____Y ____N?
     b. If yes, list the parts of the product which can be post-consumer recycled into raw materials for the product and the parts which can be postconsumer recycled into other types of items. Provide percentage amounts in relation to complete (100%) product.

Postconsumer—Raw	_Postconsumer—Other_	_Percentage_
_____	_____	_____
_____	_____	_____
_____	_____	_____

     c. If yes, describe the process of separation of the parts for postconsumer recycling from the product.

     _____

     _____

     d. If yes, list current markets using recycled materials from the product.

     _____

     _____

     e. If yes, estimate the practical number of times this item can be recycled. _____

3. Describe the manufacturer's policy and program to facilitate the recycling or reuse of its product by accepting product returns at the end of their useful life.

_____

_____

IV.   TOXICITY/HAZARDOUS MATERIALS

A. Toxic/Hazardous Byproducts :
   1. List the production wastes involved with the manufacture of this item. Distinguish the production wastes between toxic and nontoxic. Provide percentage amounts in relation to complete (100%) product.

Toxic	Nontoxic	Percentage
_____	_____	_____
_____	_____	_____
_____	_____	_____
_____	_____	_____

   2. Estimate the quantity of production waste produced per unit of finished product.

_____

   3. Is reclamation of production waste done on site: ____Y ____N?
      with outside services: ____Y ____N?
      a. If outside services are used, list companies involved.

_____

_____

   4. Is wastewater reclaimed by manufacturer: ____Y ____N?
      a. If yes, describe process of recycling/reuse of wastewater.

_____

_____

_____

_____

   5. Describe the manufacturer's active steps to minimize or eliminate production wastes; include process of liquid and solid waste material treatment or reclamation if performed at manufacturing site.

_____

_____

_____

6. Describe the manufacturing procedures and chemicals involved that would be considered better than industry standard.

_____

_____

_____

B. Toxic/Hazardous Contents (carcinogens and other hazards inherent in product/material):
   1. Provide a complete chemical profile of the item; include all chemical components and provide percentage amounts in relation to complete (100%) product; identify biocides (mildewcides or in-can preservatives) and carcinogens listed by any of the following:
      a. United States Environmental Protection Agency (EPA) Carcinogen Assessment Group (CAG) list of carcinogens.
      b. Clean Air Act Sections 109, 111, and 112.
      c. The National Toxicology Program's latest published "Annual Report on Carcinogens."
      d. IARC Human Carcinogens (Groups 1, 2A, and 2B).
      e. California Proposition 65.

Chemical	Carcinogen	Percentage
_____	__ Y __ N	_____
_____	__ Y __ N	_____
_____	__ Y __ N	_____
_____	__ Y __ N	_____
_____	__ Y __ N	_____

C. Material Safety Data Sheet (MSDS):
   1. Provide Material Safety Data Sheet (MSDS).
      a. Articles: Finished products which are manufactured off-site and shipped to the project for installation while conforming to Title 29 of the Code of Federal Regulations, OSHA Hazard Communication Regulation 29CRF 1910.1200, Section (b)5 and Section (c) are defined as articles. If by being defined as an article, a MSDS has not been developed for a particular product, then provide MSDS on raw materials, goods, and items used in the fabrication of that article.

D. Outgassing/Reactivity:
   1. Chlorofluorocarbon (CFC):
      a. Are CFCs or HCFCs used in the manufacture and/or content of the item specified: ____ Y ____ N?
      b. If CFCs or HCFCs were previously used in the product and/or its manufacture, describe measures taken by manufacturer to eliminate their use.

_____

_____

_____

_____

2. Indoor Air Quality:
   a. Does the product outgas (emit) carcinogens or other hazardous substances into the air after installation, including final curing/drying: ____Y ____N?
   b. If yes, submit IAQ test report.

E. Electromagnetic Radiation:

1. Does the product emit electromagnetic radiation: ____Y ____N?

2. If yes, at what rate per hour? _____

3. If yes, describe methods for installation, use, and maintenance of product to minimize generation of and occupant exposure to electromagnetic radiation.

   _____

   _____

F. Compliance with Regulations (Environmental Statutory Compliance):
   1. Does the manufacturer meet all federal, state, and local environmental laws, including laws governing air emissions, wastewater treatment, and solid waste disposal/treatment: ____Y ____N?
   2. Has the manufacturer met the above criteria for the previous five years: ____Y ____N?
   3. List these applicable standards.

   _____

   _____

   _____

   4. Does the product meet applicable industry standards, such as ASTM, Green Seal, manufacturing standards, LA or NY research report numbers, and UL approvals:

   ____Y ____N? List these standards._____

   _____

   _____

   _____

   _____

V.   PERFORMANCE—INSTALLATION

A. Environmental Procedures/Precautions:
   1. Describe special procedures and precautions to be used while handling and installing the product:

   _____

   _____

   _____

   _____

   _____

2. Identify accessories, such as fasteners, sealers, and adhesives that are nontoxic (or less toxic than industry standard), energy efficient, or recycled or recyclable products?

_____

_____

_____

_____

B. Installation Energy:
   1. Product Transport: List the means to transport the finished product to the construction site.

_____

_____

   2. Installation: List energy means and describe energy requirements for installation of the product.

_____

_____

C. Construction Waste:
   1. List the recommended method(s) for proper products disposal; stipulate preferred method and restrictions that might apply.

_____

_____

_____

   2. Comment on the environmental impact of the product as a waste material.

_____

_____

_____

   3. Packaging:
      a. Describe packaging for the product.

_____

_____

_____

      b. Does manufacturer accept return of used packaging for reuse: ____Y ____N?
      c. If yes, state limitations and procedures for packaging return.

_____

_____

_____

VI.   PERFORMANCE—OPERATIONS

    A. Maintenance

        1. Describe the recommended cleaning and maintenance procedures for the product using products that have minimal VOC emission.

            _____

            _____

            _____

        2. Estimate the useful life expectancy for this product.

            _____

        3. Are replacement parts available: ____Y ____N?

          a. If yes, can replacement parts be installed in the field: ____Y ____N?

        4. Provide a copy of the life cycle analysis for this product.

        5. Provide a copy of the manufacturer's warranty for this product.

    B. Energy Efficiency (energy required to operate/maintain):

        1. Estimate BTUs required to operate the product:

            when new? _____;

            after five years? _____;

            after ten years? _____.

    C. Compliance with Regulations (Environmental Statutory Compliance):

        1. Does the product meet all federal, state, and local environmental laws, including laws governing energy efficiency and air emissions: ____Y ____N?

        2. Has the product met the above criteria for the previous five years: ____Y ____N?

        3. List these applicable standards.

            _____

            _____

            _____

            _____

            _____

VII.   CORPORATE COMMITMENT

    A. Corporate Environmental Policy:

        1. Provide copy of manufacturer's stated environmental policies.

END OF ENVIRONMENTAL IMPACT QUESTIONNAIRE

> SPECIFIER NOTE: THIS DOCUMENT IS INTENDED TO BE A GUIDE FOR EVALUAT-
> ING INDOOR AIR QUALITY ISSUES RELATIVE TO BUILDING PRODUCTS.
> LANGUAGE IS PRESENTED FOR EXAMPLE ONLY AND NO WARRANTY IS MADE
> AS TO COMPLETENESS OR ACCURACY OF INFORMATION CONTAINED HEREIN.

INDOOR AIR QUALITY EMISSION TEST REPORT

I. DIRECTIONS

   A. Complete the following questionnaire and submit for review to:

   _____

   _____

   _____

   _____

   B. Relate information concerning only one product, material, or accessory item per test report.

   C. It is not expected that the manufacturer will have addressed all of the environmental concerns expressed in the Indoor Air Quality Emission Test Report.
      1. Respond to every question even if response is "not available," "not applicable," or "no."
      2. Attach additional sheets as required. Reference additional sheets to correspond with the question number.

II. IDENTIFICATION

   A. Material/Product: _____

   Brand Name: _____

   Manufacturer: _____

   What is the primary use or application for this product? _____

   _____

   _____

   B. Testing Laboratory:

   Name: _____

   Phone number: _____

   Address: _____

   Contact Person: _____

III. TEST PARAMETERS AND PROCEDURES

   A. Test Objectives: Describe the purpose of the testing and the intended use of the results:

   _____

_____

_____

B. Facilities and Equipment:
   1. Describe the facilities and equipment; indicate sensitivity of the analytical system.

_____

_____

_____

_____

C. Experimental Design:
   1. Describe test conditions including temperature, humidity, air exchange rate, and test materials loading.

   Temperature: _____

   Humidity: _____

   Air Exchange Rate: _____

   Test Materials Loading: _____

   General Test Conditions: _____

   _____

   _____

D. Sample Description:
   1. Describe the sample(s) tested including the type of material(s) or product(s), brand name or other identification as appropriate, size or quantity tested, and sample selection process (e.g., random).

   Material/Product: _____

   Brand Name: _____

   Manufacturer: _____

   Size/Quantity: _____

   Sample Selection Process: _____

   _____

   2. For wet samples or samples applied to a substrate, describe the substrate and methods to attach the sample to the substrate and to seal the sample edges.

   Substrate: _____

   Attachment Methods: _____

   Sealing Methods: _____

   _____

   _____

E. Experimental Procedures: Describe the experimental procedures used during testing including details of the sampling and analysis techniques.

1. Identify date(s) of testing: _____

2. Identify duration of exposure: _____

3. Were standardized test procedures such as ASTM D5116, *Guide for Small Scale Environmental Chamber Determination of Organic Emissions from Indoor Materials/Products*, used: _____ Y _____ N?

    a. If yes, cite standards: _____

       _____

       _____

       _____

       _____

    b. If no, describe the experimental procedures used during testing and analysis:

       _____

       _____

       _____

       _____

IV.   TEST RESULTS

A. Data Analysis: Describe the accuracy of the test results.

_____

_____

_____

_____

_____

B. Discussion and Conclusions:
1. Discuss the relevance of the findings and provide conclusions. For example, describe the effect of temperature and/or air exchange rate on emission factors. Note any anomalies and describe data treatment to address such data.

_____

_____

_____

_____

_____

_____

_____

2. List all substances identified in a sample of the air emitted from product; indicate amounts detected in parts per million (ppm); identify carcinogens that appear on any of the following lists:
   a. United States Environmental Protection Agency (EPA) Carcinogen Assessment Group (CAG) list of carcinogens.
   b. Clean Air Act Sections 109, 111, and 112.
   c. The National Toxicology Program's latest published "Annual Report on Carcinogens."
   d. IARC Human Carcinogens (Groups 1, 2A, and 2B).
   e. California Proposition 65.

Substance	*Carcinogen*	*ppm*
_____	__ Y __ N	_____
_____	__ Y __ N	_____
_____	__ Y __ N	_____
_____	__ Y __ N	_____
_____	__ Y __ N	_____
_____	__ Y __ N	_____
_____	__ Y __ N	_____

3. Provide instructions, requirements, or recommendations on minimizing the impact of emissions from the products on workers installing the items and on indoor air quality in the completed building. Include information on original installation of the item, maintenance, and eventual removal from the facility.

   Installation: _____

   _____

   _____

   _____

   Maintenance: _____

   _____

   _____

   _____

   Removal/disposal: _____

   _____

   _____

   _____

C. Other reports: If other reports and evaluations have been performed for the product, submit copies.

END OF INDOOR AIR QUALITY EMISSION TEST REPORT

SPECIFIER NOTE: THIS DOCUMENT IS INTENDED TO BE A FORMAT GUIDE FOR INCORPORATING ENVIRONMENTAL ISSUES INTO STANDARD CONSTRUCTION SPECIFICATIONS. TOPICS OTHER THAN ENVIRONMENTAL TOPICS ARE NOT ADDRESSED.

ENVIRONMENTAL SPECIFICATIONS SECTION FORMAT

SECTION 00000

TITLE

PART 1—GENERAL

1.01—SUMMARY

    A. Section Includes:
        1. [_____].
           x. Environmental requirements for work of this section.

1.02—REFERENCES

SPECIFIER NOTE: STANDARDS ARE BEING DEVELOPED RAPIDLY BY MANY SEGMENTS OF THE BUILDING INDUSTRY TO SUPPORT MARKET DEMANDS FOR PRODUCTS AND SERVICES THAT ADDRESS ENVIRONMENTAL ISSUES. VERIFY CURRENT STANDARDS APPROPRIATE TO [TITLE OF SECTION]. THE FOLLOWING ARE EXAMPLES.

    A. American Society of Heating, Refrigerating and Air Conditioning Engineers (ASHRAE):
        1. ASHRAE/IES 90.1: Energy-Efficient Design of New Buildings Except Low-rise Residential Buildings.

    B. ASTM International (ASTM):
        1. ASTM C618: Specification for Fly Ash and Raw or Calcined Natural Pozzolan for Use as a Mineral Admixture in Portland Cement Concrete.
        2. ASTM D5116: Guide for Small Scale Environmental Chamber Determination of Organic Emissions from Indoor Materials/Products.
        3. ASTM E2114: Standard Terminology for Sustainability Relative to the Performance of Buildings.

C. Green Seal:
   1. GS5: Environmental Standard for Compact Fluorescent Lamps.
   2. GS6: Environmental Standard for Water-efficient Fixtures.

D. Forest Stewardship Council:
   1. Smart Woods Program.

E. Scientific Certification Systems (SCS):
   1. Forest Conservation Program.

1.03—SUBMITTALS

SPECIFIER NOTE: VERIFY GREEN SUBMITTAL REQUIREMENTS. FOR PROPRI-
ETARY SPECIFICATIONS, SUBMITTAL OF MANUFACTURER'S PRODUCT DATA
MAY NOT BE REQUIRED. VERIFY THAT REVIEWER HAS THE EXPERTISE RE-
QUIRED TO ASSESS THE SUBMITTALS.

A. Submit manufacturer's product data, including:
   1. Emission data: Conduct materials testing according to the general guidelines of ASTM
      D5116.
   2. Material Safety Data Sheets.
   3. Recycled Content Data: Indicate percentage of preconsumer and postconsumer recycled
      contents.
   4. Energy performance data.
   5. Corporate environmental statement of manufacturer.
   6. Maintenance data.

B. Submit certification evidencing compliance with requirements for:
   1. Sustainably harvested wood.
   2. Low-flow water fixtures.

1.0X—ENVIRONMENTAL REQUIREMENTS

SPECIFIER NOTE: THIS ARTICLE SPECIFIES ENVIRONMENTAL PERFORMANCE
REQUIREMENTS. LOCATE PARAGRAPH 1.0X AT END OF PART 1.
FORMAT IS COORDINATED WITH ASTM E2129, STANDARD PRACTICE FOR DATA
COLLECTION FOR SUSTAINABILITY ASSESSMENT OF BUILDING ELEMENTS.
COORDINATE REQUIREMENTS WITH MATERIALS SPECIFICATIONS UNDER PART
2; WHERE PRESCRIPTIVE SPECIFICATIONS ARE USED AND SUBSTITUTIONS ARE
NOT ALLOWED, QUALITY CONTROL REQUIREMENTS UNDER THIS PARAGRAPH
MAY BE REDUNDANT. NEVERTHELESS, USE OF THIS PARAGRAPH WILL HELP
CLARIFY GREEN ISSUES FOR THE CONTRACTOR.

A. Resource Management:

1. Renewable Resources:
   a. Wood: Provide products from sustainably harvested wood/sustainably managed forest as certified under the Forest Stewardship Council Smart Woods Program or the SCS Forest Conservation Program.
   b. Water: Provide equipment that minimizes water usage.
      (1) Water closets, lavatory faucets, and faucet aerators: Certified under GS 6.
2. Managed Resources:
   a. Aluminum: Products containing aluminum manufactured from raw materials obtained in areas currently or historically supporting tropical rain forests are not permitted.
3. Recycled Content: Provide [Title of Section] manufactured from recycled materials.
   a. Preconsumer recycled content: Minimum __ percent of complete product.
   b. Concrete: Type F or Type C fly ash in accordance with ASTM C618 may be used as a substitute for a maximum of 20% of Portland cement.
4. Reuse/Recyclability/Disposal: Provide [Title of Section] for which secondary markets or leasing programs exist.
   a. Carpet: Furnished and installed by manufacturer under separate contract. Coordinate installation with carpet manufacturer.

B. Toxicity/Hazardous Materials:

1. Toxic/Hazardous Contents: Products containing carcinogens listed by any of the following will not be permitted.
   a. EPA-CAG list of carcinogens.
   b. Clean Air Act, Sections 109, 111, and 112.
   c. The National Toxicology Program's latest published "Annual Report on Carcinogens."
   d. IARC—Human Carcinogens (Groups 1, 2A, and 2B).
2. Outgassing/Reactivity:
   a. Formaldehyde: Products containing urea-formaldehyde will not be permitted.
   b. Chlorofluorocarbons (CFC): Products and equipment requiring or using CFC during the manufacturing process will not be permitted. Products and equipment requiring or using CFC during normal operation will not be permitted.
   c. Volatile Organic Compounds (VOC):
      (1) Paints, Coatings, Sealers: Comply with South Coast Air Quality Management District (SCAQMD) rules and regulations.

C. Performance:

SPECIFIER NOTE: INCLUDE REQUIREMENTS FOR ENERGY EFFICIENCY, ENVIRONMENTAL IMPACT OF ACCESSORIES, AND MAINTENANCE DURING OPERATIONS. INCLUDE REQUIREMENTS FOR EFFICIENCY OF INSTALLATION, MINIMIZATION OF CONSTRUCTION WASTE AND/OR RECLAMATION OF CONSTRUCTION WASTE. COORDINATE WITH ENVIRONMENTAL PROCEDURES IN PART 3.

FOLLOWING ARE EXAMPLES.

1. Energy Efficiency: Provide equipment that is energy efficient as demonstrated by comparative industry standards.
   a. Lamps and Ballasts:
      (1) Compact Fluorescent Lamps: Certified under GS5.
   c. HVAC System: Minimum __ EER (energy efficiency rating) as referenced in ASHRAE 90.1.
   d. Motors: [_____].
   e. Appliances: [_____].
2. Environmental Impact of Accessories:
   a. Adhesives: Nontoxic, water-based.
   b. Concrete placement accessories:
      (1) Formwork: Reuse forms to greatest extent possible without damaging structural integrity of concrete and without damaging aesthetics of exposed concrete.
      (2) Mixing equipment: Return excess concrete to supplier; minimize water used to wash equipment.
      (3) Moisture curing: Prevent water runoff.
3. Maintenance:
   a. Products that require toxic or hazardous materials for maintenance will not be permitted.

    4. Construction waste:
      a. Provide products from manufacturers with reclamation program for packaging.
      b. Provide products from manufacturers with reclamation program for construction scrap and waste materials.

PART 2—PRODUCTS

> SPECIFIER NOTE: IDENTIFY SPECIFIC MANUFACTURERS, MATERIALS, FINISHES AND FABRICATION REQUIREMENTS IN APPROPRIATE PART 2 PARAGRAPHS. BECAUSE NEW TECHNOLOGIES AND PRODUCTS MAY BE DIFFICULT TO LOCATE, CONSIDER IDENTIFYING CONTACT PERSON AND PHONE NUMBER FOR GREEN PRODUCTS.

PART 3—EXECUTION

3.0X—ENVIRONMENTAL PROCEDURES

> SPECIFIER NOTE: SPECIFY GREEN INSTALLATION REQUIREMENTS UNDER THIS PARAGRAPH. LOCATE PARAGRAPH 3.0X AT END OF PART 3.
> FOLLOWING ARE EXAMPLES.

A. Indoor Air Quality:
    1. Temporary ventilation: During and immediately after installation of products/materials that may negatively impact indoor air quality of completed Work, provide temporary ventilation as specified in Section 01352, IAQ Management.
    2. Cleaning: Use nontoxic materials and procedures.

B. Construction Waste Management: As specified in Section 01351, Waste Management, and as follows:
    1. Reuse of packaging by manufacturer: Coordinate reclamation of packaging with [Title of Section] manufacturer.
    2. Reuse of scrap and waste materials by manufacturer: Sort as required by manufacturer and coordinate reclamation of scrap and waste materials with [Title of Section] manufacturer.

END OF SECTION

SPECIFIER NOTE: THIS SECTION IS SIMILAR TO THE STANDARD SECTION 01230, ALTERNATES, BUT EMPHASIZES ENVIRONMENTAL CONSIDERATIONS FOR MATERIALS AND PRODUCTS. EDIT TO SUIT LOCATION AND PROJECT.
LANGUAGE IS PRESENTED FOR EXAMPLE ONLY AND NO WARRANTY IS MADE AS TO COMPLETENESS OR ACCURACY OF INFORMATION CONTAINED HEREIN. REFERENCES TO MANUFACTURERS IN THIS SECTION DO NOT REPRESENT A GUARANTY, WARRANTY, OR ENDORSEMENT THEREOF.

SECTION 01231

ENVIRONMENTAL ALTERNATES

PART 1—GENERAL

1.1—SUMMARY

    A. Section includes: Alternates to be submitted to Owner with Bid.
       1. Submission procedures.
       2. Documentation of changes to Contract Sum/Price and Contract Time.

SPECIFIER NOTE: EDIT BELOW TO SUIT PROJECT. COORDINATE WITH BID FORM.

    B. Related Documents:
       1. Agreement: Incorporating monetary value of accepted Alternates.
       2. [Instructions To Bidders,] [Bid Form,] [Supplements to Bid Forms]: Requirements for Alternates.

1.2—DEFINITIONS

    A. Alternate: The net amount to be added to or deducted from the Base Bid Price for work identified in Schedule of Alternates.

1.3—SUBMISSION REQUIREMENTS

    A. Extent of Alternates:
       1. Determine the full extent of Work affected by proposed Alternates.
       2. Coordinate related work and modify surrounding work to integrate the Work of each Alternate.
          a. Include as part of each Alternate, miscellaneous devices, accessory objects and similar items incidental to or required for a complete installation whether or not mentioned as part of the Alternate.

    B. Submission Form: Complete Schedule of Alternates below and attach to Bid.
       1. Substitutions are permitted. Submit a request for substitution for any manufacturer not named in accordance with Section 01600, Product Requirements.

C. Schedule: A Schedule of Alternates is included at the end of this Section. Specification Sections referenced in the Schedule contain requirements for materials and methods necessary to achieve the Work described under each Alternate.
   1. Alternates describe environmental requirements.
   2. Conform to Contract Documents for requirements for performance, appearance, workmanship and materials not modified under the Alternate Bids.

1.4—SELECTION AND AWARD OF ALTERNATES

A. Acceptance or Rejection: Alternates quoted on Schedule of Alternates and attached to Bid will be reviewed and accepted or rejected at the Owner's option. None, any, or all Alternates may be accepted or rejected by the Owner.

B. Bids will be evaluated on the Base Bid. After selection of a Contractor, consideration will be given to Alternates and Base Bid Price adjustments.

C. Accepted Alternates will be identified in the Owner-Contractor Agreement.

PART 2—PRODUCTS—(NOT USED)

PART 3—EXECUTION

SPECIFIER NOTE: SCHEDULE OF ALTERNATES INCLUDES POSSIBLE OPTIONS. PRODUCTS AND MANUFACTURERS ARE EXAMPLES ONLY AND NO WARRANTY OF SUITABILITY IS GIVEN BY THEIR INCLUSION HEREIN. EDIT TO SUIT PROJECT. EDIT ALTERNATES BELOW BY ADDING AND/OR DELETING ALTERNATES FOR THE SPECIFIC CONDITIONS AND REQUIREMENTS OF THE PROJECT SITE.

3.1—SCHEDULE OF ALTERNATES

A. Alternate Number 1: State the amount to be added to or deducted from the Base Bid Price if degradable, natural-fiber erosion control blankets are provided for the erosion control blankets and erosion control geotextiles as specified in Section 02370, Slope Protection and Erosion Control.
   1. WS072, WS072B, WS052, or CFS072B by GreenFix America (800-929-2184).
   2. Or equal.
      Add: _____ dollars, or Deduct: _____ dollars.

B. Alternate Number 2: State the amount to be added to or deducted from the Base Bid Price if reinforcing steel fabricated from minimum 90% postconsumer recycled steel is provided for reinforcing bars and wire as specified in Section 03200, Concrete Reinforcement.
   1. SMI-Texas (210-372-8200).
   2. Or equal.
      Add: _____ dollars, or Deduct: _____ dollars.

C. Alternate Number 3: State the amount to be added to or deducted from the Base Bid Price if expansion joint fillers fabricated from 100% postconsumer recycled newsprint is provided in lieu of expansion joint fillers as specified in Section 03300, Cast-in-Place Concrete.
   1. Homex 300 by Homosote (800-257-9491).

2. Or equal.
   Add: _____ dollars, or Deduct: _____ dollars.

D. Alternate Number 4: State the amount to be added to or deducted from the Base Bid Price if mortar mix furnished in reusable bulk bags is provided for the mortar specified in Section 04100, Masonry Mortar and Grout. Submit documentation from mortar mix manufacturer that mortar packaging from installed materials is reused or recycled.
   1. SpecMix (612-490-1665).
   2. Or equal.
      Add: _____ dollars, or Deduct: _____ dollars.

E. Alternate Number 5: State the amount to be added to or deducted from the Base Bid Price if sustainably harvested wood as certified in accordance with Forest Stewardship Council (FSC) Principles and Criteria is provided in lieu of lumber as specified in Section 06100, Rough Carpentry. Submit documentation of FSC-accredited certification for installed materials.
   1. Good Wood Alliance (802-862-4448).
   2. Or equal.
      Add: _____ dollars, or Deduct: _____ dollars.

F. Alternate Number 6: State the amount to be added to or deducted from the Base Bid Price if 100 percent remelt steel fasteners are provided in lieu of fasteners as specified in Section 06100, Rough Carpentry.
   1. Maze Nails (815-223-8290).
   2. Or equal.
      Add: _____ dollars, or Deduct: _____ dollars.

G. Alternate Number 7: State the amount to be added to or deducted from the Base Bid Price if sustainably harvested wood as certified in accordance with Forest Stewardship Council (FSC) Principles and Criteria is provided in lieu of lumber as specified in Section 06175, Wood Trusses. Submit documentation of FSC-accredited certification for installed materials.
   1. Good Wood Alliance (802-862-4448).
   2. Or equal.
      Add: _____ dollars, or Deduct: _____ dollars.

H. Alternate Number 8: State the amount to be added to or deducted from the Base Bid Price if sustainably harvested wood as certified in accordance with Forest Stewardship Council (FSC) Principles and Criteria is provided in lieu of lumber as specified in Section 06200, Finish Carpentry. Submit documentation of FSC-accredited certification for installed materials.
   1. Good Wood Alliance (802-862-4448).
   2. Or equal.
      Add: _____ dollars, or Deduct: _____ dollars.

I. Alternate Number 9: State the amount to be added to or deducted from the Base Bid Price if 100 percent remelt steel fasteners are provided in lieu of fasteners as specified in Section 06200, Finish Carpentry.
   1. Maze Nails (815-223-8290).
   2. Or equal.
      Add: _____ dollars, or Deduct: _____ dollars.

J. Alternate Number 10: State the amount to be added to or deducted from the Base Bid Price if organic asphalt shingles with membrane fabricated from minimum 50% recycled cellulose in shingle mat substrate are provided in lieu of fiberglass shingles as specified in Section 07310, Shingles. Color as approved by Owner from manufacturer's standard palette. Submit samples for initial selection purposes in form of manufacturer's color charts or chips showing full range of colors, textures, and patterns available.
1. Atlas (770-933-4461).
2. Certainteed (800-274-8530).
3. Tamko (800-641-4691).
4. Or equal.
   Add: _____ dollars, or Deduct: _____ dollars.

K. Alternate Number 11: State the amount to be added to or deducted from the Base Bid Price if walkway pads fabricated from minimum 90% postconsumer recycled rubber tires are provided in lieu of walkway pads as specified in Section 07510, Built-up Bituminous Roofing.
1. Roof-Gard Pads by Humane Manufacturing (800-369-6263).
2. Or equal.
   Add: _____ dollars, or Deduct: _____ dollars.

L. Alternate Number 12: State the amount to be added to or deducted from the Base Bid Price if walkway pads fabricated from minimum 90% postconsumer recycled rubber tires are provided in lieu of walkway pads as specified in Section 07550, Modified Bituminous Membrane Roofing.
1. Roof-Gard Pads by Humane Manufacturing (800-369-6263).
2. Or equal.
   Add: _____ dollars, or Deduct: _____ dollars.

M. Alternate Number 13: State the amount to be added to or deducted from the Base Bid Price if tile manufactured from recycled glass is provided in lieu of ceramic tile as specified in Section 09310, Ceramic Tile. Color as approved by Owner from manufacturer's standard palette. Submit samples for initial selection purposes in form of manufacturer's color charts or chips showing full range of colors, textures, and patterns available.
1. Prominence by GTE (717-724-8323).
2. Traffic Tile by Terra Green Ceramics (317-935-4760).
3. Or equal.
   Add: _____ dollars, or Deduct: _____ dollars.

N. Alternate Number 14: State the amount to be added to or deducted from the Base Bid Price if 1/8″-thick linoleum sheet with natural jute backing is provided in lieu of vinyl tile and vinyl sheet flooring as specified in Section 09650, Resilient Flooring. Color as approved by Owner from manufacturer's standard palette. Submit samples for initial selection purposes in form of manufacturer's color charts or chips showing full range of colors, textures, and patterns available.
1. Marmoleum by Forbo Industries (800-842-7839)
2. DLW Linoleum by Gerbert (717-299-5035)
3. Or equal.
   Add: _____ dollars, or Deduct: _____ dollars.

O. Alternate Number 15: State the amount to be added to or deducted from the Base Bid Price if carpet manufactured from postconsumer recycled plastic or postconsumer recycled carpet is provided in lieu of carpet as specified in Section 09680, Carpet. Color as approved by Owner from manufacturer's standard palette. Submit samples for initial selection purposes in form of manufacturer's color charts or chips showing full range of colors, textures, and patterns available.

1. Image Carpets (800-722-2504).
2. Interface (800-336-0225).
3. Or equal.

   Add: _____ dollars, or Deduct: _____ dollars.

END OF SECTION

This is a guidance document with sample specification language intended to be inserted into project specifications on this subject as appropriate to the agency's environmental goals. Certain provisions, where indicated, are required for U.S. federal agency projects. Sample specification language is numbered to clearly distinguish it from advisory or discussion material. Each sample is preceded by identification of the typical location in a specification section where it would appear using the SectionFormat™ of the Construction Specifications Institute.

SECTION 01351—WASTE MANAGEMENT

SPECIFIER NOTE: This section includes requirements for waste management. This section represents data quality objectives and waste management consistent with ASTM D5792 for typical commercial construction. This section does not address environmental remediation, abatement, regulatory requirements, or requirements for environmental impact statements/reports. Edit to suit location and project.

PART 1—GENERAL

1.1—SUMMARY

    A. Section includes:
        1. Special requirements for waste management during [deconstruction,] [renovation,] construction operations.
           a. Protect the environment, both on-site and off-site, during [deconstruction,] [renovation,] and construction operations.
           b. Prevent environmental pollution and damage.
           c. Maximize source reduction, reuse and recycling of solid waste.
        2. Monitoring requirements.

    B. Related Sections:
        1. Section 01300, Administrative Requirements: Environmental Manager and Contractor training requirements.
        2. Section 01400, Quality Control: Meetings and project coordination.

1.2—DEFINITIONS

    A. Definitions pertaining to sustainable development: As defined in ASTM E2114.

1.3—QUALITY ASSURANCE

    A. Maximize use of source reduction and recycling procedures outlined in ASTM D5834.

SPECIFIER NOTE: Green building rating systems typically include strategies to reduce construction waste. USGBC-LEED™ v2.1, for example, includes credits for diversion of waste at 50 percent and at 75 percent by weight. Green Globes—US also provides points for a construction, demolition, and renovation waste management plan.

    B. Diversion Goals: A minimum [50] [75] percent by weight of total project solid waste to be diverted from landfill.

1.4—PRECONSTRUCTION MEETING

    A. After award of Contract and prior to the commencement of the Work, schedule and conduct meeting with Owner and Architect to discuss the proposed Waste Management Plan and to develop mutual understanding relative to details of environmental protection.

1.5—SUBMITTALS

    A. Solid Waste Management Plan: Not less than 10 days before the Preconstruction meeting, prepare and submit a Solid Waste Management Plan including, but not limited to, the following:
        1. List of the recycling facilities, reuse facilities, municipal solid waste landfills and other disposal area(s) to be used. Include:
            a. Name, location, and phone number.
            b. Copy of permit or license for each facility.
        2. Identify materials that cannot be recycled or reused. Provide explanation or justification.
        3. Revise and resubmit Plan as required by Owner.
            a. Approval of Contractor's Plan will not relieve the Contractor of responsibility for compliance with applicable environmental regulations.

    B. Progress Documentation: Document solid waste disposal and diversion. Include the quantity by weight of waste generated; waste diverted through sale, reuse, or recycling; and waste disposed by landfill or incineration. Identify landfills, recycling centers, waste processors, and other organizations that process or receive the solid waste.
        1. Document on form in Appendix A of this Section, or similar form as approved by Owner.
        2. With each Application for Payment, submit updated Documentation for solid waste disposal and diversion.
        3. With each Application for Payment, submit manifests, weight tickets, receipts, and invoices specifically identifying the Project and waste material.

    C. Record Submittals: With Record Submittals as specified in Section 01780, submit the following:
        1. Summary of solid waste disposal and diversion. Submit on form in Appendix A of this Section, or similar form as approved by Owner.

PART 2—PRODUCTS

PART 3—EXECUTION

3.1—SOLID WASTE MANAGEMENT

A. Develop and implement a waste management program in accordance with ASTM E1609 and as specified herein.

B. Collection: Implement a recycling/reuse program that includes separate collection of waste materials of the following types as appropriate to the project waste and to the available recycling and reuse programs in the project area:
1. Land clearing debris.
2. Asphalt.
3. Concrete.
4. Metal.
   a. Ferrous.
   b. Nonferrous.
5. Wood, nails, and staples allowed.
6. Debris.
7. Glass, colored glass allowed.
8. Paper.
   a. Bond.
   b. Newsprint.
   c. Cardboard and paper packaging materials.
9. Plastic.

SPECIFIER NOTE: Many types of plastics may be mixed together to make plastic lumber. However, some facilities operate predominantly for the consumer sector and require separation of plastic by consumer types. Milk jugs are generally fabricated from HDPE; plastic wrap and plastic bags are generally fabricated from LDPE; plastic soda bottles are generally fabricated from PET.

---

   a. Type 1: Polyethylene Terephthalate (PET, PETE).
   b. Type 2: High-density Polyethylene (HDPE).
   c. Type 3: Vinyl (Polyvinyl Chloride or PVC).
   d. Type 4: Low Density Polyethylene (LDPE).
   e. Type 5: Polypropylene (PP).
   f. Type 6: Polystyrene (PS).
   g. Type 7: Other. Use of this code indicates that the package in question is made with a resin other than the six listed above, or is made of more than one resin listed above, and used in a multi-layer combination.
10. Gypsum.
11. Paint and paint cans.
12. Carpet.
13. Insulation.
14. Others as appropriate.

SPECIFIER NOTE: Identify local recycling centers and waste haulers. Sources for this information include state solid waste offices and environmental protection agency (EPA) regional offices, waste management division. List centers that accept material identified above for recycling/reuse.

The following are examples.

   C. Recycling/Reuse: Maximize recycling and reuse of materials.
      1. Recycling/Reuse on project site: [Coordinate with Architect.] [As indicated on Drawings.] [Items to be reused include: xxxx.]
      2. Recycling/Reuse off project site: The following is a partial list for Contractor's information only. For more information, contact the State Department of Environmental Quality and the local Integrated Solid Waste Management Office.
         a. Habitat for Humanity, a non-profit housing organization that rehabilitates and builds housing for low-income families. Sites requiring donated materials vary. Contact the national hotline (800) HABITAT.
         b. Materials For The Arts (MFA) sponsored by the Department of Cultural Affairs. MFA is a materials exchange that accepts waste and excess materials from private donors and distributes them to various non-profit art organizations throughout the City. Contact xxxxxxxxxxxxxxx.
         c. Michigan Department of Environmental Quality; 517-373-1322.
         d. Michigan Recycling Coalition (MRC). The MRC is an organization whose members consist of recycling coordinators and professionals in Michigan; 517-485-WRIN (9746) or 517-371-7073.
         e. California Materials Exchange (CAL-MAX) Program sponsored by the California Integrated Waste Management Board; (916) 255-2369.

   D. Handling:
      1. Clean materials that are contaminated prior to placing in collection containers. Deliver materials free of dirt, adhesives, solvents, petroleum contamination, and other substances deleterious to recycling process.
      2. Arrange for collection by or delivery to the appropriate recycling or reuse facility.
      3. Hazardous Waste and Hazardous Materials: Handle in accordance with applicable regulations. Coordinate with Section 01411.

SPECIFIER NOTE: Avoid composting diseased vegetation and animal waste (from carnivorous animals) in situ. Because the operations of commercial composting facilities are monitored and controlled to maintain the high temperatures required in the thermophyllic phase of composting (the thermophyllic phase of the average residential composting pile is only 4–7 days and relies on thermophyllic bacteria that function at 104 degrees–170 degrees F and that are extremely efficient at processing compostables) commercial composting can accept diseased vegetation and, in many cases, all types of animal waste. However, composting in situ is not generally so well controlled. If temperatures in the pile do not get hot enough to kill the undesirable organisms, those organisms can re-infest new vegetation when the compost is applied.

E. Composting: In accordance with State Extension Service recommendations and as follows:
   1. Moisture content: Maintain between 35 percent and 60 percent.
   2. Carbon to nitrogen (C/N) ratio: Maintain at approximately 30 to 1 by weight.
   3. Do not compost meat or dairy products on site.

SPECIFIER NOTE: Changes to the material properties of a plastic within a compost unit can affect the degradation of other materials and the resulting composition and appearance of the composed material. Edit below to suit location and project.

   4. Where the proposed Waste Management Plan incorporates composting of plastics, assess the potential effect of each type of plastic to be included on the composting process in accordance with ASTM D5509 or ASTM D5512.

END OF SECTION

SPECIFIER NOTE: Edit below to suit project.

APPENDIX A

SUMMARY OF SOLID WASTE DISPOSAL AND DIVERSION

Project Name: _____   Project Number: _____

Contractor Name: _____   License Number: _____

Contractor Address: _____

Solid Waste Material	Date Material Disposed/ Diverted	Amount Disposed/ Diverted (ton or cu. yd)	Municipal Solid Waste Facility (name, address, & phone number)	Recycling/ ReuseFacility (name, address, & phone number)	Comments (if disposed, state why not diverted)
Land Clearing Debris					
Asphalt					
Concrete					
Metal					
Wood					
Debris					
Glass					
Clay brick					
Paper/ Cardboard					
Plastic					
Gypsum					
Paint					
Carpet					
Other:					

Signature: _____   Date: _____

SECTION 01352—INDOOR AIR QUALITY (IAQ) MANAGEMENT

SPECIFIER NOTE: THIS SECTION INCLUDES REQUIREMENTS FOR IAQ MANAGE-
MENT DURING CONSTRUCTION. COORDINATE WITH REQUIREMENTS OF OTHER
SECTIONS; VERIFY THAT PRODUCTS AND INSTALLATION METHODS SPECIFIED
IN OTHER SECTIONS ARE ENVIRONMENTALLY APPROPRIATE. EDIT TO SUIT LO-
CATION AND PROJECT.

PART 1—GENERAL

1.1—SUMMARY

    A. Section includes:
       1. Special requirements for Indoor Air Quality (IAQ) management during construction op-
          erations.
       2. Procedures for testing baseline IAQ. Baseline lAQ requirements specify maximum in-
          door pollutant concentrations for acceptance of the facility.
       3. Requirements for Independent Materials Testing of specific materials anticipated to
          have measurable impact on IAQ.

SPECIFIER NOTE: COORDINATE REQUIREMENTS SPECIFIED UNDER THIS SEC-
TION WITH WORK SPECIFIED UNDER RELATED SECTIONS. EDIT BELOW TO SUIT
PROJECT.

    B. Related Sections:
       1. Section 01300—Administrative Requirements: Environmental Manager and Contractor
          training requirements.
       2. Section 01400—Quality Control: Meetings and project coordination.
       3. Section 01780—Closeout Submittals: Cleaning and final submittals.
       4. Section 01810—Commissioning

1.2—DEFINITIONS

SPECIFIER NOTE: VERIFY VENTILATION REQUIREMENTS FOR INDOOR AIR
QUALITY. ADEQUATE REQUIREMENTS FOR ONE MATERIAL MAY NOT BE ADE-
QUATE FOR ANOTHER. MATERIALS/PRODUCTS THAT GENERALLY REQUIRE
TEMPORARY VENTILATION FOR OFFGASSING INCLUDE: ADHESIVES, WOOD
PRESERVATIVES, COMPOSITE WOOD PRODUCTS, PLASTICS, WATERPROOFING,
INSULATION, FIREPROOFING, SEALANTS/CAULKING, ACOUSTICAL CEILINGS,
RESILIENT FLOORING, CARPET, PAINTING, SEALERS/COATINGS, WALL COVER-
INGS, MANUFACTURED CASEWORK, AND FURNITURE.
FOR MORE INFORMATION AND INFORMATION ON CURRENT FEDERAL ACTIVI-
TIES FOR IAQ, CONTACT EPA INDOOR AIR QUALITY INFORMATION CLEARING
HOUSE (800) 438-4318/(202) 484-1307; NATIONAL PESTICIDES TELECOMMUNICA-
TION NETWORK (800) 858-7378; NATIONAL INSTITUTE FOR OCCUPATIONAL
SAFETY AND HEALTH (800) 35-NIOSH; AND THE DEPARTMENT OF ENERGY (DOE)
OFFICE OF CONSERVATION AND RENEWABLE ENERGY (800) DOE-3732.

A. Definitions pertaining to sustainable development: As defined in ASTM E2114.

B. Adequate ventilation: Ventilation, including air circulation and air changes, required to cure materials, dissipate humidity, and prevent accumulation of dust fumes, vapors, or gases.

C. Environmental pollution and damage: The presence of chemical, physical, or biological elements or agents which adversely affect human health or welfare; unfavorably alter ecological balances; or degrade the utility of the environment for aesthetic, cultural, or historical purposes.

D. Hazardous Materials: Any material that is regulated as a hazardous material in accordance with 49 CFR 173 requires a Material Safety Data Sheet (MSDS) in accordance with 29 CFR 1910.1200 or which during end use, treatment, handling, storage, transportation or disposal meets or has components which meet or have the potential to meet the definition of a Hazardous Waste in accordance with 40 CFR 261. Throughout this specification, hazardous material includes hazardous chemicals.
   1. Hazardous materials include: pesticides, biocides, and carcinogens as listed by recognized authorities, such as the Environmental Protection Agency (EPA) and the International Agency for Research on Cancer (IARC).

E. Indoor Air Quality (IAQ): The composition and characteristics of the air in an enclosed space that affect the occupants of that space. The indoor air quality of a space refers to the relative quality of air in a building with respect to contaminants and hazards and is determined by the level of indoor air pollution and other characteristics of the air, including those that impact thermal comfort such as air temperature, relative humidity and air speed.

F. Interior final finishes: Materials and products that will be exposed at interior, occupied spaces; including flooring, wallcovering, finish carpentry, and ceilings.

G. Packaged dry products: Materials and products that are installed in dry form and are delivered to the site in manufacturer's packaging, including carpets, resilient flooring, ceiling tiles, and insulation.

H. Wet products: Materials and products installed in wet form, including paints, sealants, adhesives, and special coatings.

1.3—QUALITY ASSURANCE

A. Inspection and Testing Lab Qualifications: Minimum of 5 years experience in performing the types of testing specified herein.

1.4—PRECONSTRUCTION MEETING

A. After award of Contract and prior to the commencement of the Work, schedule and conduct meeting with Owner and Architect to discuss the proposed IAQ Management Plan and to develop mutual understanding relative to details of environmental protection.

1.5—SUBMITTALS

A. Indoor Air Quality (IAQ) Management Plan: Not less than 10 days before the Preconstruction meeting, prepare and submit an IAQ Management Plan including, but not limited to, the following:
   1. Schedule for application of interior finishes.
   2. Revise and resubmit Plan as required by Owner.

a. Approval of Contractor's Plan will not relieve the Contractor of responsibility for compliance with applicable environmental regulations.

B. Baseline Indoor Air Quality (IAQ) Test Reports.

SPECIFIER NOTE: VERIFY IAQ REQUIREMENTS FOR MATERIALS AND PRODUCTS INCORPORATED INTO PROJECT. COORDINATE WITH DIVISIONS 2-16 AS APPROPRIATE. FOLLOWING ARE EXAMPLES. EDIT TO SUIT PROJECT.

C. Independent Materials Testing Reports. Submit for the following products:
1. Emissions:
   a. Fireproofing material on appropriate substrate.
   b. Ceiling tile.
   c. Resilient flooring.
   d. Carpet including adhesive and concrete flooring.
   e. Interior paint on appropriate substrate, including any primer coat.
   f. Wallcovering.
   g. Raised flooring.
2. Lethal Toxic Potency:
   a. Ceiling tile.
   b. Resilient flooring.
   c. Carpet including adhesive and concrete flooring.
   d. Wallcovering.
   e. Raised flooring.
   f. Office equipment.
3. Microbial Growth:
   a. Fireproofing material on appropriate substrate.
   b. Ceiling tile.
   c. Wallcovering.

D. Product Data:
1. Submit product data for filtration media used during construction and during operation. Include Minimum Efficiency Reporting Value (MERV).

SPECIFIER NOTE: COORDINATE WITH SECTIONS 01611 AND 01830.

E. Material Safety Data Sheets: Submit MSDSs for inclusion in Operation and Maintenance Manual for the following products. Coordinate with Section 01830.
1. Adhesives.
2. Floor and wall patching/leveling materials.
3. Caulking and sealants.
4. Insulating materials.
5. Fireproofing and firestopping.
6. Carpet.
7. Paint.
8. Clear finish for wood surfaces.
9. Lubricants.
10. Cleaning products.

PART 2—PRODUCTS (NOT USED)

PART 3—EXECUTION

3.1—INDOOR AIR QUALITY (IAQ) MANAGEMENT

> SPECIFIER NOTE: USGBC-LEED™ V2.1 INCLUDES CREDIT FOR AN IAQ MANAGE-
> MENT PLAN CONSISTENT WITH SMACNA IAQ GUIDELINES, INCLUDING THE EL-
> EMENTS HEREIN. ALTERNATELY, USGBC-LEED™ V2.1 INCLUDES CREDIT FOR
> BASELINE IAQ TESTING. VERIFY WITH USGBC INTERPRETATION OF ACCEPT-
> ABLE MANAGEMENT PLANS AND TESTING PROTOCOLS.

A. During construction, comply with SMACNA IAQ Guidelines for Occupied Buildings under Construction.

B. HVAC Protection: To the greatest extent possible, isolate and/or shut down the return side of the HVAC system during construction. When ventilation system must be operational during construction activities, provide temporary filters.

C. Source Control: Provide low- and zero-VOC materials as specified.

D. Pathway Interruption: Isolate areas of work as necessary to prevent contamination of clean or occupied spaces. Provide pressure differentials and/or physical barriers to protect clean or occupied spaces.

E. Housekeeping: During construction, maintain project and building products and systems to prevent contamination of building spaces.
   1. Protect stored on-site and installed absorptive materials from moisture damage.
   2. Provide minimum 48 hour pre-ventilation of packaged dry products prior to installation. Remove from packaging and ventilate in a secure, dry, well-ventilated space free from strong contaminant sources and residues. Provide a temperature range of 60 degrees F minimum to 90 degree F maximum continuously during the ventilation period. Do not ventilate within limits of Work unless otherwise approved by Architect.
   3. Provide adequate ventilation during and after installation of interior wet products and interior final finishes.
   4. Provide filtration media with a Minimum Efficiency Reporting Value (MERV) of 13 as determined by ASHRAE 52.2 during construction and during Owner occupancy. Coordinate with work of Division 15.

F. Scheduling: Schedule construction operations involving wet products prior to packaged dry products to the greatest extent possible.

G. Flush-Out: Provide minimum 2-week flush-out of the building immediately prior to occupancy. Flush out with 100% outside air. Replace all media filters after flush-out.
   1. Supply airflow at 6 air changes per hour when outside temperatures are between 55 degrees F and 85 degrees F and humidity is between 30 percent and 60 percent. Supply a minimum of 1.5 air changes per hour when conditions are not within this range.

3.2—INDOOR AIR QUALITY (IAQ) BASELINE

SPECIFIER NOTE: USGBC-LEED™ V2.1 INCLUDES CREDIT FOR AN IAQ MANAGE-
MENT PLAN CONSISTENT WITH SMACNA IAQ GUIDELINES, INCLUDING THE EL-
EMENTS HEREIN. ALTERNATELY, USGBC-LEED™ V2.1 INCLUDES CREDIT FOR
BASELINE IAQ TESTING. VERIFY WITH USGBC INTERPRETATION OF ACCEPT-
ABLE MANAGEMENT PLANS AND TESTING PROTOCOLS.

A. Coordinate with commissioning as specified in Section 01810. Upon verification of HVAC
   system operation, perform baseline IAQ testing.
   1. Perform testing for minimum 3 locations in each air handling zone. Perform in the
      breathing zone; between 4' and 7' from the floor.
   2. Collect air samples on three consecutive days during normal business hours (between
      the hours of 8:00 a.m. and 5:00 p.m.) with building operating at normal HVAC rates. Av-
      erage the results of each three-day test cycle to determine compliance or noncompliance
      of indoor air quality for each air handling zone tested.
   3. Sample and record outside air levels of formaldehyde and TVOC contaminants at out-
      side air intake of each respective air handling unit simultaneously with indoor tests to
      establish basis of comparison for these contaminant levels.

B. Baseline IAQ shall conform to the following standards and limits:
   1. Carbon Monoxide: Not to exceed 9 ppm.

SPECIFIER NOTE: CARBON DIOXIDE CONCENTRATIONS CAN ASSIST IN EVALU-
ATION OF EXPECTED LEVELS OF OCCUPANT COMFORT IN TERMS OF HUMAN
BODY ODOR, LEVELS OF CONTAMINANTS RELATED TO OCCUPANT ACTIVITY,
AND SUFFICIENCY OF VENTILATION RATES RELATIVE TO OCCUPANCY. THE
MAXIMUM CONCENTRATION OF 800 PPM IS BASED ON AN OPEN OFFICE OCCU-
PANCY. EDIT TO SUIT LOCATION AND PROJECT.

   2. Carbon Dioxide: Set points not to exceed [530 ppm higher than outdoor ambient levels.]
      [800 ppm.] [xxxx.] Assess indoor Carbon Dioxide concentrations in accordance with
      ASTM D6245.
   3. Airborne Mold and Mildew: Simultaneous indoor and outdoor readings.
   4. VOCs and particulates: Monitor VOCs (volatile organic compounds) in indoor air in ac-
      cordance with ASTM D6345. Indoor room air concentration levels, emission rates, and
      qualities of the listed contaminants shall not exceed the following limits. The levels do
      not account for contributions from office furniture, occupants, and occupant activities.

MAXIMUM INDOOR AIR CONCENTRATION STANDARDS

Indoor Contaminants	Allowable Air Concentration Levels
Formaldehyde	<20 micrograms per cubic meter above outside air concentrations
Total Volatile Organic Compounds (TVOC)	<200 micrograms per cubic meter above outside air concentrations
4-Phenylcyclohexene (4~PC)	<3 micrograms per cubic meter
Total Particulates (PM)	<20 micrograms per cubic meter
Regulated Pollutants	<NAAQS

C. Test Reports: Prepare test reports showing the results and location of each test, a summary of the HVAC operating conditions, a listing of any discrepancies and recommendations for corrective actions, if required.
   1. Include certification of test equipment calibration with each test report.
   2. If any test fails the standard, the Contractor is responsible to ventilate the building with 100% outside air until the building passes both air quality tests and duct inspections. Retesting shall be performed at no additional expense to the Owner.

3.3—INDEPENDENT MATERIALS TESTING

A. Emissions: Indicate type and rate of emissions in a 24-hour period at 35 degrees C and 50% relative humidity per unit of product. Indicate type and rate of emissions under fire conditions.
   1. Small Scale Chamber: Test and report emissions from products and materials indicated in accordance with ASTM D5116.
   2. Full Scale Chamber: Test and report emissions from products and materials indicated in accordance with ASTM D6670.

B. Lethal Toxic Potency: Test for lethal toxic potency of smoke produced from the materials and products indicated under fire conditions in accordance with ASTM E1678.
   1. Report results in accordance with Section 13 of ASTM E1678.

C. Support of Microbial Growth: Test and report in accordance with ASTM D6329. Indicate susceptibility of product or material to colonization and amplification of microorganisms. Identify microorganisms and conditions of testing.
   1. Normal conditions: Perform testing at 35 degrees C and 50% relative humidity.
   2. Extreme conditions: Perform worst case scenarios screening tests by providing an atmosphere where environmental conditions may be favorable for microbial growth.

END OF SECTION

SECTION 01354—ENVIRONMENTAL MANAGEMENT

SPECIFIER NOTE: THIS SECTION INCLUDES REQUIREMENTS FOR THE PROTEC-
TION OF NATURAL RESOURCES. THIS SECTION EMPHASIZES AN INTEGRATED
TEAM APPROACH TO ADDRESS ENVIRONMENTAL ISSUES. THIS SECTION DOES
NOT ADDRESS ENVIRONMENTAL REMEDIATION, ABATEMENT, REGULATORY
REQUIREMENTS, OR REQUIREMENTS FOR ENVIRONMENTAL IMPACT STATE-
MENTS/REPORTS. COORDINATE WITH REQUIREMENTS OF OTHER SECTIONS;
VERIFY THAT PRODUCTS AND INSTALLATION METHODS SPECIFIED IN OTHER
SECTIONS ARE ENVIRONMENTALLY APPROPRIATE.
EDIT TO SUIT LOCATION AND PROJECT.

PART 1—GENERAL

1.1—SUMMARY

    A. Section includes:
       1. Special requirements for environmental management during construction operations.
       2. Monitoring requirements.

SPECIFIER NOTE: COORDINATE REQUIREMENTS SPECIFIED UNDER THIS SEC-
TION WITH WORK SPECIFIED UNDER RELATED SECTIONS. EDIT BELOW TO SUIT
PROJECT.

    B. Related Sections:
       1. Section 01300—Administrative Requirements: Environmental Manager and Contractor
          training requirements.
       2. Section 01400—Quality Control: Meetings and project coordination.
       3. Section 01780—Closeout Submittals: Cleaning and final submittals.
       4. Section 02230—Site Clearing: Removal and storage of existing vegetation and topsoil.

1.2—DEFINITIONS

    A. Definitions pertaining to sustainable development: As defined in ASTM E2114.

    B. Environmental pollution and damage: The presence of chemical, physical, or biological el-
       ements or agents that adversely affect human health or welfare; unfavorably alter ecologi-
       cal balances; or degrade the utility of the environment for aesthetic, cultural, or historical
       purposes.

1.3—PRECONSTRUCTION MEETING

    A. After award of Contract and prior to the commencement of the Work, schedule and conduct
       meeting with Owner and Architect to discuss the proposed Environmental Protection Plan
       and to develop mutual understanding relative to details of environmental protection.

1.4—SUBMITTALS

   A. Environmental Protection Plan: Not less than 10 days before the Preconstruction meeting, prepare and submit an Environmental Protection Plan.

      1. Format: At a minimum, address the following elements:

         a. Identification of Project.

         b. Identification and contact information for Environmental Manager.

         c. General site information.

         d. Summary of Plan.

         e. Procedures to address water resources.

         f. Procedures to address land resources.

         g. Procedures to address air resources.

         h. Procedures to address fish and wildlife resources.

         i. Monitoring procedures.

      2. Revise and resubmit Plan as required by Owner.

         a. Approval of Contractor's Plan will not relieve the Contractor of responsibility for compliance with applicable environmental regulations.

   B. Reports for Field Quality Control.

PART 2—PRODUCTS (NOT USED)

PART 3—EXECUTION

3.1—ENVIRONMENTAL PROTECTION

   A. Protection of natural resources: Comply with applicable regulations and these specifications. Preserve the natural resources within the Project boundaries and outside the limits of permanent Work performed under this Contract in their existing condition or restore to an equivalent or improved condition as approved by Owner.

> SPECIFIER NOTE: GREEN BUILDING RATING SYSTEMS OFTEN INCLUDE PROVISIONS FOR MINIMIZING DISTURBANCE OF THE SITE'S TOPOGRAPHY, SOILS AND VEGETATION. USGBC-LEED™ V2.1, FOR EXAMPLE, INCLUDES CREDIT FOR REDUCED SITE DISTURBANCE, LIMITING SITE DISTURBANCE TO MAXIMUM 40 FEET BEYOND THE BUILDING PERIMETER, 5 FEET BEYOND SOLID PAVING, AND 25 FEET BEYOND PERVIOUS PAVING. GREEN GLOBES—US ALSO PROVIDES POINTS FOR ACCOMMODATING THE BUILDING'S FUNCTIONS, WHILE MINIMIZING DISTURBANCES.

      1. Confine demolition and construction activities to [work area limits indicated on the Drawings] [maximum 40 feet beyond the building perimeter, 5 feet beyond solid paving, and 25 feet beyond pervious paving].

         a. Disposal operations for demolished and waste materials that are not identified to be salvaged, recycled, or reused:

           (1) Remove debris, rubbish, and other waste materials resulting from demolition and construction operations, from site.

(2) No burning permitted.

(3) Transport materials with appropriate vehicles and dispose off-site to areas that are approved for disposal by governing authorities having jurisdiction.

(4) Avoid spillage by covering and securing loads when hauling on or adjacent to public streets or highways. Remove spillage and sweep, wash, or otherwise clean project site, streets, or highways.

2. Water resources:

   a. Comply with requirements of the National Pollutant Discharge Elimination System (NPDES) and the State Pollutant Discharge Elimination System (SPDES).

   b. Oily substances: Prevent oily or other hazardous substances from entering the ground, drainage areas, or local bodies of water.

      (1) Store and service construction equipment at areas designated for collection of oil wastes.

   c. Mosquito abatement: Prevent ponding of stagnant water conducive to mosquito breeding habitat.

   d. Prevent runoff from site during demolition and construction operations.

   e. Stream Crossings: [Equipment will not be permitted to ford live streams.] [Equipment will be permitted to ford live streams if temporary culverts or bridges are constructed for the purpose. Remove temporary culverts and bridges upon completion of work and repair the area to its original condition, unless otherwise accepted in writing by Architect.]

SPECIFIER NOTE: COORDINATE BELOW WITH WORK SPECIFIED IN DIVISION 2, SITEWORK.

---

3. Land resources: Prior to construction, identify land resources to be preserved within the Work area. Do not remove, cut, deface, injure, or destroy land resources including trees, shrubs, vines, grasses, topsoil, and landforms without permission from Owner.

   a. Earthwork: As specified in Division 2 and as follows:

      (1) Erodible soils: Plan and conduct earthwork to minimize the duration of exposure of unprotected soils, except where the constructed feature obscures borrow areas, quarries, and waste material areas. Clear areas in reasonably sized increments only as needed to use the areas developed. Form earthwork to final grade as shown. Immediately protect side slopes and back slopes upon completion of rough grading.

      (2) Erosion and sedimentation control devices: Construct or install temporary and permanent erosion and sedimentation control features as required.

SPECIFIER NOTE: FOR OLD-GROWTH AND OTHER SIGNIFICANT TREES AND PLANTS, IT MAY BE USEFUL TO HAVE A MORE AGGRESSIVE APPROACH TO PROTECTION THAN THE STANDARD PROHIBITIONS. THE FOLLOWING IS AN EXAMPLE.

---

   b. Tree and plant protection: As specified in Division 2 and as follows:

          (1) Prior to start of construction, tag each tree and plant scheduled to remain with value as approved by Owner. In the event of damage to tree or plant, Owner may at Owner's discretion, deduct the indicated value of the damaged tree or plant from the Contract Sum.

    4. Air Resources: Comply with IAQ Management Plan and as follows:

      a. Prevent creation of dust, air pollution, and odors.

      b. Sequence construction to avoid disturbance to site to the greatest extent possible.

      c. Use mulch, water sprinkling, temporary enclosures, and other appropriate methods to limit dust and dirt rising and scattering in air to lowest practical level.

          (1) Do not use water when it may create hazardous or other adverse conditions such as flooding and pollution.

      d. Store volatile liquids, including fuels and solvents, in closed containers.

      e. Properly maintain equipment to reduce gaseous pollutant emissions.

    5. Fish and Wildlife Resources: Manage and control construction activities to minimize interference with, disturbance of, and damage to fish and wildlife.

      a. Do not disturb fish and wildlife.

      b. Do not alter water flows or otherwise significantly disturb the native habitat related to the project and critical to the survival of fish and wildlife, except as indicated or specified.

3.2—FIELD QUALITY CONTROL

  A. General:

    1. Comply with requirements of agencies having jurisdiction and as specified herein.

    2. Provide field practices, shipping, and handling of samples in accordance with ASTM D4840.

    3. Coordinate with Section 01411—Environmental Regulatory Requirements.

  B. Field Quality Control Reports: Provide in accordance with approved Environmental Protection Plan.

  C. Water: Develop and implement a water monitoring program for surface and ground water on the project site in accordance with ASTM D5851. Establish baseline water quality. Determine study scale and sampling frequency as appropriate to project and location. Immediately report to [Owner] [Architect] [agency having jurisdiction] when sampling indicates increase from established baseline.

> SPECIFIER NOTE: ACIDITY AND ALKALINITY ARE USED TO ASSIST IN ESTABLISHING LEVELS OF CHEMICAL TREATMENT TO CONTROL SCALE, CORROSION, ETC. THE CHARACTERISTICS ARE ALSO CRITICAL IN ESTABLISHING SOLUBILITY OF SOME METALS, TOXICITY OF SOME METALS, AND THE BUFFERING CAPACITY OF SOME WATERS.

    1. Test surface and ground water for acidity and alkalinity in accordance with ASTM D1067.

SPECIFIER NOTE: THE EROSION POTENTIAL OF A SOIL IS OF CONCERN IN VEGE-TATED CHANNELS, ROAD EMBANKMENTS, DAMS, LEVEES, SPILLWAYS, CON-STRUCTION SITES, ETC.

2. Assess potential effects of soil management practices on soil loss in accordance with ASTM D6629. Assess erodibility of soil with dominant soil structure less than 7 to 8 cm in accordance with ASTM D5852.
3. Monitor sediment in surface waters [on the project site] [directly impacted by the project whether on site or off site] in accordance with ASTM D6145. Establish baseline sediment and related flow data prior to start of construction operations. Determine study scale and sampling frequency as appropriate to project and location. Immediately report to [Owner] [Architect] [agency having jurisdiction] when sampling indicates increase from established baseline.
4. Monitor plant nutrients, nitrogen and phosphorus in surface waters [on the project site] [directly impacted by the project whether on site or off site] in accordance with ASTM D6146. Establish nitrogen and phosphorus baselines prior to start of construction operations. Determine study scale and sampling frequency as appropriate to project and location. Immediately report to [Owner] [Architect] [agency having jurisdiction] when sampling indicates increase from established baseline.
5. Where water quality test kits are used in the water monitoring program, use in accordance with ASTM D5463.
6. Report results of water testing in accordance with ASTM D596.

SPECIFIER NOTE: FOLLOWING ARE EXAMPLES. EDIT TO SUIT LOCATION AND PROJECT.

D. Toxicity:
1. Assess potential effects on plant growth and bioaccumulation in accordance with ASTM D5435 for the following materials:
   a. Paint.
   b. Sealants.
   c. Adhesives.
   d. Below-grade waterproofing.
   e. Roofing.
   f. Hydraulic fluids and lubricants.
2. Assess potential effects on the establishment and maintenance of aquatic organisms in accordance with ASTM E1023 for the following materials. Effects to be considered include: biological, chemical, physical, and toxicological properties of a material.
   a. Paint.
   b. Sealants.
   c. Adhesives.
   d. Below-grade waterproofing.

    e. Roofing.

    f. Hydraulic fluids and lubricants.

3. Assess potential effects on the establishment and maintenance of terrestrial plant communities in accordance with ASTM E1963 for the following materials. Effects to be considered include: biological, chemical, physical, and toxicological properties of a material.

    a. Paint.

    b. Sealants.

    c. Adhesives.

    d. Below-grade waterproofing.

    e. Roofing.

    f. Hydraulic fluids and lubricants.

4. Obtain site samples for assessment of terrestrial plant communities with sampling methods in accordance with ASTM E1923.

E. Ecosystems:

1. Monitor wetland functions in accordance with ASTM E1983.

    a. For constructed wetlands, assess the hydrologic and biogeochemical functions.

    b. For existing wetlands and restored wetlands, assess the hydrologic, biogeochemical, and habitat functions.

END OF SECTION

This is a guidance document with sample specification language intended to be inserted into project specifications on this subject as appropriate to the agency's environmental goals. Certain provisions, where indicated, are required for U.S. federal agency projects. Sample specification language is numbered to clearly distinguish it from advisory or discussion material. Each sample is preceded by identification of the typical location in a specification section where it would appear using the SectionFormat™ of the Construction Specifications Institute.

SECTION 01611—ENVIRONMENTAL REQUIREMENTS FOR PRODUCTS

SPECIFIER NOTE: Coordinate with Section 01600. Section 01600—Product Requirements, addresses general requirements for delivery, storage, and handling. Sometimes, it also specifies general requirements for materials and equipment identified as new. New materials include those manufactured with recycled content. New materials do not include materials salvaged or purchased for reuse.

For general information related to toxicity of various substances, refer to the Agency for Toxic Substances and Disease Registry (ATSDR), an agency of the U.S. Department of Health and Human Services. ATSDR is directed by congressional mandate to perform specific functions concerning the effect on public health of hazardous substances in the environment. These functions include health consultations concerning specific hazardous substances, health surveillance and registries, information development and dissemination, and education and training concerning hazardous substances. Refer to: http://www.atsdr.cdc.gov/

Also, the Centers for Disease Control and Prevention (CDC) scientifically considers all factors that affect the health of the nation. The interaction between people and their environments, natural as well as human-made, continues to emerge as a major issue concerning public health; therefore, the CDC promotes the Designing and Building Healthy Places program; refer to http://www.cdc.gov/healthyplaces/default.htm.

Edit to suit project if incorporating reused materials.

1.1—SUMMARY

A. Section includes:
1. Environmental requirements for products.

1.2—DEFINITIONS

A. Definitions pertaining to sustainable development: As defined in ASTM E2114.

B. Biobased Materials: Fuels, chemicals, building materials, or electric power or heat produced from biomass as defined by the Biomass Research and Development Act of 2000. Minimum biobased content shall be as defined by the U.S. Department of Agriculture pursuant to the U.S. Farm Bill May 2002.

SPECIFIER NOTE: According to the June 7, 2002, draft of the USDA Biobased Products—Definitions and Descriptions, *biobased content* is the weight of the biobased material divided by the total weight of the product and expressed as a percentage by weight.

      1. Biobased content: The weight of the biobased material divided by the total weight of the product and expressed as a percentage by weight.

    C. Chain of Custody: Process whereby a product or material is maintained under the physical possession or control during its entire life cycle.

SPECIFIER NOTE: EO 13101 defines Environmentally Preferable Products as "products and services that have a lesser or reduced effect on the environment. . . . This comparison may consider raw materials acquisition, production, manufacturing, packaging, distribution, reuse, operation, maintenance, or disposal of the product."

    D. Environmentally preferable products: Products and services that have a lesser or reduced effect on the environment in comparison to conventional products and services. Refer to EPA's Final Guidance on Environmentally Preferable Purchasing for more information, http://www.epa.gov/epp/guidance/finalguidancetoc.htm.

    E. Stewardship: Responsible use and management of resources in support of sustainability.

    F. Sustainability: The maintenance of ecosystem components and functions for future generations.

1.3—SUBMITTALS

    A. With Record Submittals as specified in Section 01780, submit the following:
      1. Affirmative Procurement Reporting Form. Submit on form in Appendix A of this Section, or similar form as approved by Owner.

SPECIFIER NOTE: Following are examples. Coordinate with Divisions 2–16 as appropriate. Edit to suit project.

      2. Submit environmental data in accordance with Table 1 of ASTM E2129 for the following products:
        a. Masonry
        b. Finish Carpentry
        c. Plastic Fabrications
        d. Building Insulation
        e. Roofing
        f. Joint Sealers
        g. Wood and Plastic Doors
        h. Windows

    i. Skylights
    j. Glazed Curtain Wall
    k. Gypsum Board
    l. Tile
    m. Acoustical Ceilings
    n. Resilient Flooring
    o. Carpet
    p. Wallcoverings
    q. Paints and Coatings
    r. Toilet Compartments
    s. Loading Dock Equipment
    t. Office Equipment
    u. Furnishings and Accessories
    v. Renewable Energy Equipment
    w. Elevators
    x. Plumbing fixtures and equipment
    y. HVAC equipment
    z. Lighting equipment

SPECIFIER NOTE: Material Safety Data Sheets (MSDS) are required under the OSHA (Occupational Safety and Health Administration) Hazard Communication Standard 1910.1200; refer to http://www.osha.gov/pls/oshaweb/owadisp.show_document?p_table=STANDARDS&p_id=10099.

According to OSHA, a MSDS must include the following information (1910.1200(g)(2)):

- Product name

- Chemical and common name(s) of all ingredients which have been determined to be health hazards or physical hazards

- Physical and chemical characteristics of the hazardous chemical (such as vapor pressure, flash point)

- Physical hazards of the hazardous chemical, including the potential for fire, explosion, and reactivity

- Health hazards of the hazardous chemical

- Primary route(s) of entry

- OSHA permissible exposure limit (Threshold Limit)

- Whether the chemical is listed in the National Toxicology Program (NTP) Annual Report on Carcinogens or the International Agency for Research on Cancer (IARC) Monographs, or by OSHA

- Precautions for safe handling and use

- Control measures, such as appropriate engineering controls, work practices, or personal protective equipment

---

- Emergency and first aid procedures
- Date of preparation of the material safety data sheet or the last change to it
- Name, address, and telephone number of the chemical manufacturer, importer, employer, or other responsible party preparing or distributing the MSDS

There is no OSHA-specified format for a MSDS. However, the American National Standards Institute (ANSI) has developed recommendations for a standard format (ANSI Z400.1) that is commonly used. The ANSI standard includes 16 sections. The first ten address the specific requirements under OSHA; the last six identify information that OSHA does not require but that may be useful for green buildings.

---

3. Material Safety Data Sheets (MSDS): For each product required by OSHA to have an MSDS, submit an MSDS. MSDS shall be prepared [no earlier than June 1998] [within the previous five years] [xxxx]. Include information for MSDS Sections 1–16 in accordance with ANSI Z400.1 and as follows:
   a. Section 1: Chemical Product and Company Identification.
   b. Section 2: Composition/Information on Ingredients.
   c. Section 3: Hazards Identification.
   d. Section 4: First Aid Measures.
   e. Section 5: Firefighting Measures.
   f. Section 6: Accidental Release Measures.
   g. Section 7: Handling and Storage.
   h. Section 8: Exposure Controls/Person Protection.
   i. Section 9: Physical and Chemical Properties.
   j. Section 10: Stability and Reactivity Data.
   k. Section 11: Toxicological Information. Include data used to determine the hazards cited in Section 3. Identify acute data, carcinogenicity, reproductive effects, and target organ effects. [Provide written description of the process used in evaluating chemical hazards relative to preparation of the MSDS.]
   l. Section 12: Ecological Information. Include data regarding environmental impacts during raw materials acquisition, manufacture, and use. Include data regarding environmental impacts in the event of an accidental release.
   m. Section 13: Disposal Considerations. Include data regarding the proper disposal of the chemical. Include information regarding recycling and reuse. Indicate whether or not the product is considered hazardous waste according the U.S. EPA Hazardous Waste Regulations 40 CFR 261.
   n. Section 14: Transportation Information. Identify hazard class for shipping.
   o. Section 15: Regulatory Information. Identify federal, state, and local regulations applicable to the material.
   p. Section 16: Other Information. Include additional information relative to recycled content, biobased content, and other information regarding environmental and health impacts. [Identify the date MSDS was prepared.]

SPECIFIER NOTE: Life Cycle Assessment (LCA) tools are evolving in the marketplace. While they may provide useful overall information, most remain limited especially in their capacity to address toxicity and human health issues.

To be of value for the Owner, LCAs for competing products must have comparable goals, objectives, system boundaries, functional units, and methodologies.

The BEES (Building for Environmental and Economic Sustainability) software, developed by the National Institute of Standards and Technology (NIST) Building and Fire Research Laboratory with support from the EPA Environmentally Preferable Purchasing Program, measures the environmental performance of building products by using the life-cycle assessment approach specified in ISO 14000 standards. Version 3.0 of the Windows-based tool, aimed at designers, builders, and product manufacturers, includes actual environmental and economic performance data for nearly 200 building products. Refer to http://www.bfrl.nist.gov/oae/software/bees.html. ASTM E1991 provides general guidance for developing an LCA; it does not delineate specific requirements or procedures. Verify with Owner the project goals for utilizing LCAs; identify objectives, system boundaries, functional units, and methodologies. Identify products requiring LCA data submittals and coordinate with Divisions 2–16 as appropriate.

Following are examples.

4. Life Cycle Assessment (LCA): For the following products, submit LCA data developed in accordance with [ASTM E1991] [ISO 14040] [xxxx]; and where BEES data exists, submit BEES 3.0c analysis using [100 percent] [50 percent] [xxxx] Environmental Performance Weighting and the [EPA Scientific Advisory Board] [Harvard University] [Equal] [xxxx] Environmental Impact Category Weights.
   a. Masonry
   b. Finish Carpentry
   c. Plastic Fabrications
   d. Building Insulation
   e. Roofing
   f. Joint Sealers
   g. Wood and Plastic Doors
   h. Windows
   i. Skylights
   j. Glazed Curtain Wall
   k. Gypsum Board
   l. Tile
   m. Acoustical Ceilings
   n. Resilient Flooring
   o. Carpet
   p. Toilet Compartments
   q. Loading Dock Equipment
   r. Office Equipment
   s. Furnishings and Accessories
   t. Renewable Energy Equipment

u. Elevators
v. HVAC equipment
w. Lighting equipment

SPECIFIER NOTE: ASTM D4840 specifies chain of custody documentation for laboratory samples. However, the language in ASTM D4840 is consistent with general chain-of-custody procedures for building products.

Some sustainability certification programs do not necessarily provide formalized chain-of-custody documentation, but rather require audited conformance with the sustainability program requirements through third party reviews. For such programs, a letter of conformance by the independent third party review organization demonstrating compliance with the sustainability certification program may be considered adequate documentation.

Following are examples. Coordinate with Divisions 2–16 as appropriate. Edit to suit project.

---

5. Chain of Custody: Submit chain-of-custody documentation for sustainable forestry for the following products:
   a. Rough Carpentry
   b. Finish Carpentry
   c. Wood Doors
   d. Windows
   e. Wood Flooring
   f. Furnishings and Accessories

1.4—SUBSTITUTIONS

A. Notify Owner when Contractor is aware of materials, equipment, or products that meet the aesthetic and programmatic intent of Contract Documents, but which are more environmentally responsible than materials, equipment, or products specified or indicated in the Contract Documents.
   1. Requirements of Section 01600—Product Requirements, apply except prior to submitting detailed information required under Section 01600, submit the following for initial review by Owner and Architect:
      a. Product data, including manufacturer's name, address, and phone number.
      b. Description of environmental advantages of proposed substitution over specified product.

1.5—PACKAGING

A. Where Contractor has the option to provide one of the listed products or equal, preference shall be given to products with minimal packaging and easily recyclable packaging as defined in ASTM D5834.

B. Maximize use of source reduction and recycling procedures outlined in ASTM D5834.

SPECIFIER NOTE: The EPA Comprehensive Procurement Guidelines (CPG) are part of EPA's continuing effort to promote the use of materials recovered from solid waste. The EPA CPG is authorized by Congress under Section 6002 of the Resource Conservation and Recovery Act (RCRA). EPA is required to designate products that are or can be made with recovered materials, and to recommend practices for buying these products. EPA's Recovered Materials Advisory Notices (RMANs) recommend recycled-content levels for CPG. The paperboard and packaging category covers two major types of board: containerboard, used to make corrugated shipping containers, and paperboard, used in a wide variety of packaging applications such as folding cartons, blister cards, beverage carriers, book and report covers, mailing tubes, and video cassette boxes, to name just a few. Refer to http://www.epa.gov/cpg/products/paperbrd.htm.

Green building rating systems often include credit for materials of recycled content. USGBC-LEED™ v2.1, for example, includes credit for materials with recycled content, calculated on the basis of preconsumer and postconsumer percentage content. In version 2.0, recycled content was defined as minimum 20% postconsumer OR minimum 40% preconsumer (postindustrial). In version 2.1, recycled content is defined as minimum 5% postconsumer OR minimum 10% of combined postconsumer and 1/2 preconsumer (postindustrial). Assuming all recycled content is preconsumer under version 2.1, this amounts to a minimum of 20% preconsumer. Additional credit is awarded under 2.1 for increasing minimums to 10% and 40% respectively.

Green Globes—US also provides points for reused building materials and components and for building materials with recycled content.

Note: The USGBC-LEED™ credit is applicable only in terms of the total value of all materials in the project.

Verify with manufacturer for product availability and recycled content.

C. Provide minimum [45] [xxxx] % postconsumer recycled content and minimum 100% recovered fiber content of industrial paperboard in accordance with EPA's Comprehensive Procurement Guidelines and ASTM D5663.

D. Provide minimum [10] [15] [xxxx] % postconsumer recycled content and minimum [10] [xxxx] [100] % recovered fiber content of carrier board in accordance with EPA's Comprehensive Procurement Guidelines and ASTM D5663.

E. Provide minimum [5] [20] [xxxx] % postconsumer recycled content and minimum [5] [40] [xxxx] % recovered fiber content of brown papers (e.g., wrapping papers and bags) in accordance with EPA's Comprehensive Procurement Guidelines and ASTM D5663.

1.6—ENVIRONMENTALLY PREFERABLE PRODUCTS

SPECIFIER NOTE: The EPA provides guidance on Environmentally Preferable Purchasing; refer to www.epa.gov/oppt/epp/guidance/finalguidancetoc.htm

A. Provide environmentally preferable products to the greatest extent possible.
1. To the greatest extent possible, provide products and materials that have a lesser or reduced effect on the environment considering raw materials acquisition, production, manufacturing, packaging, distribution, reuse, operation, maintenance, and/or disposal of the product.

PART 2—PRODUCTS (NOT USED)

PART 3—EXECUTION

END OF SECTION

APPENDIX A

SPECIFIER NOTE: The Comprehensive Procurement Guidelines (CPG) program is authorized by Congress under Section 6002 of the Resource Conservation and Recovery Act (RCRA) and Executive Order 13101. EPA is required to designate products that are or can be made with recycled/recovered materials, and to recommend practices for buying these products. Once a product is designated, federal agencies are required to purchase it with the highest recovered material content level practicable.

Farm Security and Rural Investment Act of 2002 (FSRIA) http://www.usda.gov/farmbill/ was signed into law on May 13, 2002. Section 9002 provides for preferred procurement of biobased products by Federal agencies. Federal agencies are required to purchase biobased products, as defined in regulations to implement the statute, for all items costing over $10,000. The USDA is proposing guidelines for designating items made from biobased products that would be afforded preferred procurement status.

AFFIRMATIVE PROCUREMENT REPORTING FORM

Project Name: _____   Project Number: _____

Contractor Name: _____   License Number: _____

Contractor Address: _____

Product	Total $ value provided	Total $ value w/ recycled content Pre-consumer	Total $ value w/ recycled content Post-consumer	Total $ value w/ biobased content	Exempted indicate 1,2,3,4	Comments
Hydraulic Mulch (paper-based)						
Hydraulic Mulch (wood-based)						
Compost						

Product	Total $ value provided	Total $ value w/ recycled content Pre-consumer	Total $ value w/ recycled content Post-consumer	Total $ value w/ biobased content	Exempted indicate 1,2,3,4	Comments
Parking Stops (Concrete w/fly ash, slag cement, or low cement content)						
Parking Stops (Plastic/Rubber)						
Patio Blocks/ Rubber						
Patio Blocks/ Plastic						
Playground Surfaces						
Concrete w/fly ash						
Concrete w/slag cement						
Concrete w/low cement content						
Plastic lumber						
Building Insulation						
Rock Wool						
Fiberglass						
Loose Fill/ Spray On						

Product	Total $ value provided	Total $ value w/ recycled content Pre-consumer	Total $ value w/ recycled content Post-consumer	Total $ value w/ biobased content	Exempted indicate 1,2,3,4	Comments
Perlite Comp Board						
Plastic Rigid Foam						
Glass Fiber Reinf Foam						
Phenolic Rigid Foam						
Ceramic tile						
Resilient flooring						
Floor Tiles/ Rubber						
Floor Tiles/ Plastic						
Running Tracks						
Carpet (PET)						
Paint						
Reprocessed Latex Paint White and Light Colors						
Reprocessed Latex Dark Colors						
Consolidated						

Product	Total $ value provided	Total $ value w/ recycled content Pre-consumer	Total $ value w/ recycled content Post-consumer	Total $ value w/ biobased content	Exempted indicate 1,2,3,4	Comments
Latex Paint						
toilet/shower partitions (plastic)						
Other						

CERTIFICATION

I hereby certify the information provided herein is accurate and that the requisition/procurement of all materials listed on this form comply with current EPA standards for recycled/recovered materials content.

The following exemptions may apply to the nonprocurement of recycled/recovered content materials:

1. The product does not meet appropriate performance standards.
2. The product is not available within a reasonable time frame.
3. The product is not available competitively (from two or more sources).
4. The product is only available at an unreasonable price (compared with a comparable nonrecycled content product.).

Signature: _____ Date: _____

> SPECIFIER NOTE: THIS SECTION IS A SAMPLE SECTION THAT MAY BE USED FOR CONTROLLING THE SUBMITTAL OF SUBSTITUTION REQUESTS DURING BIDDING AND CONSTRUCTION. IT SHOULD BE EDITED TO SUIT A SPECIFIC PROJECT AND LOCATION. LANGUAGE IS PRESENTED FOR EXAMPLE ONLY AND NO WARRANTY IS MADE AS TO COMPLETENESS OR ACCURACY OF INFORMATION CONTAINED HEREIN.

SECTION 01630

PRODUCT SUBSTITUTION PROCEDURES

PART 1—GENERAL

1.01—SECTION INCLUDES

    A. Contractor's options in selection of products.

    B. Requests for substitution of products.

1.02—RELATED REQUIREMENTS

    A. Document 00200—Instructions to Bidders: Times for submittal of requests for substitutions during the Bidding period.

    B. Document 00700—General Conditions: Times for submittal of requests for substitutions during the Bidding period.

    C. Section 01310—Project Management and Coordination: Coordination of construction.

    D. Section 01334—Shop Drawings, Product Data, and Samples: Product data submittals.

    E. Section 01770—Closeout Procedures: Record documents; operation and maintenance data.

1.03—OPTIONS

    A. Products Specified by Reference Standards or by Description Only: Any product meeting those standards.

    B. Products Specified by Naming One or More Manufacturers with a Provision for Substitutions: Submit a request for substitution for any manufacturer not specifically named.

    C. Products Specified by Naming Several Manufacturers: Products of named manufacturers meeting specifications; *no* options, *no* substitutions.

    D. Products Specified by Standard of Comparison: Products of named manufacturer; submit a request for substitution for any manufacturers not specifically named meeting specifications.

1.04—LIMITATIONS ON SUBSTITUTIONS

    A. Requests for substitutions of products will be considered only during bidding up to 14 days prior to the date of bid opening. Requests received after receipt of bids will be considered only in case of Product unavailability or other conditions beyond control of Contractor, his subcontractors or suppliers. Contractor shall order Products sufficiently in advance of date they will be needed on project to avoid necessity for submission of a substitution request.

B. Substitutions will not be considered when indicated on shop drawings or product data submittals without separate formal request, when requested directly by subcontractor or supplier, or when acceptance will require substantial revision of Contract Documents.

C. Substitute products shall not be ordered or installed without written acceptance.

D. Only one (1) request for substitution for each product will be considered. When substitution is not accepted, provide specified product.

E. Architect/Engineer will determine acceptability of substitutions.

1.05—REQUESTS FOR SUBSTITUTIONS

A. Submit separate request for each substitution. Document each request with complete data substantiating compliance of proposed substitution with requirements of Contract Documents.

B. Identify product by Specifications section and Article numbers. Provide manufacturer's name and address, trade name of product, and model or catalog number. List fabricators and suppliers as appropriate.

C. Attach product data as specified in Section 01334.

D. List similar projects using product, dates of installation, and names of Architect/Engineer and Owner.

E. Give itemized comparison of proposed substitution with specified product, listing variations, and reference to Specifications section and Article numbers.

F. Give quality and performance comparison between proposed substitution and the specified product.

G. Give cost data comparing proposed substitution with specified product and amount of net change to Contract Sum.

H. List availability of maintenance services and replacement materials.

I. State effect of substitution on construction schedule, and changes required in other work or products.

1.06—CONTRACTOR REPRESENTATION

A. Request for substitution constitutes a representation that Contractor has investigated proposed product and has determined that it is equal to or superior in all respects to specified product.

B. Contractor will provide the same Warranty for substitution as for specified product.

C. Contractor will coordinate installation of accepted substitute, making such changes as may be required for Work to be complete in all respects.

D. Contractor certifies that cost data presented is complete and includes all related costs under this Contract.

E. Contractor waives claims for additional costs related to substitution that may later become apparent.

1.07—SUBMITTAL PROCEDURES

A. Submit three (3) copies of request for substitution.

B. Architect/Engineer will review Contractor's requests for substitutions with reasonable promptness.

C. Acceptance by the Architect/Engineer, if given, will be made by addendum issued no later than seven (7) days prior to receipt of bids.

D. No substitutions are allowed under the Lump Sum Base Bid unless approved by addendum.

E. For accepted products, submit shop drawings, product data, and samples under provisions of Section 01334.

PART 2—PRODUCTS—*(NOT USED)*

PART 3—EXECUTION—*(NOT USED)*

<u>END OF SECTION</u>

BIDDER'S/GENERAL CONTRACTOR'S SUBSTITUTION REQUEST FORM

To: Name of Architect/Engineer _____

Project: Name of Project _____

We hereby submit for your consideration the following product instead of the specified item for the above project:

Drawing No.: Drawing Title: _____

Section: Paragraph: Specified Item: _____

Proposed Substitution: _____

Attach complete technical data, including laboratory tests, if applicable. Include complete information on changes to Drawings and/or Specifications which proposed substitution will require for its proper installation.

Fill in blanks below:

A. Does the substitution affect dimensions shown on Drawings?

   Yes __   No __   If yes, clearly indicate changes below.

   _____

   _____

   _____

B. Will the undersigned pay for changes to the building design, including engineering and detailing costs caused by the requested substitution? Yes __   No __   If no, fully explain below.

   _____

   _____

C. What effect does substitution have on other Contracts or trades?

   _____

D. Manufacturer's guarantees of the proposed and specified items are:

   Same   Different   (explain on attachment)

E. Itemized comparison of specified item(s) with the proposed substitution; list significant variations:

   _____

   (Use separate sheet if necessary)

F. Accurate cost data comparing proposed substitution with product specified:

   _____

   _____

   (Use separate sheet if necessary)

G. Reasons for substitution:

_____

_____

_____

H. What effect does substitution have on construction schedule?

_____

I. Designation of maintenance services and sources:

_____

(Attach additional sheets if required)

CERTIFICATION OF EQUAL PERFORMANCE
AND ASSUMPTION OF LIABILITY FOR EQUAL PERFORMANCE,
EQUAL DESIGN AND COMPATIBILITY WITH ADJACENT MATERIALS.

The undersigned states that the function, appearance and quality are equal or superior to the specified item.

Signature shall be a person having authority to legally bind their firm to the above terms. Failure to provide legally binding signature will result in retraction of approval.

Submitted by: For Use by Architect/Engineer:

_____   [__] Accepted   [__] Accepted As Noted

Firm (Contractor):   [__] Not Accepted   [__] Received Too Late

_____   By: _____

Address:_____   Date: _____

_____   Remarks: _____

Signature and Title: _____

_____   _____

Date: _____   _____

Telephone: _____   _____

END OF FORM

This is a guidance document with sample specification language intended to be inserted into project specifications on this subject as appropriate to the agency's environmental goals. Certain provisions, where indicated, are required for U.S. federal agency projects. Sample specification language is numbered to clearly distinguish it from advisory or discussion material. Each sample is preceded by identification of the typical location in a specification section where it would appear using the SectionFormat™ of the Construction Specifications Institute.

SECTION 06100—ROUGH CARPENTRY

SPECIFIER NOTE:

Resource management: Wood is a renewable resource. Forests provide many environmental benefits, including habitats, potential sources for medicines, and climatic control. Many certified sources of sustainably harvested wood are available. Nonsustainable harvesting of wood can produce soil erosion, pollutant runoff, increased levels of atmospheric carbon dioxide, global warming, and habitat loss.

Forest Certification Standards in North America include:

- The American Tree Farm System, developed by the American Forest Foundation; refer to www.treefarmsystem.org/aboutfarming/whatis.cfm

- Canada's National Sustainable Forest Management Standard; refer to http://certifiedwood .csa.ca

- ISO 14001, developed by the International Organization for Standardization. Although not a forest-specific standard, ISO offers a special technical report ISO 14061 that is specific to forestry and assists with implementation of ISO 14001 in forestry; refer to www.iso.ch

- The Principles for Natural Forest Management developed by The Forest Stewardship Council; for Canada visit www.fsccanada.org, for the USA visit http://fscus.org/certification/ index.html

- The Sustainable Forestry Initiative® created through the American Forest and Paper Association and currently managed by the Sustainable Forestry Board (an independent entity established to manage SFI); refer to www.afandpa.org/Content/NavigationMenu/Environment_ and_Recycling/SFI/SFI.htm

Most trees in the United States are referred to as either hardwoods or softwoods. Hardwood trees are deciduous trees that, with a few exceptions, lose their leaves in the fall or winter. Softwood forest types are conifers and evergreens such as pines, spruces, firs, and junipers. Wood that is used in construction of buildings is primarily softwood.

Much of America's hardwoods, such as oaks, are found along the East Coast. Softwood trees are concentrated in the West and South. Douglas fir is the dominant softwood in the West, while Southern pines, such as loblolly and shortleaf, are the most abundant softwoods in the South. Quaking aspen, a hardwood, is the most widely distributed tree species in North America.

The term *engineered wood product* (EWP) refers to a wood-based product that has a set of design properties assigned to it. EWPs are often manufactured as a combination of smaller pieces of wood that together create larger high-strength structural elements or components. Engineered wood components include plywood, oriented strand board (OSB), composite wood panels, glue laminated beams, structural composite lumber, including laminated veneer lumber and parallel strand lumber, as well as I-joists and metal plate connected wood trusses. An additional subcomponent of structural composite lumber includes laminated strand lumber. Finger-jointed lumber, which is interchangeable with solid sawn lumber, is also considered an EWP. Finger-jointed lumber or end-jointed lumber is permitted to be used interchangeably with solid-sawn members of the same species and grade. However, when finger-jointed lumber is marked STUD USE ONLY or VERT USE ONLY, such lumber shall be limited to use where any bending or tension stresses are of short duration.

Engineered wood products are typically prefabricated, not site-fabricated.

Engineered wood products are frequently more efficient in construction of assemblies than solid sawn lumber due to the lower coefficient of variance of EWPs. EWP assemblies tend to be more resource efficient than assemblies constructed of solid sawn members.

Toxicity/IEQ: Adhesive binders used in engineered wood products are any of several synthetic resins that pose varying degrees of human health risks. Refer to Section 06070, Wood Treatment, for information regarding treated wood.

Performance: Wood is a natural building and efficient building material that changes over time. The structural design characteristics of wood change over time as a result of changes in weather and other growing factors. These changes in structural design values of various wood species are recorded through a in-grade testing program of lumber and published periodically in ANSI/AF&PA's National Design Specification© (NDS©) for Wood Construction. For efficient resource use of solid sawn lumber, it is recommended that the least acceptable grade of lumber be specified to suit the purpose. As an alternate to new solid sawn lumber, reclaimed lumber can be used because it performs comparably to new lumber if properly graded by a grading agency in accordance with American Lumber Standards Committee grading rules. Further, the use of engineered wood products can result in resource efficiencies than might be expected of conventional lumber/timber construction. However, engineered wood products might be more difficult to recycle than standard, solid sawn lumber due to the binders used in the manufacture of the engineered wood product.

PART 1—GENERAL

1.1—SUMMARY

    A. This Section includes:
        1. Framing with dimension lumber.
        2. Engineered wood products.
        3. Wood furring, grounds, nailers, and blocking.

    B. Related Sections:
        1. Section 06070—Wood Treatment.
        2. Section 06160—Sheathing.

1.2—SUBMITTALS

    A. Product data. Unless otherwise indicated, submit the following for each type of product provided under work of this Section:

SPECIFIER NOTE: Green building rating systems often include credit for materials of recycled content. USGBC-LEED™ v2.1, for example, includes credit for materials with recycled content, calculated on the basis of preconsumer and postconsumer percentage content, and it includes credit for use of salvaged/recovered materials.

Green Globes—US also provides points for reused building materials and components and for building materials with recycled content.

    1. Recycled Content:

        a. Engineered Wood Products: Indicate recycled content; indicate percentage of preconsumer and postconsumer recycled content per unit of product. Indicate relative dollar value of recycled content product to total dollar value of product included in project.

SPECIFIER NOTE: Salvaged lumber is lumber that had been previously utilized and has been salvaged for reuse. Salvaged lumber may also be referred to as *reclaimed lumber*.

        b. Salvaged Lumber: Provide documentation certifying products are from salvaged lumber sources.

SPECIFIER NOTE: Recovered lumber is lumber that had been previously harvested but which had been abandoned in transit to riverbeds or lakes.

        c. Recovered Lumber: Provide documentation certifying products are from recovered lumber sources.

SPECIFIER NOTE: Specifying local materials may help minimize transportation impacts; however, it may not have a significant impact on reducing the overall embodied energy of a building material because of efficiencies of scale in some modes of transportation.

Green building rating systems frequently include credit for local materials. Transportation impacts include: fossil fuel consumption, air pollution, and labor. USGBC-LEED™ v2.1 includes credits for materials harvested and manufactured within a 500-mile radius from the project site.

Green Globes—US also provides points for materials that are locally manufactured.

    2. Local/Regional Materials:

        a. Indicate location of manufacturing facility; indicate distance between manufacturing facility and the project site.

        b. Indicate location of extraction, harvesting, and recovery; indicate distance between extraction, harvesting, and recovery and the project site.

        c. Indicate relative dollar value of local/regional materials to total dollar value of product included in project.

SPECIFIER NOTE: Green building rating systems may include credit for low-emitting materials. USGBC-LEED™ v2.1, for example, includes credits for low-emitting materials, including: adhesives and sealants, paints and coatings, carpets, and composite wood and agrifiber products. Under LEED™ v2.1, adhesives are to comply with California's South Coast Air Quality Management District (SCAQMD) #1168; architectural sealants are to comply with Bay Area Resources Board, reg. 8, rule 51; carpet with the Carpet and Rug Institute's Green Label; and, composite wood and agrifiber products are to contain no added urea-formaldehyde. Both the Adhesive and Sealant Council (ASC) and the SCAQMD have indicated that low-VOC adhesives may have performance difficulties in extreme temperature and humidity conditions. Green Seal certified environmentally preferable products are also available. Green Seal, an independent, nonprofit organization, certifies low-emitting products using internationally recognized methods and procedures. Green Seal certification meets the criteria of ISO 14020 and 14024, the environmental standards for eco-labeling set by the International Organization for Standardization (ISO); the U.S. Environmental Protection Agency's criteria for third-party certifiers of environmentally preferable products; and the criteria for bona fide eco-labeling bodies of the Global Ecolabeling Network.

Engineered wood products manufactured in accordance with ANSI standards are also available. For example, the Composite Panel Association's (CPA) Standard for Particleboard, ANSI A208.1, includes maximum formaldehyde emissions for different grades of particleboard; ANSI A208.2, the Composite Panel Association's Standard for MDF, covers MDF for interior applications and includes maximum formaldehyde emission level for different grades of MDF.

3. VOC data:
  a. Adhesives:
    (1) Submit manufacturer's product data for adhesives. Indicate VOC limits of the product. Submit MSDS highlighting VOC limits.
    (2) Submit Green Seal Certification to GS-36 and description of the basis for certification.
    (3) [Submit manufacturer's certification that products comply with SCAQMD #1168.] Submit manufacturer's certification that products comply with SCAQMD Rule 1168 in areas where exposure to freeze/thaw conditions and direct exposure to moisture will not occur. In areas where freeze/thaw conditions do exist or direct exposure to moisture can occur, submit manufacturer's certification that products comply with Bay Area AQMD Reg. 8, Rule 51 for containers larger than 16 oz and with California Air Resources Board (CARB) for containers 16 oz or less.
  b. Engineered Wood Products: Provide documentation that composite wood and agrifiber products [are third-party certified as meeting ANSI standard requirements for formaldehyde emissions] [contain no added urea-formaldehyde resins.]
    (1) ANSI A208.1–1999, Particleboard
    (2) ANSI A208.2–2002, Medium Density Fiberboard (MDF) for Interior Applications

SPECIFIER NOTE: Green building rating systems typically include credit for sustainably harvested wood. USGBC-LEED™ v2.1, for example, includes credit for use of sustainably harvested wood certified under Forest Stewardship Council Guidelines. Under LEED™ v2.1, a minimum of 50% of wood-based materials and products incorporated into the Project must be certified in accordance with the Forest Stewardship Council Guidelines. To qualify for this credit, wood-based materials and products must constitute at least 2% of the total value of all materials for the building.

Green Globes—US also provides points for wood products that originate from certified sources, such as Forest Stewardship Council, Sustainable Forestry Initiative, and the CSA Sustainable Forest Management Program.

    B. Letter of Certification(s) for Sustainable Forestry:
      1. Forest Stewardship Council (FSC): Provide letter of certification signed by lumber supplier. Indicate compliance with FSC "Principles for Natural Forest Management" and identify certifying organization.
        a. Submit FSC certification numbers; identify each certified product on a line-item basis.
        b. Submit copies of invoices bearing the FSC certification numbers.
      2. Sustainable Forestry Board: Provide letter of certification signed by lumber supplier. Indicate compliance with the Sustainable Forestry Board's "Sustainable Forestry Initiative" (SFI) and identify certifying organization.
        a. Submit SFI certification numbers; identify each certified product on a line-item basis.
        b. Submit copies of invoices bearing the SFI certification numbers.
      3. Canadian Standards Association (CSA): Provide letter of certification signed by lumber supplier. Indicate compliance with the CSA and identify certifying organization.
        a. Submit CSA certification numbers; identify each certified product on a line-item basis.
        b. Submit copies of invoices bearing the CSA certification numbers.

1.3—QUALITY ASSURANCE

    A. Sustainably Harvested Wood: Certification Organizations shall be accredited by the [Forest Stewardship Council] [Sustainable Forestry Board] [Canadian Standards Association] [xxxxxxxx].

    B. Recycled Content Materials: Where recycled lumber materials are used for structural applications, include lumber certification and quality grading.

    C. Engineered Wood Products:
      1. Determine formaldehyde concentrations in air from wood products under test conditions of temperature and relative humidity in accordance with ASTM D6007 or E1333.
      2. Determine Volatile Organic Compounds (VOC), excluding formaldehyde, emitted from manufactured wood-based panels in accordance with ASTM D6330.

PART 2—PRODUCTS

2.1—MATERIALS

    A. Lumber:
      1. Resource Management:

      a. Virgin Lumber: Lumber fabricated from old growth timber is not permitted. Provide sustainably harvested; certified or labeled in accordance with [FSC] [SFI] [CSA] [xxxxx] guidelines.

      b. Salvaged Lumber: Lumber from deconstruction or demolition of existing buildings or structures. Unless otherwise noted, salvaged lumber shall be delivered clean, de-nailed, and free of paint and finish materials, and other contamination.

      c. Recovered Lumber: Previously harvested lumber pulled from riverbeds or otherwise abandoned. Unless otherwise noted, recovered lumber shall be delivered clean and free of contamination.

   B. Engineered Wood Products:
     1. Toxicity/IEQ:
      a. Products shall contain no added urea-formaldehyde.

2.2—ACCESSORIES

   A. Adhesive:
     1. Toxicity/IEQ: Comply with applicable regulations regarding toxic and hazardous materials, GS-36 for Commercial Adhesive, [South Coast Air Quality Management District Rule 1168] [Bay Area AQMD Reg. 8, Rule 51 for containers larger than 16 oz and with California Air Resources Board (CARB) for containers 16 oz or less], and as specified.

   B. Fasteners:
     1. Recycled Content: Fabricated from 100% remelted steel.

PART 3—EXECUTION

3.1—INSTALLATION

   A. Install as indicated and in accordance with the National Association of Home Builders (NAHB) Advanced Framing Techniques: Optimum Value Engineering.

3.X—SITE ENVIRONMENTAL PROCEDURES

   A. Indoor Air Quality:
     1. Temporary ventilation: Provide temporary ventilation during work of this Section.
      a. During and immediately after installation of treated wood, engineered wood products, and laminated wood products at interior spaces, provide temporary ventilation.

   B. Waste Management: As specified in Section 01351—Waste Management, and as follows:
     1. Select lumber sizes to minimize waste; reuse scrap lumber to the greatest extent possible. Clearly separate scrap lumber for use on site as accessory components, including shims, bracing, and blocking.
     2. Do not leave any wood, shavings, sawdust, etc., on the ground or buried in fill. Prevent sawdust and wood shavings from entering the storm drainage system.
     3. Do not burn scrap lumber that has been pressure treated.
      a. Do not send lumber treated with pentachlorophenol, CCA, or ACA to co-generation facilities or waste-to-energy facilities.

END OF SECTION

This is a guidance document with sample specification language intended to be inserted into project specifications on this subject as appropriate to the agency's environmental goals. Certain provisions, where indicated, are required for U.S. federal agency projects. Sample specification language is numbered to clearly distinguish it from advisory or discussion material. Each sample is preceded by identification of the typical location in a specification section where it would appear using the SectionFormat™ of the Construction Specifications Institute.

SECTION 10170 - PLASTIC TOILET COMPARTMENTS

SPECIFIER NOTE:

Resource management: Refer to Section 06600—Plastic Fabrications.

Toxicity/IEQ: Refer to Section 06600—Plastic Fabrications.

Performance: Plastic partitions perform as well or better than most toilet partitions. They are water resistant, graffiti resistant, and nonabsorbent, with plastic face sheets permanently fused to plastic core.

PART 1—GENERAL

1.1—SUMMARY

    A. Work Includes:
        1. Solid plastic toilet compartments, [floor mounted, head rail braced] [xxxx].
        2. Solid plastic urinal screens, [wall mounted with floor-mounted pilaster brace] [xxxx].
        3. Attachment hardware.

    B. Related Sections:
        1. Section 06100—Rough Carpentry: Framing and plates within walls for partition attachment.
        2. Section 10810—Toilet Accessories: Coordinate compartment installation with subsequent accessory installation.

1.2—REFERENCES

    A. American National Standards Institute (ANSI):
        1. ANSI A117.1, Specifications for Making Buildings and Facilities Accessible to and Usable by Physically Handicapped People.

1.3—SUBMITTALS

    A. Product data. Unless otherwise indicated, submit the following for each type of product provided under work of this Section:

SPECIFIER NOTE: Green building rating systems often include credit for materials of recycled content. USGBC-LEED™ v2.1, for example, includes credit for materials with recycled content, calculated on the basis of preconsumer and postconsumer percentage content, and it includes credit for use of salvaged/recovered materials.

Green Globes—US also provides points for reused building materials and components and for building materials with recycled content.

1. Recycled Content:
   a. Indicate recycled content; indicate percentage of preconsumer and postconsumer recycled content per unit of product.
   b. Indicate relative dollar value of recycled content product to total dollar value of product included in project.

SPECIFIER NOTE: Specifying local materials may help minimize transportation impacts; however it may not have a significant impact on reducing the overall embodied energy of a building material because of efficiencies of scale in some modes of transportation.

Green building rating systems frequently include credit for local materials. Transportation impacts include: fossil fuel consumption, air pollution, and labor. USGBC-LEED™ v2.1 includes credits for materials harvested and manufactured within a 500-mile radius from the project site.

Green Globes—US also provides points for materials that are locally manufactured.

2. Local/Regional Materials:
   a. Indicate location of manufacturing facility; indicate distance between manufacturing facility and the project site.
   b. Indicate location of extraction, harvesting, and recovery; indicate distance between extraction, harvesting, and recovery and the project site.
   c. Indicate relative dollar value of local/regional materials to total dollar value of product included in project.

B. Submit environmental data in accordance with Table 1 of ASTM E2129 for products provided under work of this Section.

C. Operating and Maintenance Manuals Submittals:

SPECIFIER NOTE: The marking system indicated below is intended to provide assistance in identification of products for making subsequent decisions as to handling, recycling, or disposal.

1. Verify that plastic products to be incorporated into the Project are labeled in accordance with ASTM D1972. Where products are not labeled, provide product data indicating polymeric information in Operation and Maintenance Manual.
   a. Type 1: Polyethylene Terephthalate (PET, PETE).
   b. Type 2: High-density Polyethylene (HDPE).
   c. Type 3: Vinyl (Polyvinyl Chloride or PVC).
   d. Type 4: Low-density Polyethylene (LDPE).
   e. Type 5: Polypropylene (PP).
   f. Type 6: Polystyrene (PS).

g. Type 7: Other. Use of this code indicates that the package in question is made with a resin other than the six listed above, or is made of more than one resin listed above, and used in a multilayer combination.

1.4—QUALITY ASSURANCE

A. Regulatory Requirements: Conform to ANSI A117.1 code for access for the handicapped operation of toilet compartment door and hardware.

PART 2—PRODUCTS

2.1—MATERIALS

A. Solid plastic compartments and screens: water resistant; graffiti resistant; non-absorbent; with plastic face sheets permanently fused to plastic core; 1″-thick panels unless otherwise indicated.

SPECIFIER NOTE: EPA Comprehensive Procurement Guidelines (CPG) 2002 recommend 20–100% postconsumer recycled content for plastic toilet partitions.

---

1. Recycled Content: Minimum [20] [xxxx] % postconsumer recycled content.

B. Pilaster Shoes: 3″ high; [Aluminum] [Stainless Steel] [One piece molded HDPE] [xxxx].

SPECIFIER NOTE: USGBC-LEED™ v2.1 includes credit for materials with recycled content, calculated on the basis of preconsumer and postconsumer percentage content. In version 2.0, recycled content was defined as minimum 20% postconsumer OR minimum 40% preconsumer (postindustrial). In version 2.1, recycled content is defined as minimum 5% postconsumer OR minimum 10% combined postconsumer and 1/2 preconsumer (postindustrial). Assuming all recycled content is preconsumer under version 2.1, this amounts to a minimum of 20% preconsumer. Additional credit is awarded under 2.1 for increasing minimums to 10% and 40% respectively.
Note: The USGBC-LEED™ credit is applicable only in terms of the total value of all materials in the project.
Verify with manufacturer for product availability and recycled content.

---

1. Recycled Content: Minimum [5] [10] [xxxx] % postconsumer recycled content, or minimum [20] [40] [xxxx] % preconsumer recycled content at contractor's option.

C. Attachments:
1. Screws and Bolts: Stainless steel; tamper proof type.
2. Wall Mounting Brackets: Continuous, full height, [aluminum] [stainless steel] [heavy duty plastic] [xxxx]. In accordance with toilet compartment manufacturer's instructions.

D. Hardware: Chrome plated nonferrous cast pivot hinges, gravity type, adjustable for door close positioning; nylon bearings; black anodized aluminum door latch; door strike and keeper with rubber bumper; cast-alloy chrome-plated coat hook and bumper, [xxxx].

2.3—FABRICATION

A. Solid Plastic: 1/4″ radius beveled edges.

B. Hardware and Attachments: Pre-drilled by manufacturer; provide for protection of dissimilar metals.
  1. Floor-mounted Anchorage: Corrosion-resistant anchoring assemblies with threaded rods, lock washers, and leveling adjustment nuts at pilasters for structural connection to floor. Provide shoes at pilasters to conceal anchorage.

2.4—FINISHES

A. Compartments and Screens: Color as selected by [Architect] [Owner] from manufacturer's standard colors.

B. Pilaster Shoes: Color to match core of solid plastic compartments and screens.

PART 3—EXECUTION

3.1—EXAMINATION

A. Verification of Conditions: Verify that field measurements, surfaces, substrates and conditions are as required, and ready to receive Work.
  1. Verify correct spacing of plumbing fixtures.
  2. Verify correct location of built-in framing, anchorage, and bracing.

B. Report in writing to [Architect] [Owner] prevailing conditions that will adversely affect satisfactory execution of the Work of this Section. Do not proceed with Work until unsatisfactory conditions have been corrected.

3.2—INSTALLATION

A. Install partitions secure, rigid, plumb, level, and square in accordance with manufacturer's printed instructions.
  1. Provide for adjustment due to minor floor variations.
  2. Install adjacent components for consistency of line and plane.

B. Maintain 1/2″ space between wall and panels and between wall and pilasters. Attach panel brackets securely to walls using anchor devices.

C. Attach panels and pilasters to bracket with through-sleeve tamperproof bolts and nuts. Locate head rail joints at pilaster center lines.

D. Anchor urinal screen panels to walls and anchored to floor in accordance with manufacturer's printed instructions to suit supporting wall construction.

E. Conceal floor fastenings with pilaster shoes.

F. Equip each door with hinges, one door latch, and one coat hook and bumper. Align hardware to uniform clearance at vertical edges of doors, not exceeding 1/4″.
  1. Provide hardware at handicapped toilet with operating hardware complying with ANSI A117.1.

3.3—CONSTRUCTION

A. Interface with Other Work:
   1. Coordinate placement of support framing and anchors in walls.

B. Site Tolerances:
   1. Maximum Variation from True Position: 1/4″.
   2. Maximum Variation from Plumb: 1/8″.

3.4—ADJUSTING

A. Adjust and align hardware to uniform clearance at vertical edge of doors, not exceeding 3/16″.

B. In-swinging Doors: Adjust hinges to locate doors in partial open position when unlatched.

C. Out-swinging Doors: Adjust hinges to gently return doors to closed position.

D. Adjust adjacent components for consistency of line or plane.

END OF SECTION

Sample Contracts

The growth in the number of projects requiring green building design and construction services has led to the issuance of the first contract forms to address this specialized area of expertise. In response to the demand, the American Institute of Architects (AIA) has issued two new contract forms for use by architects. The contract forms included in this appendix are:

- AIA Document B211-2004, Standard Form of Architect's Services: Commissioning
- AIA Document B214-2004, Standard Form of Architect's Services: LEED® Certification

  AIA Documents are protected by U.S. copyright law and international treaties and are reproduced here by permission. Unauthorized reproduction or distribution of an AIA document, or any portion of it, may result in severe civil and criminal penalties and will be prosecuted to the maximum extent possible under the law.
  The contract forms are available for purchase from the American Institute of Architects or your local AIA component.

The American Institute of Architects
1735 New York Avenue NW
Washington, DC 20006-5292
(800) AIA-3837; (202) 626-7300; fax (202) 626-7547
www.aia.org

AIA® Document B211™–2004

Standard Form of Architect's Services: Commissioning

for the following PROJECT:
(Name and location or address)

THE OWNER:
(Name and address)

THE ARCHITECT:
(Name and address)

If this Standard Form of Architect's Services modifies an existing Owner-Architect agreement, provide the date of that agreement:

TABLE OF ARTICLES

1   PROJECT ADMINISTRATION SERVICES

2   SUPPORTING SERVICES

3   COMMISSIONING SERVICES

4   SCHEDULE OF SERVICES

5   OTHER SERVICES

6   MODIFICATIONS

This document has important legal consequences. Consultation with an attorney is encouraged with respect to its completion or modification.

This document provides the Architect's scope of services only and must be used with an owner-architect agreement. It may be used with AIA Document B141™–1997, *Standard Form of Agreement Between Owner and Architect*, to provide the Architect's sole scope of services, or with B141 in conjunction with other standard form services documents. It may also be used with G606™–2000, *Amendment to the Professional Services Agreement*, to create a modification to any owner-architect agreement.

ARTICLE 1   PROJECT ADMINISTRATION SERVICES

§ 1.1 The Architect shall consult with the Owner, research applicable criteria, attend Project meetings, communicate with members of the Project team, and issue progress reports. The Architect shall coordinate the services provided by the Architect and the Architect's consultants with those services provided by the Owner and the Owner's consultants.

§ 1.2 The Architect shall prepare, and periodically update, a schedule of Commissioning Services that shall identify milestone dates for decisions required of the Owner, services furnished by the Architect, and completion of documentation provided by the Architect. The Architect shall coordinate the Commissioning Services schedule with the Owner's Project schedule.

§ 1.3 The Architect shall make a presentation to explain the Commissioning Services to representatives of the Owner.

§ 1.4 The Architect shall assist the Owner by conducting Discovery Sessions as designated in Article 4, Schedule of Services.

1

§ 1.5 The Architect shall submit commissioning documentation to the Owner at intervals appropriate to the process for purposes of evaluation and approval by the Owner. The Architect shall be entitled to rely on approvals received from the Owner to complete the Commissioning Services.

ARTICLE 2   SUPPORTING SERVICES
§ 2.1 Unless specifically designated otherwise in Article 6, the services in this Article shall be provided by the Owner or the Owner's consultants.

§ 2.2 The Owner shall identify the systems to be commissioned and furnish a program setting forth the Owner's objectives, schedule, constraints and criteria, system requirements and relationships, special equipment and site requirements.

§ 2.3 The Owner shall provide to the Architect data necessary for the Commissioning Services which may include design drawings, construction documents, record drawings, shop drawings and submittals, operation and maintenance manuals, master plans, operation costs, operation budgets, and pertinent records relative to historical building data, building equipment, furnishings and repairs.

§ 2.4 The Owner shall provide access to the property, buildings, and personnel necessary for the Architect to provide the Commissioning Services. The personnel shall conduct tours and walk-throughs and explain the facility's original, current and anticipated future use.

§ 2.5 The Owner shall furnish the services of design consultants, testing agencies, and contractors necessary to allow the Architect to provide the Commissioning Services.

ARTICLE 3   COMMISSIONING SERVICES
§ 3.1 COMMISSIONING PLAN
§ 3.1.1 The Architect shall prepare a Commissioning Plan based on the systems to be commissioned, program and schedule. The Commissioning Plan will describe the commissioning process for the Project and may contain a description of the objectives of the commissioning, a list of participants and their roles and responsibilities, an outline of the management structure, a description of how the plan is to be implemented, the commissioning schedule, specific details about design reviews, a list of systems and components being commissioned and reporting formats.

§ 3.2 DESIGN INTENT DOCUMENT
§ 3.2.1 The Architect shall prepare a Design Intent Document with information provided by the Owner and the Owner's consultants and contractors. The Design Intent Document will describe the performance criteria for the systems to be commissioned. The performance criteria described in the Design Intent Document shall be quantifiable and measurable through objective testing.

§ 3.2.2 The Architect shall revise the Design Intent Document to reflect any changes approved by the Owner as a Change in Services.

§ 3.3 DESIGN REVIEW
§ 3.3.1 The Architect shall review the design of the systems to be commissioned for the limited purpose of determining if the systems as designed will achieve the requirements of the Design Intent Document. The Architect's review shall be made with such reasonable promptness as to cause no delay in the activities of the Owner or Owner's consultants, while allowing sufficient time in the Architect's professional judgment to permit adequate review. Review of the design is not conducted for the purpose of determining the accuracy and completeness of the design documents and other details such as quality of materials, appearance, dimensions, quantities and costs. Upon completion of the review, the Architect shall issue written comments and recommendations.

§ 3.4 COMMISSIONING SPECIFICATIONS
§ 3.4.1 The Architect shall review the Contract Documents and recommend modifications necessary for coordination with the commissioning requirements and processes, which may include equipment submittals, operation and maintenance manuals, system readiness tests, and personnel training.

§ 3.4.2 The Architect shall provide Commissioning Specifications for inclusion in the Contract Documents, which will define the contractor's responsibilities related to commissioning. The Commissioning Specifications will identify systems to be commissioned and may include detailed checklists, test procedures, required test results and warranty requirements.

§ 3.5 SHOP DRAWING AND SUBMITTAL REVIEW

§ 3.5.1 The Architect shall review contractors' submittals, such as Shop Drawings, Product Data and Samples for the systems to be commissioned, for the limited purpose of evaluating the system's ability to achieve the requirements of the Design Intent Document. The Architect's review shall be made with such reasonable promptness as to cause no delay in the Work or in the activities of the Owner, Owner's consultants or contractors, while allowing sufficient time in the Architect's professional judgment to permit adequate review. Review of such submittals is not conducted for the purpose of determining the accuracy and completeness of other details such as dimensions and quantities, or for substantiating instructions for installation or performance of equipment or systems, all of which remain the responsibility of the contractor as required by the Contract Documents. The Architect's review shall not constitute approval of safety precautions or, unless otherwise specifically stated by the Architect, of any construction means, methods, techniques, sequences or procedures.

§ 3.5.2 Upon completion of the review, the Architect shall issue written comments for those submittals that deviate from the requirements of the Design Intent Document. The Owner may choose to accept the deviations, in which case the Architect shall revise the Design Intent Document and the related Commissioning Specifications as a Change in Services.

§ 3.6 COMMISSIONING MEETINGS

§ 3.6.1 The Architect shall conduct and document commissioning coordination meetings with the Owner, Owner's consultants, contractors and subcontractors, whose systems are included in the Commissioning Specifications. The Architect shall coordinate these meetings with the Project schedule. The commissioning meetings are identified in Article 4, Schedule of Services.

§ 3.7 REVIEW OF DOCUMENTATION DURING CONSTRUCTION

§ 3.7.1 During construction the Architect shall review documentation such as meeting minutes, field reports, minor changes in the Work, Construction Change Directives, and Change Orders related to the systems to be commissioned. The Architect shall report to the Owner changes that will prevent the systems from performing as required by the Design Intent Document. The Owner may choose to accept the changes, in which case the Architect shall revise the Design Intent Document and the related Commissioning Specifications as a Change in Services.

§ 3.8 OPERATIONS AND MAINTENANCE MANUAL REVIEW

§ 3.8.1 Prior to the start of operator training, the Architect shall review the operations and maintenance manuals submitted by the contractors for the systems to be commissioned for conformance with the Commissioning Specifications.

§ 3.9 OPERATOR TRAINING

§ 3.9.1 The Architect shall review contractors' planning, scheduling, content and documentation for operator training sessions for conformance with the Commissioning Specifications.

§ 3.9.2 The Architect shall provide operator systems training including the requirements of the Design Intent Document, special design features, operating sequences and limitations, Functional Performance Test procedures, and maintenance cycles of the various systems. This training will begin before the contractor demonstrates the system performance using the Functional Performance Tests. During the commissioning of the systems, the Architect shall provide operator field training by having the operators assist in the verification of the Functional Performance Tests.

§ 3.9.3 The Architect shall observe contractors' training and maintain a training log for inclusion into the Final Commissioning Report. The training log will include the attendees names, training dates, system or equipment on which training was performed, and the name, title and contact information of the trainer.

§ 3.10 TEST REPORT REVIEW

§ 3.10.1 Before the start of Functional Performance Testing, the Architect shall observe a portion of the system readiness tests and shall review the system readiness test reports required by the Contract Documents for the systems to be commissioned. The Architect shall report to the Owner any observed deficiencies for correction prior to the start of Functional Performance Testing.

§ 3.11 FUNCTIONAL PERFORMANCE TESTING AND DOCUMENTATION

§ 3.11.1 The Architect shall direct, observe and document the Functional Performance Tests for each system to be commissioned. The Functional Performance Tests shall follow the procedures included in the Commissioning

Specifications. The Architect shall submit Functional Performance Test reports for each system to the Owner for review.

§ 3.12 DEFICIENCY CORRECTION
§ 3.12.1 The Architect shall generate a Corrective Action Report for each deficiency identified during Functional Performance Testing. The Architect shall maintain a log of the Corrective Action Reports. Each deficiency shall be resolved by the appropriate contractor and, after correction of the deficiency, the Architect shall direct, observe, and document re-testing to confirm that the deficiency has been corrected as a Change in Services.

§ 3.13 FINAL COMMISSIONING REPORT
§ 3.13.1 The Architect will prepare a Final Commissioning Report including the Commissioning Plan, Design Intent Document, Commissioning Specification, blank Functional Performance Test procedure forms, system readiness tests reports, Functional Performance Test reports, Corrective Action Reports and log, and operator training plans and log.

§ 3.14 POST OCCUPANCY REVIEW
§ 3.14.1 The Architect shall meet with the Owner prior to one year after the date of Substantial Completion to review the operations and performance of the commissioned systems and to make appropriate recommendations to the Owner.

ARTICLE 4   SCHEDULE OF SERVICES
§ 4.1 Commissioning Services beyond the following limits shall be provided by the Architect as a Change in Services in accordance with the accompanying Owner-Architect agreement:

   .1   Commissioning Meetings
        .1   up to   (   ) Discovery Sessions
        .2   up to   (   ) Commissioning Services Presentations
        .3   up to   (   ) Design Meetings
        .4   up to   (   ) Pre-bid Meetings
        .5   up to   (   ) Pre-construction Meetings
        .6   up to   (   ) Construction Meetings
        .7   up to   (   ) Warranty Meetings
        .8   up to   (   ) Post Occupancy Review Meetings
   .2   up to   (   ) reviews of each Shop Drawing, Product Data item, sample or similar submittal of the contractor.
   .3   up to   (   ) Training Sessions
   .4   up to   (   ) reviews of readiness test reports submitted by contractors.
   .5   up to   (   ) visits to the site by the Architect over the duration of the Project during construction.
   .6   up to   (   ) inspections for any portion of the Work to be commissioned to determine whether such portion of the Work is ready for Functional Performance Testing.
   .7   up to   (   ) Functional Performance Tests of each system to be commissioned.
   .8   up to   (   ) Corrective Action Reports for each system to be commissioned.

§ 4.2 The following Commissioning Services shall be provided by the Architect as a Change in Services in accordance with the accompanying owner-architect agreement:

   .1   review of a contractor's submittal out of sequence from the submittal schedule agreed to by the Architect;
   .2   responses to a contractor's requests for information where such information is available to the contractor from a careful study and comparison of the Contract Documents, field conditions, other Owner-provided information, contractor-prepared coordination drawings, or prior Project correspondence or documentation;
   .3   evaluation of substitutions proposed by the Owner's consultants or contractors and making subsequent revisions to the Design Intent Document and Commissioning Specifications resulting therefrom; or
   .4   Commissioning Services provided 60 days after the originally scheduled date for completion of the Commissioning Services in the Commissioning Services schedule.

ARTICLE 5   OTHER SERVICES

§ 5.1 In addition to the Commissioning Services described above, the Architect shall provide the following other services only if specifically designated below as the Architect's responsibility. The Architect shall perform such other services in accordance with a service description provided in Section 5.2 or attached as an exhibit to this services document.

(Designate the other services the Architect shall provide in the second column of the table below. In the third column indicate whether the service description is located in Section 5.2, or in an exhibit attached to this services document. If in an exhibit, identify the exhibit.)

Services		Responsibility (Architect, Owner or Not Provided)	Location of Service Description (Section 5.2 below or an exhibit attached to this document and identified below)
§ 5.1.1	Data Collection		
§ 5.1.2	Owner Supplied Data Analysis		
§ 5.1.3	Measurement and Verification Studies		
§ 5.1.4	Existing Facilities Surveys		
§ 5.1.5	Programming		
§ 5.1.6	Identification of Systems to be Commissioned		
§ 5.1.7	Sustainable Design Studies		
§ 5.1.8	LEED Certification		
§ 5.1.9	Detailed Cost Estimating		
§ 5.1.10	Value Analysis		
§ 5.1.11	Special Bidding or Negotiations		
§ 5.1.12	On-site Project Representation		
§ 5.1.13	Construction Management		
§ 5.1.14	Record Drawings		
§ 5.1.15	Post Occupancy Evaluations		
§ 5.1.16	Other		

§ 5.2   DESCRIPTIONS OF OTHER SERVICES

(Insert a description of each designated other service the Architect shall provide if not included in an exhibit attached to this document and identified in the table above.)

ARTICLE 6 MODIFICATIONS
§ 6.1 Modifications to this Standard Form of Architect's Services: Commissioning Services, if any, are as follows:
(In the space below, provide any modifications or refer to an exhibit attached to this document.)

6

▲AIA® Document B214™–2004

Standard Form of Architect's Services: LEED® Certification

for the following PROJECT:
(Name and location or address)

THE OWNER:
(Name and address)

THE ARCHITECT:
(Name and address)

If this Standard Form of Architect's Services modifies an existing Owner-Architect agreement, provide the date of that agreement:

TABLE OF ARTICLES

1   PROJECT ADMINISTRATION SERVICES

2   SUPPORTING SERVICES

3   LEED CERTIFICATION SERVICES

4   SCHEDULE OF SERVICES

5   MODIFICATIONS

This document has important legal consequences. Consultation with an attorney is encouraged with respect to its completion or modification.

This document provides the Architect's scope of services only and must be used with an owner-architect agreement. It may be used with AIA Document B141™–1997, *Standard Form of Agreement Between Owner and Architect,* to provide the Architect's sole scope of services, or with B141 in conjunction with other standard form services documents. It may also be used with G606™–2000, *Amendment to the Professional Services Agreement,* to create a modification to any owner-architect agreement.

ARTICLE 1 PROJECT ADMINISTRATION SERVICES
§ 1.1 The Architect shall consult with the Owner, research applicable criteria, attend Project meetings, communicate with members of the Project team, and issue progress reports. The Architect shall coordinate the services provided by the Architect and the Architect's consultants with those services provided by the Owner and the Owner's consultants.

§ 1.2 The Architect shall submit LEED certification documentation to the Owner at intervals appropriate to the LEED certification process for purposes of evaluation and approval by the Owner. The Architect shall be entitled to rely on approvals received from the Owner to complete the LEED Certification Services.

ARTICLE 2 SUPPORTING SERVICES
§ 2.1 Unless specifically designated in Article 5, the services in this Article shall be provided by the Owner or the Owner's consultants.

§ 2.2 The Owner shall furnish a program setting forth the Owner's objectives, schedule, constraints and criteria, including system requirements and relationships, special equipment and site requirements.

1

§ 2.3 The Owner shall provide to the Architect data necessary for the LEED Certification Services which may include design drawings, construction documents, record drawings, shop drawings and other submittals, operation and maintenance manuals, master plans, operation costs, operation budgets, pertinent records relative to historical building data, building equipment and furnishing and repair records.

§ 2.4 The Owner shall provide access to the property, buildings, and personnel necessary for the Architect to provide the LEED Certification Services. The personnel shall conduct tours and walk-throughs and explain the facility's original, current and anticipated future use.

§ 2.5 The Owner shall furnish the services of design consultants, testing agencies, and contractors necessary to allow the Architect to provide the LEED Certification Services.

ARTICLE 3   LEED CERTIFICATION SERVICES
§ 3.1 PREDESIGN WORKSHOP
The Architect shall conduct a predesign workshop with the Owner, the Owner's consultants, and the Architect's consultants at which the participants will review the U.S. Green Building Council's (USGBC's) Leadership in Energy and Environmental Design (LEED) Green Building Rating System. The participants will also examine each LEED credit utilizing the appropriate Green Building Rating System Project Checklist as a template for establishing green building goals, identify potential LEED points, examine strategies for implementation, assess the impact on the Owner's program and budget, and determine the LEED points to be targeted.

§ 3.2 LEED CERTIFICATION PLAN
§ 3.2.1 The Architect shall prepare a LEED Certification Plan based on the LEED points targeted. The LEED Certification Plan will describe the LEED certification process and may contain a description of the green building goals established, LEED points targeted, implementation strategies selected, list of participants and their roles and responsibilities, description of how the plan is to be implemented, certification schedule, specific details about design reviews, list of systems and components to be certified, and certification documentation required.

§ 3.2.2 The Architect shall revise the LEED Certification Plan as the design and construction of the Project progresses to reflect any changes approved by the Owner, as a Change in Services.

§ 3.3 LEED CERTIFICATION DOCUMENTATION
§ 3.3.1 The Architect shall organize and manage the LEED design documentation and certification process.

§ 3.3.2 The Architect shall review the LEED certification process and regularly report progress to the Owner.

§ 3.3.3 The Architect shall provide the services of LEED accredited professionals necessary for certification of the Project.

§ 3.3.4 The Architect shall register the Project with the USGBC. Registration fees charged by the USGBC shall be a reimbursable expense.

§ 3.3.5 The Architect shall prepare submittals for Credit Rulings from the USGBC for interpretation of credit language, principles, or implementation strategies. Credit Ruling fees charged by the USGBC shall be a reimbursable expense.

§ 3.3.6 The Architect shall prepare and submit a LEED Certification Application for the Project to the USGBC, including required calculations and documentation for each LEED credit claimed, in accordance with the LEED Certification Plan.

§ 3.3.7 The Architect shall prepare responses and submit additional documentation required by comments or questions received from the USGBC after review of the original submission for certification.

§ 3.4 LEED CERTIFICATION SPECIFICATIONS
The Architect shall provide specifications that incorporate LEED requirements for inclusion in the Contract Documents. The Contract Documents shall define the Contractor's responsibilities and documentation requirements related to LEED certification, including Construction Waste Management, Construction Indoor Air Quality, and obtaining materials credits.

§ 3.5 LEED CERTIFICATION SERVICES DURING BIDDING

§3.5.1 The Architect shall conduct a pre-bid meeting to review the differences between current standard construction practices and LEED principles, procedures, and requirements.

§ 3.5.2 The Architect shall prepare responses to questions from prospective bidders and provide clarifications and interpretations of the Bidding Documents related to LEED certification in the form of addenda.

§ 3.5.3 The Architect shall consider requests for substitutions, if permitted by the Bidding Documents, and shall prepare addenda identifying approved substitutions related to LEED certification.

§ 3.5.4 The Architect shall assist the Owner in bid validation or proposal evaluation and determination of the successful bid or proposal, if any, related to LEED certification.

§ 3.6 LEED CERTIFICATION SERVICES DURING CONTRACT ADMINISTRATION

§ 3.6.1 The Architect shall review properly prepared, timely requests by the Contractor for additional information about the Contract Documents related to LEED certification. A properly prepared request for additional information about the Contract Documents shall be in a form prepared or approved by the Architect and shall include a detailed written statement that indicates the specific Drawings or Specifications in need of clarification and the nature of the clarification requested.

§ 3.6.2 If deemed appropriate by the Architect, the Architect shall, on the Owner's behalf, prepare, reproduce and distribute supplemental Drawings, Specifications and information in response to requests for information by the Contractor related to LEED certification.

§ 3.6.3 The Architect, as a representative of the Owner, shall visit the site at intervals appropriate to the stage of the Contractor's operations, or as otherwise agreed by the Owner and the Architect in Article 4, to become generally familiar with and to keep the Owner informed about the progress of the portions of the Work related to LEED certification. However, the Architect shall not be required to make exhaustive or continuous on-site inspections to check the quality or quantity of the Work. The Architect shall neither have control over or charge of, nor be responsible for, the construction means, methods, techniques, sequences or procedures, or for safety precautions and programs in connection with the Work, since these are solely the Contractor's rights and responsibilities under the Contract Documents.

§ 3.6.4 The Architect shall at all times have access to the Work wherever it is in preparation or progress.

§ 3.6.5 The Architect shall review and approve or take other appropriate action upon the Contractor's submittals such as Shop Drawings, Product Data and Samples, but only for the limited purpose of checking for conformance with requirements for LEED certification. The Architect's action shall be taken with such reasonable promptness as to cause no delay in the Work or in the activities of the Owner, Owner's consultants or Contractor, while allowing sufficient time in the Architect's professional judgment to permit adequate review. Review of such submittals is not conducted for the purpose of determining the accuracy and completeness of other details such as dimensions and quantities, or for substantiating instructions for installation or performance of equipment or systems, all of which remain the responsibility of the Contractor as required by the Contract Documents. The Architect's review shall not constitute approval of safety precautions or, unless otherwise specifically stated by the Architect, of any construction means, methods, techniques, sequences or procedures. The Architect's approval of a specific item shall not indicate approval of an assembly of which the item is a component.

§ 3.6.6 The Architect shall review properly prepared, timely requests by the Owner, Owner's consultants or Contractor for changes in the Work related to LEED certification. A properly prepared request for a change in the Work shall be accompanied by sufficient supporting data and information to permit the Architect to make a reasonable determination without extensive investigation or preparation of additional drawings or specifications. If the Architect determines that requested changes in the Work are not materially different from the requirements for LEED certification, the Architect shall recommend an order for a minor change in the Work be issued or recommend to the Owner that the requested change be denied.

§ 3.6.7 If the Architect determines that implementation of the requested changes would result in a material change to the LEED certification, the Architect shall notify the Owner, who may authorize further investigation of such change.

Upon such authorization, and based upon information furnished by the Contractor, if any, the Architect shall make a recommendation to the Owner regarding the implementation of the requested changes.

§ 3.7 FINAL LEED CERTIFICATION REPORT
The Architect shall prepare a Final LEED Certification Report documenting the LEED rating the Project achieved, including the LEED Certification Plan, LEED Certification Documentation submitted, LEED Certification Reviews received from the USGBC, together with the specific LEED points that the Project is recognized as having received, all clarifications or interpretations of credits, and any re-certification requirements.

ARTICLE 4   SCHEDULE OF SERVICES
§ 4.1 LEED Certification Services beyond the following limits shall be provided by the Architect as a Change in Services in accordance with the accompanying Owner–Architect Agreement:

.1   up to   (   ) revisions to the LEED Certification Plan.
.2   up to   (   ) meetings during development of the design and Contract Documents
.3   up to   (   ) reviews of each Shop Drawing, Product Data item, sample and similar submittal of the Contractor.
.4   up to   (   ) visits to the site by the Architect over the duration of the Project during construction.
.5   up to   (   ) submittals to the USGBC
.6   up to   (   ) responses to the USGBC's comments and questions

§ 4.2 The following LEED Certification Services shall be provided by the Architect as a Change in Services in accordance with the accompanying Owner–Architect Agreement:

.1   review of a Contractor's submittal out of sequence from the submittal schedule agreed to by the Architect;
.2   responses to the Contractor's requests for information where such information is available to the Contractor from a careful study and comparison of the Contract Documents, field conditions, other Owner-provided information, Contractor-prepared coordination drawings, or prior Project correspondence or documentation;
.3   Change Orders and Construction Change Directives requiring evaluation of proposals, including the preparation or revision of Instruments of Service;
.4   providing consultation concerning replacement of Work resulting from fire or other cause during construction;
.5   evaluation of an extensive number of claims submitted by the Owner's consultants, the Contractor or others in connection with the Work;
.6   evaluation of substitutions proposed by the Owner's consultants or contractors and making subsequent revisions to Instruments of Service resulting therefrom; or
.7   preparation of design and documentation for alternate bid or proposal requests proposed by the Owner;

ARTICLE 5   MODIFICATIONS
§ 5.1 Modifications to this Standard Form of Architect's Services: LEED certification, if any, are as follows:
(In the space below, provide any modifications or refer to an exhibit attached to this document.)

GLOSSARY

Note: For additional definitions, the authors recommend that readers refer to ASTM E2114, Standard Terminology for Sustainability Relative to the Performance of Buildings, published by ASTM International. The standard contains terms and definitions pertaining to sustainable development and, in particular, to sustainability relative to the performance of buildings.

1,1,1-Trichloroethane Included in fabric and carpet manufacture and in a variety of cleaners, it is observed offgassing. 1,1,1-Trichloroethane is considered capable of causing fertility problems and developmental defects and may also have health impacts on wildlife. Chlorinated solvents such as 1,1,1-Trichloroethane deplete stratospheric ozone.

Abatement Reduction of the degree or intensity of, or elimination of pollution. (As defined by the EPA.)

Acetone A moderately toxic, highly volatile, and flammable solvent used in nail polish removers, glues, paint strippers, and other products. Considered less toxic than aromatic hydrocarbons such as toluene and xylene, it causes symptoms similar to, but slightly more severe than, those of ethyl alcohol.

Acid Leachates Water that has become acidic after seepage through landfills; potentially damaging to fish habitats, drinking water supplies, and so on.

Acrylics A family of plastics used for fibers, rigid sheets, and paints and caulkings.

Action Levels (1) Regulatory levels recommended by EPA for enforcement by FDA and USDA when pesticide residues occur in food or feed commodities for reasons other than the direct application of the pesticide. As opposed to *tolerances*, which are established for residues occurring as a result of proper usage, action levels are set for inadvertent residues resulting from previous legal use or accidental contamination. (2) In the Superfund program, the existence of a contaminant concentration in the environment high enough to warrant action or trigger a response under SARA and the National Oil and Hazardous Substances Contingency Plan. The term is also used in other regulatory programs. (As defined by the EPA.)

Activated Carbon A highly adsorbent form of carbon used to remove odors and toxic substances from liquid or gaseous emissions. In waste treatment, it is used to remove dissolved organic matter from waste drinking water. It is also used in motor vehicle evaporative control systems. (As defined by the EPA.)

Acute Exposure A single exposure to a toxic substance that may result in severe biological harm or death. Acute exposures are usually characterized as lasting no longer than a day, as compared to longer, continuing exposure over a period of time. (As defined by the EPA.)

Acute Toxicity The ability of a substance to cause severe biological harm or death soon after a single exposure or dose. Also, any poisonous effect resulting from a single short-term exposure to a toxic substance. (As defined by the EPA.)

Administrative Order   A legal document signed by EPA directing an individual, business, or other entity to take corrective action or refrain from an activity. It describes the violations and actions to be taken and can be enforced in court. Such orders may be issued, for example, as a result of an administrative complaint whereby the respondent is ordered to pay a penalty for violations of a statute. (As defined by the EPA.)

Adsorption   Removal of a pollutant from air or water by collecting the pollutant on the surface of a solid material; for example, an advanced method of treating waste by which activated carbon removes organic matter from wastewater. (As defined by the EPA.)

Advanced Treatment   A level of wastewater treatment more stringent than secondary treatment; requires an 85 percent reduction in conventional pollutant concentration or a significant reduction in nonconventional pollutants. Sometimes called *tertiary treatment*. (As defined by the EPA.)

Advanced Wastewater Treatment   Any treatment of sewage that goes beyond the secondary or biological water treatment stage and includes the removal of nutrients such as phosphorus and nitrogen and a high percentage of suspended solids. (As defined by the EPA.)

Aeration   A process that promotes biological degradation of organic matter in water. The process may be passive (as when waste is exposed to air) or active (as when a mixing or bubbling device introduces the air). (As defined by the EPA.)

Aerobic   Life or processes that require, or are not destroyed by, the presence of oxygen.

Aerobic Treatment   Process by which microbes decompose complex organic compounds in the presence of oxygen and use the liberated energy for reproduction and growth. Such processes include extended aeration, trickling filtration, and rotating biological contactors.

Agricultural Pollution   Farming wastes, including runoff and leaching of pesticides and fertilizers; erosion and dust from plowing; improper disposal of animal manure and carcasses; crop residues and debris. (As defined by the EPA.)

Air Pollutant   Any substance in air that could, in high enough concentration, harm humans, other animals, vegetation, or material. Pollutants may include almost any natural or artificial composition of airborne matter capable of being airborne. They may be in the form of solid particles, liquid droplets, gases, or in combination thereof. Generally, they fall into two main groups: (a) those emitted directly from identifiable sources, and (b) those produced in the air by interaction between two or more primary pollutants, or by reaction with normal atmospheric constituents, with or without photoactivation. Exclusive of pollen, fog, and dust, which are of natural origin, about 100 contaminants have been identified. Air pollutants are often grouped in categories for ease in classification; some of the categories are solids, sulfur compounds, volatile organic chemicals, particulate matter, nitrogen compounds, oxygen compounds, halogen compounds, radioactive compounds, and odors. (As defined by the EPA.)

Air Pollution   The presence of contaminants or pollutant substances in the air that interfere with human health or welfare or produce other harmful environmental effects. (As defined by the EPA.)

Air Quality Standards   The level of pollutants prescribed by regulations that are not to be exceeded during a given time in a defined area. (As defined by the EPA.)

Airborne Particulates   Total suspended particulate matter found in the atmosphere as solid particles or liquid droplets. Chemical composition of particulates varies widely, depending on location and time of year. Sources of airborne particulates include dust, emissions from industrial processes, combustion products from the burning of wood and coal, combustion products associated with motor vehicle or nonroad engine exhausts, and reactions to gases in the atmosphere. (As defined by the EPA.)

Algae Simple rootless plants that grow in sunlit waters in proportion to the amount of available nutrients. They can affect water quality adversely by lowering the dissolved oxygen in the water. They are food for fish and small aquatic animals.

Alternative Compliance A policy that allows facilities to choose among methods for achieving emission reduction or risk reduction, instead of command-and-control regulations that specify standards and how to meet them. Use of a theoretical emissions bubble over a facility to cap the amount of pollution emitted while allowing the company to choose where and how (within the facility) it complies. (As defined by the EPA.)

Alternative Fuels Substitutes for traditional liquid, oil-derived motor vehicle fuels like gasoline and diesel. Includes mixtures of alcohol-based fuels with gasoline, methanol, ethanol, compressed natural gas, and others.

Ammonia Substance used extensively in large industrial refrigeration applications, highly poisonous to humans. Ammonia is a gas that is intensely irritating to the skin, eyes, and the respiratory tract, even in low concentrations. Household ammonia is a 5 percent to 10 percent solution of ammonia in water and, like other types of cleaning products with ammonia, it gives off ammonia gas vapors. Environmental impact from household use probably is minimal, although use of ammonia-based fertilizers can lead to groundwater pollution with nitrates. Ammonia reacts with chlorine bleach to produce toxic and irritating chloramines.

Anaerobic A life or process that occurs in, or is not destroyed by, the absence of oxygen.

Aquifer An underground geological formation or group of formations containing water. Aquifers are sources of groundwater for wells and springs.

Asbestos (1) From the Greek adjective meaning "unquenchable"; the name for a number of extremely hardy fibrous silicate minerals that occur in rock formations throughout the world. Includes chrysotile, amosite, crocidolite, tremolite, anthophylite, and actinolite. (2) A mineral fiber that can pollute air or water and cause cancer or asbestosis when inhaled. EPA has banned or severely restricted its use in manufacturing and construction.

Asbestos Abatement Procedures to control fiber release from asbestos-containing materials in a building or to remove them entirely, including removal, encapsulation, repair, enclosure, encasement, and operations and maintenance programs.

ASHRAE Standard 62 Ventilation for Acceptable Indoor Air Quality. Details two methods for compliance: the Ventilation Rate Procedure and the Indoor Air Quality Procedure. Rapidly becoming the standard of care for building ventilation and indoor air quality.

Assay A test for a specific chemical, microbe, or effect. (As defined by the EPA.)

Attainment Area An area considered to have air quality as good as or better than the national ambient air quality standards as defined in the Clean Air Act. An area may be an attainment area for one pollutant and a nonattainment area for others. (As defined by the EPA.)

Background Level (1) The concentration of a substance in an environmental media (air, water, or soil) that occurs naturally or is not the result of human activities. (2) In exposure assessment, the concentration of a substance in a defined control area, during a fixed period of time before, during, or after a data-gathering operation. (As defined by the EPA.)

Bacteria Microscopic living organisms that can aid in pollution control by metabolizing organic matter in sewage, oil spills, or other pollutants. Bacteria in soil, water, or air can also cause human, animal, and plant health problems.

Bacteria Sink Porous materials that allow the growth of biological contaminants within the material.

Bake-out A process used to remove VOCs from a building by elevating the temperature in the unoccupied, fully furnished, and ventilated building.

Banking A system for recording qualified emission reductions for later use in bubble, offset, or netting transactions. (As defined by the EPA.)

BEN EPA's computer model for analyzing a violator's economic gain from not complying with the law.

Bentonite A colloidal clay, expansible when moist, commonly used to provide a tight seal around a well casing.

Benzene A clear, colorless, flammable liquid (CH) derived from petroleum and used to manufacture DDT (a prohibited insecticide), detergents, other strains of insecticides, and motor fuels. Benzene is included in the formulation of paints, adhesives, and resins, and can offgas. Benzene is considered a carcinogen.

Beryllium A metal hazardous to human health when inhaled as an airborne pollutant. It is discharged by machine shops, ceramic and propellant plants, and foundries.

Best Management Practice (BMP) Methods that have been determined to be the most effective, practical means of preventing or reducing pollution from nonpoint sources. (As defined by the EPA.)

Bioaccumulants Substances that increase in concentration in living organisms as they take in contaminated air, water, or food, because the substances are very slowly metabolized or excreted. (As defined by the EPA.)

Bioaccumulation See *Biological Magnification*.

Bioassay A test to determine the relative strength of a substance by comparing its effect on a test organism with that of a standard preparation. (As defined by the EPA.)

Biodegradable Capable of decomposing under natural conditions.

Biodiversity Refers to the variety and variability among living organisms and the ecological complexes in which they occur. Diversity can be defined as the number of different items and their relative frequencies. For biological diversity, these items are organized at many levels, ranging from complete ecosystems to the biochemical structures that are the molecular basis of heredity. Thus, the term encompasses different ecosystems, species, and genes. (As defined by the EPA.)

Biological Contaminants Contaminants that include bacteria, viruses, molds, pollen, animal and human dander, insect and arachnid excreta (dust mites).

Biological Control In pest control, the use of animals and organisms that eat or otherwise kill or outcompete pests. (As defined by the EPA.)

Biological Magnification The process whereby certain substances, such as pesticides and heavy metals, move up the food chain, work their way into rivers or lakes, and are eaten by aquatic organisms such as fish, which in turn are eaten by large birds, animals, or humans. The substances become concentrated in tissues or internal organs as they move up the chain. (As defined by the EPA.)

Biological Oxygen Demand (BOD) An indirect measure of the concentration of biologically degradable material present in organic wastes. It usually reflects the amount of oxygen consumed in five days by biological processes breaking down organic waste. (As defined by the EPA.) The greater the BOD, the greater the degree of pollution.

Biomass All of the living material in a given area; often refers to vegetation. (As defined by the EPA.)

Biome Entire community of living organisms in a single major ecological area. (As defined by the EPA.)

Bioremediation Use of living organisms to clean up oil spills or remove other pollutants from soil, water, or wastewater; use of organisms such as nonharmful insects to remove agricultural pests or counteract diseases of trees, plants, and garden soil. (As defined by the EPA.)

Biosphere The portion of Earth and its atmosphere that can support life. (As defined by the EPA.)

Biota The animal and plant life of a given region. (As defined by the EPA.)

Blackwater Water that contains animal, human, or food waste. (As defined by the EPA.)

Bloom A proliferation of algae and/or higher aquatic plants in a body of water; often related to pollution, especially when pollutants accelerate growth. (As defined by the EPA.)

BOD5 The amount of dissolved oxygen consumed in five days by biological processes breaking down organic matter. (As defined by the EPA.) See also *Biological Oxygen Demand*.

Bog A type of wetland that accumulates appreciable peat deposits. Bogs depend primarily on precipitation for their water source and are usually acidic and rich in plant residue, with a conspicuous mat of living green moss. (As defined by the EPA.)

Borax A sodium salt of boron, used as a laundry whitener and general-purpose cleaner. Slightly less toxic than boric acid.

Boric Acid A boron compound used as an insecticide, particularly against ants and fleas. Although it is considered moderately toxic, boric acid is not volatile and thus does not emit toxic vapors. Formerly used to clean and dress wounds, boric acid is absorbed through broken skin, and deaths have occurred from that use. The major hazard from household use is accidental ingestion or inhalation of dust.

Bottle Bill Proposed or enacted legislation that requires a returnable deposit on beer or soda containers and provides for retail store or other redemption. Such legislation is designed to discourage use of throwaway containers. (As defined by the EPA.)

Bottom Ash The nonairborne combustion residue from burning pulverized coal in a boiler; the material that falls to the bottom of the boiler and is removed mechanically; a concentration of noncombustible materials, which may include toxics. (As defined by the EPA.)

British Thermal Unit (BTU) Unit of heat energy equal to the amount of heat required to raise the temperature of 1 pound of water by 1 degree F at sea level.

Bromotrifluoromethane A fire suppression agent (Halon 1301) primarily designed for areas containing delicate, expensive, or irreplaceable equipment; used because of its ability to suppress fires without leaving undesirable residue.

Brownfields Abandoned, idled, or underused industrial and commercial facilities/sites where expansion or redevelopment is complicated by real or perceived environmental contamination. They can be in urban, suburban, or rural areas. EPA's brownfields initiative helps communities mitigate potential health risks and restore the economic viability of such areas or properties. (As defined by the EPA.)

Building-Related Illness Diagnosable illness whose cause and symptoms can be directly attributed to a specific pollutant source within a building (e.g., Legionnaire's disease, hypersensitivity, pneumonitis.) (As defined by the EPA.) Building-related illnesses are generally considered more serious than sick building syndrome (SBS) conditions and are clinically verifiable diseases that can be attributed to a specific source or pollutant within a building. The symptoms of the disease persist after leaving the building, unlike SBS, where the occupant experiences relief shortly after leaving the building. See also *Sick Building Syndrome.*

Butyls Synthetic rubber resins used for flexible sheet products and durable, solvent-based caulkings.

Byproduct Material, other than the principal product, generated as a consequence of an industrial process or as a breakdown product in a living system. (As defined by the EPA.)

Cadmium (Cd) A heavy metal that accumulates in the environment.

Carbon Dioxide (CO^2) A colorless, odorless gaseous product of human respiration.

Carbon Monoxide (CO) A colorless, odorless, poisonous gas produced by incomplete fossil fuel combustion. Found in soldering, in gas appliances, and in other combustion sources. Carbon monoxide can slow down the brain and reflexes and dim the vision. Most people don't realize how little carbon monoxide it takes for the human body to be poisoned. Only 50 parts of CO per million parts of air, by volume, is considered dangerous. Carbon monoxide doesn't suffocate; rather, it kills you by chemical action. It's an asphyxiant; it combines directly with the blood so the body can't carry oxygen to the tissues.

Carbon Tetrachloride (CCl4) Compound consisting of one carbon atom and four chlorine atoms. Once widely used as a industrial raw material, as a solvent, and in the production of CFCs. Use as a solvent ended when it was discovered to be carcinogenic.

Carboxyhemoglobin Hemoglobin in which the iron is bound to carbon monoxide (CO) instead of oxygen. (As defined by the EPA.)

Carcinogen Any substance that can cause or aggravate cancer. (As defined by the EPA.)

Carrying Capacity (1) In recreation management, the amount of use a recreation area can sustain without loss of quality. (2) In wildlife management, the maximum number of animals an area can support during a given period. (As defined by the EPA.) The term is commonly used by environmentalists to refer to the planetary capacity for human population growth and impact.

CAS Registration Number A number assigned by the Chemical Abstract Service to identify a chemical.

Categorical Exclusion A class of actions that either individually or cumulatively would not have a significant effect on the human environment and therefore would not require preparation of an environmental assessment or environmental impact statement under the National Environmental Policy Act (NEPA). (As defined by the EPA.)

Chemical Stressors Chemicals released to the environment through industrial waste, auto emissions, pesticides, and other human activity that can cause illnesses and even death in plants and animals. (As defined by the EPA.)

Chemical Treatment Any technology that uses chemicals or a variety of chemical processes to treat waste.

ChemNet Mutual aid network of chemical shippers and contractors that assigns a contracted emergency response company to provide technical support if a representative of the firm whose chemicals are involved in an incident is not readily available. (As defined by the EPA.)

Chlorinated Hydrocarbons (1) Chemicals containing only chlorine, carbon, and hydrogen. These include a class of persistent, broad-spectrum insecticides that linger in the environment and accumulate in the food chain. Among them are DDT, aldrin, dieldrin, heptachlor, chlordane, lindane, endrin, Mirex, hexachloride, and toxaphene. Another example is TCE, used as an industrial solvent. (2) Any chlorinated organic compound including chlorinated solvents such as dichloromethane, trichloromethylene, or chloroform.

Chlorinated Solvent An organic solvent containing chlorine atoms (e.g., methylene chloride and 1,1,1-trichloromethane). Chlorinated solvents are found in aerosol spray containers, highway paint, and dry cleaning fluids.

Chlorination The application of chlorine to drinking water, sewage, or industrial waste to disinfect or to oxidize undesirable compounds.

Chlorine A chemical used to purify water, and a bleaching agent. A movement begun in Europe to ban products containing chlorine has spread to the United States. Concerns focus on the discharge of organic compounds into oceans and waterways.

Chlorofluorocarbons (CFCs) A family of inert, nontoxic, and easily liquefied chemicals used in refrigeration, air conditioning, packaging, insulation, or as solvents and aerosol propellants. Because CFCs are not destroyed in the lower atmosphere, they drift into the upper atmosphere, where their chlorine components destroy ozone.

Chlorophenoxy A class of herbicides that may be found in domestic water supplies and that causes adverse health effects.

Chronic Effect An adverse effect on a human or animal whereby symptoms recur frequently or develop slowly over a long period. (As defined by the EPA.)

Chronic Exposure Multiple exposures occurring over an extended period or over a significant fraction of an animal's or human's lifetime—usually seven years to a lifetime. (As defined by the EPA.)

Chronic Toxicity The capacity of a substance to cause long-term poisonous health effects in humans, animals, fish, and other organisms. (As defined by the EPA.)

Cistern Small tank or storage facility used to store water for a home or farm; often used to store rainwater.

Class I Area Under the Clean Air Act, a Class I area is one in which visibility is protected more stringently than under the national ambient air quality standards; includes national parks, wilderness areas, monuments, and other areas of special national and cultural significance. (As defined by the EPA.)

Class I Substance One of several groups of chemicals with an ozone depletion potential of 0.2 or higher, including CFCS, halons, carbon tetrachloride, and methyl chloroform (listed in the Clean Air Act), and HBFCs and ethyl bromide (added by EPA regulations). (As defined by the EPA.)

Class II Substance A substance with an ozone depletion potential of less than 0.2. All HCFCs are currently included in this classification. (As defined by the EPA.)

Clearcut Harvesting all the trees in one area at one time, a practice that can encourage fast rainfall or snowmelt runoff, erosion, sedimentation of streams and lakes, and flooding, and that destroys vital habitat. (As defined by the EPA.)

Climate Change Also referred to as *global climate change*, the term sometimes refers to all forms of climatic inconsistency, but because the Earth's climate is never static, the term is more properly used to imply a significant change from one climatic condition to another. In some cases, *climate change* is used synonymously with *global warming*; scientists, however, tend to use the term in the wider sense to include natural changes in climate as well. (As defined by the EPA.)

Closed-Loop Recycling Reclaiming or reusing wastewater for nonpotable purposes in an enclosed process. (As defined by the EPA.)

Code of Federal Regulations (CFR) Document that codifies all rules of the executive volumes, known as *titles*. Title 40 of the CFR (referenced as 40 CFR) lists all environmental regulations.

Cogeneration The consecutive generation of useful thermal and electric energy from the same fuel source.

Coliform Index A rating of the purity of water based on a count of fecal bacteria.

Commissioning The startup phase for a new or remodeled building. This phase includes testing and fine-tuning the HVAC and other systems to assure proper functioning and adherence to design criteria. Commissioning also includes preparation of the system operation manuals and instruction of the building maintenance personnel.

Compost The relatively stable humus material produced from a composting process by which bacteria in soil mixed with garbage and degradable trash break down the mixture into organic fertilizer.

Composting The controlled biological decomposition of organic material in the presence of air to form a humuslike material. Controlled methods of composting include mechanical mixing and aerating, ventilating the materials by dropping them through a vertical series of aerated chambers, and placing the compost in piles in the open air and mixing it or turning it periodically.

Compressed Natural Gas (CNG) An alternative fuel for motor vehicles; considered one of the cleanest because of low hydrocarbon emissions and because its vapors are relatively non-ozone-producing. However, vehicles fueled with CNG do emit a significant quantity of nitrogen oxides.

Conservation Preserving and renewing, when possible, human and natural resources. The use, protection, and improvement of natural resources according to principles that ensure their highest economic or social benefits. (As defined by the EPA.)

Conservation Easement Easement that restricts a landowner to land uses that are compatible with long-term conservation and environmental values. (As defined by the EPA.)

Constructed Wetland Any designed system that approximates natural wetlands, uses aquatic plants, and can be used to treat wastewater or runoff.

Contaminant Any physical, chemical, biological, or radiological substance or matter that has an adverse effect on air, water, or soil. (As defined by the EPA.)

Copper Naphthenate One of the copper compounds used as a wood preservative. Because of its relatively low acute toxicity to humans, it is considered a safer alternative to pentachlorophenol and creosote. Copper compounds, including copper naphthenate, are highly toxic to aquatic organisms. Copper accumulates in soils and concentrates in marine and fresh water organisms.

Criteria Pollutants The 1970 amendments to the Clean Air Act required EPA to set National Ambient Air Quality Standards for certain pollutants known to be hazardous to human health. EPA has identified and set standards to protect human health and welfare for six pollutants: ozone, carbon monoxide, total suspended particulates, sulfur dioxide, lead, and nitrogen oxide. The term *criteria pollutants* derives from the requirement that the EPA describe the characteristics and potential health and welfare effects of these pollutants. It is on the basis of these criteria that standards are set or revised. (As defined by the EPA.)

Cryptosporidium A protozoan microbe associated with the disease cryptosporidiosis in humans. The disease can be transmitted through ingestion of drinking water, person-to-person contact, or other pathways, and can cause acute diarrhea, abdominal pain, vomiting, and fever. It can be fatal, as it was in the Milwaukee episode.

Cumulative Exposure The sum of exposures of an organism to a pollutant over a period. (As defined by the EPA.)

Degree-day A rough measure used to estimate the amount of heating required in a given area; defined as the difference between the mean daily temperature and 65 degrees F. Degree-days are also calculated to estimate cooling requirements.

Department of Energy (DOE) The DOE originated with the race to develop the atomic bomb during World War II and resulted in the Atomic Energy Commission. By the mid-1970s, the Atomic Energy Commission was abolished and two new agencies were created: the Nuclear Regulatory Agency, to regulate the nuclear power industry, and the Energy Research and Development Administration, to manage the nuclear weapon, naval reactor, and energy development programs. However, the extended energy crisis of the 1970s soon demonstrated the need for unified energy organization and planning. In 1977, the Department of Energy assumed the responsibilities of the Federal Energy Administration, the Energy Research and Development Administration, the Federal Power Commission, and parts and programs of several other agencies. Today, the DOE mission includes ensuring the energy security of the nation, maintaining the safety of its nuclear stockpile, and developing energy innovations and technology.

Diatomaceous Earth (Diatomite) A chalklike material (fossilized diatoms) used to filter out solid waste in wastewater treatment plants; also used as an active ingredient in some powdered pesticides. Both natural diatomaceous earth (DE) and swimming pool grade come from the same fossil sources, but they are processed differently. The pool grade is chemically treated and partially melted, and consequently contains crystalline silica, which can be a respiratory hazard.

Diazinon An insecticide. In 1986, the EPA banned its use on open areas such as sod farms and golf courses because it posed a danger to migratory birds. The ban did not apply to agricultural, home lawn, or commercial establishment uses.

Dibenzofurans A group of organic compounds, some of which are toxic.

Dichloro-Diphenyl-Trichloroethane (DDT) The first chlorinated hydrocarbon insecticide chemical name. It has a half-life of 15 years and can collect in fatty tissues of certain animals. The EPA banned registration and interstate sale of DDT for virtually all but emergency uses in the United States in 1972 because of its persistence in the environment and accumulation in the food chain.

Dinoseb A herbicide that is also used as a fungicide and insecticide. It was banned by the EPA in 1986 because it poses the risk of birth defects and sterility.

Dioxin Any member of a family of compounds known chemically as dibenzo-p-dioxins. Concern about these compounds arises from their potential toxicity as contaminants in commercial products. Tests on laboratory animals indicate that dioxins are among the more toxic anthropogenic (man-made) compounds.

Dissolved Oxygen (DO) The oxygen freely available in water; it is vital to fish and other aquatic life and for the prevention of odors. DO levels are considered a most important indicator of a water body's ability to support desirable aquatic life. Secondary and advanced waste treatment are generally designed to ensure adequate DO in waste-receiving waters.

Ecological Impact The effect of a human-caused or natural activity on living organisms and their nonliving (abiotic) environment. (As defined by the EPA.)

Ecological Indicator A characteristic of an ecosystem that is related to or derived from a measure of biotic or abiotic variable that can provide quantitative information on ecological structure and function. An indicator can contribute to a measure of integrity and sustainability. (As defined by the EPA.)

Ecology The relationship of living things to one another and their environment, or the study of such relationships. (As defined by the EPA.)

Ecosphere The biobubble that contains life on earth, in surface waters, and in the air. (As defined by the EPA.)

Ecosystem The interacting system of a biological community and its nonliving environmental surroundings. (As defined by the EPA.)

Electric and Magnetic Fields (EMF) See *Electromagnetic Spectrum.*

Electromagnetic Spectrum A continuum of electric and magnetic radiation, encompassing all wavelengths from electricity, radio, and microwaves, at the low-frequency end to infrared, visible light, and ultraviolet light in the midrange, to x-rays and gamma rays at the high-frequency end of the spectrum.

Embodied Energy The total energy that a product may be said to contain, including all energy used in growing, extracting, and manufacturing it, and energy used to transport it to the point of use. The embodied energy of a structure or system includes the embodied energy of its components plus the energy used in construction.

Emission Pollution discharged into the atmosphere from smokestacks, other vents, and surface areas of commercial or industrial facilities; from residential chimneys; and from motor vehicle, locomotive, or aircraft exhausts. (As defined by the EPA.)

Emissions Trading The creation of surplus emission reductions at certain stacks, vents, or similar emissions sources, and the use of this surplus to meet or redefine pollution requirements applicable to other emissions sources. This allows one source to increase emissions when another source reduces them, maintaining an overall constant emission level. Facilities that reduce emissions substantially may bank their credits or sell them to other facilities or industries. (As defined by the EPA.)

Encapsulation The treatment of asbestos-containing material with a liquid that covers the surface with a protective coating or embeds fibers in an adhesive matrix to prevent their release into the air. (As defined by the EPA.)

Endangered Species Animals, birds, fish, plants, or other living organisms threatened with extinction by anthropogenic (human-caused) or other natural changes in their environment. Requirements for declaring a species endangered are contained in the Endangered Species Act. (As defined by the EPA.)

Endangerment Assessment A study to determine the nature and extent of contamination at a site on the National Priorities List and the risks posed to public health or the environment. The EPA or the state conducts the study when a legal action is to be taken to direct potentially responsible parties to clean up a site or pay for it. An endangerment assessment supplements a remedial investigation. (As defined by the EPA.)

End-of-the-Pipe Technologies such as scrubbers on smokestacks and catalytic converters on automobile tailpipes that reduce emissions of pollutants after they have formed. (As defined by the EPA.)

Endrin A pesticide toxic to freshwater and marine aquatic life that produces adverse health effects in domestic water supplies.

Energy Management System A control system capable of monitoring environmental and system loads and adjusting HVAC operations accordingly in order to conserve energy while maintaining comfort. (As defined by the EPA.)

Energy Recovery Obtaining energy from waste through a variety of processes (e.g., combustion).

Environmental Assessment An environmental analysis, prepared pursuant to the National Environmental Policy Act (NEPA), assessing the potential environmental and cumulative impacts of a project and possible ways to minimize its effects on the environment.

Environmental Audit An independent assessment of the current status of a party's compliance with applicable environmental requirements or of a party's environmental compliance policies, practices, and controls. (As defined by the EPA.)

Environmental Chamber A stainless-steel, nonreactive testing device with a known air volume and dynamically controlled air change rate, temperature and humidity. Emission rates are commonly determined by placing materials or furniture in a small or large stainless-steel environmental chamber and then measuring the release of volatile vapors from the products over a specified period. Rates are measured in $\mu g/m^2 \cdot hr$ (micrograms per square meter per hour) or $mg/m^2 \cdot hr$ (milligrams per square meter per hour).

Environmental Equity/Justice Equal protection from environmental hazards for individuals, groups, or communities regardless of race, ethnicity, or economic status. Applies to the development, implementation, and enforcement of environmental laws, regulations, and policies, and implies that no population of people should be forced to shoulder a disproportionate share of negative environmental impacts of pollution or environmental hazard due to a lack of political or economic strength.

Environmental Fate The destiny of a chemical or biological pollutant after release into the environment.

Environmental Fate Data Data that characterize a pesticide's fate in the ecosystem, considering factors that foster its degradation (light, water, microbes), pathways, and resultant products.

Environmental Impact Statement A document required of federal agencies by the National Environmental Policy Act (NEPA) for major projects or legislative proposals significantly affecting the environment. A tool for decision making, it describes the positive and negative effects of the undertaking and cites alternative actions.

Environmental Indicator A measurement, statistic, or value that provides a proximate gauge or evidence of the effects of environmental management programs or of the state or condition of the environment.

Environmental Protection Agency (EPA) The EPA was established in 1970 to consolidate the federal government's environmental regulatory activities under the jurisdiction of a single agency. Its mission is to protect human health and to safeguard the natural environment. It ensures that federal environmental laws are enforced fairly and effectively.

Environmental Site Assessment The process of determining the presence of contamination on a parcel of real property. (As defined by the EPA.)

Environmental Tobacco Smoke Mixture of smoke from the burning end of a cigarette, pipe, or cigar, and smoke exhaled by the smoker. (As defined by the EPA.)

Erosion The wearing away of land surface by wind or water, intensified by land-clearing practices related to farming, residential or industrial development, road building, or logging. (As defined by the EPA.)

Ethylbenzene A part of paint formulations, and associated with some carpeting, it is observed off-gassing in the home, in office furniture products, in office buildings, and in subjects' breath. Ethylbenzene is a chronic toxin capable of causing fertility problems and developmental defects. Ethylbenzene also has potential health impacts on wildlife.

Eutrophication The slow aging process during which a lake, estuary, or bay evolves into a bog or marsh and eventually disappears. During the later stages of eutrophication, the water body is choked by abundant plant life due to higher levels of nutritive compounds such as nitrogen and phosphorus. Human activities can accelerate the process. (As defined by the EPA.)

Evapotranspiration The loss of water from the soil both by evaporation and by transpiration from the plants growing in the soil.

Exotic Species A species that is not indigenous to a region.

Feedstocks The raw material used in manufacturing a product, such as the oil or gas used to make a plastic.

Fluorides Gaseous, solid, or dissolved compounds containing fluorine that result from industrial processes. Excessive amounts in food can lead to fluorosis.

Fluorocarbons (FCs) Any organic compound analogous to hydrocarbon in which one or more hydrogen atoms are replaced by fluorine. Once used in the United States as a propellant for domestic aerosols, FCs are now found mainly in coolants and some industrial processes. FCs containing chlorine are called chlorofluorocarbons (CFCs). They are believed to be modifying the ozone layer in the stratosphere, thereby allowing more harmful solar radiation to reach the Earth's surface. (As defined by the EPA.)

Flush-out A process used to remove VOCs from a building by operating the building's HVAC system at 100 percent outside air for a specific period.

Fly ash Very fine ash waste collected from the flue gases of burning coal, smelting, or waste incineration.

Formaldehyde A colorless, gaseous compound used in an aqueous solution as a preservative, disinfectant, and curing agent. It is used widely in the production of adhesives, plastics, preservatives, fabric treatments, and other materials, and is commonly emitted by indoor materials made with its compounds. It is highly irritating if inhaled and is now listed as a probable human carcinogen. Urea formaldehyde and gaseous byproducts are detrimental to human health. Formaldehyde earned notoriety through its widespread use as a component in urea formaldehyde insulation. Formaldehyde exposure causes sensitization in a significant fraction of people exposed. Formaldehyde causes cancer in animal tests.

Friable Capable of being crumbled, pulverized, or reduced to powder by hand pressure.

Fungi Parasitic lower plants (including molds and mildew) that lack chlorophyll and need organic material and moisture to germinate and grow.

General Services Administration (GSA) One of the three central management agencies in the federal government (the Office of Personnel Management and the Office of Management and Budget are the others). GSA provides the buildings and supplies that enable federal employees to accomplish their work. It also provides workspace, security, furniture, equipment, supplies, tools, computers, and telephones. GSA negotiates contracts that account for $40 billion of goods and services bought annually from the private sector.

Geothermal/Ground Source Heat Pump Underground coils used to transfer heat from the ground to the inside of a building.

Global Warming An increase in the near-surface temperature of the Earth. Global warming occurred in the distant past as the result of natural influences, but the term is most often used to refer to the warming predicted to occur as a result of increased emissions of greenhouse gases. Scientists generally agree that the Earth's surface has warmed by about 1 degree F in the past 140 years. The Intergovernmental Panel on Climate Change (IPCC) recently concluded that increased concentrations of greenhouse gases are causing an increase in the Earth's surface temperature and that increased concentrations of sulfate aerosols have led to relative cooling in some regions, generally over and downwind of heavily industrialized areas. (As defined by the EPA.)

Graywater Domestic wastewater composed of washwater from kitchen, bathroom, and laundry sinks, tubs, and washers. (As defined by the EPA.)

Greenhouse Effect The warming of the Earth's atmosphere attributed to a buildup of carbon dioxide or other gases; some scientists think this buildup allows the sun's rays to heat the Earth while making the infrared radiation atmosphere opaque to infrared radiation, thereby preventing a counterbalancing loss of heat. (As defined by the EPA.)

Greenhouse Gas A gas, such as carbon dioxide or methane, that contributes to potential climate change. (As defined by the EPA.)

Groundwater The supply of freshwater found beneath the Earth's surface, usually in aquifers, which supply wells and springs. Because groundwater is a major source of drinking water, there is growing concern over contamination from leaching agricultural or industrial pollutants or leaking underground storage tanks. (As defined by the EPA.)

Groundwater Disinfection Rule A 1996 amendment of the Safe Drinking Water Act requiring the EPA to promulgate national primary drinking water regulations requiring disinfection as for all public water systems, including surface waters and groundwater systems. (As defined by the EPA.)

Habitat The place where a population (e.g., human, animal, plant, microorganism) lives; includes its surroundings, both living and nonliving. (As defined by the EPA.)

Habitat Indicator A physical attribute of the environment measured to characterize conditions necessary to support an organism, population, or community in the absence of pollutants; for example, salinity of estuarine waters or substrate type in streams or lakes. (As defined by the EPA.)

Hazard (1) Potential for radiation, a chemical, or other pollutant to cause human illness or injury. (2) In the pesticide program, the inherent toxicity of a compound. Hazard identification of a given substance is an informed judgment based on verifiable toxicity data from animal models or human studies. (As defined by the EPA.)

Hazard Assessment Evaluation of the effects of a stressor or the determination of a margin of safety for an organism conducted by comparing the concentration that causes toxic effects with an estimate of exposure to the organism. (As defined by the EPA.)

Hazard Communication Standard An OSHA regulation requiring chemical manufacturers, suppliers, and importers to assess the hazards of the chemicals they make, supply, or import and to inform employers, customers, and workers of these hazards through MSDS information. (As defined by the EPA.)

Hazard Evaluation A component of risk evaluation that involves gathering and evaluating data on the types of health injuries or diseases that may be produced by a chemical and on the conditions of exposure under which such health effects are produced. (As defined by the EPA.)

Hazardous Air Pollutants Air pollutants that are not covered by ambient air quality standards but that, as defined in the Clean Air Act, may present a threat of adverse human health effects or adverse environmental effects. Such pollutants include asbestos, beryllium, mercury, benzene, coke oven emissions, radionuclides, and vinyl chloride. (As defined by the EPA.)

Hazardous Chemical An EPA designation for any hazardous material requiring an MSDS under OSHA's Hazard Communication Standard. Such substances are capable of producing fires and explosions or adverse health effects like cancer and dermatitis. Hazardous chemicals are distinct from hazardous waste. (As defined by the EPA.)

Hazardous Ranking System (HRS) The principal screening tool used by the EPA to evaluate risks to public health and the environment associated with abandoned or uncontrolled hazardous waste sites. The HRS calculates a score based on the potential of hazardous substances spreading from the site through the air, surface water, or groundwater, and on other factors such as density and proximity of human population. This score is the primary factor for determining whether the site should be on the National Priorities List, and, if so, the ranking it should have compared to other sites on the list. (As defined by the EPA.)

Hazardous Substance (1) Any material that poses a threat to human health or the environment. Typical hazardous substances are toxic, corrosive, ignitable, explosive, or chemically reactive. (2) Any substance listed by the EPA, that, if spilled in a designated quantity in the waters of the United States or otherwise released into the environment, must be reported to the EPA. (As defined by the EPA.)

Hazardous Waste Byproducts of society that can pose a substantial or potential hazard to human health or the environment when improperly managed. Possesses at least one of four characteristics (ignitability, corrosivity, reactivity, or toxicity), or appears on special EPA lists. (As defined by the EPA.)

Hazardous Waste Landfill An excavated or engineered site where hazardous waste is deposited and covered. (As defined by the EPA.)

Hazards Analysis Procedures used to (a) identify potential sources of release of hazardous materials from fixed facilities or transportation accidents; (b) determine the vulnerability of a geographical area to a release of hazardous materials; and (c) compare hazards to determine which present greater or lesser risks to a community. (As defined by the EPA.)

Hazards Identification Providing information on which facilities have extremely hazardous substances, what those chemicals are, how much there is at each facility, how the chemicals are stored, and whether they are used at high temperatures. (As defined by the EPA.)

Heat Island Effect A dome of elevated temperatures over an urban area caused by structural and pavement heat fluxes and pollutant emissions. (As defined by the EPA.)

Heat Pump An electric device with both heating and cooling capabilities. It extracts heat from one medium (the heat source) at a lower temperature and transfers it to another (the heat sink) at a higher temperature, thereby cooling the first and warming the second. (As defined by the EPA.)

Heavy Metals Metallic elements with high atomic weights (e.g., mercury, chromium, cadmium, arsenic, and lead) that can damage living things at low concentrations and tend to accumulate in the food chain. (As defined by the EPA.)

Heptachlor An insecticide banned from use on some food products in 1975 and from all of them in 1978. It was allowed for use in seed treatment until 1983. More recently, it was found in milk and other dairy products in Arkansas and Missouri where dairy cattle were illegally fed treated seed.

High-Efficiency Particulate Arrestance (HEPA) A designation for very fine air filters (usually exceeding 98 percent atmospheric efficiency), typically used only in surgeries, clean rooms, or other specialized applications.

Hydrogen Sulfide A very odorous, toxic, and explosive gas produced by some bacteria in the absence of oxygen. Produces acids on contact with water.

Indicator (1) In biology, a biological entity or processes or community whose characteristics show the presence of specific environmental conditions. (2) In chemistry, a substance that shows a visible change, usually of color, at a desired point in a chemical reaction. (3) A device that indicates the result of a measurement; for example, a pressure gauge or a movable scale. (As defined by the EPA.)

Indoor Air Pollution Chemical, physical, or biological contaminants in indoor air. (As defined by the EPA.)

Indoor Air Quality (IAQ) According to the EPA (Environmental Protection Agency) and NIOSH (National Institute of Occupational Safety and Health) good indoor air quality includes introduction and distribution of adequate ventilation air, control of airborne contaminants, and maintenance of acceptable temperature and relative humidity. According to ASHRAE Standard 62, good indoor air quality is defined as "air in which there are no known contaminants at harmful concentrations as determined by cognizant authorities and with which a substantial majority (80 percent or more) of the people exposed do not express dissatisfaction."

Integrated Design A process used to design a building in a manner that promotes sustainability. The process encourages all members of the building team to work together from the earliest stages of project development to achieve high performance and sustainability in the design. Also called *whole building design.*

Integrated Pest Management (IPM) A mixture of chemical and other, nonpesticide, methods to control pests. (As defined by the EPA.) IPM commonly refers to an environmentally sound system of controlling landscape pests, which includes well-timed nontoxic treatments and an understanding of the pest's life cycle.

Invasive Commonly used to refer to an exotic plant adapted to similar growing conditions as those found in the region to which it is imported. Because such a species usually has no natural enemies (pests, diseases, or grazers), it flourishes so strongly that it disrupts the native ecosystem and forces out native plant species, resulting in habitat loss, water table modification, and other serious problems.

Joint and Several Liability Under CERCLA, this legal concept relates to the liability for Superfund site cleanup and other costs on the part of more than one potentially responsible party (i.e., if there were several owners or users of a site that became contaminated over the years, they could all be considered potentially liable for cleaning it up). (As defined by the EPA.)

Lagoon (1) A shallow pond where sunlight, bacterial action, and oxygen work to purify wastewater; also used for storage of wastewater or spent nuclear fuel rods. (2) Shallow body of water, often separated from the sea by coral reefs or sandbars. (As defined by the EPA.)

Landfills (1) Sanitary landfills are disposal sites for nonhazardous solid wastes spread in layers, compacted to the smallest practical volume, and covered by material applied at the end of each operating day. (2) Secure chemical landfills are disposal sites for hazardous waste, selected and designed to minimize the chance of release of hazardous substances into the environment. (As defined by the EPA.)

LC 50/Lethal Concentration Median-level concentration, a standard measure of toxicity that tells how much of a substance is needed to kill half a group of experimental organisms in a given time. (As defined by the EPA.)

LD 50/Lethal Dose The dose of a toxicant or microbe that will kill 50 percent of the test organisms within a designated period. The lower the LD 50, the more toxic the compound. (As defined by the EPA.)

Leachate Water that collects contaminants as it trickles through wastes, pesticides, or fertilizers. Leaching may occur in farming areas, feedlots, and landfills, and may result in hazardous substances entering surface water, groundwater, or soil. (As defined by the EPA.)

Leachate Collection System A system that gathers leachate and pumps it to the surface for treatment. (As defined by the EPA.)

Lead (Pb) A heavy metal that is hazardous to health if breathed or swallowed. It was once used in oil-based paints and printing inks, and still is used in some motor fuels, some pigments, and solders. Older homes may contain layers of lead-bearing paint, which pose a toxic hazard if disturbed. Many lead compounds cause cancer. Like other metals, lead is not biodegraded in the environment.

Legionella A genus of bacteria, some species of which cause a type of pneumonia called Legionnaires' Disease.

Lethal Dose Low (Ldlo) The lowest dose in an animal study at which lethality occurs. (As defined by the EPA.)

Level of Concern (LOC) The concentration in air of an extremely hazardous substance above which there may be serious immediate health effects to anyone exposed to it for short periods. (As defined by the EPA.)

Life Cycle Cost An accounting method that extends beyond capital cost into maintenance and replacement costs, environmental costs, and so on.

Life Cycle of a Product All stages of a product's development, from extraction of fuel for power to production, marketing, use, and disposal. (As defined by the EPA.)

Lifetime Average Daily Dose Figure for estimating excess lifetime cancer risk. (As defined by the EPA.)

Lifetime Exposure Total amount of exposure to a substance that a human would receive in a lifetime (usually assumed to be 70 years).

Limit of Detection (LOD) The minimum concentration of a substance being analyzed that has a 99 percent probability of being identified. (As defined by the EPA.)

Lindane A pesticide that causes adverse health effects in domestic water supplies and is toxic to freshwater fish and aquatic life.

Low-Emissivity (low-E) Windows Technology that reduces the amount of energy loss through windows by inhibiting the transmission of radiant heat while allowing sufficient light to pass through.

Material Safety Data Sheet (MSDS) A compilation of information required under the OSHA Communication Standard on the identity of hazardous chemicals, health, and physical hazards, exposure limits, and precautions. Section 311 of SARA requires facilities to submit MSDSs under certain circumstances.

Materials Recovery Facility (MRF) A facility that processes residentially collected, mixed recyclables into new products available for market.

Maximum Acceptable Toxic Concentration For a given ecological effects test, the range (or geometric mean) between the no observable adverse effect level and the lowest observable adverse effects level. (As defined by the EPA.)

Maximum Tolerated Dose The maximum dose an animal species can tolerate for a major portion of its lifetime without significant impairment or toxic effect other than carcinogenicity. (As defined by the EPA.)

Mercury (Hg) Heavy metal that can accumulate in the environment, and is highly toxic if breathed or swallowed. See *Heavy Metals*.

Methane A colorless, nonpoisonous, flammable gas created by anaerobic decomposition of organic compounds. A major component of natural gas used in the home.

Microclimate (1) Localized climate conditions within an urban area or neighborhood. (2) The climate around a tree or shrub or a stand of trees. (As defined by the EPA.)

Montreal Protocol Treaty, signed in 1987, governing stratospheric ozone protection and research and the production and use of ozone-depleting substances. It provides for the end of production of ozone-depleting substances such as CFCs. Under the protocol, research groups continue to assess the ozone layer. The Multilateral Fund provides resources to developing nations to promote the transition to ozone-safe technologies.

Moratorium During the negotiation process, a period of 60 to 90 days during which the EPA and potentially responsible parties may reach settlement but no site response activities can be conducted. (As defined by the EPA.)

Multiple Chemical Sensitivity (MCS) A diagnostic label for people who suffer multisystem illnesses as a result of contact with or proximity to airborne agents and other substances. (As defined by the EPA.)

Mutagen/Mutagenicity A mutagen is an agent that causes a permanent genetic change in a cell other than that occurring during normal growth. Mutagenicity is the capacity of a chemical or physical agent to cause such permanent changes. (As defined by the EPA.)

National Ambient Air Quality Standards (NAAQS) Standards established by the EPA that apply for outdoor air throughout the country. See *Criteria Pollutants, State Implementation Plans, Emissions Trading*.

National Emissions Standards for Hazardous Air Pollutants (NESHAPS) Emissions standards set by the EPA for an air pollutant not covered by NAAQS that may cause an increase in fatalities or in serious, irreversible, or incapacitating illnesses. Primary standards are designed to protect human health; secondary standards are designed to protect public welfare (e.g., building façades, visibility, crops, and domestic animals). (As defined by the EPA.)

National Estuary Program A program established under the Clean Water Act Amendments of 1987 to develop and implement conservation and management plans for protecting estuaries and restoring and maintaining their chemical, physical, and biological integrity, as well as controlling point and nonpoint pollution sources. (As defined by the EPA.)

National Institute of Occupational Safety and Health (NIOSH) An agency of the Centers for Disease Control of the Department of Health and Human Services. NIOSH is the research arm of OSHA, the Occupational Safety and Health Administration.

National Pollutant Discharge Elimination System (NPDES) A provision of the Clean Water Act that prohibits discharge of pollutants into waters of the United States unless a special permit is issued by the EPA, a state, or, where delegated, a tribal government on a Native American reservation. (As defined by the EPA.)

National Priorities List (NPL) The EPA's list of the most serious uncontrolled or abandoned hazardous waste sites identified for possible long-term remedial action under Superfund. The list is based primarily on the score a site receives from the Hazard Ranking System. The EPA is required to update the NPL at least once a year. A site must be on the NPL to receive money from the Trust Fund for remedial action. (As defined by the EPA.)

National Response Center The federal operations center that receives notifications of all releases of oil and hazardous substances into the environment. Open 24 hours a day, it is operated by the U.S. Coast Guard, which evaluates all reports and notifies the appropriate agency. (As defined by the EPA.)

Native Describing a plant whose presence and survival in a specific region is not due to human intervention. Certain experts argue that plants imported to a region by prehistoric peoples should be considered native. The term for plants that are imported and then adapt to survive without human cultivation is *naturalized*.

Nonaqueous Phase Liquid Contaminants that remain undiluted as the original bulk liquid in the subsurface; for example, spilled oil. (As defined by the EPA.)

Nonpoint Sources Diffuse pollution sources (i.e., without a single point of origin or not introduced into a receiving stream from a specific outlet). The pollutants are generally carried off the land by stormwater. Common nonpoint sources are agriculture, forestry, urban, mining, construction, dams, channels, land disposal, saltwater intrusion, and city streets. (As defined by the EPA.)

Occupational Safety and Health Administration (OSHA) OSHA, which resides under the U.S. Department of Labor, implements the provisions of the 1970 Occupational Safety and Health Act. It establishes and enforces protective standards for employees in the workplace.

OECD Guidelines Testing guidelines prepared by the Organization of Economic and Cooperative Development of the United Nations. They assist in preparation of protocols for studies of toxicology, environmental fate, and so on. (As defined by the EPA.)

Offgas/Outgas A process of evaporation or chemical decomposition through which vapors are released from materials.

Oxidizer Any agent or process that receives electrons during a chemical reaction.

Ozonation/Ozonator Ozonation is the application of ozone to water for disinfection or for taste and odor control. The ozonator is the device that does this.

Ozone (O_3) Found in two layers of the atmosphere, the stratosphere and the troposphere. In the stratosphere (the atmospheric layer 7 to 10 miles or more above the Earth's surface), ozone is a natural form of oxygen that provides a protective layer shielding the Earth from ultraviolet radiation. In the troposphere (the layer extending up 7 to 10 miles from the Earth's surface), ozone is a chemical oxidant and major component of photochemical smog. It can seriously impair the respiratory system and is one of the most widespread of all the criteria pollutants for which the Clean Air Act required the EPA to set standards. Ozone in the troposphere is produced through complex chemical reactions of nitrogen oxides, which are among the primary pollutants emitted by combustion sources; hydrocarbons, released into the atmosphere through the combustion, handling, and processing of petroleum products; and sunlight. (As defined by the EPA.)

Ozone Depletion Destruction of the stratospheric ozone layer, which shields the Earth from ultraviolet radiation harmful to life. This destruction of ozone is caused by the breakdown of certain chlorine- or bromine-containing compounds (chlorofluorocarbons or halons), which break down when they reach the stratosphere and then catalytically destroy ozone molecules. (As defined by the EPA.)

Ozone Hole A thinning break in the stratospheric ozone layer. Designation of such depletion as an ozone hole is made when the detected amount of depletion exceeds 50 percent. Seasonal ozone holes have been observed over both the Antarctic and Arctic regions, part of Canada, and the extreme northeastern United States. (As defined by the EPA.)

Ozone Layer The protective layer in the atmosphere, about 15 miles above the ground, that absorbs some of the sun's ultraviolet rays, thereby reducing the amount of potentially harmful radiation that reaches the Earth's surface. (As defined by the EPA.)

Pathogens Microorganisms (e.g., bacteria, viruses, or parasites) that can cause disease in humans, animals and plants.

Pay-as-You-Throw Systems under which residents pay for municipal waste management and disposal services by weight or volume collected, not a fixed fee. (As defined by the EPA.)

Peak Electricity Demand The maximum electricity used to meet the cooling load of a building or buildings in a given area.

Peak Levels Levels of airborne pollutant contaminants much higher than average or occurring for short periods in response to sudden releases.

Phenols Organic compounds that are byproducts of petroleum refining, tanning, and textile, dye, and resin manufacturing. Low concentrations cause taste and odor problems in water; higher concentrations can kill aquatic life and humans.

Phosphates Certain chemical compounds containing phosphorus.

Photochemical Smog Air pollution caused by chemical reactions of various pollutants emitted from different sources.

Photosynthesis The manufacture by plants of carbohydrates and oxygen from carbon dioxide mediated by chlorophyll in the presence of sunlight.

Photovoltaic Having the capacity to generate electricity from the energy of sunlight by means of photocells.

Phytoplankton That portion of the plankton community composed of tiny plants; for example, algae, diatoms.

Phytoremediation Low-cost remediation option for sites with widely dispersed contamination at low concentrations. (As defined by the EPA.)

Phytotoxic Harmful to plants.

Phytotreatment (Phytoremediation) The cultivation of specialized plants that absorb specific contaminants from the soil through their roots or foliage. This reduces the concentration of contaminants and incorporates them into biomasses that may be released into the environment when the plant dies or is harvested. (As defined by the EPA.)

Plasticizers Chemicals added to soft plastics to preserve their flexibility. These agents offgas slowly, eventually rendering the plastic brittle.

Point Source A stationary location or fixed facility from which pollutants are discharged; any single identifiable source of pollution (e.g., a pipe, ditch, ship, ore pit, factory smokestack). (As defined by the EPA.)

Pollutant Generally, any substance introduced into the environment that adversely affects the usefulness of a resource or the health of humans, animals, or ecosystems. (As defined by the EPA.)

Pollution Generally, the presence of a substance in the environment that, because of its chemical composition or quantity, prevents the functioning of natural processes and produces undesirable environmental and health effects. Under the Clean Water Act, for example, the term is defined as the man-made or -induced alteration of the physical, biological, chemical, and radiological integrity of water and other media. (As defined by the EPA.)

Pollution Prevention (1) The identification of areas, processes, and activities that generate excessive waste products or pollutants, the goal being to reduce or prevent them through alteration or elimination of a process. Such activities, consistent with the Pollution Prevention Act of 1990, are conducted across all EPA programs and can involve cooperative efforts with such agencies as the departments of Agriculture and Energy. (2) The EPA has initiated a number of voluntary programs in which industrial or commercial partners join with the agency in promoting activities that conserve energy, conserve and protect water supplies, reduce emissions or find ways of utilizing them as energy resources, and reduce the waste stream. Among these are Agstar, to reduce methane emissions through manure management; Climate Wise, to lower industrial greenhouse gas emissions and energy costs; and Coalbed Methane Outreach, to boost methane recovery at coal mines; Design for the Environment, to foster the inclusion of environmental considerations in product design and processes; Energy Star programs, to promote energy efficiency in commercial and residential buildings, office equipment, transformers, computers, office equipment, and home appliances; Environmental Accounting, to help businesses identify environmental costs and factor them into management decision making; Green Chemistry, to promote and recognize cost-effective breakthroughs in chemistry that prevent pollution; Green Lights, to spread the use of energy-efficient lighting technologies; Indoor Environments, to reduce risks from indoor air pollution; Landfill Methane Outreach, to develop landfill gas-to-energy projects; Natural Gas Star, to reduce methane emissions from the natural gas industry; Ruminant Livestock Methane, to reduce methane emissions from ruminant livestock; Transportation Partners, to reduce carbon dioxide emissions from the transportation sector; Voluntary Aluminum Industrial Partnership, to reduce perfluorocarbon emissions from the primary aluminum industry; WAVE, to promote efficient water use in the lodging industry; and Wastewi$e, to reduce business-generated solid waste through prevention, reuse, and recycling. (As defined by the EPA.)

Polychlorinated biphenyls (PCB) Organo-halogen compounds, or compounds containing chlorine, bromine, or fluorine with organic chemicals. In construction, polychlorinated biphenyls are commonly found in fluorescent light fixture ballasts and electrical power transformers.

Polyethylene Terephthalate (PET) A polyester plastic used widely in soft drink bottles.

Polymer A natural or synthetic chemical structure where two or more like molecules are joined to form a more complex molecular structure (e.g., polyethylene in plastic). (As defined by the EPA.)

Polyvinyl Chloride (PVC) (1) A polymer derived from oil or liquid natural gas and salt (sodium chloride). The liquid natural gas or petroleum is refined and reacted with chlorine from the salt to form vinyl chloride monomer. Vinyl chloride monomer, a known carcinogen, is polymerized to form PVC resin. (2) A tough, environmentally indestructible plastic that releases hydrochloric acid when burned. (As defined by the EPA.)

Postconsumer Describing a reclaimed waste product that has already served a purpose to a consumer, such as used newspaper. Waste from industrial processes is not considered postconsumer.

Preconsumer Materials/Waste Materials generated in manufacturing and converting processes, such as manufacturing scrap and trimmings and cuttings. Includes print overruns, over-issue publications, and obsolete inventories. (As defined by the EPA.)

Project XL An EPA initiative to give states and the regulated community the flexibility to develop comprehensive strategies as alternatives to multiple current regulatory requirements in order to exceed compliance and increase overall environmental benefits. (As defined by the EPA.)

Pyrethrum and Pyrethrins Pyrethrum, an insecticide, is made from powdered flowers of the chrysanthemum family. Pyrethrin is the active ingredient in pyrethrum. Some people are acutely sensitive to pyrethrum. Adverse reactions range from contact dermatitis and asthmalike attacks to anaphylactic reactions with peripheral vascular collapse. As early as 1934, a cross-reaction of ragweed allergies and pyrethrum sensitivities was noted in the medical literature. Some pyrethrum formulations include petrochemicals as solvents and propellants, as well as synergists to make them more toxic. Pyrethrum and pyrethrins are used for pest control.

Radon A colorless, naturally occurring, radioactive, inert gas formed by radioactive decay of radium atoms in soil or rocks. Trace radon emissions may be detected after excavating into subsoil for building foundations.

Rainwater Harvesting The practice of collecting, storing, and using precipitation from a catchment area, such as a roof.

Recharge The process by which water is added to a zone of saturation, usually by percolation from the soil surface (e.g., the recharge of an aquifer). (As defined by the EPA.)

Recharge Rate The quantity of water per unit of time that replenishes or refills an aquifer. (As defined by the EPA.)

Reclamation In recycling, the restoration of materials found in the waste stream to a beneficial use, which may be for purposes other than the original use. (As defined by the EPA.)

Recombinant Bacteria A microorganism whose genetic makeup has been altered by the deliberate introduction of new genetic elements. The offspring of these altered bacteria also contains these new genetic elements; that is, they breed true. (As defined by the EPA.)

Recombinant DNA The new DNA formed by combining pieces of DNA from different organisms or cells.

Recycle/Reuse Minimizing waste generation by recovering and reprocessing usable products that might otherwise become waste (e.g., recycling aluminum cans, paper, and bottles, etc.). (As defined by the EPA.)

Red Tide A proliferation of a marine plankton that is toxic and often fatal to fish, perhaps stimulated by the addition of nutrients. A tide can be red, green, or brown, depending on the coloration of the plankton.

Remediation (1) Cleanup or other methods used to remove or contain a toxic spill or hazardous materials from a Superfund site. (2) For the Asbestos Hazard Emergency Response program, abatement methods including evaluation, repair, enclosure, encapsulation, or removal of greater than 3 linear feet or square feet of asbestos-containing materials from a building. (As defined by the EPA.)

Renewable Describing a product that can be grown or naturally replenished or cleansed at a rate that exceeds human depletion of the resource.

Reuse Using a product or component of municipal solid waste in its original form more than once; for example, refilling a glass bottle that has been returned or using a coffee can to hold nuts and bolts. (As defined by the EPA.)

Riparian Habitat Areas adjacent to rivers and streams with a differing density, diversity, and productivity of plant and animal species relative to nearby uplands. (As defined by the EPA.)

Riparian Rights Entitlement of a landowner to certain uses of water on or bordering the property, including the right to prevent diversion or misuse of upstream waters. Generally a matter of state law. (As defined by the EPA.)

Risk A measure of the probability that damage to life, health, property, or the environment will occur as a result of a given hazard. (As defined by the EPA.)

Risk Assessment Qualitative and quantitative evaluation of the risk posed to human health or the environment by the actual or potential presence or use of specific pollutants. (As defined by the EPA.)

Risk Characterization The last phase of the risk assessment process that estimates the potential for adverse health or ecological effects to occur from exposure to a stressor and evaluates the uncertainty involved. (As defined by the EPA.)

Runoff That part of precipitation, snowmelt, or irrigation water that runs off the land into streams or other surface water. It can carry pollutants from the air and land into receiving waters. (As defined by the EPA.)

Sand Filters Devices that remove some suspended solids from sewage. Air and bacteria decompose additional wastes that filter through the sand so cleaner water drains from the bed. (As defined by the EPA.)

Secondary Effect Action of a stressor on supporting components of the ecosystem, which in turn impacts the ecological component of concern. (As defined by the EPA.)

Secondary Treatment The second step in most publicly owned waste treatment systems, during which bacteria consume the organic parts of the waste. This is accomplished by bringing together waste, bacteria, and oxygen in trickling filters or in the activated sludge process. This treatment removes floating and settleable solids and about 90 percent of the oxygen-demanding substances and suspended solids. Disinfection is the final stage of secondary treatment. (As defined by the EPA.)

Semivolatile Organic Compounds Organic compounds that volatilize slowly at standard temperature (20 degrees C and 1 atm pressure). (As defined by the EPA.)

Septic System An on-site system designed to treat and dispose of domestic sewage. A typical septic system consists of a tank that receives waste from a residence or business and a system of tile lines or a pit for disposal of the liquid effluent (sludge) that remains after decomposition of the solids by bacteria in the tank and that must be pumped out periodically.

Septic Tank An underground storage tank for wastes from homes not connected to a sewer line. Waste goes directly from the home to the tank.

Shading Coefficient The amount of the sun's heat transmitted through a given window compared with that of a standard 1/8-inch-thick single pane of glass under the same conditions.

Sick Building Syndrome (SBS) Syndrome whereby occupants of a building experience acute health or comfort effects that appear linked to time spent therein, but where no specific illness or cause can be identified. Complaints may be localized in a particular room or zone or spread throughout the building. (As defined by the EPA.)

Sink Place in the environment where a compound or material collects. (As defined by the EPA.) In buildings, surfaces that tend to capture volatile compounds from air and release them later. Carpets, gypsum board, ceiling tile, and upholstery are all sinks.

Sinking Generally, in buildings, the absorption of VOCs by sinks (soft building materials). See *Adsorption, Sink.*

Solvents Found in adhesives, coal tar pitch and coal tar roofing, metal cleaners, putty, impermeable paints and coatings, pipe cements (polyurethane resins), wire coverings, transformers. Aliphatic hydrocarbons, aromatic hydrocarbons, petroleum naphtha, tetrachloroethylene, toluene are found in solvents.

Source Reduction Reducing the amount of materials entering the waste stream from a specific source by redesigning products or patterns of production or consumption (e.g., using returnable beverage containers). Synonymous with waste reduction. (As defined by the EPA.)

Species (1) A reproductively isolated aggregate of interbreeding organisms having common attributes and usually designated by a common name. (2) An organism belonging to such a category. (As defined by the EPA.)

Superfund The program operated under the legislative authority of CERCLA and SARA that funds and carries out EPA solid waste emergency and long-term removal and remedial activities. These activities include establishing the National Priorities List, investigating sites for inclusion on the list, determining their priority, and conducting and/or supervising cleanup and other remedial actions. (As defined by the EPA.)

Surface Runoff Precipitation, snowmelt, or irrigation water in excess of the amount that can infiltrate the soil surface and be stored in small surface depressions; a major transporter of nonpoint source pollutants in rivers, streams, and lakes. (As defined by the EPA.)

Sustainable Describing practices and communities that meet the needs of present generations without compromising those needs for future generations. To be truly sustainable, a human community must not decrease biodiversity, must not consume resources faster than they are renewed, must recycle and reuse virtually all materials, and must rely primarily on resources of its own region. Ecological/environmental sustainability is defined by the EPA as the maintenance of ecosystem components and functions for future generations.

Tertiary Treatment Advanced cleaning of wastewater that goes beyond the secondary or biological stage, removing nutrients such as phosphorus, nitrogen, and most BOD and suspended solids. (As defined by the EPA.)

Thermal Pollution Discharge of heated water from industrial processes that can kill or injure aquatic organisms. (As defined by the EPA.)

Thermal Stratification The formation of layers of different temperatures in a lake or reservoir. (As defined by the EPA.)

Threshold The dose or exposure level below which a significant adverse effect is not expected. (As defined by the EPA.)

Threshold Level Time-weighted average pollutant concentration values, exposure beyond which is likely to adversely affect human health. (As defined by the EPA.)

Threshold Limit Value (TLV) The concentration of an airborne substance to which an average person can be repeatedly exposed without adverse effects. TLVs may be expressed in three ways: (a) TLV-TWA, time-weighted average, based on an allowable exposure averaged over a normal 8-hour workday or 40-hour workweek; (b) TLV-STEL, short-term exposure limit or maximum concentration for a brief specified period, depending on a specific chemical (TWA must still be met); and (c) TLV-C, ceiling exposure limit or maximum exposure concentration not to be exceeded under any circumstances (TWA must still be met). (As defined by the EPA.)

Tight Buildings Buildings designed to let in minimal infiltration air in order to reduce heating and cooling energy costs. In actuality, buildings typically exhibit leakage on the same order as required ventilation; however, this leakage is not well distributed and cannot serve as a substitute for proper ventilation.

Total Dissolved Solids (TDS) All material that passes the standard glass river filter; now called *total filtrable residue*. Term is used to reflect salinity.

Total Petroleum Hydrocarbons (TPH) Measure of the concentration or mass of petroleum hydrocarbon constituents present in a given amount of soil or water. The word *total* is misleading; few, if any, procedures for quantifying hydrocarbons can measure all of them in a given sample. Volatile ones are usually lost in the process and not quantified, and nonpetroleum hydrocarbons sometimes appear in the analysis.

Total Suspended Particles (TSP) A method of monitoring airborne particulate matter by total weight.

Total Suspended Solids (TSS) A measure of the suspended solids in wastewater, effluent, or water bodies, determined by tests for total suspended nonfilterable solids.

Total Volatile Organic Compound (TVOC) Compound measured in $\mu g/m^3$ (micrograms per cubic meter).

Toxaphene Chemical that causes adverse health effects in domestic water supplies and is toxic to freshwater and marine aquatic life.

Toxicant A harmful substance or agent that may injure an exposed organism. (As defined by the EPA.)

Toxic Chemical Any chemical listed in the EPA rules as "subject to Section 313 of the Emergency Planning and Community Right-to-Know Act of 1986." (As defined by the EPA.)

Toxic Chemical Release Form Information form required of facilities that manufacture, process, or use (in quantities above a specific amount) chemicals listed under SARA, Title III. (As defined by the EPA.)

Toxicity The degree to which a substance or mixture of substances can harm humans or animals. Acute toxicity involves harmful effects in an organism through a single or short-term exposure. Chronic toxicity is the ability of a substance or mixture of substances to cause harmful effects over an extended period, usually on repeated or continuous exposure, sometimes lasting for the entire life of the exposed organism. Subchronic toxicity is the ability of the substance to cause effects for more than one year but less than the lifetime of the exposed organism. (As defined by the EPA.)

Toxicity Assessment Characterization of the toxicological properties and effects of a chemical, with special emphasis on establishment of dose-response characteristics. (As defined by the EPA.)

Toxicity Testing Biological testing (usually with an invertebrate, fish, or small mammal) to determine the adverse effects of a compound or effluent. (As defined by the EPA.)

Toxic Pollutants Materials that cause death, disease, or birth defects in organisms that ingest or absorb them. The quantities and exposures necessary to cause these effects can vary widely. (As defined by the EPA.)

Toxic Release Inventory Database of toxic releases in the United States compiled from SARA, Title III, Section 313 reports. (As defined by the EPA.)

Toxic Substance A chemical or mixture that may present an unreasonable risk of injury to health or the environment. (As defined by the EPA.)

Toxic Waste A waste that can produce injury if inhaled, swallowed, or absorbed through the skin. (As defined by the EPA.)

Trichloroethylene Found in solvents and used in the formulations of paints, varnishes, lacquers, and dyes, trichlorethylene is observed offgassing. It is considered a carcinogen and a chronic toxin, and can cause fertility problems and developmental defects.

Troposphere The layer of the atmosphere closest to the Earth's surface.

United States Postal Service (USPS) For the last decade, the United States Postal Service has been committed to sustainable principles. In 1993, the Postmaster General issued the USPS *Environmental Policy and Guiding Principles,* which can be summarized as follows: Meet or exceed all applicable environmental laws; incorporate environmental considerations into the business planning process; foster the sustainable use of natural resources by promoting pollution prevention reducing waste, recycling, and reusing material; expect every employee to take ownership and responsibility for the USPS's environmental objectives; work with customers to address mutual environmental concerns; measure progress on protecting the environment; encourage suppliers, vendors, and contractors to comply with similar environmental protection policies. The USPS has developed a Green Addendum to the USPS specifications that specifies low-VOC and recycled-content products. In 1998, the USPS opened the first green post office, in Fort Worth, Texas.

Urban Runoff Stormwater from city streets and adjacent domestic or commercial properties that carries pollutants into the sewer systems and receiving waters. (As defined by the EPA.)

Urethanes A family of plastics (polyurethanes) used for varnish coatings, foamed insulations, highly durable paints, and rubber goods.

Variable Air Volume (VAV) A method of modulating the amount of heating or cooling effect delivered to a building by the HVAC system. The flow of air is modulated, rather than the temperature. VAV systems typically consist of VAV boxes that throttle supply airflow to individual zones, some mechanism to control supply fanflow to matchbox demand, and the interconnecting ductwork and components.

Vinyl Chloride A chemical compound used in producing some plastics; believed to be oncogenic.

Volatile Describing any substance that evaporates readily.

Volatile Organic Compound (VOC) Any organic compound that participates in atmospheric photochemical reactions, except those designated by EPA as having negligible photochemical reactivity. Volatile organic compounds are chemical compounds based on carbon and hydrogen structures and are vaporized at room temperatures.

Waste Exchange Arrangement by which companies exchange their wastes for the benefit of both parties.

Waste Stream The total flow of solid waste from homes, businesses, institutions, and manufacturing plants that is recycled, burned, or disposed of in landfills or segments thereof, such as the residential waste stream or the recyclable waste stream. (As defined by the EPA.)

Watershed The land area that drains into a stream; the watershed for a major river may encompass a number of smaller watersheds that ultimately combine at a common point. (As defined by the EPA.)

Watershed Approach A coordinated framework for environmental management that focuses public and private efforts on the highest-priority problems within hydrologically defined geographic areas, taking into consideration both groundwater and surface water flow. (As defined by the EPA.)

Watershed Area A topographic area within a line drawn to connect the highest points uphill of a drinking water intake into which overland flow drains. (As defined by the EPA.)

Wetlands An area saturated by surface water or groundwater, with vegetation adapted for life under those soil conditions, such as swamps, bogs, fens, marshes, and estuaries. (As defined by the EPA.)

Xenobiota Any biotum displaced from its normal habitat; a chemical foreign to a biological system.

Xeriscape A landscaped area designed with water-efficient choices in planting and irrigation. It encompasses seven basic principles to conserve water and protect the environment: planning and design, use of well-adapted plants, soil analysis, practical turf areas, use of mulches, appropriate maintenance, and efficient irrigation.

Xylene Found in paints, varnishes, lacquers, solvents, xylenes are included in the formulations of paints, adhesives, and some furniture products and are observed offgassing. Xylenes are considered chronic toxins capable of causing fertility problems and developmental defects. Xylenes also have potential health impacts on wildlife.

INDEX